DATE DUE

MAY 8 2004		
GAYLORD		PRINTED IN U.S.A.

PRINCIPLES

of

CATHOLIC THEOLOGY

Edward J. Gratsch, S.T.D., Editor
John R. Civille, S.T.D.
Ralph J. Lawrence, S.T.D.
Donald G. McCarthy, Ph.D.

ALBA · HOUSE NEW · YORK

SOCIETY OF ST. PAUL, 2187 VICTORY BLVD., STATEN ISLAND, NEW YORK 10314

Library of Congress Cataloging in Publication Data

Principles of Catholic theology.

   Bibliography: p.
   Includes index.
   1. Theology, Catholic. 2. Christian ethics—Catholic authors. I. Gratsch, Edward J.
BX1751.2.P74   230'.2   80-26272
ISBN 0-8189-0407-0

Nihil Obstat:
John J. Jennings, S.T.D.

Imprimatur:
†Daniel E. Pilarczyk, S.T.D., Ph.D.
Vicar General, Archdiocese of Cincinnati
Nov. 16, 1979

The Nihil Obstat and Imprimatur are
a declaration that a book or pamphlet is considered
to be free from doctrinal or moral error. It it is not implied
that those who have granted the Nihil Obstat and
Imprimatur agree with the contents,
opinions or statements expressed.

Designed, printed and bound in the United States of
America by the Fathers and Brothers of the
Society of St. Paul, 2187 Victory Boulevard,
Staten Island, New York 10314, as part of their
communications apostolate.

2 3 4 5 6 7 8 9 (Current Printing: first digit).

Dedicated to the faculty and students,
past and present, of Mt. St. Mary's
Seminary of the West, Norwood, Ohio, on the
occasion of its sesquicentennial (1829-1979).

CONTENTS

PART 1 (THE CALL)
DOGMATIC THEOLOGY

PART 2 (THE RESPONSE)
MORAL THEOLOGY

ABBREVIATIONS

AAS	*Acta Apostolicae Sedis*
AER	*American Ecclesiastical Review*
CBQ	*Catholic Biblical Quarterly*
CIC	*Codex Iuris Canonici* (The Code of Canon Law)
CSEL	*Corpus scriptorum ecclesiasticorum latinorum* (Vienna)
CT	*The Church Teaches*, St. Louis, 1955, B. Herder Book Co.
DB	J. McKenzie, *Dictionary of the Bible*, Milwaukee, 1965, Bruce Publ. Co.
DBT	X. Léon Dufour, *Dictionary of Biblical Theology*, 2nd ed., New York, 1973, The Seabury Press.
DS	H. Denziger and A. Schönmetzer, *Enchiridion Symbolorum*, 34th ed.
HD	A. Harnack, *History of Dogma*, New York, 1961, Dover Publications, 7 vols.
JBC	*The Jerome Biblical Commentary*, Englewood Cliffs, 1968, Prentice-Hall.
NAB	*The New American Bible*, New York, 1970, P.J. Kenedy & Sons.
NCE	*New Catholic Encyclopedia*
ODCC	F. Cross (ed.), *The Oxford Dictionary of the Christian Church*, 2nd ed., 1974, Oxford University Press.
PG	J. Migne, *Patrologia graeca*
PL	J. Migne, *Patrologia latina*
SM	*Sacramentum Mundi*, New York, 1968, Herder and Herder, 6 vols.
ST	St. Thomas Aquinas, *Summa Theologica*

TCC   J. Neuner, S.J., and H. Roos, S.J., *The Teaching of the Catholic Church*, Staten Island, 1967, Alba House.

TD   K. Rahner and H. Vorgrimler, *Theological Dictionary*, New York, 1965, Herder and Herder.

TDNT   G. Kittel (ed.), *Theological Dictionary of the New Testament*, Grand Rapids, 1964, Wm. B. Eerdmans Publ. Co.

Th.Dig.   *Theology Digest*

TS   *Theological Studies*

ACKNOWLEDGEMENTS

Scripture texts used in this work are taken from the *New American Bible* copyright © 1970, by the Confraternity of Christian Doctrine, Washington, D.C., and are used by permission of copyright owner.
All rights reserved.

Quotations from the systematic index of Denziger-Schönmetzer, *Enchiridion Symbolorum Definitionum et Declarationum* (34th ed.) are used with permission of the publisher, Verlag Herder, Freiburg.

PRINCIPLES OF CATHOLIC THEOLOGY

PART 1
THE CALL

DOGMATIC THEOLOGY

INTRODUCTION

The purpose of this volume of systematic theology—which includes both dogmatic and moral theology—is to provide students with a concise and up-to-date synthesis of Catholic theology. A synthesis brings together ideas that may be considered in isolation and shows how they are related in a logically consistent way. Through a synthesis one achieves a better understanding of individual ideas. Here is an example. One can come to know a student in isolation by sharing a room with him or her on a college campus; but one can come to know an individual still better by observing how he or she interacts with other students as a member of the college community. A synthesis studies the interaction of ideas as parts of a conceptual whole.

Naturally this relatively short volume is restricted to the most general ideas of a theological synthesis; but it offers suggestions for reading in greater depth by providing a bibliography which introduces each chapter.

This volume is divided up into two main parts. The first part studies the divine call to fellowship with the one and triune God; the second part, the human response to that call. Part 1, which is concerned with the divine call, is dogmatic in character. After preliminary remarks about revelation and theology, it takes up the reality of God, the beginning and end of all things and the primary subject of theology. The divine essence is one; yet, there are three really distinct persons in the one God, Father, Son, and Holy Spirit. God is the creator of all things other than Himself— angels, the material world, and human beings. God conferred many benefits on the human race through His Son, our Lord Jesus Christ. Because the human race had fallen from grace, the Son of God became man, suffered, died, and rose from the dead to restore us to God's friendship. To communicate the fruits of His redemption to the human race, Jesus gave us His Church and sacraments. The first part of this volume concludes with a discussion of eschatology or the last things. Those who share in the fruits of Christ's redemption are admitted to fellowship with God in heaven; those who do not share in those fruits are denied that fellowship.

Part 2 of this volume, which deals with the human response to the divine call, is devoted to moral theology. Men and women are the images of God. They are images of God because they are responsible agents endowed with intellect and will. Using their God-given faculties, they must appropriate for themselves the fruits of Christ's redemption and make their way to God. Hence, Part 2 is concerned with the human acts by which God's rational creatures meet this responsibility.

This volume is concerned with the principles of *Catholic* theology. In other words, it treats primarily the development of theology in the Roman Catholic tradition. But the authors of this volume have also included references to non-Catholic theological systems for the purposes of comparison and contrast.

The primary object of theological study is God who has revealed Himself to the human race principally through His Son, Jesus Christ. Indeed, theology, the noblest of the sciences, clarifies the meaning of human existence as no other science can!

Chapter 1

REVELATION

Bibliography: *TCC* nos. 1-74h; Vatican II, *Dei Verbum*, Constitution on Divine Revelation; W. Bulst, S.J., *Revelation*, New York, 1965, Sheed and Ward. Transl. by B. Vawter, C.M.; several authors, *Revelation* in the *NCE* 12, 436-448; G. Moran, F.S.C., *Theology of Revelation*, New York, 1966, Herder and Herder; L. Monden, S.J., *Signs and Wonders*, New York, 1966, Desclee Company. Transl. from the French; J. Macquarrie, *Principles of Christian Theology*, New York, 1966, Charles Scribner's Sons, 75-93 (a non-Catholic work); M. Schmaus, *God in Revelation*, New York 1968, Sheed and Ward; several authors, *Revelation*, in *SM* 5, 342-359; G. McCool (ed.), *A Rahner Reader*, New York 1975, The Seabury Press, 1-130. For the history of revelation: J. McKenzie, *Revelation* in *DB* 735-738; B. Rigaux, P. Grelot, *Revelation* in *DBT* 499-505; R. Latourelle, *Theology of Revelation*, Staten Island, 1966, Alba House; A. Dulles, S.J., *Revelation Theology*, New York 1969, Herder and Herder; K. Rahner, S.J., *Foundations of Christian Faith*, New York, 1978, The Seabury Press, 138-175.

Catholic theology employs both reason and revelation as tools or channels of information, as the means of reaching its conclusions. Reason, of course, is man's native power of comprehending, inferring, or thinking. Revelation means God's self-disclosure. God reveals Himself through creation (Rm 1:20). This revelation is natural. God has also revealed Himself through the prophets and especially through His divine Son, Jesus Christ (Heb 1:1-2). This revelation is supernatural. It is supernatural revelation which is the subject of this chapter because, along with reason, it is the tool of theology.

The Teaching of the Church

The teaching of the Church about revelation was formulated especially by two ecumenical councils, the First and Second Vatican Councils. The First Vatican Council (1869-70) taught infallibly a number of important ideas on this subject. Human reason, it said, can discover the existence of God with certainty. Divine revelation helps human beings to know better the religious and moral truths of the natural order; however, revelation is absolutely necessary if they are to know their supernatural end. Man believes what God has revealed simply because God has revealed it. Miracles and prophecies afford proof of the fact of divine revelation. The assent to divine revelation is a work of grace. Revelation contains mysteries; but reason enlightened by faith can achieve some understanding of those mysteries. There can be no real conflict between human reason and revelation. Reason can demonstrate the foundations of faith which is the appropriate human response to revelation. The content of revelation or the deposit of faith has been entrusted to the Church to be kept faithfully and declared infallibly.[1]

The Second Vatican Council (1962-65), reflecting the mind of the Catholic bishops throughout the world, reaffirmed all that the First Vatican Council had taught about revelation. Moreover, Vatican II taught that God has revealed Himself in history by the words and deeds of the prophets and especially of His divine Son (Heb 1:1-2). The obedience of faith is to be given to the God who has revealed Himself, an obedience by which human beings commit themselves freely to God, offering Him the full submission of intellect and will. Christ commissioned the apostles and bishops to teach what God has revealed. With the help of the Holy Spirit the Church grows in its understanding of this revelation. The apostolic preaching is reflected in the life or tradition of the Church and in her sacred books, the Bible. The sacred books have both God and man as their authors. These books teach without error that truth which God wanted written down for the sake of salvation.[2]

Vatican II taught that God's plan of salvation for mankind has been revealed in both the Old and New Testaments of the Bible. The principal purpose of the Old Testament was to prepare the Jewish people for the coming of Christ. The four Gospels of the New Testament give witness to the life and teaching of Jesus Christ, the incarnate Son of God and our savior, through whom God has revealed Himself in the most explicit way. With the four Gospels, the New Testament also contains the epistles of St. Paul and other apostolic writings which clarify the Christian message. The Church encourages the reading and study of the Bible. The study of the Bible must be, as it were, the *soul of theology*.[3]

Systematic Reflection

Revelation means God's disclosure of Himself to the human race. It is the conviction of Catholics based upon the Scriptures (Ws 13:1-9; Rm 1:20) and the teaching of the First Vatican Council[4] that God reveals Himself through creation. The famous five "ways" of the medieval theologian Thomas Aquinas (1225-74) are an attempt to show how creation reveals the existence of God and His invisible attributes.[5] This kind of revelation may be described as natural. Because creation reveals God to be One who is personal and distinct from His creatures, Catholics do not look to the monistic and pantheistic religions of the East for the ultimate explanation of reality. It is supernatural revelation, however, with which we are particularly concerned here and now. Supernatural revelation means God's speaking to men and women in such a way that they know God is speaking to them. Such revelation is supernatural in the sense that it is an utterly gratuitous communication.

The conception of revelation as God's speaking to men and women was expressed by the Epistle to the Hebrews: "In times past, God spoke in fragmentary and varied ways to our fathers through the prophets; in this, the final age, he has spoken to us through his Son" (Heb 1:1-2). Probably the author of the Epistle to the Hebrews is thinking of God's total message to men and women through His Son's person, word, and deeds. Actually the message of God is communicated to them by words and deeds having an inner unity. The deeds wrought by God in the history of salvation manifest and confirm the teaching and realities signified by the words, while the words proclaim the deeds and clarify the mystery contained in them. When, therefore, revelation is described as God's speaking to men and women, speaking is to be understood in a large sense as the communication of a message by word and deed. However, the definition of revelation as God's speaking emphasizes the indispensable role of words in manifesting and interpreting the hidden deeds of God.

If revelation is conceived as God's speaking to mankind, the implications are tremendous. To speak is to manifest one's thoughts immediately and directly to another. Accordingly, revelation affords men and women the opportunity of personal contact with God. It invites a response from those whom God addresses. It assuages the intensity of man's desire to know God better. If God speaks to His creatures, He speaks at a specific moment in time and history; and it is possible to compose the history of revelation. Those individuals whom God addresses may be called upon to communicate His message to those who have not heard it.

The last point suggests the distinction between immediate and mediate revelation. *Immediate* revelation takes place when God speaks to an individual without using another human being as a messenger. The conversations between God and Moses as recorded in the Pentateuch are examples of immediate revelation. *Mediate* revelation is that form of revelation whereby God uses a human being as a messenger to speak to another human being. The message given by God to the Israelites through Moses and recorded in the Pentateuch was mediate revelation as far as the Israelites were concerned. Mediate revelation adds to the concept of immediate revelation only the intervention of a legate who speaks on behalf of God. God endows His legates with evident signs that serve to identify them as messengers of God.[6]

What are these evident signs? They are miracles. Only God can identify those who speak in His name. He does so by working miracles in support of those who claim to be His messengers. A miracle is a uniquely divine sign. It is a supernatural event of which only God could be the main cause, for instance, the instantaneous cure of a diseased limb. Miracles are the credentials of God's ambassadors.

Jesus claimed to speak for God in a unique manner. The strongest evidence for His claim lies in the miracles of His own life; the greatest miracle being His resurrection from the dead.[7] It is interesting to observe that the founders of other world religions worked no miracles. The lives of the Buddha, Confucius, and Muhammad are devoid of the miraculous. Indeed, the Buddha and Confucius taught a set of moral principles and values without claiming a revelation from God. Muhammad claimed to be the "seal of the prophets," the last and greatest of the prophets; but he explicitly denied that he had the capacity to work miracles.[8] Jesus, then, is the summit of God's revelation to mankind; and Catholics expect no new public revelation after Him.

The message of Jesus contains a body of religious and ethical truths which man can discover by his own native intelligence. The existence of a personal God who is endowed with certain attributes is one of these truths. God's caring for His creatures and man's obligation to avoid stealing and adultery are other examples of truths which can be discovered by human reason alone. Jesus taught these truths so that His followers might know them easily and surely.

The Christian message also contains mysteries such as the most holy Trinity and the incarnation of the Son of God. We should not be surprised. God chose to speak about Himself in human language. Human language is a reflection of human ideas which are derived initially from created reality through the senses. Created reality, however, is a very imperfect reflection of God. When God chose to speak about Himself in human words, these words necessarily described Him in an exceedingly imperfect manner so that considerable obscurity remains even after the revelation of mysteries such as the most holy Trinity and the incarnation of the Son of God. Nevertheless, the revelation of what remains mysterious still throws some light upon divine reality. We now know, for example, about the personal relationships in God which would have been hidden from us had not God revealed them.

Jesus enjoined His followers to preach His message about God to others—indeed throughout the course of history until the end of time. The command of Jesus to preach to others what He Himself had taught was one of the first steps in the foundation of the Church. The Church is a group of persons committed to God through Jesus Christ and bent upon spreading the good news revealed by God through Him. What the Church preached in obedience to the command of Christ was reflected in the life of the Church—its beliefs, its way of life, and its worship. The life of the Church as it reflects the teaching of Jesus is called tradition by Catholics. Subsequently, the Church felt the need of a written record of its preaching and belief. This need gave rise to the New Testament portion of the Bible. The result is that the message of Jesus is preserved in the tradition of the Church and its Bible.

It is the conviction of Catholics[9] that Jesus established a living teaching authority or magisterium which is charged with preserving and interpreting the revealed word of God to be found in tradition and the Bible. The magisterium consists of the Pope, the bishop of Rome, and the bishops in communion with him. The Pope and the bishops are the successors of the original apostolic college made up of Peter and the other apostles. The magisterium "is not above the word of God, but serves it, teaching only what has been handed on, listening to it devoutly, guarding it scrupulously and explaining it faithfully by divine commission and with the help of the Holy Spirit. It draws from this one deposit of faith everything which it presents for belief as divinely revealed."[10]

Occasionally, the magisterium solemnly defines a dogma; that is, it declares in solemn fashion what God has revealed in a particular instance. A definition of this nature is not an addition to the deposit of faith, but a clarification of what God has revealed. Dogmas revealed by God and defined by the Church always retain their original sense. They express incompletely (but not falsely) the permanent reality. The Church can and does grow in its understanding of revealed truth by realizing more fully its implications. There can never be any fundamental disagreement between revealed truth and the conclusions of human reason. God employs both revelation and reason as means of revealing Himself; and God cannot contradict Himself.

The History of Revelation

Prior to the coming of Christ, God gradually revealed Himself by word and deed. This revelation culminated in God's revelation of Himself to mankind through His incarnate Son. Thereafter, theologians isolated and studied different aspects of revelation in accordance with the needs of their times. This section traces the development of revelation in history and identifies the various aspects of revelation investigated and stressed by theologians at different periods of history.

In the Old Testament Yahweh revealed Himself as a living God (Jos 3:10; Is 37:4). He did so in several ways. He manifested Himself as the lord of history, especially in the events surrounding the exodus of Israel from Egypt (Ex 14:18; Jr 7:22; Ho 11:1). Yahweh manifested himself as the lord of creation which disclosed His wisdom and sovereign power (Jb 26:1-13; Pr 8:23-31; Ws 13:1-9). Yahweh also revealed Himself as a judge who judged the nations, the enemies of Israel (Is 13; Am 1-2:3), and Israel too (Ezk 6:13-14; 7:9; etc.) for their crimes.

Yahweh, however, employed still other means of self-disclosure which clarified His deeds and intentions. He entered a covenant with the Israelites of which Moses was the mediator. This covenant established standards of conduct for Israel. Beyond this, Yahweh spoke to the Israelites through the prophets. In this manner He disclosed His plans for the destiny of Israel. Finally, God instructed the Israelites through the wisdom philosophers who revealed Yahweh's will for man in the ordinary events of life.

The pivotal event between the Old Testament and the New Testament is the incarnation of the Son of God. "In times past, God spoke in fragmentary and varied ways to our fathers through the prophets; in this, the final age, He has spoken to us through His Son" (Heb 1:1-2). What Jesus revealed to us about His Father was proclaimed by the apostles and the Church under the influence of the Holy Spirit. Along with His Father Jesus Himself became the object of revelation. At the end of history, however, what we now accept in faith will give way to the immediate vision of God.

The Synoptic Gospels make it clear that Jesus is the Son of God who sends the Spirit upon those who believe in Him (Mt 3:13-17; Mk 1:9-11; Lk 3:21-22). Jesus came to fulfill the Law and the prophets (Mt 5:17-20). The central theme of Jesus' message was the kingdom of God, a theme which Jesus accepted from the Old Testament and expanded upon. The Acts of the Apostles represents the apostles as witnesses and heralds of Christ. It is the Holy Spirit who assures the accuracy of the apostolic testimony (Ac 1:8; 2:1-21).

In the apostolic letters of the New Testament we read that God reveals Himself through nature (Rm 1:19-20). Christ, the spotless lamb of God, was revealed for our sake in the last days (1 P 1:20). He took away sins once and for all by His sacrifice (Heb 9:26). The grace of God has been manifested to us in Christ Jesus (2 Tm 1:10). The justice of God which works through faith in Jesus Christ has been made known (Rm 3:22). This mystery had been hidden for many ages (Rm 16:25). Jesus will be revealed even more clearly at the Parousia (1 Cor 1:7; 2 Th 1:7).

The theme of revelation is quite prominent in the Gospel of John. For John, Jesus is the self-manifestation of God, the Word of God, the only Son, ever at the Father's side, the one who has revealed Him (Jn 1:1-17). Jesus testified to what He had seen (Jn 3:11-13). He who has seen Jesus has seen the Father; for Jesus and the Father are in each other (Jn 14:9-11). The Holy Spirit reminds the disciples of all that Jesus told them (Jn 14:26) and guides them to all truth (Jn 16:13). All these approaches to the central mystery of revelation are like complementary views of the same landscape, each view illuminating one aspect of the total reality.

The theme of revelation is quite prominent in the writings of the Fathers too. The Fathers are the ancient writers who have been accepted by the Church as authoritative witnesses to its teaching and practice. Justin the Martyr, writing at Rome toward the middle of the second century, maintained that all who lived by reason were in some sense Christians. However, they often contradicted themselves because their knowledge was partial inasmuch as they were ignorant of Christ, the Word of God.[11] At the end of the second century, Irenaeus of Lyons expressed a common patristic idea when he wrote that God revealed Himself first through creation, then through the Law and the prophets, and finally through Christ, His incarnate Son.[12] For Clement of Alexandria (d. 213) there were three testaments—philosophy, Law and the Gospel. All three testaments were derived from one and the same Logos. Philosophy prepared the Greeks to accept Christ, and the Law prepared the Jews to receive Him.[13]

In opposition to the heresy of Eunomius (d. 394) who asserted that human beings could comprehend the divine essence once it had been revealed, the Cappadocian Fathers—Basil (d. 379), Gregory of Nazianzen (d. 390), and Gregoy of Nyssa (d. 394)—stressed the incomprehensibility of God here below even after revelation. For Augustine (354-430), Christ is the Word of God, the image of the Father, the one who reveals the Father's will. The apostles and the Church are witnesses to Christ. These preserve and hand on what Christ taught. The external preaching of the word of God by the Church is accompanied by the illumination of the Holy Spirit opening the human heart to accept it.[14]

The 12th and 13th centuries were the golden age of Scholasticism. The term commonly designates the systems of speculative thought which employed reason to demonstrate the harmony between natural and supernatural truth. There were two main traditions within Scholasticism. One took its inspiration from Augustine, and the other employed the philosophy of Aristotle in the exposition of the Christian faith.

Bonaventure (1221-74), a member of the Franciscan order, is representative of the first tradition. Following Augustine, Bonaventure saw revelation as the illuminating activity of God or the subjective illumination of the human spirit which is the result of the external preaching of the word of God and the inner testimony of the Holy Spirit.[15]

Thomas Aquinas (1225-74) is representative of the other (Aristotelian) tradition of Scholasticism. He taught that revelation was absolutely necessary if man was to direct his life toward the vision of God, a goal that could be known only through revelation. However, revelation was also necessary if man was to secure a good grasp of natural religious and ethical truth.[16] (Divine revelation is authenticated by external signs, especially, miracles and prophecies, which identify those who speak in God's name.)[17] Aquinas, following Augustine, recognized the need for a divinely infused light to adhere to revealed truth. The principal truths revealed by God are set forth in the articles of the creed;[18] however, a profession of faith terminates not at the words of the creed but at the reality behind them.[19] Aquinas distinguished various stages of revelation: before the Law, under the Law, and under grace.[10] Finally, in the section of his *Summa Theologiae* which he devoted to Christ,[21] he spoke at considerable length about the revelatory function of the incarnate Word.

Martin Luther (1483-1546) set the Reformation on its course. In 1517 he began to teach his well-known doctrine that sinners are justified by faith alone (*sola fide*); that is, men are saved by confidence in the sufficiency of Christ's death on Calvary to reconcile them with God. For Luther, the Bible was the word of God and the sole norm of faith. All dogmas and all teachers, living and dead, were to be judged by the Bible (*sola Scriptura*). Luther rejected the authority of Popes and councils to interpret the Bible because, he said, Popes and councils had contradicted each other. John Calvin (1509-64), a younger contemporary of Luther and deeply indebted to him for his theological ideas, also believed that the Scriptures were the necessary and sufficient source of man's knowledge of God. All that was required for salvation was in the Bible and in it alone.

The position of Luther and Calvin provoked a reaction from the Council of Trent (1545-63), the 19th ecumenical council, and from Catholic theologians such as Robert Bellarmine (1542-1621). These were at pains to explain and defend two ideas: that the revealed word of

God is preserved *both* in the tradition of the Church *and* its Bible, that the magisterium or living teaching authority of the Church is charged with interpreting the revealed word of God in tradition and the Bible.[22]

Deism was a system of natural religion which was first developed in England in the late seventeenth and eighteenth centuries. The Englishman, J. Toland (1670-1722), wrote the classical exposition of Deism, *Christianity Not Mysterious* (1696). In it he said that God's revelation is not above the comprehension of human reason, for revelation comes from the Author of reason.

Different views of revelation were to be found among *European Protestants* in the nineteenth century. The German theologian, F. Schleiermacher (1768-1834), defined religion as the feeling of absolute dependence upon the infinite. Revelation was an original insight into man's dependence upon God. Christ had had such an insight.[23] A German theologian, A. Ritschl (1822-89), stressed the idea that God is in Christ *pro me*, for my salvation. An abstract knowledge of divine revelation without a value judgment about its profoundly personal significance means little.[24] A. Sabatier (1839-1901) propagated the theories of Schleiermacher and Ritschl in France. He held that revelation was the subjective consciousness of man's relationship with God.[25] Modernists of the Catholic Church who wished to bring the teaching of the Church abreast of the times held similar views about the nature of revelation. A. Loisy (1857-1940), a French priest, called revelation man's acquired consciousness of his relationship with God;[26] and G. Tyrrell (1861-1909), an English priest, thought of revelation as an emotion and experience. It was not to be identified with the intellectual content of that experience.[27]

There was, of course, a strong current of orthodox thought within the Catholic Church of the nineteenth century. J. Möhler (1796-1838) of the Tübingen school of Germany stressed the role of the Church as the extension of Christ in preaching the revealed word of God.[28] J. Newman (1801-90), the English cardinal, held that revelation is necessarily mysterious, that it may be nonetheless consistent with reason, that it must be embraced because it comes from God who can neither deceive nor be deceived.[29] Finally, the Jesuit professors of the Gregorian University, Rome—G. Perrone, C. Schrader, J. Franzelin, and others—helped to prepare the way for the dogmatic statements of Vatican I (1869-70) about revelation.

At the end of the nineteenth and the beginning of the twentieth centuries the science of comparative religion made considerable strides under the influence of evolutionary ideas and the greatly increased factual knowledge of other religions. This science discovered certain similarities between Christian revelation and other world religions. German-speaking Protestant theologians continued their study of revelation. K. Barth (1886-1968) rejected all natural theology and held that God's sole revelation is in Jesus Christ to whom the Scriptures and the Church bear witness.[30] R. Bultmann (1884-1976) held that divine revelation enables individuals to understand themselves and summons them to authentic existence.[31] O. Cullmann (1902-) developed the idea of salvation history (*Heilsgeschichte*) which is concerned with God's redemptive activity in history.[32] W. Pannenberg (1928-) attributes an important role to reason in verifying revelatory events.[33] J. Moltmann (1926-) has forced Christian theology to recognize the essential place of eschatology and hope in revelation.[34]

During the first half of the twentieth century the Catholic teaching on revelation was often set forth in Latin manuals which adhered strictly to the position of Vatican I about the supernaturalism, irreformability and transcendence of revelation. C. Pesch, S.J. (1853-1925), H. Dieckmann, S.J. (1880-1928), R. Garrigou-Lagrange, O.P. (1877-1964), and A. Tanquerey (1854-1932) were among those who composed such manuals. In 1940 R. Guardini (1885-1968), the preacher and liturgist, published an important monograph in which he examined the historical and personalist aspects of revelation.[35] Other theologians, for example, C. Boyer, S.J., and H. de Lubac, S.J., were concerned with the development of revealed dogmas. Did new dogmas arise by logical deduction from other dogmas explicitly defined by the Church or by what might be called quantum leaps in some cases?

K. Rahner, S.J. (1904-), one of the most influential of contemporary Catholic theologians, has also written about revelation. Already in the consciousness of his own finiteness man is implicitly aware of infinite Being. This awareness is a kind of natural revelation. Still it is not apparent from this consciousness whether the infinite Being wishes to draw near to man or keep him at a distance. But God reveals Himself further in the depths of the spiritual person. Such revelation is a "state of mind'' produced by grace—not knowledge by a consciousness. However, this non-reflexive consciousness is translated in the course of time into objective, reflex consciousness in the form of propositions. Divine revelation is expressed climactically in the incarnation of God's Son and without substantial error in the Judaeo-Christian tradition and only imperfectly in other religions. The Church is the body which receives and announces God's absolute revelation in Christ.[36]

Footnotes

1. *TCC* nos. 31-48.
2. *Dei verbum*, Divine Revelation, ch. 1-3.
3. *Ibid.* ch. 4-6.
4. *TCC* no. 31.
5. *ST* 1a2.3.
6. It must be noted, however, that signs are not for the ill-disposed but for the well-disposed to evoke or confirm faith.
7. Is the personality of the founder of the religion a reason for adhering to it? Unquestionably the personality of the founder—whether it be the Buddha, Jesus or Muhammad—exercises a powerful attraction upon the faithful; but the truth of his teaching, whether it be perceived by oneself or attested to by God, must be decisive.
8. As a matter of fact, Muhammad did believe that his dictation of the Koran was miraculous. It is difficult to understand, though, how this belief can be justified.
9. The reasons for this conviction will be given later in the pages dealing with the Church.
10. *Dei verbum* no. 10.
11. 1 *Apology* 46; 2 *Apology* 10.
12. *Against Heresies* 4, 6, 6.
13. *Stromata* 1, 28, 1-3; 6, 41, 7-42, 1.
14. *On the Gospel of John* tr. 26, 5.8; *On the Grace of Christ* 1, 10.11.14.15.
15. Cf. Latourelle, *op. cit.* 155-159.
16. *ST* 1a.1.1.
17. *CG* 3.154.
18. *ST* 2a2ae.1.6-9.
19. *ST* 2a2ae.1.2.ad 2.
20. *ST* 2a2ae.174.6.
21. *ST* 3.1-39.
22. *TCC* nos. 80-86.
23. *Religion, Speeches to its Cultured Despisers* 1799 (ET 1893); *The Christian Faith* 1821-2 (ET 1928).
24. *The Christian Teaching on Justification and Reconciliation* 1870-74 (ET 1872, 1900).
25. *Outlines of a Philosophy of Religion* 1896 (ET 1897).
26. *Autour d'un petit livre* 1903.
27. *Through Scylla and Charybdis* 1907.
28. *Symbolik* 1832 (ET 1843).
29. *Idea of a University* 1853.
30. *Church Dogmatics* 1932 ff. (ET 1936 ff.).
31. *New Testament and Mythology* 1941 (ET 1953).

32. *Christ and Time* 1946 (ET 1951); *Salvation in History* 1965 (ET 1967).
33. *Revelation as History* 1961 (ET 1968).
34. *Theology of Hope* 1965 (ET 1967).
35. *Die Offenbarung* 1940.
36. *Revelation* in *TD* 409-413.

Chapter 2

THEOLOGY

Bibliography: *TCC* nos. 11, 29, 43, 74c, 74h, 126c, 352-3, 398h-i; Vatican II, *Optatam Totius*, Priestly Formation, 16; Intern. Theol. Comm., *Theses on the Relationship betw. the Eccl. Magisterium and Theology*, 1976; H. Vorgrimler, *Dogmatic vs. Biblical Theology*, Baltimore, 1964, Helicon Press; G. Van Ackeren, *Theology* in the *NCE* 14, 39-49; J. Macquarrie, *Principles of Christian Theology*, New York, 1966, Charles Scribner's Sons, 1-36 (a non-Catholic work); M. Schmaus, *God in Revelation*, New York, 1968, Sheed and Ward, 255-295; R. Latourelle, S.J., *Theology, Science of Salvation*, Staten Island, 1969, Alba House; C. Ernst, *Theological Methodology* in *SM* 6, 218-224; K. Rahner, *Theology* in *SM* 6, 233-245; B. Lonergan, *Method in Theology*, New York, 1972, Herder and Herder; G. McCool, *A Rahner Reader*, New York, 1975, Seabury Press, 66-130; W. Pannenberg, *Theology and the Philosophy of Science*, Philadelphia, 1976, Westminster Press. Trans. by F. McDonagh. For the history of theology: A. Harnack, *History of Dogma*, New York, 1961, Dover Publications, Inc., 7 vols. in 4; P. De Letter, *Theology, History of* in the *NCE* 14, 49-58; L. Berkhof, *The History of Christian Doctrines*, Edinburgh, 1976, The Banner of Truth Trust; Y. Congar, O.P., *A History of Theology*, Garden City, 1968, Doubleday & Co. Transl. and ed. by H. Guthrie, S.J.; K. Rahner, *Theology, History* in *SM* 6, 240-245; G. Maloney, S.J., *A History of Orthodox Theology since 1453*, Belmont, 1976, Nordland Publishing Co.

Theology is the study of God and His relation to the world. However, a distinction must be made between natural theology and supernatural theology. Natural theology employs reason alone in its study of God; and it is a part of philosophy. Supernatural theology on the other hand employs both reason and revelation in its study of God. *Theology in the strict sense is supernatural theology and this is what is meant when the word is used without qualification.*

Sometimes theology is defined as faith seeking understanding: *fides quaerens intellectum.* In other words, it is man's attempt to comprehend better what God has revealed and man has accepted in faith. This definition does not differ essentially from the definition given in the preceding paragraph. Theology can also be defined as the science of the faith. In this case, the word, science, means a systematized, organized body of knowledge.

The Teaching of the Church

The First Vatican Council (1869-70) spoke optimistically about the possibility of theologizing. Reason enlightened by faith, it said, can achieve a partial but profitable understanding of divine mysteries. Such an understanding is possible in two ways: by comparing and contrasting the mysteries with what reason knows naturally and by studying the relation of the mysteries to one another and the ultimate end of man.[1]

In his encyclical letter which begins with the Latin words, *Humani Generis* (1950), Pope Pius XII dealt with the subject of theology among others. He noted that the terminology employed by theologians and even by the magisterium can be improved in certain instances. He praised the contribution of Scholastic theology to the theological enterprise. Theologians, he said, must always return to the sources of divine revelation; for it belongs to them to point out how the teaching of the magisterium is to be found either explicitly or implicitly in the Scriptures and tradition. It is the magisterium as distinct from the faithful themselves and theologians which is ultimately responsible for preserving and interpreting the deposit of faith.[2]

The Second Vatican Council (1962-65) spoke repeatedly of theology and theologians. According to the council, the study of Scripture must be the soul of theology.[3] Theological inquiry must maintain close contact with its own times; and theologians should seek continually for more suitable ways of communicating doctrine to their contemporaries.[4] The council noted that there are differences between the East and the West in the theological expression of doctrine; but these differences are often complementary rather than conflicting.[5] The council also spoke its mind about theological education:

"Dogmatic theology should be so arranged that Biblical themes are proposed first of all. Next there should be opened up to the students what the Fathers of the Eastern and Western Church have contributed to the faithful transmission and development of the individual truths of revelation. The further history of dogma should also be presented, account being taken of its relation to the general history of the Church. Then by way of making the mysteries of salvation known as thoroughly as they can be, students should learn to penetrate them more deeply with the help of speculation under the guidance of St. Thomas. Students should learn too how these mysteries are interconnected and how they are present and active in the liturgy and the whole life of the Church. Let them learn to seek solutions to human problems in the light of revelation, to apply the eternal truths of revelation to the changeable conditions of human affairs, and to communicate them in a way suitable to their contemporaries.

"Other theological disciplines should also be renewed by livelier contact with the mystery of Christ and the history of salvation. Special care should be taken to develop moral theology so that, nourished to a greater degree by scriptural teaching, it may show forth the nobility of the Christian calling and the obligation in charity to bear fruit for the life of the world. . . . "[6]

Finally, the council made it clear that in the last resort it is the Pope and the bishops, not theologians, who tell us how we are to understand what has been revealed.[7]

Systematic Reflection

Our concern here is supernatural theology. Supernatural theology employs both reason and revelation as it studies God and His relation to the world. The word, theology (from the Greek *theologia* meaning the science of God), indicates that God is the primary object of theology; creatures are the secondary object of theology; theology is concerned with them insofar as they are related to God.

Theology is the conscious effort of the Christian to establish the fact of revelation, to acquire a knowledge of revelation by the methods of scholarship, to penetrate, clarify, and interpret revelation, to make appropriate applications of it to life, to discover created analogies useful for illustrating revealed mysteries, to arrange revealed truths in a systematic order, and to answer objections against the whole of revelation or against particular revealed truths. Because theology serves the revealed word of God in these ways, theology can be called the science of salvation; and it is closely tied to the living magisterium of the Church which preserves and interprets the word of God as it is enshrined in Sacred Scripture and tradition.

Theology presupposes faith. Faith is an obedience by which a person entrusts himself freely to God, offering the full submission of intellect and will to God who reveals, and freely assenting to the truth revealed by Him.[8] In other words, theology supposes commitment to the realities which it studies. This commitment is a lived experience which begets a connaturality with things divine and a penetration into them that is unavailable to the unbeliever.

Theology is a science in the sense that it is an organized body of knowledge. As a science, theology is both speculative and practical. It is speculative because it contemplates God and the things of God. This is especially true of dogmatic theology. Theology is practical because it directs human beings to God, their ultimate end. This is especially true of moral theology.[9] Because theology is concerned with God as He has disclosed Himself through revelation, because theology directs human beings to God who is their ultimate end, it is superior to all other sciences which are primarily concerned with creatures and more immediate ends.[10] Theology uses the other sciences wherever this is helpful toward attaining its own objectives. Theology corrects the other sciences when these contradict theological teachings that are certain. But theology rightly revises its own mere opinions in the light of more certain evidence from the other sciences.

One can "do" theology in several ways. For example, one can "do" either positive or scholastic theology. Both types of theology rely upon reason and revelation; but positive theology examines the deposit of revelation, that is, Scripture and tradition, in order to find out what God has actually disclosed about Himself. For this purpose, the theologian must call upon the science of hermeneutics to discover the meaning of the relevant texts. Under the category of positive theology we can distinguish Biblical, patristic, conciliar, and other types of theology. Scholastic (also called speculative) theology examines the truths of revelation in order to explain, develop, and systematize them and defend them in the light of reason. For this purpose, the theologian often calls upon some philosophy for assistance. In the past, the theologian often employed Platonic or Aristotelian philosophy to this end; but today there is a tendency to make greater use of what are called existentialist philosophies. Obviously, both positive and scholastic theology are necessary and both are to be found in most theological writings.

One can "do" dogmatic or moral theology. Both are grounded in the revelation of God in Christ. However, dogmatic theology is concerned with the core of Christian revelation—with such fundamental doctrines as the triune God, creation, the fall of man, the incarnation and redemption, the Church, sacraments, and eschatology. On the other hand, moral theology, including ascetical and mystical theology, is concerned with the goal of human conduct and the means of achieving it.

Some authors have argued for a form of theology called "kerygmatic." This form of theology centers on Christ and is primarily oriented toward preaching and catechizing. ("Kerygmatic" is derived from *kerygma*, a Greek word which came to be applied to the preaching of the Gospel.) Still the consensus of opinion seems to be that any legitimate theology must pursue the goals emphasized by the kerygmatic theologians, that consequently a distinct form of kerygmatic theology is unnecessary and undesirable.

The role of analogy lies at the heart of the theological enterprise. There is a similarity—a very imperfect one, to be sure—between God and His creatures, especially His rational creatures. This similarity exists because God is the cause of creatures. By exploiting this similarity through a study of creatures and purging his concepts of creaturely imperfection, the theologian can arrive at a better understanding of divine mysteries. For example, Jesus taught us to think of God as our Father. By comparing an earthly father with our heavenly Father and abstracting from the limitations that circumscribe an earthly father, the theologian can achieve a better understanding of God. This comparison is a kind of natural analogy; but there is also a supernatural analogy or analogy of faith by which the theologian compares divine mysteries among themselves to understand them better. Both kinds of analogy were commended by Vatican I. In any event, theological understanding will always remain imperfect and analogous (but not false), since the ideas which human beings use to think about God are derived initially from creatures.

Theology inevitably bears the mark of its time. It reflects the theologian's secular knowledge, methodology, philosophy, historical situation, *Weltanschauung*, and terminology. For example, in the Hellenistic milieu of the fourth and fifth centuries theologians used Platonic philosophy and Greek terms to elucidate the mysteries of Christianity. The theology of the Counter-Reformation reflects the controversies with Protestants. The modern world is increasingly dominated by a scientific spirit; and the human race has passed from a rather static concept of reality to a more dynamic, evolutionary one.[11] Theologians have not remained unaffected. These temporal elements need to be weighed carefully in order to determine what is and what is not of permanent significance in theological statements.

Theological knowledge is capable of growth. Just as the Church can come to a fuller knowledge of revelation by a deeper understanding of its implications, so the theologian can come to a deeper understanding of his science in the same way. The ever changing experience of the whole Church fosters such development. Individuals change; discoveries are made; new movements burgeon; one type of society yields to another; an older culture is replaced by a newer one. As the faithful attempt to respond to the word of God in a new context, they and the theologian achieve new insights into revelation and theology. These new insights affect both dogmatic and moral theology.

Often the dialectical tension between orthodoxy and heresy is an important factor in the development of theology. When God's revealed word poses a problem, theologians may offer contradictory solutions. The Church is led to examine the problem and the tentative solutions. What was unclear and doubtful is clarified; a solution (incomplete but not false) is given. Dogmatic and theological development occurs. A great Christological controversy of the past offers an example. The theologians of the fourth century asked, "Who is Christ?" Arius and his supporters held that Christ was the creature of the Father. Athanasius and his supporters hotly disagreed with Arius. The Council of Nicea (325) took up the problem and affirmed the divinity of Christ. The matter was clarified for subsequent generations.

When the theologian reflects upon the historical development of theology, he discerns certain processes at work. For example, he notes the transposition of the Gospel from the thought patterns of one culture to those of another—from the Semitic to the Hellenistic, from the medieval to the modern Western and to other cultures. The possibility of such a transposition is implicit in the command of Christ to preach the Gospel to all nations. The theologian also notes the gradual process by which an understanding of revelation achieves the status of a Church dogma. In this way, the ancient understanding of the person of Christ was gradually clarified as a dogma by the first ecumenical councils of the Church.

An important task of the theologian is to show how the truths that have been defined as dogmas of the Church have evolved from their original expression in revelation. The Church is charged with the preservation of the Gospel of Christ to the exclusion of innovations. Hence, it is the responsibility of the Church to point out how its dogmatic definitions maintain continuity with the Gospel of Christ. It is the task of the theologian to identify and demonstrate this continuity.

Theology has an important bearing upon preaching; and in this respect theologians and pastors are collaborators. It is the duty of the pastors of the Church to preach the word of God to their people. The word of God as it is preserved in the Bible and tradition is expressed in language that is often symbolic, tied to a particular culture, and conditioned by a specific historical context. The theologian will attempt to fathom the meaning of this language so that the pastors of the Church can present it to their people in ordinary language.

Theology can strengthen one's spiritual life. It is concerned primarily with God as He has disclosed Himself to mankind. Theology is, as it were, an inventory of the blessings which God has conferred upon the human race. Like revelation, theology is a summons to respond to God's love. Sound theology preserves one from the doctrinal errors which are injurious to spirituality. The doctors of the Church offer convincing evidence of the salutary effects of theological study.

As the theologian studies the revealed word of God, he receives invaluable assistance from the magisterium. The magisterium is the living teaching office of the Church vested in the Pope and bishops. The magisterium is ultimately responsible for preserving and interpreting the revealed word. In very specific circumstances this teaching office can be exercised in an infallible manner. Even when they do not speak infallibly but only as authentic teachers, the Pope and the bishops can rightly expect assent from the faithful in matters of faith and morals.[12]

A Survey of Catholic Theology

At the center of the theology of the Old Testament is a basic personal reality, Yahweh. Israel encountered Yahweh through cult, revelation, history, nature, wisdom, institutions, and the promise of the future.[13] The Pentateuch speaks of Yahweh's covenant with Israel. The Law has been given to Israel; by observing it Israel will continue to be the people of God and live. The prophets remind Israel of its ancient call by Yahweh and they summon it to observance of the Law, especially its social demands. The prophets foresee the future, condemning or promising good. They exhort Israel to an interior dependence upon Yahweh. The Deuteronomic writers interpret the meaning of the exile for Israel. The wisdom literature interprets Yahweh's will for men in the ordinary events of life. Finally, the apocalyptic literature contrasts this evil world with the blessed world that Yahweh will bring about in the future.

In the New Testament we can distinguish three basic theologies: the Pauline (c. 35-60), the synoptic (c. 70-90), and the Johannine (c. 100). Paul's theology centers on Christ; but he views Christ primarily as a savior. Paul was not as much concerned about the intrinsic constitution of Christ as he was about the significance of Christ for man. He preached "Christ crucified." One is saved by sharing in Christ's death and resurrection through faith and baptism. In the synoptic tradition, Matthew wishes to convince Jewish readers that Jesus is the expected Messiah-king of Israel. The author is concerned with Jesus' teaching about the kingdom of heaven and the Church. Mark's Gospel revolves around the two titles, "Christ" and "Son of God." Mark displays greater interest in the works of Jesus than in His sayings. Luke portrays Christianity as a religious faith open to all. In the prologue to his Gospel, John speaks about the timeless existence of the Word and His identity with God. John explores the mysteries of belief and unbelief in Jesus and portrays Him as the victorious and exalted savior. These three Christologies are expressed in a series of titles that articulate the mystery of Christ.

The Apostolic Fathers—Barnabas, Clement of Rome, Ignatius of Antioch, Polycarp of Smyrna, and others—did little more than reflect upon the theology of the Gospels. The Greek Apologists of the second century—among them Aristides of Athens and Justin the Martyr—attempted to show the sublimity of Christianity and the absurdity of paganism. The catechetical school at Alexandria utilized the philosophy of Plato and the allegorical interpretation of the Bible. Among the best-known members of the school were Clement (d. 213) and Origen (d. 254). The Christian school at Antioch stressed the literal sense of the Bible and preferred the philosophy of Aristotle. Athanasius (d. 373) defended the divinity of the Word against the Arians. The Cappadocians (Basil and the two Gregories) elaborated a theology of the Trinity. These Greek Fathers stressed man's divinization through Christ rather than his redemption from sin.

The Latin Fathers include Tertullian, Cyprian, Ambrose, Jerome and Augustine. Tertullian (d. 220) may be said to have created the language of western theology. Cyprian (d. 258) wrote about the Church, the ministry and the sacraments. Ambrose (d. 397) wrote on moral and ascetical subjects. Jerome (d. 420) is famous for his Biblical translations and commentaries. Augustine (d. 430), possibly the greatest and most influential of all the Fathers, strove to unite faith and reason, and he devoted special attention to the doctrines of the fall and redemption, predestination, the grace of Christ, the Trinity, and the divinization of man.

Several factors contributed to the progress of theology in the *twelfth and thirteenth centuries*: the rediscovery of Aristotelian philosophy, the systematization of the patristic heritage in the *summae sententiarum*, the rise of the universities, and the foundation of the mendicant orders. The contribution of Abelard (1079-1142) was his method of *Sic et Non* by which he attempted to reconcile apparently contradictory excerpts from the Scriptures and Fathers. Peter Lombard (c. 1100-60) wrote the four books of *Sentences* which became the theological textbook of the schools. It is distinguished by its methodical orderliness, completeness, and wealth of quotations from the Greek and Latin Fathers. Thomas Aquinas (c. 1225-74) is possibly the most influential theologian in the Catholic Church by reason of his *Summa Theologiae* and other writings. He distinguished sharply between faith and reason, act and potency, and nature and supernature. Bonaventure (1221-74) stressed the mystical illumination of the faithful by God[14] and the role of will and love. The weakness of Scholastic theology was its lack of an historical sense.

The chief theological topics in the *fourteenth and fifteenth centuries* were the relationship between the Church and the State and conciliarism. There was also an interest in mysticism.

Both the Renaissance and the Reformation challenged the Catholic theologians of the Counter-Reformation in the sixteenth century. The Renaissance was hostile to scholastic theology, to its spirit and method. Martin Luther and John Calvin proposed a revolutionary reform of the Church's life and teaching. The controversies between Catholics and Protestants centered mainly on justification, the sacraments, and ecclesiology. The Catholic response came from the Council of Trent (1545-63) and from controversialists such as Robert Bellarmine (1542-1621). His method of argumentation was to contrast the Catholic and Protestant doctrines, state the precise teaching of the Church, and prove it from Sacred Scripture, the Fathers, the practice of the Church, and agreement of theologians. Finally, he answered the difficulties that had been raised.[15] Among the theologians of this period were John Fisher (d. 1535), Melchior Cano (d. 1560), Peter Canisius (d. 1597), Domingo Banez (d. 1604), Francis Suarez (d. 1617), and John of St. Thomas (d. 1644). The latter three produced distinguished commentaries on the *Summa* of Aquinas among other writings.

During the late *seventeenth and eighteenth centuries* theological manuals made their appearance. These combined positive, scholastic and controversial theology. There was a trend toward specialization and the theological disciplines—dogmatic, moral, and pastoral theology, patrology, history of dogma, etc.—were separated. Denis Petau (1583-1652) is known as the "Father of Positive Theology."[16] Alphonsus Liguori (1696-1787) composed his celebrated *Theologia Moralis* (1753). John Mansi (1692-1769) published his collection of conciliar documents.[17] The eighteenth century was the age of the Enlightenment with its rationalistic criticism of religion and rejection of traditional values.

The *nineteenth century* was the age of Romanticism which reawakened an interest in the past and an awareness of human solidarity. It encouraged Catholic theologians of the Tübingen school to return to the Scriptural and patristic sources of the past and to study the Church as a communion. Theology began to regain a sense of history and development.

The Ultramontanist movement pressed for the reassertion of papal authority. The movement triumphed at Vatican I (1869-70) which solemnly defined papal primacy and infallibility. Pope Leo XIII (d. 1903) was important for theology because he fostered a revival of Thomism, issued directives for the study of Holy Scripture, and published encyclicals on social questions. Modernism was the name given to a conglomeration of ideas having to do with Biblical criticism and the philosophy of religion. These ideas were defended by some thinkers in France, England, and Italy; but they were condemned by Pope Pius X.[18]

The first half of the twentieth century was notable for neo-Scholasticism and the vigorous Biblical and liturgical movements. However, the Second Vatican Council (1962-65) was a watershed. *Today* theology tends to be historical. Modern theologians are keenly aware of salvation history, of God's intervention in human history for our salvation. They are aware too that the dogmas and theological conclusions of the past were formulated in a particular historical context. This context needs to be studied in order to separate the kernel of truth from the cultural shell in which it is enclosed. Theologians wish to trace the development of theological thought over the past in order to understand better the current stage of development.

Today theology tends to be existentialist. It is especially concerned with the experience of human beings in the contemporary world. Theology recognizes the diversity of this experience according to time, place and culture. This diversity of experience gives rise to multitude of theologies such as liberation theology, "black" theology, theology of hope, Western theology, and so forth. "Theological enquiry should seek a profound understanding of revealed truth without neglecting close contact with its own times."[19]

Today theology is characterized by dialogue. Vatican II did much to stimulate dialogue among representatives of the Catholic Church and representatives of other groups. Other groups too—non-Catholic Christians, religious non-Christians, humanists, atheists, philosophers, scientists, artists, and others—have certain insights into the truth. The effect of dialogue among these groups is to clarify their insights for the participants. Theologians are among the principal beneficiaries.

Today theology is searching for a synthesis of its various branches. Throughout the nineteenth and twentieth centuries many theologians devoted themselves to individual disciplines. Specialization was widely cultivated. In some cases, the result was unfortunate: theology became a collection of unrelated insights without a unified point of view. To overcome this unfortunate result, there is need of a more systematic, a more synthetic approach to the subject.

Among the important questions and interests which occupy contemporary theologians some are connected with dogmatic theology: words and events as vehicles of revelation, the "I-Thou" relationship established by revelation, the reassessment of Biblical data, the development of dogma, hermeneutics, theological pluralism, God-free humanism, the origin of man, man as fallen and estranged, the effects of redemption, the consequences of Christ's humanity in terms of His human knowledge, uncreated and created grace, the Church as a communion, the Church and the modern world, the boundaries of the Church, ecumenism, the sacraments as encounters with Christ and eschatology.

Other questions and interests are connected with moral theology: faith as the response of the whole person to God, fundamental option, responsible freedom, natural law, theology of work, theology of hope, social justice, liberation theology, business and medical ethics, birth control, technology and industrialization, secularity, and the future.

Footnotes

1. *TCC* no. 43.
2. Nos. 16-21. Cf. *TCC* nos. 74c-g, 398h-i.
3. *Dei Verbum*, Divine Revelation, no. 23.
4. *Gaudium et Spes*, The Church Today, no. 62.
5. *Unitatis Redintegratio*, Ecumenism, no. 17.
6. *Optatam Totius*, Priestly Formation, no. 16.
7. *Lumen Gentium*, The Church, no. 25; *Dei Verbum*, Divine Revelation, no. 10.
8. *Dei Verbum*, Divine Revelation, no. 5.
9. *ST* 1a.1.4.
10. *ST* 1a.1.5.
11. *Gaudium et Spes*, The Church Today, nos. 5-6.
12. *Lumen Gentium*, The Church, no. 25.
13. Cf. J. McKenzie, *A Theology of the Old Testament*, Garden City, 1974, Doubleday.
14. *Itinerarium Mentis in Deum*:

15. His chief work was *Disputationes de Controversiis Christianae Fidei* 1586-93.
16. *Dogmata Theologica* 1643-50.
17. *Sacrorum Conciliorum Nova et Amplissima Collectio* 1758-98.
18. *Lamentabili* 1907; *Pascendi* 1907.
19. *Gaudium et Spes*, The Church Today, no. 62.

Chapter 3

GOD AND GOD-TALK

Bibliography: P. Berger, *A Rumor of Angels*, Garden City, 1968, Doubleday & Co.; J. Macquarrie, *God-Talk*, New York, 1967, Harper & Row; E. Mascall, *The Openness of Being*, Philadelphia, 1971, Westminster; *ST* 1a.1-26; J. Murray, S.J., *The Problem of God*, New Haven, 1964, Yale University Press; *NCE, God*, 6, 535-572; K. Rahner, S.J., *Foundations of Christian Faith*, New York, 1978, Seabury, 44-89.

God-talk is an English translation of the word "theology;" for theology, in the proper sense of the term, is discourse about God. Other disciplines which are called theological receive this name from the relation that they bear to the study of God Himself. What is to be presented in this section on God is therefore theology, or God-talk, in the strictest sense of the word.

The study of God properly begins with a study of God-talk, since one must seriously ask the question, whether it is possible to talk about God, and if so, how one can do so. What sort of talk is God-talk? It may surprise the theological neophyte to learn that God-talk is a problem, since people do in fact talk about God. Yet, the fact remains, that God is a wholly transcendent being, not of the created order, while all human talk exists in the context of the created order, and expresses human experience with the finite. Philosophers are therefore quick to remind us that predication about God will fall short of the truth about Him, so long as language remains limited by the finiteness of human knowledge and experience. And therefore God-talk is a special kind of talk, no matter how ordinary it may seem to those who use it.

A public stir was created, especially in the English-speaking world, in the early 1960's when a number of prominent theologians alleged that God had died. Since this was a most unusual thing for God to do, the matter was discussed, not only in theological journals and books, but even in news magazines and papers. As it turned out, nothing had happened to God, but much had happened to the language about God; and that in turn had created the illusion of His demise "in our cosmos, in our history, in our *Existenz*."[1] This so-called radical Christian theology ranged from the moderately revisionist views of men like Bishop John A.T. Robinson (1919-)[2] to the hard radical views of the death-of-God proponents like Thomas J.J. Altizer (1927-), William Hamilton (1924-), and Paul M. Van Buren (1924-).[3] Perhaps the real honesty of Bishop Robinson's *Honest to God* lay in its recognition that something was wrong with our God-talk, and not with God Himself. The Bishop of Woolwich wanted to revise our images and concepts of God, to make them more relevant to modern man. His adversaries, among whom were E.L. Mascall (1905-) and C.S. Lewis (1898-1963), also believed that God-talk must be relevant; but they believed that *traditional* God-talk, if not misunderstood, is perennially relevant.[4] The Catholic Church shares that belief. The official magisterium teaches it; and one of the Church's greatest theologians, Thomas Aquinas (1225-74), espoused a philosophy of God-talk which has remained unsurpassed in its ability to bridge the gap between finite language and the infinite Subject of theological discourse. It seems quite reasonable to suppose, that if Thomas' doctrine on analogy had been more respected in the theology of the early 1960's, much of the confusion about God's alleged death might have been avoided. After a brief look at the doctrine of Thomas, we shall return to these death-of-God thinkers for a critique in the light of that doctrine.

Analogous God-Talk

When Thomas discusses the divine names in his theological summa, he raises the question, "whether what is said of God and creatures is univocally predicated of them."[5] In his reply Thomas denies that such predication is univocal. The fundamental reason is the gulf between God as creator and His creatures. In God all perfection exists in total wholeness and simplicity; in creatures the divine perfection is only mirrored in a finite reflection of the Infinite. The divine essence is indeed the pattern for all things created, and the divine will is the efficient cause of their coming to be. Yet the gulf between cause and effect between pattern and image, is of such a kind as to preclude univocal predication at both ends. God remains in the *order* of the infinite; creatures stand in the *order* of the finite. One cannot, therefore, predicate properly of the infinite God, by using language that belongs to the finite creatures. The local butcher is alive; so is his dog, and so is his geranium. The term "alive" is used univocally of all three subjects, even though one is human, a second is a dumb animal, and another still is a plant. But if one asks whether God is "alive," the reply becomes a problem of predication. If the question means, does God have life like the life of these three beings, then the answer should be "no;" for God will never die, nor did God ever begin to live. His life is from eternity. On the other hand, one cannot say that God is not alive (except for those who espouse the death-of-God theology), for that statement would say something false about God. God-talk, then, is a special kind of predication. Nevertheless, it is predication *with meaning*. Thomas makes this point clearly when he insists that predication about God and about creatures is not equivocal. "Because if that were so," said Thomas, "it follows that from creatures nothing could be known or demonstrated about God at all; for the reasoning would always be exposed to the fallacy of equivocation. Such a view is against the philosophers, who proved many things about God, and also against what the Apostle says: 'The invisible things of God are clearly seen being understood by the things that are made' (Rm 1:20). Therefore it must be said that these names are said of God and creatures in an analogous sense, that is, according to proportion."[6]

Equivocal predication, in Thomas' view, would rule out proofs for the existence of God. When Thomas comes to the question of proving that God exists, he will offer proofs based upon God's causal relation to the created universe. And so he tells us that predication about God and creatures is one of proportional analogy. That means that words used to describe perfections in creatures can also be applied to God, but with all the limitation removed from the concept, and with the superlative excellence of the concept implied as it applies to God. So, God and the butcher are both alive. But God's life has none of the finiteness found in human life, and human life is but a shadow of that fullness of life which is life divine. God's life is the pattern and source for all created life; it exceeds the created effect far more than human words can express. Yet the bond of predication by analogy is there, precisely because the creature is made on the pattern of the Uncreated.

Thomas' own example of proportional analogy in the created order itself is the example of health. We all know what is meant by a "healthy" animal. Deprived of health, the animal is said to be sick. The veterinarian may prescribe some medicine to restore the animal to health. The medicine itself, Thomas noted, picks up the name of health; it is called "healthful" medicine, because it caused health in the animal. Moreover, the veterinarian may examine the urine of the animal after he has treated it for its illness; if the urine is what it should be, he will say that it is "healthy" urine. This is so, because it is the effect of the health in the animal. Thomas then went on to show that "healthy" is properly predicated of the animal; for it is the living animal that properly has health. Health belongs to life. But the term is also used to denote two non-living things: and this is so, because one of them is the cause of health, and the other is the effect of health in the being that properly can be called healthy. Hence, the term, health, applies to these two non-living beings by way of proportional analogy.

Since God is the cause and pattern for all things created, He is the proper subject for predication of all perfection. Creatures share the names of the perfections in God by reason of the bond of causality that links them to their creator. God is good, we say. Goodness in its ultimate and unlimited perfection is found in God alone. This divine goodness is reflected in good creation, for whatever good there is in creatures owes its source to the divine goodness. We often try to show this eminence of perfection in God by attaching to the names of the divine perfections or attributes a word such as "all;" God is all-good, God is all-loving, God is almighty. Evil, which by definition is the absence of some perfection, does not have its pattern not its efficient cause in God. God is surely the source of those beings that bear evil, but the evil as such has its source, not in God, but in the defective causality of secondary, created causes. A hole in a bucket is not a part of the bucket; it is rather the absence of a part that should be there.

It is now opportune for us to return to the chief death-of-God theologians and to examine their thought in the light of this theology of analogous God-talk which we have expounded according to the mind of

Thomas Aquinas. Thomas Altizer's God died an historical death, and one may suspect that it was univocal God-talk that caused it. "We must realize that the death of God is an historical event, that God died in our cosmos, in our history in our *Existenz*."[7] In another article, entitled "The sacred and the profane: a dialectical understanding of Christianity," Altizer says, " 'God is dead' are words that only truly may be spoken by the Christian, not by the religious Christian who is bound to an eternal and unmoving Word, but by the radical Christian who speaks in response to an Incarnate Word that empties Itself of Spirit so as to appear and exist as flesh."[8] The article abounds in Hegelian ideas about the eventual entithetic meeting of flesh and Spirit; but of interest to us here is the assumption that God (Word and Spirit) interacts with the world of flesh on univocal terms. Marius Victorinus (c. 355) wrote in the fourth century: "That the Logos was made flesh, however, does not mean that the Logos was corrupted and turned into flesh. . . . The whole man, therefore, was assumed, and having been assumed was also made free."[9] While this ancient writer did not know the sophisticated doctrine of proportional analogy, he sensed by faith that God remains unaltered by even the profound mystery of the Incarnation. Defective God-talk made it possible for Altizer to find God dead as the result of His being made flesh for our salvation. Right he was in saying that the Christian who accepts an eternal and unmoving Word cannot say "God is dead."

A similar univocal view of God-and-creatures muddied the waters of theology for William Hamilton. He was never able to see God and divine causality as belonging to a distinct *order* or reality. For him, God was at best the finest of causes and first of agents in the *same* order as creation. Thus he observes the absence of the God who fills the gaps where lesser causes are unable to function. Granted, many people think of God in that way. They pray only when all other helps fail. God is their last resort in crises. But the educated theologian really should have a more developed view of God. Yet, we find that Hamilton said: "God is not in the realm of the necessary at all; he is not a necessary being, he is not necessary to avoid despair or self-righteousness. . . . It is not true to say, with Luther, *entweder Gott oder Abgott*. It is not true to say with Ingmar Bergman, 'Without God, life is an outrageous terror.' It is not true to say that there are certain areas, problems, dimensions of life today that can only be faced, solved, illumined, dealt with by a religious perspective. . . . We trust the world, not God, to be our need fulfiller and problem solver, and God, if he is to be for us at all, must come in some other role."[10] If God is not actually dead in Hamilton's view, He is surely missing in action. But the action that Hamilton wants to see from God is precisely the action of a super-cause made of cosmic stuff. But God is not the man from Krypton who occasionally sallies forth from the telephone booth to intervene in human affairs when evils threaten good people. That God can intervene in a special way in nature is the belief of all people who think that miracles are possible. But it is not true, that God is absent or silent whenever He is not intervening after the manner of a miraculous cause. God is *totally* involved as First Cause in His created universe at all times; He is no less the cause of the cure of the blindness of a modern patient in a surgical ward than He was of the cure of the blind man in the Gospel (Jn 9). Through Jesus His Son He acted by way of miracle; through the modern surgeon He still acts by way of nature's course. The hospital chaplain with the oil of the sick in his hands mystically joins the patients to their God, the *total* master and cause of all that exists. He is not really a member of a healing "team," no matter how useful the term has become in hospital practice. What He offers the patient is not one *additional* help toward recovery of health; He offers a whole different *order* from that of the others on the team. His holy oil is not a substitute for pills and scalpels; they belong to the order of creation. The Spirit of the Lord belongs to the order of the Uncreated. It borders on blasphemy to say that patient X does not need to be anointed, because the doctor's expertise will bring him health without divine aid. No, it is to be hoped that the doctor is an expert; but God does not enter the picture merely as a flying Superman. His causal power is at work in the very mind and hands of the doctor. He made both doctor and patient out of nothing! The priest brings to the patient a special mystical bond with God Himself. When priests fail to see this as their role, they are easy victims of a vocation crisis. Even when Mother Nature and all the hospital staff point out a patient whose only future is death itself, the priest is the one person who doesn't call the patient a "hopeless" case. His mystical touch may not beget a miraculous cure. Such miracles are rare. But his mystical touch offers a hope beyond death itself: the priest offers the seeds of resurrection.

For an expanded consideration of these concerns, one would do well to read E.L. Mascall's fourth chapter in *The Secularization of Christian-*

ity, entitled, "Science, the secular and the supernatural,"[11] as well as
C.S. Lewis' book on *Miracles*, about which Dr. Mascall wrote, "I
should like to make Lewis' *Miracles* required reading for all New
Testament scholars."[12]

If univocal God-talk played a role in leading astray Altizer and
Hamilton, it was equivocal God-talk that caused the death of Paul Van
Buren's God. Linguistic analysts, like their progenitors, the logical
positivists, are unable to find any meaning in the word "God" or in
sentences in which God appears as a topic of reference. Paul Van Buren
approaches theology from this standpoint.[13] William Hamilton had this
to say about Van Buren's approach: "Van Buren is inclined to assume
that analytical philosophy has made all language about God impossible.
He is not talking about the deterioration of our experience of God, and he
is not talking about the loss of the sacred. He is talking about words, and
how hard it is to find the right ones. 'Simple literal theism' is out, he says,
and so is the kind of sophisticated and qualified non-objective theism that
he finds in Ogden, Tillich, Karl Jaspers, and that he ought to find in
Bishop Robinson."[14] So, the title of his book that placed him squarely
among the death-of-God theologians, *The Secular Meaning of the
Gospel*, is very apt and descriptive of his method. Sentences about God,
while grammatically akin to sentences about creatures, are not of the
same nature. "My child loves me" and "my God loves me" seem to be
two similar statements; but linguistic analysts tell us that they are not. For
the child is verifiable by empirical examination; but God is not verifiable
at all. Therefore the second sentence is an apparent statement about a
subject called "God" but in reality can be understood only if "God" is a
symbol for something else which is verifiable empirically. "God exists"
does not tell a truth nor a falsehood about God; it is simply meaningless,
we are told. If, however, one recasts such God-statements so as to make
them have a true meaning for verifiable humanity, then those statements
acquire a meaning. Thus, "God raised up Christ from the dead" could be
recast to mean: "The disciples after the death of Jesus had an Easter
experience that made Jesus come alive in their hearts and preaching."
Thus the Gospel about "God" acquires meaning when it receives its
"secular meaning."

Names are not "applied to God and creatures in a purely equivocal
sense," wrote Thomas Aquinas. "Because if that were so, it follows that

from creatures nothing could be known or demonstrated about God at all, for the reasoning would always be exposed to the fallacy of equivocation."[15]

For a sentence to be meaningful, it is only required that it can be understood, not necessarily by everyone, but by those who have a basic knowledge of the terms used in it. And the knowledge need only be basic. "Bertha is pregnant" is a statement that can be understood, not only by a gynecologist, but by anyone who knows where babies come from. "John is pregnant with a new book" can also be understood by these same people as a metaphor based on birth. For a statement about God to have meaning, it is only necessary that those to whom it is made have a basic, or minimal, understanding of what one means by "God." It is not necessary to have some great theological education, nor even to have in mind the God whom Jews and Christians worship. In fact, it is this basic, or minimal idea of God that forms the subject of the traditional proofs for the existence of God. We turn now to that consideration.

God and the Philosophers

The Second Vatican Council reaffirmed the teaching of Vatican I, when it said: "The Sacred Synod professes that 'God, the first principle and last end of all things, can be known with certainty from the created world, by the natural light of human reason.' "[16] The council further makes allusion to the teaching of Paul in Rm 1:20, where the apostle points to the effects of God's deeds in creation as pointers to God Himself. Tatian the Syrian (c. 165/175) imitated Paul in pointing to God's existence and nature through His creation. "Our God has no introduction in time. He alone is without beginning, and is Himself the beginning of all things. God is a spirit, not attending upon matter, but the Maker of material spirits and of the appearances which are in matter. He is invisible and untouchable, being Himself the Father of both sensible and invisible things. This we know by the evidence of what He has created; and we perceive His invisible power by His works."[17] This "philosophical" or "natural" theology, which we meet from the earliest days of the Church, found formal expression in the writings of later philosophers, of whom Thomas Aquinas is one of the best known. In his great *Summa*, Thomas offers five proofs for the existence of God.[18] These proofs are called "cosmological" because they are all based upon the evidence of the cosmos which God created. Thomas explained his method in his reply to the question, whether it can be demonstrated that God exists. "When an effect is better known to us than its cause, from the effect we proceed to the knowledge of the cause. From every effect the existence of its proper cause can be demonstrated, so long as its effects are better known to us; because since every effect depends upon its cause, if the effect exists, the cause must pre-exist. Hence the existence of God, insofar as it is not self-evident to us, can be demonstrated from those of His effects which are known to us."[19] Recall an old saying: where there is smoke there is fire.

When Aquinas presented his five cosmological proofs, he argued that the cosmic realities which we observe have a primal cause, albeit a cause that is invisible and untouchable, as Tatian would say. His argument from the order of efficient causes, for example, concludes: "Therefore it is necessary to admit a first efficient cause, to which everyone gives the name of God."[20] Sloppy theological thinking has had as much to do with the rejection of Thomas' arguments as has anti-Scholastic prejudice among the rejectors. All too often the careless thinker will present these arguments of the Angelic Doctor, and then go on to assume that Thomas has conclusively proved the existence of the God who spoke to Moses from the burning bush. Not so! The argument proves no more than the premises warrant. It proves the existence of a first efficient cause: no more than that. Since this cause is commonly considered to be "divine" and "supreme," it is called "God" by common consent. But the proof says nothing about Moses, burning bushes, nor anything pertaining to the history of salvation by the God who called Abraham and who sent His Son into the world as our Savior. To give the term "God" the minimal meaning that it has in the five proofs, and then to shift the meaning as the conclusion is drawn to the enriched sense that the term "God" has in the Sacred Scriptures, is pure logical fallacy. The cosmological arguments offered by Thomas can prove nothing more than the existence of a primal cosmological "god" who is the first mover, prime efficient cause, ultimate perfection, and so on. What we learn about this "supreme being" through Sacred Scripture comes, not from unaided human reason, but from the revelation by which "God wished to manifest and communicate both Himself and the eternal decrees of His will concerning the salvation of mankind. He wished, in other words, 'to share with us divine benefits which entirely surpass the powers of the human mind to understand.' "[21] Even some of the things that human reason might be able to discover about God without special revelation are illumined by God's word, spoken to us through divine revelation. Vatican II taught "that it is to His revelation that we must attribute the fact 'that those things, which in themselves are not beyond the grasp of human reason, can, in the present condition of the human race, be known by all men with ease, with firm certainty, and without the contamination of error.'"[22]

Thomas had no monopoly on offering proofs for God's existence; nor does the whole company of those who offer cosmological proofs. One of the best known proofs for God's existence, besides those of Thomas, is the proof espoused by Anselm of Canterbury (c. 1033-1109), in his work, *Proslogium*.[23] Here he presented his "ontological" proof, which fundamentally asserted that God's existence is self-evident from the very notion of the term "God." Thomas rejected this proof as valid. The argument of Anselm was stated in summary form by Thomas in this way: "Those things are said to be self-evident which are known as soon as the terms are known. . . . Thus, when the nature of the whole and of a part are known, it is at once recognized that every whole is greater than its part. But as soon as the signification of the word 'God' is understood, it is at once seen that God exists. For by this word is signified that thing than which nothing greater can be conceived. But that which exists actually and mentally is greater than that which exists only mentally. Therefore, since as soon as the word 'God' is understood it exists mentally, it also follows that it exists actually. Therefore, the proposition 'God exists' is self-evident." In refutation Thomas said: "Perhaps not everyone who heard this word 'God' understands it to signify something than which nothing greater can be thought, seeing that some have believed God to be a body. Yet, granted that everyone understands that by this word 'God' is signified something than which nothing greater can be thought, nevertheless, it does not therefore follow that he understands that what the word signifies exists actually, but only that it exists mentally. Nor can it be argued that it actually exists, unless it be admitted that there actually is something than which nothing greater can be thought; and this precisely is not admitted by those who hold that God does not exist."[24]

Karl Barth (1886-1968) rejected natural or philosophical theology as human arrogance attempting to discover the God who can be known only by the revelation that He has given. Rejecting the notion of the analogy of being, he saw philosophical assertions about God to be equivalent to equivocation. Yet, he wrote a book about Anselm, and had some pleasant things to say about the *Proslogium*.[25] But Barth interpreted Anselm, not as proving that God exists from the light of natural reason, but rather as illuminating faith, which is God's free gift. The *Proslogium* was faith seeking understanding. "God gave Himself as the object of his knowledge and God illumined him that he might know Him as object. Apart from this event there is no proof of the existence, that is, of the reality of God. But in the power of this event there is proof which is worthy of gratitude. It is truth that has spoken and not man in search of faith. . . . Just because it is the science of faith about faith, theology possesses light, but it is not the light of the theologian's faith."[26]

Official Catholic teaching disagrees with Barth; human reason can discover the existence of God by its own light. Yet, the magisterium has never said which arguments are valid ones. Not even the five proofs of Aquinas have received this declared approval. We must, moreover, readily admit, that while it is possible for the human mind to find God's existence philosophically, fallen humanity is excessively prone to worship idols, the works of human hands. If we must disagree with Barth about the principles of natural theology, we must also agree with him that God's grace and revealing Word have saved humanity from the pit of death. God wanted us "to have access to the Father, through Christ the Word made flesh, in the Holy Spirit, and thus become sharers in the divine nature."[27]

Human reason is limited in what it can say about God, apart from the light of special revelation. Reason may discover the existence of a primal cause of the visible universe (Thomas), the Supreme Being whose very idea includes existence (Anselm), but the premises warrant only a minimal notion of God. Thomas does not hesitate to derive a number of additional divine attributes from the data of reason, and some theologians may be surprised at how much he claims can be known by reason's light. Yet, for all that, he was trying to adhere to the premises of the five proofs as he did this. He saw these attributes contained in the notion of God in the five ways.

After the Enlightenment had enthroned the Goddess Reason, there came a reaction in both literature and theology that sought to exalt the non-rational side of humanity. The Romanticism of a writer like Samuel Taylor Coleridge (1772-1834)[28] was paired in theology with the work of Friedrich Schleiermacher (1768-1834). This Father of German Liberalism looked, not to reason, but to *religious feeling* or intuition as the basis for religion: one comes to a feeling of absolute dependence upon the One God, and in this experience the person validates religious commitment and piety.[29] Rudolph Otto (1869-1937) followed Schleiermacher's lead in his *Idea of the Holy*, written in 1917. Meanwhile Albrecht Ritschl (1822-89) and his Ritschlian followers stressed the *ethical* side of humanity, and gave Liberalism a new direction for the late nineteenth and twentieth centuries. The humanism which characterized much of the Liberal movement led eventually to a rationalistic approach to faith and the sources of revelation that disturbed many Christians: a lesson to serve as a warning to theologians of every age, that philosophy is neither to be despised on the one hand, nor to be exalted above revelation on the other. In His revelation, God has spoken to us. His revealed word is the basis for the theological considerations that are now before us.

Footnotes

1. T. Alitzer, "America and the Future of Theology," *Radical Theology and the Death of God*, Indianapolis, 1966, Bobbs-Merrill, 11.
2. *Honest to God*, Philadelphia, 1963, Westminster. Also *see* H. Cox, *The Secular City*, New York, 1965, Macmillan.
3. T. Altizer, *The Gospel of Christian Atheism*, Philadelphia, 1966, Westminster; W. Hamilton, *The Christian Man*, Philadelphia, 1961, Westminster; W. Hamilton, *The New Essence of Christianity*, New York, 1961, Association Press; P. Van Buren, *The Secular Meaning of the Gospel*, New York, 1963, Macmillan.
4. *See* D. Edwards (ed.), *The Honest to God Debate*, Philadelphia, 1963, Westminster, 91-95; and E. Mascall, *The Secularization of Christianity*, New York, 1966, Holt Rinehart & Winston.
5. *ST* 1a.13.5.
6. *Ibid.*
7. *Radical Theology and the Death of God*, 11.
8. *Ibid.*, 54.

9. *Against Arius* 1,45; 3,3.
10. W. Hamilton, "The Death of God Theologies Today," *Radical Theology and the Death of God*, 40-41.
11. *Op. cit.*, 190-192.
12. *Ibid.*, 237. Lewis' book is *Miracles*, New York, 1947, Macmillan.
13. P. Van Buren, *The Secular Meaning of the Gospel: Based on an Analysis of Its Language*.
14. *Radical Theology and the Death of God*, 32-33.
15. *ST* 1a.13.5.
16. Vatican II, *Dei Verbum* no. 6; Vatican I, *Dogm. Const. on Cath. Faith* 2.
17. *Oratio ad Graecos* 4.
18. *ST* 1a.2.3.
19. *ST* 1a.2.2.
20. *ST* 1a.2.3, the second proof.
21. Vat. II, *Dei Verbum* no. 6; Vat. I, *Dogm. Const. on Cath. Faith* 2.
22. *Ibid.*
23. S. Deane has translated this into English: Saint Anselm, *Basic Writings*, La Salle, 1961, Open Court, 1-34.
24. *ST* 1a.2.1, obj. 2 and ad 2.
25. Anselm, *Fides Quaerens Intellectum* (1931), Cleveland, 1962, World Meridian.
26. *Ibid.*, 171.
27. *Dei Verbum* no. 2.
28. Author of "The Rime of the Ancient Mariner," an other-worldly, non-logical poetic piece.
29. See *Religion: Speeches to Its Cultured Despisers* (1799), New York, 1958, Harper and Row.

Chapter 4

FATHER, SON, AND HOLY SPIRIT

Bibliography: E. Fortman, S.J., *The Triune God*, Philadelphia, 1971, Westminster; V. Lossky, *In the Image and Likeness of God* (1967), New York, Saint Vladimir's Seminary Press; *ST* 1a.27-43; *NCE, Trinity, Holy*, 14, 295-306.

The teaching of the Catholic Church regarding the God whom Christians worship can be found in a sort of compendium in these excerpts from Pope Paul VI's *Credo of the People of God*.[1] "We believe in the one only God, Father, Son, and Holy Spirit. . . . We believe that this only God is absolutely one in His infinitely holy essence as also in His perfections, in His omnipotence, His infinite knowledge, His providence, His will and His love. He is the *He who is*, as He revealed to Moses (Ex 3:14); and He is *Love*, as the Apostle John teaches us (1 Jn 4:8): so that these two names, Being and Love, express ineffably the same divine reality of Him who wished to make Himself known to us, and who 'dwelling in light inaccessible' (1 Tm 6:16), is in Himself above every name, above every thing and above every created intellect. God alone can give us right and full knowledge of this reality by revealing Himself as Father, Son, and Holy Spirit, in whose eternal life we are by grace called to share, here below in the obscurity of faith and after death in eternal light. The mutual bonds which eternally constitute the three persons, who are each one and the same divine Being, are the blessed inmost life of God thrice holy, infinitely beyond all that we can conceive in human measure. . . . We believe then in the Father who eternally begets the Son, in the Son, the Word of God, who is eternally begotten, in the Holy Spirit, the uncreated person who proceeds from the Father and the Son as their eternal love. Thus in the three divine persons, co-eternal and co-equal, the life and beatitude of God perfectly one superabound and are consummated in the supreme excellence and glory proper to uncreated Being, and always 'there should be venerated Unity in the Trinity and Trinity in the Unity.'[2] We believe in Our Lord Jesus Christ, who is the Son of God. He is the eternal Word, born of the Father before time began, and one in substance with the Father (*homoousios to Patri*), and through Him all things were made. . . . We believe in the Holy Spirit, who is Lord and giver of life, who is adored and glorified with the Father and the Son. He spoke to us by the prophets; He was sent by Christ after His resurrection and His ascension to the Father; He illuminates, vivifies, protects and guides the Church. . . ."[3]

Symbolic Theology

In the preceding chapter our concern was with the God of the philosophers. We were concerned with the role of human reason in the discovery and validation of the God who is primal cause of the world which we experience. That branch of theology is therefore called "philosophical" or "natural" theology. Now we are to begin the study of systematic theology in regard to God, by introducing into our study the revealed teaching that God gives us about Himself. So, this theological enterprise is often called "symbolic" theology, because it is based upon the Church's *creed*; and "symbol" is a Greek word meaning "creed."

The God of philosophers and the God of revelation are not two Gods; one and the same God, known to us by the light of reason in a limited way, becomes known to us in illuminated richness through the revealed word that God speaks to us. Before the advent of Jesus, God spoke to His people of election in the Law of Moses, in the oracles of the prophets, and in the wisdom of the sages. In the fullness of time, He sent His Son, the divine Wisdom incarnate, to fulfill the Law and the prophets, and to plant His Word in the Church as the seed of a new and everlasting covenant. His revelation, expressed in word and writing by His apostles, lives on in the Church which is guided by its teachers, the bishops united with one another and their head, Peter's successor, who in turn are in the special care of the Holy Spirit, Advocate and Sanctifier.

Christians believe in the Father, the Son, and the Holy Spirit. They receive baptism in these names, and worship these persons as God. In the history of religions, a community of three deities would rank low among polytheistic cultures. But Christianity is unique: it does not have three deities; it has only one God. It is this one God who is Father and Son and Holy Spirit. This is the Christian mystery of the Holy Trinity. Christianity inherits its belief in God's oneness from its Jewish roots. Like every observant Jew, Jesus Himself was fully familiar with the words of the *Torah*: "Hear, O Israel! The Lord is our God, the Lord alone! Therefore, you shall love the Lord your God with all your heart, and with all your soul, and with all your strength" (Dt 6:4-5). Jesus recognized that commandment as the first and greatest of the Lord's commandments. Together with the command to love one's neighbor as oneself, that is the cornerstone of the Law and the prophets (Mt 22:34-40). The monotheism of the New Testament arises, not out of the philosophical notion that there can be only one truly "supreme" being, but out of this heritage of Judaism. Side by side with its monotheism the New Testament presents a picture of Jesus as Lord, Son of Man and Son of God. While the former title is His own favorite title, a messianic designation, Jesus describes Himself unmistakably as the only Son who knows God, because He has seen the Father (Mt 11:27; Lk 10:22). Jesus is the one who, being in the form of God, emptied Himself, taking the form of a servant (Ph 2:6-7). Yes "in the beginning was the Word, and the Word was with God, and the Word was God," wrote John (Jn 1:1); and this Word who became flesh and dwelt among us (Jn 1:14) was Jesus.

Not only is Jesus divine, but so is the Holy Spirit. The divinity of the Holy Spirit, insinuated throughout the New Testament, is most clearly set forth by John. More than a cosmic force, the Spirit teaches the apostles all things (Jn 14:26), and He glorifies Jesus, because He receives of what is His and declares it to the apostles (Jn 16:14). The Spirit is sent by the Father in the name of the Son (Jn 14:26), and is unmistakably distinct from each of them. So, from the New Testament comes a mystery: three distinct persons are divine, but their divinity itself is one and not threefold. Monotheism is not discarded; rather, it is enriched. The God of Abraham is more than Abraham had ever imagined; He is Father to a divine Son and giver of a Holy Spirit, but in such wise that He retains the totality of His godhead even as He gives the totality thereof to the persons who come forth from His divine bosom. This mystery, hidden from Abraham, was all the more hidden from the philosophers who sought knowledge of God through His creation. The full mystic harmony which the divine persons exhibit in their creative work hides from the inquiry of the philosopher, seeking the knowledge of cause through effects, the richness of the personal life of the First Cause of all that exists. The philosopher, guided by the light of natural reason, beholds the harmonious action of the three divine hypostatic energies as though it were from a single person. Hence, the God of the philosophers may well appear to be a *personal* God; but the trinity of persons can be known only to those whom divine revelation has enlightened.

Theology in Development

The Fathers of the apostolic age clearly believed that Jesus was divine. Although their statements were pre-theological in that era, they declared that Jesus is God, and that His person pre-existed His incarnation. Ignatius of Antioch (died c. 110) wrote to the Ephesians: "Our God, Jesus Christ, was conceived by Mary in accord with God's plan: of the seed of David, it is true, but also of the Holy Spirit."[4] Dealing with the early heresies that aimed their shafts of error mainly at Christ, they were more concerned to show *Christ's* divinity than they were to show the divinity of the Spirit. But His divinity, already guaranteed in the New Testament, soon reached explicit assertion in Christian writings. This statement from Tertullian (c. 155—post 220), although it comes from the period after he had joined the Montanists, still has value for observing the faith of the third century: "We do indeed define that there are two, Father and Son, and with the Holy Spirit even a third, in accord with the principle of the *oikonomia*, which distinguishes as to number, lest, as your perversity would infer,[5] the Father Himself be believed to have been born and to have suffered—which, in fact, it is not lawful to believe, since it has not been handed down. That there are two Gods and two Lords, however, is a statement which we will never allow to issue from our mouth—not as if the Father and the Son were not one God, nor the Spirit God, and each of them God; but formerly two were spoken of as Gods and two as Lords, so that when Christ would come, He might both be acknowledged as God and be called Lord, because He is the Son of Him who is both God and Lord."[6]

Arguing against Praxeas, Tertullian clearly distinguishes the three persons from one another, while asserting that this distinction does not imply any division. God remains one in the threeness of Father, Son, Spirit. If it were otherwise, then the incarnate Lord who suffered on the cross would be God the Father; but tradition rejects that erroneous notion. The belief that the Father suffered for us in the flesh is not only erroneous, but it has its own name as a heresy: Patripassionism.[7] It belongs to the general corpus of modalist heresies, which found in Sabellius (*floruit* c. 215) an outstanding expositor. Thus modalism of various kinds is often called simply Sabellianism. The notion of the *oikonomia* is often associated with Sabellian modalism, and it is well to note the use of that term by Tertullian in the passage just cited.

Tertullian said that the principle of *oikonomia* distinguishes as to number. The distinction of persons as "three" seems to be a bit of "economy"—a kind of catechetical housekeeping. For Sabellius it would be that and nothing more. God, in his view, is not Trinity: He is one person who reveals Himself to His creation under three *modes* of relationship. The one divine person is named Father or Son or Spirit according to the mode in question. That is why his false doctrine is called *modalism*. Tertullian, however, made it evident that his economy did not point to modal unitarianism. The *number three* in the theology of the Christian God needs to be seen as economic and is a reminder to us that all language about God is analogous, not univocal. Even the number three, when used in God-talk, is an analogous term. Outside of God, there is no being of any rank that is one in essence and three in persons. The triuneness of God is unique; no creature can be called triune. So, the words of Tertullian make more sense than one might think at first reading.

Traditional theology uses the distinction between "economic" and "essential" to show that God is triune in Himself, and not simply in relation to the created universe. Just as philosophical theology seeks to know God's existence and attributes through observing created effects of God's acts, so symbolic theology seeks to discover the "essential" truth about God through contemplation of the "economic" role of the divine persons in salvation history. This entails a process of abstracting the essential truth from the data of revelation, so that the theologian can say what God's life and nature would be, even if God had not created anything at all. The Greeks called this process *apophasis*.[8] The historic creeds contain assertions that are in part economic and in part pure theology. The Nicene Creed of 381 says of the Second Person: "We believe in one Lord Jesus Christ, the only Son of God, eternally begotten of the Father, God from God, Light from Light, true God from true God, begotten not made, one in Being with the Father. Through Him all things were made." Further assertions follow concerning His incarnation. In the portion quoted, "Jesus Christ" and "through Him all things were made" are statements of the *oikonomia*; the others are essential truths about the Son of God, and would have been so even if He had not become incarnate as Jesus the Christ, or even if nothing had been made at all. All the statements about the incarnation are, of course, economic truths about the Son of God. If one recalls that some of the early writers, too much influenced by the philosophy of Plato, implied that the Father brought forth the Logos (the divine Word) *in order to* relate to creation through Him, one can see the vital importance of knowing where economy leaves off and *theologia* in the strictest sense begins.[9]

Tertullian, in the passage cited above, further stated that "formerly" there were two who were called Gods and Lords. He was referring to the Jewish writings, odd as that may seem. But, like many of the ancient writers, Tertullian thought that the Trinity was *foreshadowed* in the revelation to the Jews, becoming explicit in the revelation of the New Testament. Surely, the monotheism of the Jewish people is beyond question. Yet, in a passage like Psalm 110: "The *Lord* said to my *Lord*, sit at my right hand," etc. some ancient writers saw the distinction of divine persons in the one God already indicated prior to the advent of Christ. The Synoptics (Mt 22:41-46; Mk 12:35-37; Lk 20:41-44) reinforced the interpretation of this verse of the psalm as referring to the Father by the first *Lord* and to the Son by the second. Pope Paul VI, in the portion of his *Credo* which was cited at the beginning of this chapter imitating the Nicene Creed, said that the Holy Spirit spoke through the prophets. The divine inspiration of the pre-Christian inspired authors is attributed to the third person of the Trinity. While some Scripture scholars generally find this kind of interpretation annoying, one can accept it in proper theological context. It is true that before the advent of Christ the Trinity of persons was not known, not even to the inspired authors. Yet, the Trinity existed then, as it always had and always will. The Fathers would have us understand that, although hidden from the minds and eyes of all people on earth, the reality of the Trinity of persons was at work in the actions of Him whom the ancients called "Lord and God." Realizing the triune character of the God who called Abraham and who sent His own Son into the world in the fullness of time, Christian Fathers decided to read back into the Jewish writings the truth which, at the time of the writings, was veiled.

It was in this work against Praxeas that Tertullian used the word *Trinitas* (2,4), a special word to designate the unique threeness of the one God. In Greek theological language, a similar term had been born of the mind of Theophilus of Antioch (died c. 185-191). Referring to the creation account of Genesis, he wrote: "The three days before the luminaries were created are types of the *Trias* (Trinity): God, His Word, and His wisdom."[10]

Christian apologists of the second century, writing just a bit earlier than Tertullian, not only bore witness to the biblical basis for the theology of the Trinity, but they also produced examples from common things to serve as analogies for the divine mystery of trinitarian life. Justin Martyr (died c. 165) says of the Son's relation to God the Father: "We see things happen similarly among ourselves: for whenever we utter some word, we beget a word—yet, not by any cutting off, which would diminish the word in us when we utter it. We see a similar occurrence when one fire enkindles another. It is not diminished through the kindling of the other, but remains as it was; and that which was enkindled by it appears to exist by itself, not diminishing that from which it was enkindled."[11] Here we can see analogies about Word and Light, Johannine biblical themes made concrete for Justin's readers. We are reminded that the historic Nicene Creed would call the Word "Light from Light" as well as "God from God." We might also think of the Holy Saturday baptismal liturgy, where the lights of all the candles, enkindled from the sole source of the paschal candle, symbol of Christ, do not weaken the Christlight: "a flame divided but undimmed."[12]

Athenagoras of Athens (died c. 180), a contemporary of Justin, spoke of the Holy Spirit, "who works in those who speak prophetically,"[13] as "an effluence of God, flowing out and returning like a ray of the sun."[14] Further in this work, Athenagoras described the Holy Spirit as "an effluence like light from fire."[15] One might think of the Lucan account of

Pentecost (Ac 2:1-4) where the Spirit descends upon the infant Church in fiery tongues, or of several images in the liturgical sequence, *Veni Sancte Spiritus*.

The Nicene Crisis

In spite of the efforts like those just considered, the theology of the Christian God did not develop smoothly and peacefully. The desire to demystify the mystery kept appearing. Since there is an order of divine persons: Father, Son, Holy Spirit, would it not be more reasonable to see the Father as the "real" God, and to make the other two divine persons either different aspects of the Father, or sub-divine beings after the manner of the created angels? The former path was taken by the *modalist* heretics, like Sabellius. The latter path was taken by various teachers of *subordinationism*, of which Arius of Alexandria (c. 270-c.336) is the outstanding instance, and whose name became attached to his heretical brain-child, *Arianism*, never to be forgotten in theological history.

Arius, priest of the Baucalis church at Alexandria, openly taught that the Son of God was created out of nothing by the Father, and that there was a time when the Son did not exist. Notice that Arius was not talking about the *human nature* which God's Son took unto Himself in the incarnation. He was talking about the Son's *divinity*. Made, not begotten, the Son had a separate being or substance from the Father. He and the Father were not *of one substance (homoousios)* as the Fathers of Nicea would subsequently define. Arius' ideas were gaining influence at Alexandria, and about the year 318 Bishop Alexander, the Coptic pope, openly opposed his troublesome priest. Arius was undaunted, and continued to propagate his doctrine, which he believed to be the correct one. After a synod at Alexandria had declared Arius to be in error, Alexander wrote an encyclical letter in the year 324 to the bishops not of his jurisdiction, to warn them of the false teachings of the condemned Arius. The letter is a clear statement of biblical truth about the triune God; and the bishops of the East, acting in concert, were about to uphold that truth. Constantine the Great (c. 288-337), who had brought freedom to Christianity in the empire in 313, became personally interested in the Arian problem after the defeat of Licinius, which made him the sole emperor of the Roman empire. He called a council of bishops at Nicea in 325, which history reckons as the first ecumenical council of the Church. The teaching of Arius was roundly condemned by the bishops, and a credal statement was issued, namely, the Nicene Creed.

This Nicene Creed of 325, shorter than the so-called Nicene Creed of 381 which is used in the Roman Mass on Sundays and solemnities, became the touchstone of orthodoxy, as it proclaimed the full unity of the Godhead in the threeness of Father and Son and Holy Spirit. The original Nicene Creed stated this: "We believe in one God, the Father almighty, maker of all things visible and invisible. And in one Lord Jesus Christ, the Son of God; the only-begotten, begotten of the Father, that is, of the substance of the Father; God of God, Light of Light, true God of true God; begotten, not made; of the same substance (*homoousion*) as the Father; through whom all things were made, both those in heaven and on earth; who for us men and our salvation came down, took flesh, and was made man, suffered, and rose up on the third day, ascended into heaven, and will come to judge the living and the dead. And in the Holy Spirit. But those who say that there was a time when He was not, and that He was made out of what did not exist, or who say that He is of another hypostasis or substance, or that the Son of God is created or subject to change or alteration, the Catholic Church anathematizes."[16] The Father and the Holy Spirit received only brief mention at Nicea; it is evident that the creed was designed to reject the false teaching of Arius. To give theological precision to their creed, the Nicene Fathers chose the word *homoousios* to describe the unity of Being which the Father and the Son possess in undivided totality. Although the term had been in use earlier in an heretical sense, declaring a unitarian modalism in the writings of Paul of Samosata (mid-third century) the Nicene Fathers herewith gave it a new meaning, applying it to the *oneness of substance* in the Godhead. The Emperor Constantine put his authority behind this creed.

Touchstone of orthodoxy: what does this mean? Arius himself had used the word "glory" in reference to the divine quality of the persons. He said that there is a Trinity, but that it is *not of like glories*.[17] The Nicene Fathers declared the very opposite. The dogmatics of Nicea had its effect upon liturgical practice. The "Glory be to the Father," etc. assumed varied forms, some of which were Nicene and the others of which were Arian. By the way one said the prayers, one would indicate whether the Trinity was of like or unlike glories. Those who believed and prayed in the Nicene manner came to be called "Orthodox," those whose *glory* was *right*. The Arians, on the other hand, proclaimed the Trinity to be of unlike glories, and so their *glory* was not *right*.

Calling the universal Church *catholic* goes back to Ignatius of Antioch.[18] The Nicene decree used the word catholic in this same sense. After Nicea, the Churches of the East began to adopt the name "Orthodox" as their normal title, stressing their Nicene loyalty and their opposition to the Arians. The western Church, on the other hand, continued to use the name "Catholic" as its main hallmark. The predilection of Augustine (354-430) for this term firmed up its use by all those who read and honored his works. Today, the Church of the West in union with Rome calls itself Catholic; the Churches of the East who honor the Nicene faith call themselves Orthodox.

After the Council of Nicea in 325, Arianism made a powerful bid for the ascendancy over Orthodoxy. Eusebius of Nicomedia (d. 342) persuaded Constantine the Great to renege on his commitments to the Nicene faith, and the beginning of a half century of imperial meddling was under way, which would give to the Arians the political clout necessary to subvert Nicea. Subsequent emperors, especially Constantine's son Constantius (317-361), persecuted the Nicene Christians, and summoned councils filled with hand-picked Arian bishops to proclaim Arianism as true Christianity. Athanasius (c. 297-373) was exiled five times from the Coptic See of Alexandria in these persecutions; Hilary of Poitiers (c. 315-c. 367) was sent into exile for four years because of his defense of the Nicene faith. A series of councils made up of Arian Fathers condemned the Nicene Creed: Tyre in 335, Antioch in 339, Arles in 353, Milan in 355, Sirmium in 357, Rimini and Seleucia in 359. The empire was being turned into an Arian society.

During this period of well-being, Arianism had internal disagreements about trinitarian doctrine, and three distinct schools of Arian thought emerged. The radical Arians considered the Son of God to be a creature who is unlike the Father in His essence. He is not really the image of the Father at all. These were called *Anomoeans* which means dissimilarists; they were also called *Eunomians*, after Eunomius of Cyzicus (c. 333-c. 393), their chief propagandist. A moderate group of Arians had representatives among many influential people in letters and politics. They held that the Son of God, while created and distinct from the Father, had nevertheless a similarity of essence to the Father's. They were called *Homoeans* which means similarists; Acacius of Caesarea in Palestine (d. 366) was a propagator of this view. Lastly there were the *Homoiousians*, who literally made just one iota of difference in doctrine from the Nicene *Homoousians*. They were also called Semi-Arians. For them, the essence of the Son of God was so like that of the Father, that the two divine essences were quasi-identical. Some of the Nicene Fathers, and in particular Hilary, entered into serious dialogue with these people, and in some cases convinced them that their position would make full sense only if it were revised to the Nicene position. An iota of change in thought to match the iota of change in the name in some cases meant conversion to Orthodoxy. The term, Semi-Arian, shifted meaning in the course of these fifty years. By the time of the Council of 381, Semi-Arian meant those who were professing "Holy-Spirit" Arianism, also called Pneumatomachianism (Fighters against the Spirit) or Macedonianism. This last name comes, not from the Balkan nation, but from the priest Macedonius (died c. 362), who is believed to have played an important part in bringing Arian doctrine to this logical conclusion.[19] If the Son of God is not true God, made from non-being, then the same should be true of the Holy Spirit, leaving only the Father as divine monarch and true God. This development in Arianism came, as expected, in the period following Nicea.

When the Romans were routed and soundly beaten by the Visigoths in the battle at Adrianople in 378, the Arian emperor Valens (c. 328-378) was killed. The western emperor, Gratian (359-383), named Theodosius I (c. 346-395), who would be known as Theodosius the Great, to be the successor to Valens. Under the rule of Theodosius, who was a Catholic, Arian bishops were dispossessed of their powers and Orthodox bishops were returned to their sees. In the summer of 381 the Council of Constantinople was held at the behest of Theodosius. This council of eastern bishops reaffirmed the Orthodoxy of Nicea. The bishop of Rome was not represented, although he did send a message to the council through the bishop of Thessalonika. The main purpose of the council was to show to the Christian world that, although the Nicene Creed had been condemned in many synods over the past fifty years, the true Church of Christ will ever believe in the unity of the Father, Son and Holy Spirit, consubstantial with one another in undivided Godhead. This council is reckoned historically as the second ecumenical council of the universal Church.

Shortly after this important eastern council an important council was held at Aquileia in northern Italy. There, a group of bishops of the western Church, guided chiefly by Ambrose (c. 340-397), the bishop of Milan, who in turn was in touch with the bishop of Rome, Damasus (c. 305-384), ruled in favor of the Nicene Orthodoxy. The emperors Theodosius and Gratian readily supported the decrees of the two councils, and Arianism, having lost its imperial support, began to decline in influence and numbers.

Post-Nicene Theology

Although politically the Arians were dominant after the council of 325, they did not overshadow their Orthodox contemporaries in theological thought. Particularly important to this period were three men of the province of Cappadocia, who are known in patristic history simply as the "Cappadocian Fathers." These three are: Basil of Caesarea (c. 330-379), and his brother Gregory of Nyssa (died c. 394), and their friend Gregory of Nazianzus (c. 330-390). The Greek Church honors all three with titles of dignity. Basil and Gregory are honored as "Ecumenical Doctors" along with John Chrysostom; Basil is called Basil the Great; Gregory of Nazianzus is called the "Theologian," a title given to few persons in the world of theology. And Gregory of Nyssa was acknowledged in early councils as the "Father of the Fathers" and as the "Pillar of Orthodoxy." Basil, from his metropolitan see of Caesarea Mazaca, was a bulwark of Orthodoxy in the East during the trying years between the two ecumenical councils. He died just before the restoration of Orthodoxy under Theodosius the Great. The two Gregories were at the council of 381, and Gregory of Nazianzus was, for a short time, its president. Matching their zeal in action was their theological acumen.

One of the theological emphases of the Greek Church has always been the tri-personal character of the Godhead. While the West generally puts the trinitarian question this way: "There is one God; now how can He be three?" the Greek Church puts it the other way round: "There are Father, Son, and Holy Spirit; now how can these three be one?" Athanasius' emphasis was similar to that which marked the western Church. In fact, the Council of Nicea, facing an Arian attempt to divide God into two or three separate essences, placed an emphasis upon God's oneness that shifted the question as seen by the Greek Church to the opposite pole. One of the contributions of the Cappadocians in their writings was a shifting back from the emphasis on oneness to the emphasis on trinity. For this reason, some students of their works have called them "new Nicenes" and claimed that they have modified the Orthodoxy of Nicea. This charge is, however, without basis. They defined terms and developed doctrine in full accord with the Nicene Fathers, and in so doing, built a safe path for those who were to follow them in their tasks.

The western Church, as we have just noted, has approached the theology of the Trinity by using God's oneness as the starting point. This emphasis was largely due to the authority of Augustine, whose writings influenced much of western thought after his time. Father Edmund Fortman (b. 1901) said that Augustine thought "of one single divine nature susbsisting in three persons. Hence, he started his explanation of the mystery not from the Father considered as the source of the other two persons, but from the one, simple divine nature or essence which is the Trinity. . . . Never before had the divine unity been set in such strong relief in relation to the three divine persons. God, for Augustine, does not mean directly the Father, as *ho theos* did for the Greeks, but the concrete Godhead, the basic divinity unfolding itself into three persons, the Father, the Son, and the Holy Spirit. He stresses oneness rather than threeness and starts from the one divine essence rather than from the saving deed of God in Christ, which he assumes to be known. This new starting point will be very influential in all subsequent western trinitarian teaching, and will lead to a distinction between the two treatises of God, *De Deo Uno* and *De Deo Trino*."[20] While both approaches to the mystery, that of the Cappadocians and that of Augustine, are quite legitimate, the different paths taken have given quite a different character to theology in each of the Churches.

The decree of Nicea in 325 condemned those who said that the Son of God was "of another hypostasis or substance." One can see here that the two terms, hypostasis and substance, were regarded as synonyms, and were being used without accurate theological definition. The Cappadocians were more precise. They used the word *ousia* to refer to God's nature or essence, and the word *hypostasis* as equivalent to the individual or person. Thus, they established for the future the theological formula: *one ousia, three hypostases*.

The Cappadocians likewise guaranteed the full divinity of the Holy Spirit. The Council in 325 was brief about Him: "and in the Holy Spirit." This third person of the Trinity was a vague figure in the theology of the Nicene age, and His true divinity was soon denied by the Macedonian heretics. The Cappadocians made it clear that He was not merely a divine force (something like the benevolent Force of *Star Wars*), but an hypostasis equal to, yet distinct from, the Father and the Son. He was truly God.

They faced the issue of how the Holy Spirit is different from the Son, inasmuch as both come forth from the bosom of the Father. Gregory of Nazianzus, in his fifth *Theological Oration*, showed that the Holy Spirit is distinct from the Son; for although He proceeds from the Father as does the Son, yet the mode of origin differs. He is therefore not a second Son of God, nor is He *less than* the Son of God, owing to some supposed deficiency in His mode of origin. Gregory asserted the oneness of the Godhead by saying that the Son is not the Father; there is but one Father, although the Son is what the Father is. And he said that the Holy Spirit is not the Son; there is but one Son, although the Spirit is what the Son is.[21]

This unity of substance, whereby the three persons of the Trinity are present in an ineffable manner in the work of any one of the persons, is described by Latin theologians as *circuminsession*. John of Damascus (c. 675-c.749) would give this profound truth the more athletic name of *perichoresis*.[22] Both terms show the unity of operation in God while indicating that the divine person who acts is not merged hypostatically with the others.

The theological practice of the western Church which stresses the oneness of the Godhead as the starting point for considering the Trinity has led to a strong emphasis on circuminsession. Following the lead of Augustine, Latin theologians have asserted that all of God's *external* acts are common to the three persons; only in the *internal* life of God is there distinction of hypostatic activity. When one of the divine persons is said to act, this is to be understood as an *appropriation*, we are told. This means that an action of the Holy Spirit is in reality an action of all three persons, but which is "attributed" to the Spirit because of His role as Sanctifier. When, for example, the Holy Spirit overshadowed Blessed Mary (Lk 1:35) at the time of the incarnation of the Son of God, it was in reality the Blessed Trinity that overshadowed her, with the Spirit being named according to appropriation. Latin theologians have insisted, nonetheless, that the incarnation of the Word is precisely that, and not the incarnation of the three divine persons. While this approach to theology casts out all danger of subordinationism, Arian or otherwise, it runs the risk of theological modalism. Adolph von Harnack believed that he found this modalism in the theology of Augustine and of the Scholastics who followed his lead. He said that Augustine got beyond Modalism by not wanting to be a Modalist and by certain ingenious distinctions. Of the Scholastics who followed Augustine's system of thought he said that in discussing the Trinity "they do not get beyond Modalism."[23]

While the judgment of Harnack may be much too severe, it does not seem that the doctrine of appropriation limits too much the individual dynamism of the divine persons, making them for all practical purposes a Trinity only when turned inward, but a Unity when manifested outwardly, with the possible exception of the hypostatic union of the Word of God to the humanity of Jesus. It is hard to believe that the New Testament writers, or even Jesus Himself, distinguished the three persons in the Godhead for our benefit, if the distinctions have in fact no practical bearing upon our spiritual life as Christians. It makes more theological sense to take the words of the New Testament seriously, and to attribute to the divine persons their saving acts, not by appropriation, but by recognition of their being the personal and dynamic source thereof.

The Augustinian approach to trinitarian theology is quite helpful, on the other hand, when one tries to understand the divine *attributes*. This term itself is helpful to God-talk that must be analogous. God does not really "have" an intellect, a will, and various virtues; His essence is simple and admits no composition. God *is* His intellect; He *is* His will; He *is* His might and righteousness. What are faculties or qualities rooted in created human nature, are in God His very Being itself, looked at by us through *analogy* to created realities. Hence, we speak of God's will, for example, as though it were not identified with His essence, when we say: "God *has* a saving will toward us." We *attribute* to God's essence those perfections which in us are distinct realities. Hence, we call this God-talk the language of attribution.

Looking at God as Augustine did, and seeing Him as *primarily* one in essence and nature, one can readily see that all the attributes belong equally to the three persons of the Trinity. All three are of one essence; all three therefore possess the divine intellect, will, and perfections in the same fullness of Being, without any measure of greater or less. Hence, Pope Paul said: "We believe that this one only God is absolutely one in His infinitely holy essence as also in His perfections, in His omnipotence, His infinite knowledge, His providence, His will and His love." Of the divine Son, Pope Paul said: "equal therefore to the Father according to His divinity, and inferior to the Father according to His humanity."[24] This differs from what we find in certain ancient writers. Interpreting Jn 14:28, Alexander of Alexandria (d. 328) had written: "To the Father alone, however, do we ascribe the peculiar circumstance of being the Unbegotten; for the Savior Himself has said, 'My Father is greater than I.' "[25] Here it is asserted that Christ is less than the Father, even as the Son of God. If this meant that He has less of the Godhead, it would be the heresy of subordinationism. But it does not mean that. It is a Greek way of looking at the Trinity. Since the Father is the Origin and Fountain of all Godhead, He is called "greater" by reason of His being the first person. After the Arian crisis, both Greeks and Latins moved away from expressions that might hint at subordinationism.

Footnotes

1. Issued June 30, 1968, by Pope Paul VI (1897-1978).
2. Creed *Quicumque*, called the "Athanasian."
3. Translation adapted from the USCC version.
4. *Op. cit.*, 18,2.
5. The "perversity" is that of Praxeas, Tertullian's opponent.
6. *Adversus Praxeam* 13, 5-6.
7. A Latin term meaning, the Father suffered.
8. *See* Lossky, *In the Image and Likeness of God*, "Apophasis and Trinitarian Theology," 13-29.
9. For example, Hippolytus, *Refutation of all Heresies* 10, 33.
10. *To Autolycus* 2, 15.
11. *Dialogue with Trypho* 61.
12. From the Paschal *Exultet*.
13. Like the creed of 381: "Who spoke through the prophets."
14. *Supplication for Christians* 10.

15. *Ibid.* 24.
16. Translation from Jurgens, *Faith of the Early Fathers* 1, no. 651 f.
17. According to his work, *Thalia*, written around 320.
18. *To the Church of Smyrna* 8, 2.
19. Hence, the Macedonian Orthodox Church is not a contradiction in terms; it is doctrinally Orthodox, ethnically Macedonian.
20. *The Triune God* 141.
21. *Oration* 31.
22. *See* Fortman, *The Triune God* 81.
23. *History of Dogma* (1885), New York, 1961, Dover, 131 note.
24. Paul VI, *Credo of the People of God.*
25. Encyclical letter of the year 324.

Chapter 5

EMMANUEL: GOD WITH US

Bibliography: T. d'Eypernon, *The Blessed Trinity and the Sacraments*, Westminster, 1961, the Newman Press. Trans. from the French; Leo XIII, *Divinum Illud*, Encyclical Letter on the Holy Spirit; *see also* the bibliography for chapter 4 on God.

Immanent and Transcendent

The God of Israel was without doubt a transcendent God. The Jews revered His name so highly that they shied away from pronouncing it. Wherever the sacred tetragram YHWH appeared, it was read as *Adonai*, which we translate as *Lord*. This practice is observed by modern Jews when they read the Scriptures. Yet, although gloriously transcendent, this God was by no means absent. He dealt familiarly with Abraham, Isaac, and Jacob; He spoke to Moses face-to-face as it were; He led His people in pillar of fire and pillar of cloud; and He rested in the midst of His chosen ones upon the propitiatory of the Ark. God was indeed closer to His people than were any of the gods of the nations round about.

The God of the Hebrew people is the Father of our Lord Jesus Christ. He is the Father of Him, not in an adoptive sense, as He is Father to human beings who live in His grace, but as Father in the very life of the Godhead. He begets the Son by an eternal begetting. In so doing He does not *share* His divine Being with the Son; He communicates to Him the totality thereof. The Son is personally distinct from the Father, but identical to Him in Being. Justin (died c. 165) said of Him: "He ministers to the will of the Father and was begotten by the Father's will."[1] This assertion, which can be properly understood, needs clarification. It would not be said by a present-day theologian.

A number of ancient writers spoke as did Justin, asserting that the Son comes from the Father through the Father's will. Those who say this in a false sense are teachers of subordinationism—God the Father had a choice: He chose (perhaps from all eternity) to have a Son; otherwise, He would have been a one-person God. But there are those like Justin who do not mean that. Adversaries of the faith sometimes argued that the Father was *coerced* in the Christian system; He had no freedom in the matter of communicating His nature to the Son and the Spirit. The reply of the Fathers is, that God is free in all things. Regarding creation He has freedom of choice to create or not to. Regarding divine life in Himself He cannot be other than Trinity, for such is His necessary nature. But He is not unwilling to have it so. So, in begetting the Son, the Father does so willfully, that is, happily and without duress.

That the Son ministers to the Father's will may also sound subordinationist. If, however, we remember that the Father and the Son are of one identical will in their Unity, this charge may vanish. Important to us, nonetheless, is the Platonism of a number of early Fathers. Identifying the pleroma of the world of ideas as the dwelling of the Father, the Platonists regarded the Son, the divine Logos, as the intermediary between the Father and His created universe. Not only did God make the world through the Logos, but God's people are in direct touch only with the Logos who bridges the gap between the Father God and what He has made. Gone is the immanence of Abraham's God in this system of philosophy. This excessive use of a system of philosophy, as faith sought understanding, gave a false view of the Father whom we are taught to address familiarly in the Scriptures. It stands as a perennial warning to all who are so wedded to a system of thought, that they are ready to revise revelation to make it fit the system.

While some ancient authors had connected the divine origin of the Son with the divine will, later theologians in the western tradition connected it with the divine intellect, and related the origin of the Holy Spirit to the divine will. Thus they tried to show that the two "personal faculties" among the divine attributes accounted for the two persons who proceed from the first person, source of all life in God. Thomas Aquinas wrote: "The name Love in God can be taken essentially and personally.

If taken personally, it is the proper name of the Holy Ghost; as Word is the proper name of the Son. To see this, we must know that since . . . there are two processions in God, one by way of the intellect, which is the procession of the Word, and another by way of the will, which is the procession of Love; forasmuch as the former is more known to us, we have been able to apply suitable names to express our various considerations as regards that procession, but not as regards the procession of the will."[2] He then shows that, while it is simple enough to call the procession of the Son from the Source of the Godhead *birth*, it is harder to name the procession of the Spirit from His Source of Godhead. Yet, it may be called a *breathing forth* (since the Spirit means breath), or even *dilection* (since the Spirit is the terminus of divine Love). Theologians have actually put together a system, based on the Scriptures, but not fully validated by revelation, in assigning the origin of the two proceeding persons to the activity of the divine intellect and will. It is an ingenious structure; it helps to illustrate why there are two such processions and no more in God; and it ties together revealed notions about the Son of God as the Word (Jn 1) and the Spirit as the Gift of divine Love (Ep 1:14; 4:8). Clever though it is, it remains a *theologoumenon*; it cannot be ultimately verified through revelation. Moreover, it *illustrates* the truths about the Trinity; it does not prove the Trinity. Pope Paul VI made passing reference to this structure in his *Credo* when he said: "We believe . . . in the Holy Spirit, the uncreated person who proceeds from the Father and the Son as their eternal Love." It is often called the "psychological model" for the Trinity. That means that it is based upon the analogy of the faculties of the human psyche, the intellect and the will. This psychological model also has its weaknesses. It would seem that if the Son is the terminus of divine intellectual activity, then it is the Father who does all the thinking, while the Son is simply His Word; and if the Spirit is the terminus of the divine love of the Father and the Son for each other, then the Spirit is called Love, not as one who does the loving, but as the term of such loving. But the truth is, that all three persons know and understand, will and love. For the divine intellect and will are not persons as such, but are attributes of the one essence of God.

That there are three persons in God, not more not fewer, is not dependent upon any theological model, but upon the revelation of the New Testament. The oneness of this God, which is also Trinity, is likewise revealed truth. That there are in God two *processions*, where-with the Son and Spirit derive their origin from the Father is a necessary corollary to the revealed truths. The procession of the Spirit, however, is a matter of theological dispute between Latins and Greeks. The Greeks say that the Spirit proceeds from the Father alone in the essence of the Trinity; the Latins argue for His proceeding from both the Father and the Son. The Roman Church does not consider this an open question. The Second Council of Lyons in 1274 stated: "With faithful and devout profession we confess that the Holy Spirit proceeds eternally from the Father and the Son, not as from two principles, but as from one; not by two aspirations but by one. This has been the profession, preaching, and teaching of the Holy Roman Catholic Church, the mother and teacher of all the faithful, up to the present day. This is the unchangeable and true doctrine of the orthodox Fathers and Doctors, both Latin and Greek."[3]

This bold statement of doctrine, which even interpreted the minds of the Fathers both Latin and Greek, was reaffirmed essentially in the Council of Florence (1438-1445) in the Decrees for the Greeks and for the Jacobites. At this council there was some ecumenical agreement between East and West, as the eastern bishops became convinced that when the Greek Fathers spoke of the Spirit's origin from the Father as coming *through the Son*, they were saying much the same as the western theolo-gians were saying by insisting that the Spirit proceeds from the Father and the Son as from a single principle. This agreement was short-lived, however. And the dispute goes on today. As for the addition of the word *Filioque* (and the Son) in the Latin version of the historic creed of 381, the vision is not so sharp. The western Church argues that the addition is legitimate, because it expresses the truth about the Spirit's origin. But the western Church also knows that the original creed did not contain that word, and that the word *Filioque* had been added to the Latin versions of the creed by the time that the creed was made a part of the Roman Sunday Mass in the eleventh century. Greeks who are in union with the Chair of Peter are not required to "Latinize" their creed in the liturgy.

One of the best treatises on the Holy Spirit in the Trinity from the modern Orthodox viewpoint has been written by Vladimir Lossky (1903-1958).[4] In his chapter on the procession of the Holy Spirit, Lossky argued that the Latin insistence upon the *Filioque*, that is, upon the doctrine that the Spirit proceeds from the Father and the Son as from a single principle of origin, is quite logical for those who start from the presuppositions that are found in western trinitarian theology. But he asked that philosophical constructs not be allowed to put limits upon the light of revelation. If one begins from the Latin (shall we say, Augustinian) principle that God is first of all one, and must try to show the distinctness of the three persons out of that presupposition, he will be required to show a difference in the procession of the Spirit from that of the Son; otherwise, there would be two Sons. So, the Latin thinker posits a procession from a principle of origin that is not the Father alone, but Father and Son as one principle. Thus the threeness of persons is established on the basis of *four relations*, in accord with the famous teaching of the Council of Florence: "Everything is one where there is no distinction by relative opposition."[5] There are then, in the Latin system of theology, *four relations* in which the three persons of the Trinity are distinguished through opposition to one another. The Father begets the Son: *paternity* is opposite *filiation*, and these are two relations. The Father and the Son as a single principle breathe forth the Holy Spirit: *active spiration* is opposite *passive spiration*, and these are two relations. Thus the three persons are distinct from one another by reason of four relations of opposition. All else in the Godhead belongs to the oneness thereof, which is the essence in which each of these divine persons subsists. Add to the list of these four relations the quality of *unbegottenness* in God the Father, and one arrives at the *five notions* by which the hypostatic life of the Trinity is distinguished. This fifth notion is not a relation, however; for it does not declare any relation of opposition of the Father to another hypostasis. Rather it states that the Father is the beginning and fountainhead of the divine life.

Because Byzantine theology begins from the Trinity of persons rather than from the unity of the essence, the Byzantine theologian does not look for a norm for positing distinctions, but rather, accepting the distinctions as given in revelation, he looks for the norm of unity. The Byzantine theologian is content to say that the Godhead is in three hypostases, and he does not seek to establish this by a system of relations; it is simply the fact about the mystery of the personal God who dwells in light inaccessible. Lossky said this about the matter: "Every name except those of Father, Son, and Holy Spirit—even the names of 'Word' and 'Paraclete'—is inappropriate for designating the special characteristics of the hypostases in the inaccessible existence of the Trinity, and refers rather to the external aspect of God, to His manifestations, or even to His economy. The dogma of the Trinity marks the summit of theology, where our thought stands still before the primordial mystery of the existence of the personal God. Apart from the names denoting the three hypostases and the common name of the Trinity, the innumerable names which we apply to God—the *divine names* which textbook theology calls His attributes—denote God not in His inaccessible Being but in 'that which surrounds the essence' *(ta peri tis ousias)*.[6] This is the eternal radiance of the common content of the three persons, who reveal their incommunicable nature in *energies*. This technical term of Byzantine theology, denoting a mode of divine existence besides essence, introduces no new philosophical notion alien to revelation. The Bible, in its concrete language, speaks of nothing other than *energies* when it tells us of the 'glory of God'—a glory with innumerable names which surrounds the inaccessible Being of God, making Him known outside Himself, while concealing what He is in Himself. This is the eternal glory which belongs to the three persons, which the Son 'had before the world was.' And when we speak of the divine energies in relation to the human beings to whom they are communicated and given and by whom they are appropriated, this divine and uncreated reality within us is called Grace."[7]

Once again we are faced with the distinction between "theology" pure and simple, and "economy" along with an intermediate level of "manifestation." It is at the profound first level of the personal God's life that the Byzantines insist that the Spirit is from the Father alone. They are willing to say with the Cappadocian Fathers, that the Spirit is "manifested" after the Son, and that the Spirit's mission in the economy of salvation is the mission of bringing to fulfillment in the Church the work of the Son of God, Jesus Christ. The divine energies, which signal the manifestation of the individual divine hypostases, are the source of the Church's life of grace in each of its members. Byzantines do not posit a "created" grace in the soul to correspond to the uncreated indwelling of the persons. This manifestation of the divine life in grace gives the sanctified human person an intimate relationship to each of the persons. Thus the Holy Trinity in the prayer life of the Christian is experienced through grace *as triune*; it is not just a matter of addressing one or the other person *by appropriation*.

The glory of the Lord which is a biblical expression for the divine energies in manifestation played an important role in the theology of Gregory Palamas, archbishop of Thessalonika (c. 1296-1359). Gregory argued that the divine energies manifest the Godhead in an effulgence of light, which it is possible for human beings to see, God willing. The light that the apostles saw on the mount of the transfiguration was uncreated light, not a created effulgence. The divinity of Jesus became visible, not in the inaccessible essence (the most profound level of divine life), but in the manifestation of the Son of God in the divine energy. Only the blessed in beatific vision will see the very essence of God; but it is quite possible for holy persons in this life, responding to divine love, to experience a certain enlightenment which is the true vision of God, manifested in the dynamism of divine personal giving. Thus Gregory defended the claims of the Hesychast monks of Mount Athos against those who argued that no divine light shines on us this side of heaven.

Two of the divine persons are said to be *sent* into this world for its uplift from sin and its sanctification. Both East and West agree on this matter, although the Roman Church sees the *mission* of the Spirit as a kind of proof of His origin in the profound life of God from both Father and Son. Thus Pope Leo XIII (1810-1903) wrote: " 'It is expedient to you that I go: for if I go not, the Paraclete will not come to you: but if I go, I will send Him to you' (Jn 16:7). In these words He gave as the chief reason of His departure and His return to the Father the advantage which would most certainly accrue to His followers from the coming of the Holy Ghost, and at the same time He made it clear that the Holy Ghost is equally sent by—*and therefore proceeds from*—Himself and the Father.''[8] We have seen that the Byzantines put the economic Trinity with the divine missions at a level other than that on which the theologian considers God in Himself, even prior to manifestation. So, the Byzantines would agree that the Spirit is on mission from the Father and comes as the Spirit of Jesus, the Son of God. And the Son Himself is on mission from the Father: "God did not send His Son into the world to condemn the world, but that through Him the world might be saved" (Jn 3:17). The two *divine missions* in God's life among His people correspond to the *processions* in the trinitarian interior life of the Godhead. The Father is not *sent*, for He is the origin of all divine life, and has no sender in the Godhead. This does not mean that the Father is absent from His people, as some of the early Platonists thought. He is with us as

Father and Lord. We address Him with love in the prayer that Jesus taught us to say (Mt 9:9-13). By grace we are His children, and He dwells in our very souls with the Son and the Spirit. But there is no liturgical feast of God the Father. Liturgical feasts and solemnities are concerned with the *mysteries*; and these *mysteries* are celebrations of the *mission* of the divine persons whose mysteries they are.

Most of the divine mysteries are those of our Lord Jesus Christ, from His advent to His glorious ascension to the Father. The great mystery of the Holy Spirit is Pentecost, the solemnity whereon we celebrate His being sent upon the Church from the Father and the Son on high. We do not, however, celebrate liturgical days in honor of the "divinity" of either the Son or the Spirit; it is only their mysteries through mission that we so honor. Therefore, we have no feast of God the Father; for He has no mission, and we do not celebrate as such his *divinity*. Pope John XXII (1249-1334) did indeed institute a solemn feast in honor of the Most Holy Trinity. In our time it is still celebrated; it follows the Sunday of Pentecost. It does not, however, intend to honor the divinity as such, but rather to honor the three persons of the Godhead together in one solemn festival. In spite of this noble purpose, the antiphons and prayers become clumsy at times. One cannot really talk to an essence; one talks to persons. When the prayers address the oneness of God, they seem to be addressing either the essence rather than the persons, or the persons in an indeterminate way. Nonetheless, such a festival is legitimate to honor the three persons of the Trinity on a single day, so long as we pray to Father, Son, and Holy Spirit.

In our liturgical tradition, the name *God (Deus* in Latin) has the meaning of God the Father. Our translators of the prayers into English have generally substituted the word *Father* for the Latin *Deus*.[9] The prayers conclude with doxologies that laud Christ His Son and the Holy Spirit, and thus implicitly acknowledge the presence by circuminsession of the three divine persons in our midst as we pray and hear God's word.

In spite of our strong liturgical tradition, in which the three persons of the Holy Trinity are properly distinguished and recognized in our life of prayer, one still finds an ever present attitude among many Christian people that God is really just one person. The *modalism* against which Harnack warned shows up in conversation and in spontaneous prayers. One often hears the ultimate anthropomorphism used by Christians: the

Man Upstairs. God is indeed "in the highest" (Lk 2:14), but when that biblical expression becomes a sort of high-rise building, it is time to take warning from Bishop John Robinson (b. 1919) about the God "out there" and to find His immanence in His world, recognizing that He is truly "with us," our Emmanuel.[10]

In spontaneous prayers it often becomes apparent that the person praying has little idea concerning the personal object of the prayer. A prayer that ostensibly began with an address to the Father or to the Holy Spirit might go on to ask that we may be saved by that person's holy passion. This results, not from heretical leanings by the person praying, but rather from a vagueness about the person to whom the prayer is addressed. Unitarian Churches are often criticized by other Christians for having too little prayer; but the others make up for it by those prayers that are really unitarian in content, if not in intent.

One example of how confusing our life of prayer can be made by addressing ourselves to the Trinity as if the Trinity were a single hypostasis, can be found in the hymn, "Most Ancient of All Mysteries." The opening stanzas are addressed clearly to the "Most Holy Trinity." In the third stanza the singer says: "You were not born, there was no source from which your Being flowed." It is probably Arian doctrine, but a theologian would be hard put to show just what it is. The divine Being is truly communicated from the Father to the Son by the procession which Church dogma calls *birth*. God has a Son! In the hymn, however, the divine object of address is the Trinity as such; and one is left wondering who it is that was not born. Only the Son of God is born in the life of the Holy Trinity; but He surely is the object of the prayer along with the Father and Holy Spirit in the context. The point, however, to be made is, that this kind of vagueness in prayer, which is likely due to our emphasis on God's oneness, leads to difficulties.

Pope Paul VI, while beginning with God's oneness in his *Credo of the People of God*, immediately identified the Trinity in name, and devoted the greater part of that creed's statement about God to the individual persons of the Holy Trinity. Even the attributes of the one Godhead which he chooses to mention are few, and they are the ones that relate most to our salvation. In a word, his statement about God is truly pastoral. He singled out God's omnipotence (the anchor of hope), knowledge (the basis of providence), His providence itself, and His will and love (source of divine love in us). We are thus reminded that our God is not distant from us, but that the Father, Son, and Holy Spirit abide with us. We are taught to pray to the Father through the Son in the unity of the Spirit in liturgical prayers. We are further invited to pray directly to the Son and to the Spirit; this is not only the case in private prayer, but at times in liturgical prayer. In the Eucharistic liturgy the prayer before Holy Communion is addressed to God's Son, our Lord Jesus Christ. And surely no one forgets the lovely hymn for Pentecost, *Veni, creator Spiritus*. The many doxologies in the liturgies lead us in conscious prayer to each of the divine persons, especially as we conclude a prayer that has been addressed to one person alone. Thus the prayer of Christians reflects the belief of Christians.

Footnotes

1. *Dialogue* 61.
2. *ST* 1a.37.1.
3. Constitution on the Procession of the Holy Spirit, *CT* no. 308.
4. *In the Image and Likeness of God*, 71-96.
5. Decree for the Jacobites, *CT* no. 311.
6. Lossky's note refers to Gregory of Nazianzus, *Oration* 38, 7.
7. Lossky, *op. cit.,* 89-90.
8. *Divinum Illud* 1; New York, 1961, Paulist Press.
9. A notable exception is the Corpus Christi prayer, "Deus, qui nobis sub sacramento mirabili," etc. Here *Deus* means Christ.
10. *See* Robinson's *Honest to God*, ch. 1: "Reluctant Revolution."

Chapter 6

CREATION

Bibliography: B. Vawter, C.M., *A Path through Genesis, New York, 1956,* Sheed & Ward, 31-110; M. Schmaus, *Dogma 2: God and Creation,* New York, 1969, Sheed & Ward. Trans. by A. Laeuchli, W. McKenna, T. Burke; C.S. Lewis, *The Screwtape Letters,* New York, 1961, Macmillan; *ST* 1a.44-119.

The Church of Christ has been taught to "believe in one God, the Father, the almighty, maker of heaven and earth, and of all that is seen and unseen" (Nicene Creed). This insistence upon God as creator of all that exists outside Himself is important, not simply for general knowledge, but for the hope that Christians have that they will be saved. For unless God is truly almighty and in full control of the origin and destiny of the created universe, Christians could not rest assured that God is the master of their own destiny. It would always be possible for some dark, alien force to overcome God, and thus conquer Him and all His servants.

Cosmology

The question about the origin of the world is such a basic one, that it addresses itself to a variety of disciplines. The theologian hears it asked, as also do the philosopher, the geologist, the paleontologist, and the litterateur. Each one must provide some answer in keeping with the competence of his or her discipline. The so-called conflict between religion and the natural sciences has arisen from a desire to read the Bible as a book about scientific matters on the one hand, and from the desire to read archeological findings as ultimate explanations of the world on the other. Archeological studies have told us much about the world, its evolution, its age, and its long-term history. But it is for the philosopher to reflect on the data thus acquired, in order to build a theory of cosmology and cosmic origins. And it is for the theologian to reflect with the philosopher on the data, and to compare it with divine revelation. The litterateur, for his or her part, may apply the power of the imagination to the data of science, and produce valuable works of science fiction. We are presently concerned with the theologian's role in cosmology. And thus we are to bear in mind that the religious explanation of the world's origin does not contradict, nor render unnecessary, the explanation that is proper to the other disciplines.

The book called Genesis stands at the head of the five books called the Pentateuch. It opens with the Priestly account of creation (Gn 1:1-2:3). The author declares that "in the beginning God created heaven and earth," and that the earth "was void and empty (*tohu va-bohu*)." He then describes the work of creation in detail, assigning the entire genesis of the cosmos to six days, followed by a day of rest after the labor of creation. In the course of this account, which bears a closer resemblance to the work of a writer of science fiction than to that of an archeologist, the Hebrew author sets forth a religious position that contradicts the religious doctrine of the Babylonians, the nation that had held Israel captive from 587 till 537 B.C. His writing has some similarity to the other near-eastern creation stories, including the Babylonian *Enuma Elish*.[1] Yet there is a difference: and in the difference one finds the specific message of the Hebrew writer about his God.

The God of Genesis did not make the world out of some preexisting matter, not even out of the relics of slain gods. And the formless mass (tohu va-bohu) out of which He brought order and beauty was itself totally created by Him. For it came to be "in the beginning" when God created the universe, that is, heaven and earth. The six days of creation were fully under God's control; all things came into being at His word. And God pronounced what He had created to be good. The God of Genesis did not engage other gods in combat in order to bring about His world. He is quite obviously a different kind of God altogether than Marduk. The God of Genesis is indeed the almighty one.

The prophets, moreover, had made it clear to the people that the victory of Nebuchadnezzar over the Hebrews was not a victory of Marduk over the Lord. It was rather the Lord's own doing. He punished the transgressions of His people by the sword of foreigners; He let foreigners come into the very homeland of His chosen people to smite them for their faithlessness and to destroy their idols: gods that had not made heaven and earth. But when the time for deliverance came, this same God of Israel brought Babylon down; and His providential hand guided Cyrus to victory, even though Cyrus did not know his divine benefactor by name. In all of salvation history, the destiny of everyone is in God's hand.

Augustine (354-430), whose theology influenced the western Church for many centuries, gave primary importance to the religious message of the book of Genesis, although he also sought in the creation story a philosophical understanding of cosmic origins. When Augustine was yet a Manichean, he held a materialistic view of God. According to the doctrine of Manes (c. 215-275), God is a resplendent and subtle body. This primordial light which is God shines forth in the heavenly luminaries, and struggles against earthly darkness. After Augustine had become a Christian, he rejected all such pantheism, stressing the transcendent and spiritual nature of God. The light which God made on the third day in the Priestly creation account is fully a creature, and not part of God. The heavenly luminaries share in the created light, but they are not part of God. Nevertheless, all creatures have in themselves a certain *likeness* of God, since He is the pattern of their nature. God had no other pattern for created beings except His own divine image, the uncreated Word of the Father.

"In the beginning God created heaven and earth," says the opening verse of Genesis. Augustine avoided arguments about the relation of this "beginning" to the question of "time" by asserting that the beginning is to be understood as "Principle." This rendering of the phrase was natural enough, since the Latin translation for "in the beginning" was "in principio." The Principle in whom all things were created was for Augustine the Word. And that which God created in the Word was "heaven and earth." By "heaven" Augustine understood the angelic world, of which we shall later treat in this study. By "earth" he meant the corporeal world, whose order and adornment are described as a six-day work of the creator. Augustine did not have all the biblical scholar's science to help him interpret the creation story of Genesis; but he did realize that the account was to be read symbolically, not historically. He knew that God did not create in the course of a calendar week as we know it. He believed, in fact, that God's creative word achieved its effect in a single moment, and that the explanation of that single act took the form of a six-day account because six is the symbol of perfection. He argued this point on a mathematical basis, however, and thus missed the point that, in the Hebrew mentality, perfection came in sevens. "No prolongation of time was necessary for God. He could have at once created all things and then let them measure time by their appropriate movements. It is the perfection of God's work that is signified by the number six."[2] Hence, time itself is a creature, for it comes into being with the creatures that by nature need temporality.

The supremacy of God as the sole creator was fully affirmed by Augustine. There is not another God who is the independent source of evil, as the Manicheans taught. "There is no creator higher than God, no art more efficacious than the Word of God, no better reason why something should be created than that the God who creates it is good."[3] Further on he wrote: "It is no wonder that heretics, who hold that some positive evil has sprung and sprouted from an evil principle radically opposed to God, refuse to accept this explanation of creation—that a God who is good should create things that are good. They prefer to believe that God was driven, by the sheer necessity of quelling the evil one in rebellion against Him, to build the bulwarks of a material universe, and thus mingle the goodness of His nature with evil in order to coerce and conquer evil; so that the divine nature, prostituted and oppressed, is now in shameful and cruel captivity and can be purified and emancipated only with very great difficulty. Even then, one part will remain impervious to purification, and this is to be the prison and the chains to hold the conquered enemy in subjection."[4]

The Problem of Evil

"Evil has no positive nature; what we call evil is merely the lack of something that is good."[5] Augustine wrote an important point for Christian thinking about evil in that statement. Since evil has no positive nature, it does not need a dualistic principle, an anti-god to create it. It is to be found in what God created. Yet, because it is essentially a lack of goodness, it cannot claim God for its direct author; for He made what is good, not the lack thereof. While God alone is the first cause of all that is good, various creatures in their defective causalities are the cause of what is evil; for in their defective causality they produce the lack of goodness.

But evil remains a problem for us, even after we have given assent to this piece of Christian philosophy. God is almighty, and therefore we ask: since He has full control of the whole created universe, why doesn't He eliminate all evil? The question is easy to ask; it is complicated to try to answer. Augustine's Manichean friends were able to exonerate God from ill will in this matter, since He was involved in a struggle with evil that left Him no power to destroy it outright. Certain schools of process theology in modern times give similar answers; God is in the process of becoming perfect, and presently is unable to exclude all evil from His created world. While this thinking exonerates God of ill will, it condemns Him as being too weak to be the kind of God one would dare risk everything for. Total commitment is worth giving only to an almighty God!

We are left, then, with the mystery of evil. It is here in the world, and somehow God is willing that it be here. He is not its direct cause, but He does not exclude it from His world, even though He is almighty. When we look at nature, we are almost convinced that some natural evils are quite necessary for nature to function. We tell the chef that the steaks are very good; the cow that provided them would probably have preferred a vegetarian owner. Somehow this world moves toward its destiny only with evil as part of its history, not excluding moral evil. The prophet Habakkuk was troubled over the good fortune of evildoers, and wondered how their foul deeds would be repaid in justice. Job suffered evil upon evil at the hand of an adversary who felt that Job's faithfulness to God was a fair-weather friendship. Tobit also received trouble in exchange for his good deeds. The end of the tales of Job and Tobit are happy endings; but many people who try to serve God faithfully are cast in the roles of suffering, and the happy endings never materialize for them, as poverty, disease or accident bring them down to their graves. Yet, at the risk of being accused of proclaiming a religion that offers "pie in the sky," we should recall that the apostle Paul foresaw a happy ending to the tale of the Christian, one that does not occur in earthly days: "The sufferings of this present time cannot be compared with the glory that is to be revealed in us'' (Rm 8:18). Our Savior Himself died on His cross. It was in His resurrection that the true meaning of His ignominious death came to light. We are partakers in His resurrection already through our baptismal fellowship with Him.

Anthropology

The author of the book of Genesis, having set forth in the Priestly account of creation (Gn 1:1-2; 3) the work of God in six days followed by a sabbath of rest, thereupon repeated the story of creation in a tale drawn from another ancient source, namely, the Yahwist. The creator Himself in this account (Gn 2:4-25) is no longer just ''God: Elohim;'' now He is ''Lord God: Adonai Elohim.''[6] And in this account the creature man and his wife play the significant role that prompted the author to include this story in his book. For he wanted to teach his readers that, of all things created by God, mankind was superior, made in the image and likeness of the creator. In this second account of creation, it is the man who gives names to all the cattle, the birds of the air, and to every beast of the field. This is the author's way of saying that the man is lord of them all. Yet among these creatures there was not found a helper fit for him. The Lord took the rib from the man as he slept, and he fashioned woman for him. She was indeed bone of his bones and flesh of his flesh. Her dignity as woman exceeded all the dignity of the lower creation. For a man leaves his father and mother and cleaves to his wife, and they become one flesh. Woman's dignity is human dignity; and with her husband she becomes one flesh. Thus the author sets monogamy before his readers as an ideal to be cherished. Jesus would one day declare the restoration of monogamy, and would forbid divorce; and in so doing He would cite this text from Genesis (Mt 19:3-9). The Fathers of the Church would also appeal to this primordial marriage as a biblical type for the marriage of Christ to His Church. ''Just as Eve was formed from the side of the sleeping Adam, so the Church is formed from the side of Christ hanging on the cross. For His side was struck, as the Gospel says (Jn 19:34), and immediately there came out blood and water. These are the Church's twin sacraments: the water, in which the bride was purified, the blood from which she is found to have her dowry.''[7]

The Yahwistic account of creation finally presents the happy couple as naked, but not ashamed. In this simple picturesque declaration, the author of Genesis has put across the notion of a special privilege given to them that transcends the order of nature. The concupiscence, so well known and experienced by humanity in his day as in ours, is missing from this idyllic scene. They walked familiarly with God, until the day when, deceived by the serpent, they ate of the tree of knowledge of good and evil, recognized their nakedness which had become a source of shame to them, and were cast out of the garden of Eden or paradise. Garments of skin clothed their bodies as a sign of their fall from grace. This we learn from chapter 3 of Genesis. The author was not what we would call a theologian; he was closer to our notion of a catechist. And most assuredly he could not have grasped the distinction of *supernatural* gifts from *preternatural* gifts. Yet out of his Jewish catechesis the later theologians could draw building blocks for their edifice. Adam and Eve were indeed raised by God to a state above their nature. Gifts like freedom from concupiscence accompanied this unique relationship to the creator. The account of the fall in chapter 3 is also the account of the sad loss of this special status and its accompanying gifts. This fall, the *first* human sin, became likewise the source of the *original* sin, that "hereditary corruption" which is the "depravedness of a nature formerly good and pure," as Calvin (1509-1564) said.[8] But then "in Romans 5:12ff we have the prophetic completion and fulfillment of the story found in Genesis 3. Here Paul develops, in the fullness of time, the religious thinking of Israel strengthened by later revelation, in which the whole significance of Adam's fall is seen in relation to all subsequent sin to the salvation of Christ. The fulness of the New Testament would, of course, be incomprehensible without the revelation handed on by Genesis. The author of Genesis, too, knew that the sin of Adam and Eve was not theirs only, but had somehow infected the entire human race that descends from them."[9]

The restoration of paradise that we are given by the grace of Christ brings us a fullness of grace in excess of the gift that we had lost in Adam. Yet, until the eschaton arrives, the members of this Second Adam struggle through life, beset by concupiscence, temptation, sickness, and death itself. Recognizing this condition of redeemed humanity, theologians are accustomed to distinguish the *life of grace* from the *accompanying gifts* that Adam and Eve enjoyed with that divine life. The life of grace they call our *supernatural* gifts; the other gifts which are not restored to us in the pilgrim Church they call *preternatural* gifts.

Although biblical scholars and theologians constantly emphasize that the prehistoric accounts which we read in the early chapters of Genesis are an adaptation of ancient near eastern myths by the Jewish author to his purpose of putting across his divinely revealed message, there are always some people who prefer to read these chapters as eyewitness history. These are *fundamentalists*. For them, creation took one week just like the modern week; Adam began as a handful of dust; Eve began as a bony rib; and some loquacious snake talked Eve into picking a forbidden apple. They are often convinced that all books of the Bible must be given equal evaluation. To see in the serpent of Genesis the image of a serpent-god, who in turn signifies the power of Satan at work, disturbs these people; for they object that this method of interpretation allows one to *make a myth* out of Jesus' resurrection in the Gospels! If, however, we learn to read the various books of the Bible in accord with the author's mind and intent, then we need not share those fears. The garden of Eden is a long way historically and literarily from the garden of Gethsemane and the garden of Joseph's tomb.

Evolution and polygenism are two issues that require patience and careful cooperation between scientists and theologians. Religious enthusiasts of a fundamentalist bent can always be reminded of the embarrassing trial in 1925 in Dayton, Tennessee, of John T. Scopes (1901-70). This teacher was convicted of teaching falsehood contrary to the state's laws because he taught the evolution of species; and today the scientific world looks upon evolution as a theory unlikely to be discredited. Pope Pius XII (1876-1958) wrote in the encyclical letter *Humani Generis* (1950) that an inquiry into the subject of evolution by competent persons is not forbidden by the teaching authority of the Church. He did add, however, that "the Catholic faith obliges us to hold that souls are immediately created by God."[10] On the subject of polygenism, Pope Pius was firm in statement. "For the faithful cannot embrace that opinion which maintains either that after Adam there existed on this earth true men who did not take their origin through natural generation from him as from the first parent of all, or that Adam represents a certain number of first parents. Now it is in no way apparent how such an opinion can be reconciled with that which the sources of revealed truth and the documents of the teaching authority of the Church propose with regard to original sin, which proceeds from a sin actually committed by an individual Adam and which through generation is passed on to all and is in everyone as his own."[11]

Though somewhat guarded in his rejection of polygenism, by saying that it is not apparent how the idea could be reconciled to Christian doctrine, Pope Pius did put the matter quite clearly. Polygenism may be a physical possibility. If Adam evolved and reached *hominization*, why not other members of the chain of life? But the Pope said that Christian faith rules out the belief that, in the world of the present age, in which the sons and daughters of Adam inhabit this earth, there are in fact some non-Adamites. We cannot point to some human beings on earth today and say: "Christ did not die for them, nor does He call them to His Church; for the first Adam was not their father, and so the Second Adam has no role to play for them." Pope Pius also reiterated the traditional belief of the Church that the *original sin* was caused by a *first sin*. Some evolutionists are inclined to reject the *fall* of mankind. They think that mankind's fallen condition is not the result of a fall from grace, but merely the result of a failure to rise to human responsible morality. At hominization, they argue, human beings kept on acting in their inherited bestial manner. The *Credo of the People of God* (1968), issued by Pope Paul VI (1897-1978), reaffirmed the first sin of Adam as the cause of our original sin, and also God's direct action in the origin of each human soul.[12]

Since that time, Catholic theologians have attempted to interpret the original sin in terms of modern theological thought, while keeping their eyes on the official teaching of the Church's magisterium. A few examples will suffice to show the directions that have been taken by these Catholic thinkers, and to make it clear that the whole question about the original sin—its origin, its exact nature, and its elimination by the power of Christ—is far from being a theologically settled question.

Karl Rahner (1904-) had long identified Adam as the biblical symbol of a single first individual, who committed the first sin. In 1966 he moved away from the traditional position, and began to argue in favor of polygenism, which he believed to be compatible with the Church's teaching. His later position held that the original sin was the result of the sinful conduct of a group of individuals, all of whom deeply affected one another in their own sinfulness. His doctrine can be read at some length in the references cited.[13]

Two other Jesuit theologians, both professors at the Gregorian University in Rome, have likewise written about this subject to a significant degree. They are Maurizio Flick (1909-) and Zoltán Alszeghy (1915-). Their full-length book on original sin appeared in Italy in 1972. The *Biblical Theology Bulletin* in 1973 carried an article in English about this work of the two Gregorian professors, called "Original Sin Reappraised."[14] There is also in English a digest of an article written by the two professors in 1971 concerning the doctrine of the Council of Trent on original sin; this is to be found in *Theology Digest*.[15]

Flich and Alszeghy regarded original sin as a certain inability to fulfill one's moral duty. This would result necessarily in actual sin, unless the power of Christ healed this weakness. Unlike some Christian evolutionists who regarded this weakness as stemming from the origins of mankind by necessity, Flick and Alszeghy pointed to the first sin in the human race, be it the deed of one or of many, as the historic beginning of that weakness which thereafter became the heritage of all who were born into human society. These writers also felt that in the study of this question, more emphasis should be put on Christ's atoning victory over sin, less upon the sin itself. It is interesting to note that in the encyclical of Pope John Paul II, *Redemptor Hominis*, this emphasis is present, and with it, an optimism about our world, whose destiny is in the power of Christ the Redeemer.[16]

The basic lines of the doctrine on original sin are part of the tradition of the Church, and will therefore remain a part of the Church's doctrine for the future. But there are many uncertainties about the total picture wherein those basic lines are found. The theologian's work for the future lies in the study of these problems.

The Angels of the Lord

The Sacred Scriptures and the Christian tradition which they express bear witness to a part of God's creation that is unseen. This is the world of the created spirits, who remain unseen by their very nature, since the eye sees only what is corporeal. This angelic world is made up of the good angels, who are in union with God, and the bad angels, also called devils or demons, who are cut off from God by reason of a sinful fall from His grace and love.

The Second Vatican Council, speaking of the communion of saints, declared: "The Church has always believed that the apostles and Christ's martyrs . . . are closely joined with us in Christ, and she has always venerated them, together with the blessed virgin Mary and the holy angels, with a special devotion."[17] Pope Paul VI's *Credo of the People of God* includes the holy angels in the heavenly realm where Christ reigns in glory. The Sacred Scriptures mention the holy angels in many places. In modern writings, however, we occasionally encounter the opinion that the angelic world does not really exist; that it is a mythological mode of expression, signifying God's own action, or, in the case of the devils, the powers of evil lurking in this imperfect world. It is perhaps true that a more credulous age was wont to find angels and demons everywhere, even where natural causes might easily have been found to explain the so-called wonders. And even in the Scriptures themselves there are some instances where, no doubt, the angels might have turned out to be quite prosaic and corporeal, had there been a quest for the historical angel. For the word "angel" does in fact mean "messenger." God's messengers are not always and necessarily incorporeal spirits. Yet the overall picture of the angelic world in the Bible and in the Church's tradition does not warrant a total demythologizing of the world of created spirits. In fact, the honest philosopher must admit that, while one cannot prove from reason that such a world of spirits exist, unless that world manifests itself to us empirically, still one cannot prove that such a world does not exist, merely by reason of the non-empirical evidence from such a world. Surely such a world is possible; and therefore it *can* exist. The Church, taught by divine revelation, believes that it does exist.

The Scriptures are not very helpful in the creation accounts to those who want to learn when the angels came into being. This is not surprising, when we consider that both creation accounts are concerned with the visible cosmos and with the crowning glory of that cosmos, mankind. But Augustine tried to find in the first account some reference to the creation of the angelic orders. He decided that they may well be the "heaven" spoken of in the opening verse of Genesis. Recall too that he rendered "in the beginning" as meaning "in the Principle," namely, in the divine Word. So, he understood the verse to say that in the Word, God made the angelic orders and the earth.[18] Augustine advanced an alternate suggestion, saying that the angelic beings were included in the creation of the *light*. Thus they shared in the divine light which was the pattern for their own light, and bore the image of God in their knowledge.

"If, in the passage of Scripture where God says: Let there be light, and there was light, we are right in taking this light to mean the angels, then we are sure that they are made participants of His eternal light, which is nothing other than the unchangeable Wisdom by which all things were made, and which we call the only-begotten Son of God. Thus, the angels, illumined by that Light which created them, became light and were called *day* because they participated in the unchangeable Light and Day which is the Word of God, by whom they and all things were made."[19]

From this point of departure, Augustine developed his doctrine on the knowledge of the angels. The angels see God as He is in Himself. This knowledge they gain, not by a spoken word, "but by the presence in their souls of that immutable truth which is the only-begotten Word of God."[20] The later Scholastics would not have liked the expression "souls" as referring to angels, since they have no corporeal principle, but are pure spirits. Augustine further asserted that the angels who abide in this divine light have a twofold knowledge of created things. "They also know every creature not merely in itself but, still better, in the wisdom of God, in the very art by which it was created. And, therefore, they know themselves better in God than as they are in themselves, although, of course, they have this knowledge too. For these angels were created and are something different from the one who created them. Therefore . . . the knowledge which they have in Him is as clear as daylight, whereas what they have in themselves is like the twilight."[21] This distinction of the angelic knowledge, compared by Augustine to day and twilight, became a classic of subsequent theology. Aquinas in the *Summa* speaks of the twofold knowledge of the angels as *scientiá matutina* and *scientia vespertina.*[22]

The angels might matter little to the Church on earth if they had no role to play in the plan of salvation. But the Church believes that the angels, both the good and the bad, do have roles to play in human affairs. The Church regards the good angels as the messengers of the Lord, who, out of love for God and for us, do His bidding on our behalf. On October 2nd of each year the Roman rite celebrates the memorial of the Guardian Angels. The first lesson recalls the angel of the Lord who served as guardian to the chosen people of God during their sojourn toward the Promised Land (Ex 23:20-23). The response in psalm 91 again extolls the angelic role of guardianship. Finally, Jesus speaks in the Gospel (Mt 18:1-5, 10) of the angels of His beloved little ones, angels who see God's face as they guard His children. On September 29th the feast of the three great archangels is celebrated: Michael, Gabriel and Raphael. The reading from chapter 7 of Daniel shows us that myriads of angels served the enthroned Lord. An alternate reading Revelation 12:7-12, depicts in apocalyptic language the victory of Michael over Satan and his bad angels. The victory hymn shows that the power for such conquest came from the blood of the Lamb, and from the martyrdom of those who faithfully serve the Lamb of God here on earth. Again it is Jesus who speaks in the Gospel (Jn 1:47-51). He tells Nathanael that he will see heaven opened, and the angels of God descending upon the Son of Man. Like a new Jacob, Jesus will be the foundation stone of a new covenant (Gn 28:10-22).

Michael, whose name means "Who is like God?" is mentioned in Sacred Scripture four times, always as a captain of the righteous and foe of Satan (Dn 10:13; Dn 12:1; Jude 1:9; Rv 12:7-9). He also plays a similar role in some of the pseudepigraphal scriptures. Gabriel, whose name means God's servant, assisted Daniel in understanding his visions (Dn 8:15; 9:21), announced the birth of John the Baptist (Lk 1:11), and announced the incarnation of our Lord to Mary (Lk 1:26). Raphael is the divine healer, both in the meaning of his name, and in his activity. He figures prominently in the book of Tobit, and also appears in the pseudepigraphal Enoch.

The Pseudo-Dionysius, whose writings come from the late patristic period, is the source of the traditional division of the angelic world into nine choirs. In his *Celestial Hierarchy* he so divided the angelic beings, drawing upon the Scriptures for his list of names: seraphim, cherubim, thrones, dominations, virtues, powers, principalities, archangels, and angels. Only the last two choirs are sent on direct mission to human beings. Scholastic theologians took over this hierarchy from Dionysius, and developed treatises on the angels as part of their theological doctrine. The total incorporeality, or completely spiritual nature of the angels, was not always understood by Christian writers. Justin Martyr (c. 100-c. 165), for instance, thought that the angels had bodies, although of a more subtle kind than bodily objects that we know. Thomas Aquinas taught the completely spiritual nature of angels, and in accord with his peripatetic cosmology, he claimed that each angel is a separate species of spiritual being.[23]

The Gates of Hell

The gates of hell, also called the powers of death, which are not to prevail against Peter in his role as head of the apostolic college (Mt 16:18), are none other than the powers of Satan and his host of fallen angels, whom the archangel Michael defeated, and whose battle with Satan is apocalyptically described in Revelation 12. While we do not believe that every inclination to evil in our lives is the work of an angelic tempter, we do recognize the role of these enemies of God in the struggle that we have against evil. The traditional enemies of our salvation are described as the world, the flesh, and the devil.

We must remind ourselves once again than an absolute dualism is foreign to Christianity. There is no devil who is another god, opposing the good God as an equal and opposite principle of being or first causality. The devil and his cohorts were created by God, and as His creatures, they were good. Augustine, who has told us that the Word of God, the Light from Light, is the source of the angelic knowledge, adds these comments about the devils: "Once an angel rejects this light, he becomes impure. Thus, all those who are called unclean spirits are no longer light in the Lord but darkness in themselves, being deprived of a participation in His eternal light. For, evil has no positive nature; what we call evil is merely the lack of something that is good."[24] Similarly, C.S. Lewis (1898-1963) wrote in *The Screwtape Letters*: "I believe in angels, and I believe that some of these, by the abuse of their free will, have become enemies of God and, as a corollary, to us. These we may call devils. They do not differ in nature from the good angels, but their nature is depraved. *Devil* is the opposite of *angel* only as Bad Man is the opposite of Good Man. Satan, the leader or dictator of devils, is the opposite, not of God, but of Michael."[25]

With this in mind, we may, even must, speak about a certain dualism in the life of the Church, in which Satan is opposed to God and His Christ. Was not Jesus tempted by the devil, so that He might yield to the capital vices and thus lose His messianic role? Was it not the devil who, in his desire to do away with the Lord, inspired His enemies to kill Him, and put it into the heart of Judas Iscariot (Lk 22:3; Jn 13:2) to betray Him?

Somehow, the devil, after the fall of our first parents, laid claim to the title of Prince of this world. Jesus Himself spoke of him in that way. While we don't know from revelation just what this means, and do not have an understanding of the problem of evil in this world, we know that the devil does work for our ruin, and had a certain claim on us by reason of the original sin. In his struggle with Christ he was defeated. The Prince of this world has been cast out. The precious blood of the Lamb of God has broken the strength of the gates of hell. Yet, the mystery of evil continues in the time of the pilgrim Church. The radical victory won by Christ is yet to be achieved in each human being who comes into this world. His general baptism for our new birth took place on Calvary; yet each one of us has had to enter into the mystery of Calvary by an individual baptism of water, given us by the Church. And so the struggle of Satan against Christ will go on until the final eschaton, when Christ will come in glory to judge the quick and the dead, and to put all things into subjection to God the Father. Then, at last, the power of hell will come to complete defeat.

Meanwhile, our life is an optimistic one. We are not servants of Satan, but of Christ. The evil powers can do nothing that God does not permit them. And the angel who guards us, regardless of his rank in the celestial hierarchy, is fully able to defend us in the battle. For he is armed with the power of the precious blood of our Redeemer. And that makes him in Christ an image of the great Michael, the one who is like unto God.

Footnotes

1. *See* D.W. Thomas (ed.), *Documents from Old Testament Times* New York, 1961, Harper Torchbook, 3-16.
2. *The City of God* 11, 30.
3. *Ibid.*, 11, 21.
4. *Ibid.*, 11, 22.
5. *Ibid.*, 11, 9.
6. Adonai (Lord) is represented in the Hebrew text by the tetragram YHWH. Jews do not pronounce this sacred name; they read *Adonai* wherever YHWH appears.
7. Augustine, *De symbolo ad catechumenos* 6, 15.
8. *Institutes* 2, 1, 5.
9. B. Vawter, *op. cit.* 71.
10. No. 36. By *souls* is meant *human* souls only.
11. No. 37.
12. *See The Pope Speaks* 13 (1968) 276-282.
13. K. Rahner, "Evolution and Original Sin," *Concilium* 6/3 (1967) 30-35; *Idem*, "Exkurs: Erbsünde und Monogenismus," in K—H. Weger (ed.) *Theologie der Erbsünde*, Freiburg, 1970, Herder Verlag, 176-223; digest of the foregoing article, "Original Sin, Polygenism, and Freedom," *Th. Dig.* 21 (1973) 53-56.
14. L. Sabourin, S.J., "Original Sin Reappraised," *Biblical Theology Bulletin* 3 (1973) 51-81. The book: M. Flick and Z. Alszeghy, *Il Peccato Originale*, Brescia, 1972, Queriniana.
15. "What did Trent define about Original Sin?" *Th. Dig.* 21 (1973) 57-65.
16. *Redemptor Hominis*, March 15, 1979. English text in *The Pope Speaks* 24 (1979) 97-147.
17. *Lumen Gentium* no. 50.
18. *See The City of God* 11, 9.
19. *Ibid.*
20. *Ibid.*
21. *Ibid.*
22. *ST* 1a.58.6.
23. *ST* 1a.50.4.
24. *The City of God* 11, 9.
25. *Op. cit.* vii.

Chapter 7

JESUS CHRIST

Bibliography. For the teaching of the Church: *TCC* nos. 231-319. For the Scriptural material: G. Bornkamm, *Jesus of Nazareth*, New York, 1960, Harper & Row. Transl. by I. and F. McLuskey; relevant articles in the *JBC* and *NCE*; F. Durrwell, C.SS.R., *The Resurrection*, New York, 1960, Sheed and Ward. Transl. by R. Sheed; J. Guillet, S.J., *The Consciousness of Jesus*, New York, 1972, Newman Press. Transl. by E. Bonin; W. Kasper, *Jesus the Christ*, New York, 1976, Paulist Press. Transl. by V. Green; H. Küng, *On Being a Christian*, Garden City, 1976, Doubleday, 117-462. Transl. by E. Quinn. (The author, a Catholic, seems to neglect the divinity of Christ.) X. Léon-Dufour, *Jesus* in *DBT*, 263-272; J. McKenzie, *Jesus Christ* in *DB*, 432-436; G. O'Collins, S.J., *The Resurrection*, Valley Forge, 1973, The Judson Press; R. Schnackenburg, *God's Rule and Kingdom*, New York, 1963, Herder and Herder. Transl. by J. Murray; D. Senior, C.P., *Jesus*, Dayton, 1975, Pflaum Publishing Co.; B. Vawter, C.M., *This Man Jesus*, Garden City, 1975, Image Books; R. Brown, S.S., *The Birth of the Messiah*, Garden City, 1977, Doubleday & Co.

For the theological and dogmatic development: Thomas Aquinas, *ST* 3a.1-59; W. Farrell, O.P., *A Companion to the Summa*, New York, 1942, Sheed and Ward, 4; G. Aulén, *Christus Victor*, New York, 1969, the Macmillan Co.; *Idem, Jesus in Cont. Historical Research*, Philadelphia, 1976, Fortress Press, Transl. by I. Hjelm; Y. Congar, O.P., *Jesus Christ*, New York, 1966, Herder and Herder. Transl. by L. O'Neill; A. Grillmeier, S.J., *Christ in Christian Tradition*, New York, 1965, Sheed and Ward. Transl. by J. Bowden; J. Kelly, *Early Christian Doctrines*, New York, 1960, Harper & Row, 2 ed.; D. Lane, *The Reality of Jesus*, New York, 1975, Paulist Press; E. Schillebeeckx, O.P., *Christ the Sacrament*, New

York, 1963, Sheed and Ward; P. Smulders, S.J., *The Fathers on Christology*, De Pere, 1968, St. Norbert Abbey Press. Transl. by L. Roy, S.J.; G. Mooney, S.J., *Teilhard de Chardin and the Mystery of Christ*, New York, 1964, Harper & Row; J. Hayes, *Son of God to Superstar*, Nashville, 1976, Abingdon Press; K. Rahner, S.J. *Foundations of Christian Faith*, New York, 1978, Seabury Press, 176-321.

Jesus Christ is the second person of the Blessed Trinity, true God and true man, the savior of the world.

The Teaching of the Church

The Council of Nicea (325), the first ecumenical council of the Church, taught that Jesus Christ is true God. He was born of the Father and is of one substance with the Father. There never was a time when He was not.[1] The Council of Ephesus (431), the third ecumenical council, taught that there is only one person in Christ, the person of the Word.[2] The Council of Chalcedon (451), the fourth ecumenical council, recognized two distinct natures in the one person of Christ. He is perfect in divinity and perfect in humanity, being true God and true man.[3] The Third Council of Constantinople (680-681), the sixth ecumenical council, defined the existence of two active principles and two wills in Christ, a divine will and a human will. The human will is perfectly subject to the divine will and without sin.[4]

The creeds of the Church attribute to the divine person of the Word what belonged to Him according to His human nature; for example, they profess that the Son of God became man, suffered, died, and rose from the dead.[5] Because of its personal union with the Word, the human nature of Christ is endowed with special knowledge.[6] Jesus Christ is the mediator with the Father on behalf of mankind; He redeemed men and women by His sacrifice on the cross and merited all grace for them.[7]

Christology

Christology is that part of theology which is concerned with the person of Christ. The work of Christ, the atonement, will be dealt with in the following section.

References to Jesus are found in the works of three Roman historians, Suetonius (69-140), Tacitus (b. 55), and Pliny the Younger (61-113).[8] The Jewish historian, Josephus (37-100), speaks of Christ in two places;[9] but outside of the New Testament early Jewish documents which speak of Christ are sparse.

The New Testament. The Gospels are our most important source of information about the details of Jesus' life. The other New Testament writings recognize the centrality of Jesus; but they add no new details to those of the Gospels.

The exact dates of the birth and death of Jesus are unknown; but He must have lived between the death of Herod (4 B.C.) and the governorship of Pontius Pilate (26-36 A.D.) under whom He was crucified. The public life of Jesus began among the poor of Galilee and ended in the city of Jerusalem. It was confined largely to Palestine. Jesus was addressed by the people as "rabbi" which means "teacher;" hence, He was regarded as one learned in the Jewish law. The central theme of Jesus' preaching was the kingdom of God, an idea with deep roots in Jewish history. The kingdom of God signifies the reign of God, a situation in which the will of God alone prevails. The kingdom proclaimed by Jesus is already present (Mk 1:14-15), but it will be fully realized only in the future (Mt 13:40-43). The kingdom demands a radical change of heart on the part of human beings (Mk 1:15). Jesus accompanied His teaching with deeds of power. The miracles of Jesus required an incipient faith from those who were cured; but they led to a deeper faith in Jesus and His mission.

Like any other rabbi, Jesus gathered disciples or followers around Himself. They shared in His mission and were equipped with power to accomplish it. Despite considerable good will on their part, they were slow to grasp who Jesus was and what He was about. Finally, they came to recognize Him as the Messiah (Mk 8:29), a leader whom the Jewish people had long awaited. By His association with sinners and outcasts, by His critique of the Jewish law, and by His manner of teaching with authority, Jesus provoked the opposition of almost every sect in Jewish society. He considered Himself to be the last and greatest of the prophets; and He saw His own fate as a share in the cruel destiny of the rejected prophets. Jesus was executed by the Romans with the involvement of some Jews. The outcome of His passion and death was the resurrection.

There is continuity between the mission of Jesus and the mission of the Church. Nevertheless, in the preaching of the Church, "the proclaimer becomes the proclaimed." The early Christians often used titles such as Lord and messiah to express their maturing faith in Jesus. An examination of these titles reveals the development of Christology in the apostolic age.

In the apostolic preaching which is recorded in Acts, the title *Kyrios* or Lord was applied to the risen Christ, exalted by God; and it expressed the reality of Jesus' divine sonship (Ac 2:33). The title, messiah, was used in the apostolic preaching to underscore the Christian belief that Jesus was the fulfillment of Jewish messianic hopes (Ac 2:36; 17:3). The designation of Jesus as the servant of God (Ac 3:13; 4:27), a figure described in Deutero-Isaiah, was the result of Christian reflection on the meaning of salvation. Jesus was also characterized as the holy and just one (Ac 3:14), the author of life (Ac 3:15), the prophet like Moses (Ac 3:22), the stone rejected by the builders (Ac 4:11), the judge of the living and the dead (Ac 10:42; 17:30), and savior (Ac 5:31).

The titles of Jesus which are employed in the apostolic preaching of Acts recur in the Synoptic Gospels. In these Gospels Jesus appears again as the servant of God (Mk 10:45; Mt 8:16; Lk 24:26, 45-46). He is given the title of "messiah" (Mk 8:30; 14:62; 15:2 with the parallel passages in Mt and Lk). The Gospel of Matthew revolves around the concept that Jesus is the expected messiah-king of Israel. The Gospel of Mark focuses on the two titles "Christ" or "messiah" and "Son of God" (Mk 1:1). For Mark, Jesus reveals Himself as the Son of God by His exercise of divine power. In Matthew's Gospel Jesus is described as the "son of David" (Mt 1:1). In Luke's Gospel Jesus is called a savior (Lk 2:11). In all the Synoptic Gospels, Jesus refers to Himself as the "son of man" especially in two cases—in His role as judge and as the suffering servant of God (e.g., Mt 24:30; Mk 8:31; 9:11). The title is probably borrowed from Dn 7:13.

In the Pauline writings, one finds the famous Christological hymn which speaks of the preexistent Christ, His self-effacement in the incarnation, His humiliating death, and His exaltation by God, so that every tongue must proclaim Him as *Kyrios* or Lord (Ph 2:5-11). Along with "Christ" or "messiah," "Lord" is the most common Pauline title for Jesus (e.g., 1 Th 1:6; Ph 1:2). For Paul, Jesus is the messiah of the Jews (Rm 9:5; 10:4; etc.), the Son of God (1 Th 1:10; 1 Cor 1:9; etc.), the image of God (2 Cor 4:4; Col 1:15), the firstborn before all creatures (Col 1:15-16), the savior (Ph 3:20; Ep 5:23), the head of the Church (Col 1:18; Ep 1:22), and in equivalent terms, God, (Ph 2:5-11; Col 1:15; 2:9). For Paul, Christ is the "last Adam." This title is one of Paul's original contributions to the Christology of the New Testament. As the last Adam, the risen Lord is a "life-giving spirit" into whose image man must be transformed (1 Cor 15:45). Mankind is involved in the death and resurrection of Christ, just as it was involved in the disobedience of Adam (Rm 5:15-21). In Christ, the new Adam, Jew and Gentile achieve a new unity (Ep 2:15).

To a large extent, the Synoptic and Pauline titles of Christ are also found in the Johannine literature. In this literature, Jesus is the messiah (Jn 20:31; 1 Jn 2:22; Rv 11:15), the Son of God (Jn 20:31; 1 Jn 1:3; etc.), *Kyrios* or Lord (Jn 20:2; 21:7), son of man (Jn 1:51; 13:31), son of Joseph (Jn 1:46; 6:42), the prophet (Jn 6:14), the king of Israel (Jn 1:49), and savior (Jn 4:42). John the Baptist speaks of Jesus as the lamb of God (Jn 1:29, 36). This title means that Jesus is the servant of Yahweh who "is led to the slaughter like a lamb" (Is 53:7), that He is a victim similar to the Passover lamb (Jn 19:36). For John, Jesus is the Word of God (Jn 1:1-18) because He reveals the Father. The "I am" statements in the Gospel (Jn 8:24; 13:19; etc.) are an expression of Jesus' divinity.

The Fathers. At the beginning the Fathers affirmed the mysterious unity of God and man in Jesus Christ. For example, Ignatius of Antioch (died c. 110) wrote: "We have as a physician the Lord our God, Jesus the Christ, the only begotten Son and Word before time began, who afterwards became man also of Mary the virgin."[10] Ignatius opposed the heresy of Docetism (from the Gr. *dokein*, to seem) which maintained that the redeemer assumed only the appearance of a man and only appeared to suffer and die. Irenaeus of Lyons (died c. 200) repeated the thought of Ignatius: the Word who existed from the beginning with God descended from the Father and became incarnate.[11] For Hippolytus of Rome (died c. 235), the eternal Word of God was born of Mary, died, rose, ascended, and sits at the right hand of the Father.[12] Tertullian (d. after 220) argued that Jesus was one person in two substances or natures, truly God and truly man.[13] Some of the formulas that Tertullian used were used by councils and tradition after him. The Word-Christology of Alexandria saw the revelation of the Father as the heart of the work of salvation.

Clement of Alexandria (d. 215) and Origen (d. 253) are representative. Origen, for example, regarded the Son of God as the perfect image of the Father. The Son became man and the sinless soul of Jesus was the pure image of the Son. In turn, the body of Jesus was the mirror of His soul.[14] Origen gave Greek Christology the scientific terms, *physis, hypostasis, ousia, homousios,* and *theanthropos.*

Toward the end of the 3rd century, Paul of Samosata, bishop of Antioch, held that Jesus was a mere man; however, the impersonal Word or wisdom of God dwelt in Him. This opinion was a form of Adoptionism, a heresy which regarded Jesus as simply a human being who was "adopted" by God as His Son. The priest, Malchion, attempted to convice Paul of his error; but in his attempt, Malchion fell into another error by holding that Jesus was without a human soul, the God-Word taking the place of the soul. Arius (died c. 336), a priest of Alexandria, denied the divinity of Christ. Christ, the Son of God, although eternal, was the creature of the Father. This was the heresy of Arianism. The Council of Nicea (325) condemned the Arian view by asserting that the Son was of one nature, *homoousios,* with the Father. Athanasius, who became the bishop of Alexandria in 328, was the leader of the struggle against the Arians and the opponents of Nicea.[15]

Subsequently, a new controversy disturbed the Church. Diodore of Tarsus (died c. 394) apparently denied that the Son of God was born of Mary. What she bore was the man to whom the Word united Himself. The position of Theodore of Mopsuestia (d. 428), the disciple of Diodore, was ambiguous. Theodore spoke of the union between the Word and the man who is filled by Him as a moral union similar to the union between a man and his wife. Thus in Christ there seemed to be two persons. Yet, Theodore also spoke expressly of "two natures," "one person," "without confusion and without division" in Christ. Nestorius of Constantinople (d. 451), a disciple of Theodore, held that Mary was the mother of the man and the mother of Christ, but not the mother of God or *theotókos.* The great opponent of Nestorius was Cyril of Alexandria (d. 444). The Council of Ephesus condemned Nestorius' view which is the heresy of Nestorianism. For the council, the eternal Son of the Father is Himself the one who was born from Mary, died, and rose. He was the one subject of the saving mystery.[16]

Still another Christological heresy appeared, Monophysitism. The

Monophysites believed that the divine and human natures had gone to form Christ. They said, however, that the union of the two natures had given rise to a single nature in which the humanity was absorbed by the divinity, dissolved like a drop of honey in the sea. Eutyches, abbot of a monastery at Constantinople, gave this teaching its clearest formulation. In 449 Pope Leo the Great (d. 461) sent a letter to Flavian, patriarch of Constantinople, in which he opposed the teaching of Eutyches. This letter is known as the Tome of Leo.[17] It was later accepted by the Council of Chalcedon (451) as an accurate expression of the traditional teaching on the one person and two natures in Christ. The council asserted one Lord in two natures, without confusion or conversion, without division or separation, both being united in a single person or hypostasis.[18]

One further clarification was forthcoming. Did Christ have two principles of action and two wills? Sergius, patriarch of Constantinople (610-38), gave a negative answer to this question. Owing to the hypostatic union, he said, Christ could have only one principle of action and only one will, at once divine and human. This was the heresy of Monothelitism. The Third Council of Constantinople (680-681), however, gave an affirmative answer to the question by drawing the logical conclusion from Chalcedon's definition of two natures in Christ. According to III Constantinople, Christ has two principles of action and two wills which do not conflict since the human will is subordinate to the divine.[19] With this council, the development of classical Christology came to an end.

Since the patristic era, the magisterium and theologians have used certain terms in a very precise sense to elucidate the mystery of the incarnation. The *hypostatic union* is the substantial union of the human and divine natures in the one person of the Word of God. A *nature* is the permanent structure of a thing viewed as the basic principle of its activity. A nature is distinguished from a person as a part from a whole. A *person* is the subject which possesses a rational nature and is the ultimate bearer of it. An individual, rational nature is not a person unless it subsists in its own right. In this case, *subsistence* means being in and for itself without being assumed into a unity of a higher order.

The Atonement

The atonement (Eng. *at-one-ment*, bringing together) refers to man's reconciliation with God through the sacrificial death of Christ.

Under the *Old Testament* God took the initiative in reconciling sinful man to Himself. God established rites of expiation intended ultimately to reconcile man with Himself. Without repentance, however, the offering of sacrifice for sin was futile (Is 1:10-17; Ho 6:6). God promised a new and eternal covenant to replace the old one which sinful Israel had broken (Jr 31:31-34). God also prepared a servant who was "crushed for our sins" and "shall take away the sins of many and win pardon for their offenses" (Is 53:5, 12).

Under the *New Testament* God reconciled man to Himself perfectly and definitively through Jesus Christ. Jesus began His public ministry with a call to repentance for sin (Mk 1:15). He came to suffer an atoning death for all men (Mk 10:45). At the institution of the Eucharist Jesus declared the shedding of His blood to constitute a new covenant between God and His people (Lk 22:20) unto the forgiveness of sins (Mt 26:28). Jesus identified Himself with the suffering servant (Lk 22:37) of whom Isaiah spoke (53:12). This identification was proclaimed in the earliest Christian preaching (Ac 8:32-35). John the Baptist referred to Jesus as "the lamb of God who takes away the sin of the world" (Jn 1:29). Probably John was comparing Jesus to the lamb which was sacrificed at the Passover (Jn 19:14, 36).

According to Paul, Christ died for the sake of sinners (Rm 5:6, 8; 14:9; 1 Cor 15:3). God has reconciled us to Himself through Christ (2 Cor 5:18). Christ made peace between God and man through the blood of His cross (Col 1:20). Baptism incorporates the Christian into the death and resurrection of Christ, frees him from sin, and confers upon him a new life (Rm 6:3-11). Peter speaks of our deliverance by Christ's blood (1 P 1:18); and the author of Hebrews asserts that Christ's redeeming death had the character of sacrifice (Heb 9).

The *Fathers* developed the teaching of the New Testament on the atonement and posed problems which did not occur to the Biblical writers. Borrowing the idea from Paul (Rm 5:12-18), Irenaeus thought of the "recapitulation" of all things in Christ. By this he meant that mankind regained through Christ what it had lost through Adam.[20] It was impossible for the fallen human race to renew itself and attain salvation; therefore, the Son of God became man and died to accomplish both these things.[21] "God recapitulated in Himself the ancient formation of man, that He might kill sin, deprive death of its power, and vivify man."[22] One hears echoes of Irenaeus' theory of recapitulation in the writings of Hippolytus and Tertullian. Irenaeus also developed what might be called the "exchange" theory. This means that he saw the restoration of human nature in the fact that God the Son took our nature unto Himself. "For it was for this end that the Word of God was made man . . . that man, having been taken into the Word and receiving the adoption, might become the son of God."[23] The salvation of mankind is a reality because of the incarnation. Later, Athanasius was to employ this idea in his struggle with the Arians.[24]

At Alexandria, Clement spoke of Christ's laying down His life as a ransom on our behalf, redeeming us by His blood, and offering Himself as a sacrifice.[25] Origen, the disciple of Clement, thought of the death of Christ as a ransom paid to the devil who had acquired rights over humanity because of its sinfulness.[26] This idea was accepted with certain modifications by Hilary of Poitiers, Augustine, and Leo the Great. They added, however, that the devil had abused his rights when he sought to exercise them on the sinless Christ. Thus, the devil was himself conquered by the resurrection of Christ. Origen also thought of Christ as a priest who offered Himself as a sacrificial victim to the Father, thereby propitiating Him.[27] He took away sin because He Himself was without sin.[28] Writing in the same vein, Cyril of Alexandria described Christ as "a victim, priest, mediator, spotless sacrifice, and the true lamb who takes away the sin of the world."[29] Hence, according to the Fathers, the atonement of Christ was effected in two ways—through the contact of human nature with the divinity in the incarnation and through the sacrificial death of Christ on the cross.

To the *Middle Ages* belongs the famous study of the atonement, *Cur Deus Homo?* by Anselm of Canterbury (1033-1109). According to Anselm, sin is an infinite offense against God. No ordinary being of finite worth, whether man or angel, could offer adequate satisfaction to the Father for such an offense. Hence, it was necessary for a God-Man of infinite worth, Jesus Christ, to offer complete satisfaction for sin through His suffering and death. In this way, the justice of God was satisfied and God and man were reconciled.[30] Anselm's theory reflected the relationship between the feudal lord and his vassal.[31] Thomas Aquinas (1225-74) did not believe that the incarnation and death of Christ were absolutely necessary to reconcile God and man. God could have reconciled man to Himself in many other ways without sacrificing the demands of justice. However, the incarnation and death of Christ served an extremely useful purpose, namely the revelation of God's love, the instruction and encouragement of human beings, and stress upon the horror of sin.[32] Actually, the death of Christ merited the salvation of mankind, offered superabundant satisfaction for sin, had the effect of a true sacrifice, redeemed us from the slavery of sin and death, and reconciled us to God.[33]

The *Reformers of the 16th century* accepted the core of the traditional doctrine while underscoring the voluntary substitution of the sinless Christ for sinful man in His passion and death. Martin Luther (1483-1546) taught that God's only Son became man, took upon Himself the guilt and wrath of men's sins, and made His own body and blood a ransom and a sacrifice in atonement for sin. God is reconciled to all who believe in this Son.[34] John Calvin (1509-64) spoke of the expiation and satisfaction exhibited in the death of Christ after He had assumed our guilt and suffered in His soul the dreadful torments of a person condemned and lost.[35] However, the Rakovian Catechism (1609) of the Socinians denied the objective efficacy of the cross and the doctrine of penal satisfaction. It taught that the death of Christ was primarily an example to His followers.[36] During the 19th century the latter theory was developed in its essentials by Schleiermacher, Ritschl, Harnack, and Sabatier.

In the *20th century* there are two general views of the atonement. One view regards the death of Jesus as a revelation of the goodness of God and the malice of sin whereby the sinner is moved to repent and so achieves the forgiveness of his offenses.[37] A variation of this view regards the life and death of Jesus as a call to authentic existence or to be "men for others" or to believe as Jesus believed or to share His self-understanding.[38] It seems to follow from this view and its variation that the events of Jesus' life would have been without effect had there been no one to contemplate them. The other view—the one held by Catholics and many Protestants—recognizes the revelatory and inspirational character of Jesus' life and death; but it goes further. It holds that Jesus was the representative or substitute of sinful men. He took upon Himself the sins of men. His death was a voluntary sacrifice or oblation offered to God on behalf of men. It had objective value before God as satisfaction for sin.

What part does the *resurrection* have in the atonement? For many centuries, western theologians devoted greater attention to the death of Christ as an atoning event than to the resurrection. There were several reasons. First, the Scriptures do attach enormous significance to the death of Christ as an atoning event. Second, it is possible that a Platonic interest in the soul rather than in the body entailed a relative lack of interest in the bodily resurrection of Christ. Third, after Anselm's *Cur Deus Homo?* of the 11th century, theologians were concerned with the process of reconciliation as an act at once of justice and grace. The resurrection did not bulk large in Anselm's work. Fourth, the medieval devotion to the passion and death of Christ symbolized by the crucifix and way of the cross may have played its part. Nevertheless, the New Testament and especially Paul saw the death *and* resurrection of Christ as atoning acts. We have already noticed the profound importance which Paul attached to the death of Christ; but he went on to say that Jesus was ''raised up for our justification'' (Rm 4:25). Christ was raised from the dead in order that we might bear fruit for God (Rm 7:4). The resurrection of Jesus is the principle of our resurrection (2 Cor 4:14). Elsewhere, we read that the Christian is born again to a new life and hope that derive from the resurrection of Jesus Christ (1 P 1:3-4). In other words, the redemption was not complete on Good Friday. We are saved by both the death of Jesus and His resurrection.

Special Questions

1. The Reality of the Resurrection. The resurrection was more than the restoration of the slain Jesus to the conditions of the present life; rather, it conferred upon Him a new and permanent form of life in glory and power. The New Testament does not describe the actual event of the resurrection; it tells only of the empty tomb and the appearances of the risen Jesus to His disciples and Paul. The earliest list of appearances is derived from Paul writing to the Corinthians about 57 A.D. (1 Cor 15:3-8). According to the accounts, the resurrected Jesus was able to pass through closed doors; and He appeared and disappeared with an unnatural suddenness (Jn 20:19-29). His appearances to His followers caused them to fear and doubt His reality at first; yet, He was not a phantom. He spoke and ate with them. He could be seen and felt by them. Those who saw Him recognized Him as their former master, Jesus, who had been crucified (Lk 24:36-45). After His resurrection Jesus enjoyed a ''glorious'' (Ph 3:21) "spiritual" existence—freed from the possibility of decline and death (1 Cor 15:43-58). The resurrection appearances of the risen Savior are attached to different localities, namely, Jerusalem and Galilee; but it is useless to attempt a sequence of all the post-resurrection appearances of Jesus.

Surely, the bald assertion that someone has risen from the dead is for many absolutely incredible. One recalls the reaction of certain Athenians to Paul's discourse in the midst of the Areopagus. After Paul had spoken about Jesus' resurrection from the dead, "some began to sneer" (Ac 17:31-32). Yet, the assertion that *Jesus* rose from the dead becomes less incredible if one is prepared to grant certain possibilities: that human beings could have benefited by a message from God; that God could have imparted this message through agents; that the profoundly religious figure, Jesus, could have been an agent of God; that God could have guaranteed Him to all by raising Him from the dead. Of course, one who admits these possibilities is not compelled as a consequence to admit the fact of Jesus' resurrection; but he is prepared to weigh the evidence.

Some have understood the resurrection story to be a symbol of Jesus' life with God after His death. Jesus continues to live with His Father even though His body may have remained in the tomb. However, such an understanding is not faithful to the apostolic proclamation of a *bodily* resurrection. Others have attributed the apostolic proclamation of a bodily resurrection either to fraud or to credulity. In other words, the apostles were either lying or the victims of an hallucination when they claimed to have seen the risen Jesus. The difficulty with this explanation of the resurrection story is that it fails to account for the rise of the Christian Church despite Jesus' ignominious death. Despite the crushing psychological blow of Jesus' crucifixion, the apostles and the Christian Church began to proclaim Jesus as Lord and messiah. This proclamation cannot be attributed to Jesus' life which ended so disastrously. It has to be attributed to the reality of the resurrection.

Was Jesus raised from the dead or did He rise from the dead? In a number of passages of the New Testament, particularly in the Pauline writings, it is said that the Father raised Jesus from the dead (e.g., 1 Th 1:10; 1 Cor 6:14; Gal 1:1). In John, however, where the unity of the Father and Son is stressed (Jn 10:30), it is said that Jesus had the power to take up His life again after He had laid it down (Jn 10:17-18). What is the connection between the resurrection and the ascension of Jesus? If the ascension is taken to mean the glorification of Jesus at the Father's right hand, then it was an integral part of the resurrection. If the ascension is taken to mean the termination of Jesus' frequent appearances to His disciples, then it was removed from the resurrection by some time (forty days).

2. *The Knowledge of Christ.* The knowledge of Christ is the knowledge which Christ has as God and man. Thomas Aquinas distinguished four kinds of knowledge in Christ: 1) the eternal, infinite, and perfect knowledge which is proper to God; 2) the knowledge of vision proper to the blessed in heaven; 3) the infused knowledge proper to the angels; and 4) the acquired knowledge proper to men.[39] Christ possessed the knowledge proper to God because He was God. The other three kinds of knowledge are rooted in His human soul. Christ had the beatifying knowledge of the blessed in heaven because His humanity was united to the Word in a personal union, a union much more intimate than the union of the blessed in heaven with God. Christ possessed this knowledge from the inception of the incarnation. Christ had the infused knowledge proper to the angels in His capacity as head of the angels and for the perfection of His "possible" intellect. Christ also acquired knowledge by means of abstraction from sense knowledge; for example, He learned obedience from what He suffered (Heb 5:8). Christ acquired this knowledge only gradually with the passing of the years.

The theological problem of Christ's knowledge is not concerned with the infinite knowledge of Jesus as God, but with that of His human finite soul. The problem arises because Jesus seems to have been ignorant of certain important matters, an ignorance which is difficult to explain if the soul of Jesus enjoyed the vision of God. For example, some exegetes say that Jesus in His earthly life did not know Himself to be the natural Son of God. Had He known Himself to be the Son of God He could not have contained His knowledge. Yet, the Gospels reflect no historically certain claim by Jesus to be God; and His disciples did not recognize His divinity until after the resurrection.[40] Moreover, the Gospels speak of Jesus' ignorance in certain respects; for example, He did not know the exact day or hour of the final consummation (Mt 24:36).

Even though the idea presents problems, many theologians are unwilling to deny the vision of God to the human soul of Christ. The idea is too firmly rooted in Christian tradition. To deal with the theological problem of Christ's knowledge, some theologians hold that Christ's knowledge of His divine self was intuitive and inexpressible, the result of the union between His human mind and the divine person. Christ was able to articulate this knowledge to Himself and others only gradually as He acquired the necessary concepts and images through human experience.[41] One must acknowledge, however, the great difficulty of trying to understand the psychology of one who was both God and man.

Did Jesus actually express a claim to divinity? Yes. This is the most natural explanation of the Church's faith in the divinity of Christ. Generally, Christ presented His claim in a veiled manner for pedagogical reasons; and His disciples did not understand His claim until after the illuminating experience of the resurrection; but there is evidence of the claim. One expression of Jesus' claim to divinity may be seen in His custom of contrasting His own sonship with that of His disciples. He did so by referring a number of times to "my Father" (Lk 22:29; 24:49) and "your Father" (Mt 7:11; Mk 11:25). He avoided the phrase "our Father," so that He might never place Himself on the same level of adoptive sonship which the disciples enjoyed. Jesus described His unique sonship in some detail. He is the beloved son sent by His Father (Mk 12:1-12). He pre-existed so that His ancestor, David, knew Him and called Him Lord (Mk 12:35-37). He is greater than Solomon, the prophets of the Old Testament (Mt 12:41-42), and the temple (Mt 12:6). The angels of heaven serve Him (Mt 13:41; Mk 13:27). His knowledge of the Father is comparable to the Father's knowledge of Him (Mt 11:27; Lk 10:22). Jesus presents Himself as eschatological king and judge (Mt 25:34-40). As the Son, Jesus claims the prerogatives of Yahweh. A. Feuillet has drawn attention to a number of passages of the Synoptic Gospels which imply pre-existence and transcendence, particularly the use of the phrases "I am sent" (Mt 15:24; Lk 4:43) and "I have come" (Mt 5:17; Mk 2:17; etc.)[42]

For some Fathers and Aquinas, Jesus' ignorance of the day and hour of the judgment (Mk 13:30) meant only that He was unwilling to communicate His knowledge of them to His disciples (as in Ac 1:6-7). Knowing all the details of the judgment recorded in Mark and Matthew, He surely knew the time of the judgment too.[43]

3. *The Communication of Idioms.* This is a corollary of the Church's

teaching on the incarnation. Since Christ has a divine and a human nature united in the person of the Word, the properties of both natures can and must be predicated of the one divine person of Jesus Christ; for example, Christ is God, Christ is man. Furthermore, when the person of the Word is designated by a name which identifies Him as the bearer of one of the natures, the properties of the other nature can be predicated of Him; for example, God is man. The communication of idioms, therefore, is the mutual attribution of the properties of the divine and human natures of Christ and each other.

Among the rules for the communication of idioms are these: 1) In affirmative sentences concrete expressions pertaining to one nature may be predicated of concrete expressions pertaining to the other nature; for example, it is true to say that God, that is, this second person of the blessed Trinity, is man; that this man, that is, this concrete person, is God. If, however, the subject of the sentence is qualified in a specific way, the predication is illegitimate. Thus it is wrong to say that this man (Christ) as man is God. 2) In Christ abstract expressions referring to one nature cannot be predicated of abstract expressions referring to the other nature. One may not say, for example, that in Christ divinity is humanity. Such abstract expressions do not have the personal reference which legitimizes the communication of idioms. 3) Ordinarily concrete words cannot be predicated of abstract words. Hence, it is false to say that in Christ humanity is God. 4) Abstract words cannot be predicated of concrete words. One may not say that the Son of God is humanity. 5) Expressions used by heretics should be used with caution. Arius said that Christ was a creature. This statement is susceptible of a correct interpretation, but it could be misleading. To put it all briefly, what is true of the one nature cannot be said of the other except insofar as these two are one; and they are one only in the person.

4. The Modern Concept of Person. Traditionally, a person has been defined as "the individual substance of a rational nature." This definition goes back to Boethius of the sixth century; and it is consistent with the ancient conciliar understanding of a person as the bearer of a nature, a center of unity, the subject of a particular concrete existence, and the ultimate term of responsibility. This definition is sometimes described as ontological and it differs in some measure from the modern definition of a person which is largely psychological. The modern conception of a person is that of a subject which is conscious of itself, free, and a center of experience. Christ's human nature lacked nothing that characterizes a human person in the modern sense, namely, consciousness of itself, freedom, and the capacity to enter into human relationship with God and others. The implications of the psychological definition of person for the understanding and explanation of the mystery of the incarnation are not yet entirely clear.[44]

In the encylical, *Sempiternus Rex* (1951), Pope Pius XII saw no reason why the human nature of Christ should not be studied from the standpoint of psychology. However, he wrote that one must avoid the danger of viewing Christ's human nature as an independent subject which does not subsist in the person of the Word. The ancient councils plainly asserted the union of Christ's two natures in the one person. In Christ there is no "assumed man" possessing complete autonomy.[45] In 1972, the Sacred Congregation for Teaching the Faith said that the following opinions were *contrary* to the Catholic faith: 1) that the Son of God did not subsist from all eternity as distinct from the Father and the Holy Spirit; 2) that the idea of one person in Jesus Christ must be abandoned; 3) that the humanity of Christ is a human person.[46]

5. The Jesus of History and the Christ of Faith. In the 19th and early 20th centuries some scholars distinguished between the Jesus of history and the Christ of faith. The historical figure of Jesus, they said, had been transformed into the Christ of faith by the early Church which had misunderstood His person and message. These scholars attempted to recover the historical Jesus by historical and literary criticism of the Gospels. A. Harnack (1851-1930) thought that Jesus was a simple Galilean villager who taught only the fatherhood of God and the brotherhood of man. All else was an extraneous addition to Christianity.[47] R. Bultmann (1884-1976) believed that very little is known about the historical Jesus. This ignorance was unimportant for Bultmann. What was important was man's acceptance or rejection of the Church's proclamation that God had acted in Jesus.[48]

Reacting to Bultmann's position, the Post-Bultmannians pointed out that Christianity becomes a pure myth if it does not rest on the life of the historical Jesus. More recent scholarship has demonstrated the continuity between the Jesus of history and the Christ of faith. It has justified confidence in the Gospels as sources of information about Jesus. No doubt, the early Church came to appreciate the depths of Jesus' person and teaching with a clarity that the disciples did not experience prior to the resurrection. Frequently, this clarity was inserted into the Gospel accounts of the earthly life of Jesus. To what extent this occurred will always be a question; but, for excellent reasons, Vatican II held that the four Gospels "whose historical character the Church unhesitatingly asserts, faithfully hand on what Jesus Christ, while living among men, really did and taught for their eternal salvation."[49]

Twentieth Century Interpretations of Jesus

The twentieth century has produced many diverse interpretations of Jesus and His message. There are a variety of reasons. The principal sources of information about the life and teaching of Jesus are the Gospels; but some inerpreters (like Bultmann) contest the reliability of the Gospels and reconstruct the life and teaching of Jesus in their own way. Other interpreters cannot agree about the methodology for extracting the historical elements of the Gospels. Must one, for example, accept as historical only those sayings which occur in more than one form or have an Aramaic background or place Jesus and the early Christian community in a poor light? Or are there other criteria of historicity? All interpreters are influenced by their philosophical presuppositions. Thus, an interpreter who admits the possibility of miracles will view the cures of Jesus differently than one who denies the possibility of miracles.

Certain other factors—a renewal of interest in the humanity of Jesus, a greater insight into what it means to be human, a world view colored by evolutionary theory, reflection on what Christ did at the end (His atoning death and resurrection) rather than on what He did at the beginning (the incarnation), the availability of new philosophical concepts, the attempt to demythologize the Gospels, and the desire to render the Christian message more meaningful to the modern mind—all these have led some twentieth century interpreters to regard Jesus and His message in new ways.

In such works as *Die Geschichte der Synoptischen Tradition* (1921) and *Jesus* (1926), Rudolph Bultmann, the German exegete and theologian, viewed Jesus as a prophet calling men to repent and to embrace the kingdom of God. Jesus was not a divine person; rather, He was the one in whom God speaks to men in an ultimate manner. The ancient Church erred when it interpreted the person of Jesus in terms of Greek metaphysics. Karl Barth (1886-1968), the Swiss Protestant theologian and author of *Der Römerbrief* (1919) and *Church Dogmatics* (1932-67; Eng. tr. 1936-69) held that God cannot be known by unaided human reason, but only through Jesus Christ. The task of the theologian is to show how the revealing Christ tells us who God is and who we are. Barth stressed the divinity of Christ. Oscar Cullmann (1902-) of the University of Paris expounded the notion of salvation history in his *Christ and Time* (1946; Eng. tr. 1951). God has revealed Himself in the events of a relatively narow stream of sacred history the midpoint of which was Jesus Christ. Cullmann is also notable for his "functional" approach to Christology.

Pierre Teilhard de Chardin, S.J. (1881-1955), a French theologian and scientist, expressed his view of Christ in *The Phenomenon of Man* (1955; Eng. tr. 1959) and *The Divine Milieu* (1957; Eng. tr. 1960). For Teilhard, the whole universe is in an evolutionary process of "Christification" as a result of the incarnation. The risen Christ is the personal center of the entire cosmos and the point of its final consummation—its Omega point. Karl Rahner, S.J. (1904-), formerly professor of dogmatic theology at the University of Munich, recognizes the centrality of the mystery of Jesus for Christianity. He is firmly committed to the traditional teaching that Jesus is true God and true man. The task of the modern theologian, as he sees it, is to express this tradition in such a way that it can be understood by contemporary man. Rahner's writings have been collected under the title *Theological Investigations* (1954 ff; Eng. tr. 1961).

Albert Schweitzer (*The Quest of the Historical Jesus* 1906; Eng. tr. 1910) held that Jesus expected a speedy end to the world. When the end did not come, Jesus concluded that He must suffer and die in order to compel the coming of God's kingdom. C.H. Dodd (*The Apostolic Preaching*, 1936) was the spokesman for "realized eschatology." By this, he meant that the kingdom of God, which had been expected in the Old Testament and announced by Christ, had been realized in the incarnation and its consequences for mankind. Dietrich Bonhoeffer (*Letters and Papers from Prison*, 1951; Eng. tr. 1953; *The Cost of Discipleship* 1937; Eng. tr. 1948) was deeply influenced by Barth. Jesus was God's Son who became the "man for others" and the only way to a true knowledge of God.

Joseph Klausner (*Jesus of Nazareth* 1922; Eng. tr. 1925) stressed the Jewishness of Jesus. The natural environment of Nazareth, the Hebrew Scriptures, the life of the Galileans, and the *Torah*—all these were powerful influences upon Him. C.F. Potter (*The Lost Years of Jesus* 1958) examined the relationship between Christianity and the Qumran community. He believed that Jesus must have had contact with this community prior to His public ministry. Hugh Schonfield (*The Passover Plot* 1965) thought of Jesus as a messianic schemer who plotted to fulfill in His own life the predictions of the Scriptures relative to the Jewish messiah. S. Brandon (*Jesus and the Zealots* 1967) maintained that Jesus was associated with Zealot and revolutionary principles. He was crucified by Romans as a rebel against their government in Judea. James Cone (*A Black Theology of Liberation* 1970) saw Jesus as the Oppressed One whose work was that of liberating humanity from inhumanity. Through Him the oppressed are set free to be what they are. John Allegro (*The Sacred Mushroom and the Cross* 1970) connected Christianity with the ancient fertility cults of which the mushroom was a symbol. Allegro professed to find numerous references to the mushroom fertility cult in the life of Jesus. Morton Smith (*The Secret Gospel* 1973) contended that Jesus was the founder of a secret society of which the secret gnostic sects—like the Carpocratians—were the true heirs.

Piet Schoonenberg, S.J., holds that, since the incarnation, the Logos has become the second person of God's trinity—person being taken in the *modern* sense—by actuating and supporting actively the human person of Jesus.[50] For Wolfhart Pannenberg (*Jesus, God and Man* 1968), Jesus is true God and true man. Only through Jesus do we come to know God. In Jesus the end of history is truly anticipated and revealed. The resurrection of Jesus was an historical event not to be taken on faith. Hans Küng (*On Being a Christian* 1976) regards Christ as ultimately decisive, definitive, and archetypal for man's relationship to God; but he stops short of saying that Jesus is truly God.

Footnotes

1. *TCC* nos. 829-830.
2. *TCC* no. 246.
3. *TCC* no. 252.
4. *TCC* nos. 295-296.
5. *TCC* nos. 828, 829, 831.
6. *TCC* nos. 304-307, 311-313, 319a.
7. *TCC* nos. 243, 247, 293, 314-315, 718, 747.
8. Suetonius, *Life of Claudius* 25, 4; Tacitus, *Annals* 15, 44; Pliny, Letters 10, 96.
9. *Antiquities* 20,9,1; 18,3,3.
10. Letter to the Ephesians 7.
11. *Against Heresies* 3, 18, 1-2.
12. *In Cant.* 2, 8.
13. *Against Praxeas* 27.
14. H. Crouzel, *Théologie de l'image de Dieu chez Origène*, Paris, 1956, 135-142.
15. J. Kelly, *op. cit.* 158-161, 226-247; P. Smulders, *op. cit.* 57-79.
16. J. Kelly, *op. cit.* 301-330; P. Smulders, *op. cit.* 91-119.
17. *TCC* nos. 247-251.
18. J. Kelly, *op. cit.* 330-342; P. Smulders, *op. cit.* 119-139.
19. J. Kelly, *op. cit.* 343; P. Smulders, *op. cit.* 139-147.
20. *Against Heresies* 3, 18, 1.
21. *Ibid.* 3, 18, 2.
22. *Ibid.* 3, 18, 7.
23. *Ibid.* 3, 19, 1.
24. *On the Incarnation* 54.
25. *Who Is the Rich Man?* 37; *The Instructor* 1.5; 1,11.
26. *In Matt.* 16, 8.
27. *In Rom.* 3, 8; *Hom. in Num.* 24, 1.
28. *In Jo.* 28, 18.
29. *In Jo.* 11, 8. *PG* 74, 508A.
30. For an Eng. tr. of *Cur Deus Homo?* see S.W. Deane, *St. Anselm*, La Salle, 1962, Open Court Publ. Co., 171-288.
31. *See* G. Greshake, *Redemption and Freedom* in *Th. Dig.* 25 (1977) 61-65.
32. *ST* 3a.1.2.

33. *ST* 3a.48-49.
34. Epistle Sermon, 24th Sunday after Trinity.
35. *Institutes* 2, 16, 3; 2, 16, 5; 2, 16, 10.
36. *HD* 7, 146-156.
37. For names *see* G. Graystone, *Modern Theories of Atonement* in R. Gleason (ed.), *A Theology Reader*, New York 1966, The Macmillan Co., 192-222.
38. *See* G. O'Collins, S.J., *The Resurrection*, Valley Forge, 1973, The Judson Press, 125-131.
39. *ST* 3a.9.
40. *See* B. Vawter, *This Man Jesus*, Garden City, 1973, Doubleday & Co. 134.
41. See *TD, Knowledge of Christ.*
42. *See* A. Gelin (et. al.), *Son and Savior*, Baltimore, 1960, Helicon Press, 50-85; J. McKenzie, *Jesus Christ* in *DB* 435.
43. *ST* 3a.10.2.ad 1.
44. See *TD, Person*; D. Lane, *op. cit.* 112-114.
45. *TCC* no. 319b.
46. *AAS* 64 (1972) 238.
47. *Das Wesen des Christenthums* 1900.
48. *Die Geschichte der Synoptischen Tradition* 1921.
49. Vatican II, *Dei Verbum* no. 19.
50. *Th. Dig.* Autumn 1975, 224-225.

Chapter 8

MARY, MOTHER OF GOD

Bibliography. For the teaching of the Church: *TCC* nos. 320-334c; Vatican II, *Lumen Gentium*, ch. 8; NCCB, *Behold Your Mother*, Washington, 1973; Paul VI, *Marialis Cultus, L'Osservatore Romano*, April 4, 1974. For the Scriptural material: J. McKenzie, *Mary* in *DB* 551-552; C. Ceroke, O. Carm., *Mary (in the Bible)* in *NCE* 9, 335-347; M. Schmaus, *Mariology, Biblical* in *SM*, 376-383; pertinent sections in the *JBC*; A. George, S.M., *Mary* in *DBT* 338-342; M. Thurian, *Mary, Mother of All Christians*, New York, 1964, Herder and Herder; J. McHugh, *The Mother of Jesus in the NT*, London, 1975, Darton, Longman & Todd; M. Miguens, O.F.M., *The Virgin Birth*, Westminster, 1975, Christian Classics; R. Brown, *The Birth of the Messiah*, Garden City, 1977, Doubleday & Co.

For the theological and dogmatic development: P. Palmer, S.J., *Mary in the Documents of the Church*, Westminster, 1952, The Newman Press; H. Graef, *Mary, A History of Doctrine and Devotion*, New York, 1963 (vol. 1) and 1965 (vol. 2), Sheed and Ward; pertinent articles in the *NCE* (e.g., *Mariology* 9, 223-227; *Mother of God* 10, 21-24; *Immaculate Conception* 7, 378-381; *Virgin Birth* 14, 692-696; *Assumption of Mary* 1, 971-975; *Mary, Devotion to* 9, 364-368); K. Rahner, S.J., *Mary, Mother of the Lord*, New York, 1963, Herder and Herder; E. Schillebeeckx, O.P., *Mary, Mother of the Redemption*, New York, 1964, Sheed and Ward; E. Carroll, O. Carm., *Theology on the Virgin Mary: 1966-75* in *TS* 37 (1976) 253-289.

Mary is the mother of Jesus who is God and man.

The Teaching of the Church

The teaching of the councils and the Popes prior to Vatican II may be summarized in this way: Mary is truly the mother of God.[1] She conceived the Son of God by the power of the Holy Spirit.[2] Mary remained a virgin throughout her life.[3] She was free from original sin. This freedom was her immaculate conception.[4] She was distinguished by her fullness of grace[5] and her complete sinlessness.[6] She is the mediatrix of the graces merited by Christ.[7] At the end of her earthly life she was assumed body and soul into heaven.[8]

The Second Vatican Council (1962-65) reaffirmed these and other traditional doctrines of the Church about Mary. The council noted that the heavenly Father sought and obtained Mary's consent to the incarnation of His divine Son. Mary is the mother of God. She conceived the Son of God in a virginal manner and remained a virgin thereafter. As the mother of God, Mary was accorded certain extraordinary privileges—freedom from original sin and personal sin, the fullness of grace, and bodily assumption into heaven. Mary is not only the mother of God, but also the mother of men in the order of grace. Her close association with her divine Son in the redemption of mankind, in restoring men to the supernatural life of grace, justifies the latter title. Mary's part in the redemption of mankind was not demanded by the nature of things; rather, it was a free disposition of God's providence. As a mother and virgin, Mary is a type of the Church. The Church too is a mother because by her preaching she brings forth to a new life the sons who are born to her in baptism. The Church is a virgin because she keeps with virginal purity an entire faith, a firm hope, and a sincere charity.

The Church venerates Mary because she is the mother of God and the mother of men. Veneration for Mary leads one to love her and imitate her virtues. The veneration of the Church for Mary has expressed itself in a variety of ways which often reflect the cultural conditions of the faithful. In this way, the prophetic words of Mary have been verified: "All generations will call me blessed because He that is mighty has done great things for me" (Lk 1:49). Notwithstanding her privileges, Mary remains within the realm of creatures; and she is not venerated with the worship given to God. The veneration given her, however, is simply the recognition and approbation of God's work in and through her. Glorified in body and soul in heaven, Mary is a sign of hope and solace to the people of God during its sojourn on earth.[9]

Mary in the New Testament

Mary was the name of the sister of Moses (Ex 15:20); it was the name of several women in the New Testament; and it was the name of the mother of Jesus, the wife of Joseph (Mt 1:16). Matthew speaks of Mary in connection with the birth of Jesus (1:18-25), the visit of the Magi (2:11), and the flight into Egypt (2:13-23). Luke speaks of Mary in connection with the annunciation (Lk 1:26-38), the visitation (1:39-56), the birth of Jesus (2:1-19), His presentation in the temple (2:22-39), and finding Him in the temple (2:41-51). Luke portrays Mary as a pious Jewish woman obedient to the Law (2:22, 27, 39). Mary appears in Matthew (13:55) and Mark (6:3) as one well-known to the people of Nazareth; and in Matthew (12:46-50), Mark (3:31-35), and Luke (8:19-21), Mary and the kinsmen of Jesus come to visit Him during His public ministry. John speaks of Mary in connection with the wedding at Cana (2:1-11), her return to Capernaum (2:12), her presence near the cross and the commission of her care to John (19-25-27). Mary was present with the disciples in the upper room as they awaited the descent of the Spirit (Ac 1:14). The New Testament and any other reliable source are silent about the further course of her life and death. The relatively minor role which Mary plays in the Gospels reflects the generally minor role of women in Jewish life of the Biblical period.

Matthew (1:18-23) and Luke (1:26-38) state that Mary conceived her Son in a virginal manner. Some exegetes believe that this statement is not to be taken literally, that it is only an image of the truth that Jesus was God's Son from the moment of conception. These exegetes support their belief by pointing to the developed Christology implied by the virginal conception, the allegedly dubious historicity of the infancy narratives in general, and the silence of the rest of the New Testament about the matter. Other exegetes believe that the virginal conception of Jesus is to be taken literally because it is difficult to explain how the early Christians happened upon the idea of a virginal conception—unless, of course, that is what really occurred.[10] The tradition of the Church has unanimously affirmed the virginal conception of Jesus in a literal sense.

Apparently, Mary was betrothed, rather than married, to Joseph when the angel announced to her that she would conceive the Son of the Most High (Lk 1:31-32). The angel implied that she was to become a mother immediately. Therefore, Mary asked the angel, "How can this be since I do not know man?" (Lk 1:34). She was unable to understand how she could conceive a son even before she had consummated her marriage to Joseph. The angel explained that the conception would come about through the power of the Holy Spirit.

In the Gospels there are references to brothers of Jesus (Mk 3:31-32; Jn 7:3; etc.) which suggest that Mary had children other than Jesus. Still, these references could refer in the semitic world to close relations and relations by marriage. Such an interpretation would explain why Jesus dying on the cross entrusted His mother to the care of a disciple (Jn 19:25-27), why the ancient tradition thought of Mary as "ever virgin."

Luke indicates that God sought and obtained Mary's consent to the conception of Jesus (Lk 1:26-38). Yet, Mary had to grow in understanding her Son's mission in life (Lk 2:33; 49-50); and He maintained a certain detachment from her (Mt 12:46-50; etc.) perhaps to teach that carnal connection with Jesus was no substitute for faith in Him. But the New Testament praises Mary's faith: "Blest is she who trusted that the Lord's words to her would be fulfilled" (Lk 1:45). On the occasion of the annunciation, the angel addressed Mary as "full of grace" before God (Lk 1:28); in the *Magnificat* (Lk 1:46-55) Mary appears totally at the service of God and His people; and she is united with her Son as He suffers on the cross (Jn 19:25). Hence, Mary foretells that all ages to come will call her blesed (Lk 1:48). The New Testament does not explicitly mention the two terms of Mary's life, her immaculate conception and assumption.

The Development of Mariology

Mary, Mother of God. The fact that Mary is the mother of God is the basis of her greatness. The New Testament speaks of Mary as the mother of Jesus (Mt 1:18; Jn 19:25) and the mother of the Lord (Lk 1:43). But Mary can be called and is the mother of God as a consequence of the hypostatic union of divinity and humanity in the second person of the blessed Trinity. This divine person has derived His humanity from Mary and was born of her in time. Because the relationship between mother and son is a personal relationship and Mary's Son is a divine person, Mary is truly the mother of God. Just as human parents are truly the parents of their children even though the children derive only their bodies and not their souls from them, so Mary is the mother of God even though her Son derived only His humanity and not His divinity from her.

The divine maternity of Mary was contested, at least by implication, from the very beginning. Already in the apostolic age, the Docetists (from the Gr. *dokein*, to seem) maintained that Jesus had only an apparent body and only seemed to suffer and die. Hence, Mary was not really the mother of Jesus. The Fathers opposed this error by defending the reality of Jesus' humanity. In the fifth century, Nestorius (died c. 451), patriarch of Constantinople, held that there were two persons in Christ. Mary gave birth to the human person, Jesus of Nazareth, in whom the divine person dwelt. Mary, therefore, was the mother of Christ, but not the mother of God. Mary might be called *christotokos* (Christ-bearer) but not *theotokos* (God-bearer or mother of God). The most vigorous opponent of Nestorius was Cyril of Alexandria (d. 444). The Council of Ephesus (431) condemned Nestorius' view. For the council, the eternal Son of the Father is Himself the one who was born of Mary, died, and rose. He was the one subject of the saving mystery; and Mary is the mother of God or *theotokos*.

Mary's Perpetual Virginity. Closely tied to the dogma of Mary's divine maternity is the dogma of Mary's perpetual virginity. The latter dogma includes three facts: Mary's conception of Jesus without a human father, the birth of Jesus without injury to the bodily integrity of Mary, and Mary's virginity thereafter. The early creeds, including the Apostles' Creed, profess that Jesus was conceived by the Holy Spirit and born of the virgin Mary.[11] The Fathers explained that neither the old Adam nor the new Adam had a human father. Subsequently, the Church began to confess Mary as *ever* virgin; for example, in the creed of Epiphanius (c. 374).[12] Augustine spoke of Mary as "a virgin conceiving, a virgin bearing, a virgin pregnant, a virgin with child, a virgin forever."[13] The First Lateran Council (649) made the same point.[14] Mary's complete devotion to God was understood to imply renunciation of marital union. Since the 7th century, Mary's perpetual virginity has been explained as virginity—*ante partum, in partu, et post partum*: "before, in, and after the birth" of the Lord.

Mary's Sinlessness. This refers to Mary's freedom from original sin (her immaculate conception) and her freedom from actual sin. Mary's freedom from original sin, as defined by Pius IX in the bull, *Ineffabilis Deus* (1854), means that "from the first moment of her conception, by the singular grace and privilege of Almighty God, and in view of the merits of Jesus Christ, the savior of mankind, the blessed virgin Mary was kept free of all stain of original sin."[15] The argument from tradition is based upon the patristic conception of Christ as the "new Adam" and Mary as the "new Eve" (Justin Martyr and Irenaeus). With them there was a new beginning. Subsequently, the definition of Mary's divine maternity strengthened the conviction that Mary's holiness was flawless and immense (Andrew of Crete and John Damascene). The feast of Mary's conception was celebrated in the East from the sixth century. In the medieval period, the doctrine of Mary's immaculate conception was disputed. Bernard and Thomas Aquinas denied it. How, Thomas asked, could Christ be Mary's savior if she had never contracted original sin?[16] Duns Scotus argued in favor of the immaculate conception, teaching that Mary was preserved from original sin through the merits of Christ.[17] The Council of Trent (1546) explicitly declared that its decree on original sin did not include Mary.[18] Pius IX's definition of 1854 was the natural result.

Some of the Fathers contested Mary's freedom from actual sin. Tertullian, for instance, held that there was a time when Mary did not believe in her Son.[19] John Chrysostom even accused her of ambition and vainglory.[20] However, other Fathers took an entirely different stance. Hippolytus associated the sinlessness of Jesus with the sinlessness of Mary;[21] and Ephrem the Syrian sang of Jesus and Mary as "perfectly beautiful in every respect," without spot or taint.[22] As mentioned above, the definition of Mary's divine maternity strengthened the conviction that Mary's holiness was flawless and immense. According to the Council of Trent (1547), the Church holds that Mary avoided even venial sins throughout her life by a special privilege of God.[23] In the bull defining the immaculate conception (1854), Pius IX referred to Mary's sinlessness in every respect. Mary's freedom from actual sin is a dogma because it is taught as such by the ordinary and universal magisterium of the Church.

Mary's Assumption. Pius XII defined the dogma of Mary's assumption in the apostolic constitution, *Munificentissimus Deus* (1950): "At the end of her earthly life, Mary ever virgin, the immaculate mother of

God, was assumed body and soul into heavenly glory.''[24] There is no explicit reference to the dogma in the Bible; yet Pius XII insisted that the Scriptures are the ultimate foundation of this truth. The Pope pointed to Mary's intimate association with her divine Son in all things including His resurrection. The Pope left open the question whether Mary died. The definition of the assumption reflected the "almost unanimous" conviction of the bishops of the Church whom the Pope consulted before proceeding to the definition. Apparently, the assumption was unknown in the early Church; but feasts celebrating the death of Mary were observed in Palestine as early as the fifth century. In the eighth century Mary's assumption was accepted in the East by Germanus of Constantinople, Andrew of Crete, and John Damascene. There is no shortage of testimonies thereafter. Among Eastern Orthodox Christians belief in the bodily assumption of Mary is general.

Mary's Queenship. Christians have been accustomed to address Mary as a queen. They have recognized Mary as queen of creation (John Damascene), queen of heaven (Sixtus IV, Pius XII), queen of heaven and earth (Pius XI), queen of martyrs (Pius XII), and unconquered queen (the Akathistos hymn).[25] The Roman liturgy observes the feast of Mary's queenship on August 22—to underscore the connection between the queenship of Mary and her assumption (August 15). The Liturgy of the Hours is often concluded with the medieval antiphon, "Hail, holy queen." Mary's queenship rests upon her divine maternity, her cooperation with her Son in the redemption of mankind, and her personal excellence. It is true that queenship as a political institution has had its day. The point is that all creation bears the same relationship to Mary which ancient peoples had to their queens.

Mediation. This is the act of a mediator who brings conflicting parties together. Christ is the one mediator between God and men (1 Tm 2:5). By His atoning life, death, and resurrection, Christ reconciled God and men. Yet, other individuals can be called mediators too insofar as they bring God and men together in subordination to Christ. For example, one who preaches the saving message of Christ is a mediator in a certain sense because he reconciled men to God by his preaching. Men and women become mediators by praying for each other. Mary is a mediatrix because she had a role in the atonement of her Son by consenting to His incarnation, caring for Him, and sharing His sufferings on Calvary. What is more, Mary obtains for us by her prayers the fruits of reconciliation which she acquired in subordination to her Son. Several recent Popes have explicitly applied the title of mediatrix to Mary.[26]

Mary, Mother of Men. Mary is the spiritual mother of the human race because, in subordination to Christ, she gave divine life to the human race. She did so, as the preceding section noted, by cooperating with her divine Son in the redemption of mankind. The idea was known to the Fathers. For example, Peter Chrysologus (d. 450) spoke of Mary's mystical motherhood of men[27] and Gregory the Great (d. 604) thought of Mary as the mother of the Church.[28] Recent Popes have recognized Mary as the spiritual mother of mankind. Pius X[29] and Pius XII[30] regarded Mary as the mother of Christ's mystical body. Paul VI declared Mary to be "the mother of the Church, that is, of the entire Christian people, both faithful and pastors."[31] Vatican II spoke of Mary as the mother of men in the order of grace.[32]

Devotion to Mary. Devotion to Mary means love and veneration for her, invocation and imitation of her. It is based on singular position as the mother of God in the divine plan of salvation history. Devotion to Mary is called hyperdulia. It is distinct from *latria*, the worship due to God alone, and *dulia*, the worship due to lesser saints. The early Church venerated Mary as the new Eve, a virgin, and totally sinless. It invoked her intercession. The definition of Mary's divine maternity at Ephesus (431) powerfully stimulated devotion to her. The liturgical cult of Mary originated in the East with the celebration of certain feasts—the purification (celebrated at Jerusalem already in the 5th century), nativity, annunciation, and assumption. These feasts were introduced into Rome from the East about the 7th century. The oldest Marian feast to be celebrated at Rome was the octave day of Christmas, January 1, which was dominated by a Marian theme.[33]

From the 8th to the 15th centuries there was greater concentration on Mary's role as heavenly queen, spiritual mother, and all-powerful intercessor. Cathedrals were built in her honor, the *Hail Mary* was composed, the rosary was introduced, and litanies were developed. In the 16th century, the Reformers forbade in practice devotion to Mary as prejudicial to the unique mediation of Christ; but the Counter-Reformers were not slow to answer. In the 17th century, Cardinal de Bérulle (1575-1629) and the school that he founded joined the cult of Mary to the mystery of the Word made flesh. Jansenism, however, cooled Marian devotion. During the 19th century, many religious congregations were established under Mary's patronage. Marian shrines (such as Lourdes) attracted numerous pilgrims. The definition of the immaculate conception in 1854 inspired a flowering of Marian studies. In the 20th century, the Popes wrote frequently about Mary. Attention was focused on her mediation, assumption, and the Mary-Church analogy. Marian congresses were held in many places. Vatican II highly commended devotion to Mary, the mother of God, and offered useful directions for implementing it.[34]

Mariology. Mariology is that part of dogmatic theology which is concerned with Mary. Anselm of Canterbury (1033-1109) is considered to be the founder of scientific Mariology. It is customary to study Mariology as a separate treatise after Christology since Mary can be seen only in the light of Jesus. Still, Mariology can also be seen as a part of ecclesiology which deals with the Church. Tradition has long recognized the analogy between Mary and the Church and viewed Mary as a redeemed believer belonging to the Church. The fundamental principle organizing the facts and conclusions of Mariology seems to be Mary's divine maternity and her cooperation in the work of her Son. Some theologians, however, see the fundamental principle as Mary's fullness of grace or her relationship to the Church or her own perfect redemption.

Footnotes

1. *TCC* no. 234.
2. *TCC* nos. 283, 828.
3. *TCC* nos. 247, 255, 269.
4. *TCC* nos. 226, 325.
5. *TCC* nos. 329, 334.
6. *TCC* nos. 321, 760.
7. *TCC* nos. 326-334a.
8. *TCC* nos. 334bc.
9. *Lumen Gentium* ch. 8.
10. The arguments are enumerated and weighed in R. Brown, *The Virginal Conception & Bodily Resurrection of Jesus*, New York, 1973, Paulist Press, 52-68.

11. *TCC* nos. 828-831.
12. *TCC* no. 832.
13. Sermon 186.
14. DS 503.
15. Pius IX, *Ineffabilis Deus* (1854), *TCC* no. 325.
16. *ST* 3a.27.2.ad.2.
17. *In 3 Sent.* 3.1, *Per illud patet.*
18. *TCC* no. 226.
19. *On the Flesh of Christ* 7.
20. Homily 21 on St. John, 2:3; Homily 44 on St. Matthew, 12:47.
21. Fragment quoted by Theodoret, *Dialogue* 1. *PG* 10, 864-865.
22. *The Nisibis Hymn* 27.
23. *TCC* no. 321.
24. *TCC* no. 334c.
25. Cf. P. Palmer, S.J., *op. cit.* 119.
26. *Ibid.* 118.
27. Sermon 146, *On the Generation of Christ* 2. *PL52, 593.*
28. *Homilies on the Gospels* 2, 38, 3. *PL* 76, 1283.
29. *Ad Diem Illum Acta* (1905) 150-155.
30. *Mystici Corporis AAS* 35 (1943) 247-248.
31. *AAS* 56 (1964) 1015.
32. *Lumen Gentium* no. 62.
33. Cf. J. Jungmann, S.J., *Public Worship*, Collegeville, 1957, The Liturgical Press, 219-221.
34. *Lumen Gentium* nos. 66-67.

Chapter 9

GRACE

Bibliography. For the teaching of the Church: *TCC* nos. 680-807b. For the Scriptural material: J. McKenzie, *Grace* in *DB* 324-326; W. Most, *Grace (in the Bible)* in the *NCE* 6, 672-674; K. Berger, *Grace (Biblical)* in *SM* 2, 409-412; J. Guillet, S.J., *Grace* in *DBT* 218-220; E. Fortman, S.J., (ed.), *The Theology of Man and Grace*, Milwaukee, 1966, The Bruce Publ. Co., 1-80; *JBC*, pertinent entries.

For the theological and dogmatic development: *ST* 1a2ae.109-114; W. Farrell, O.P., *A Companion to the Summa*, New York, 1938, Sheed & Ward, 2, 413-433; E. Fortman, S.J., *op. cit.* 81-395; P. de Letter, S.J., *Sanctifying Grace and the Divine Indwelling* in *TS* 14 (1953) 242-272; *idem, Grace, Incorporation, Inhabitation* in *TS* 19 (1958) 1-31; H. Küng, *Justification*, New York, 1964, Thomas Nelson & Sons; E. Burke, *Grace* in the *NCE* 6, 658-672; P. Fransen, S.J., *Divine Grace and Man*, New York, 1962, Desclee Co.; K. Rahner, H. Vorgrimler, S.J., *TD* pertinent entries; R. Gleason, S.J., *Grace*, New York, 1962, Sheed and Ward; C. Meyer, *A Contemporary Theology of Grace*, Staten Island, 1971, Alba House; J. Sittler, *Essays on Nature and Grace*, Philadelphia, 1972, Fortress Press; B. Lonergan, S.J., *Grace and Freedom*, London, 1971, Darton, Longman & Todd; G. McCool, S.J., (ed.), *A Rahner Reader*, New York, 1975, The Seabury Press, 173-204; *Grace* in the *ODCC* 586-587.

Grace is a supernatural gift of God bestowed upon a person with a view to sanctification and salvation. If a gift such as prophecy or healing is bestowed upon a person for the benefit of others, it is said to be a charism. If a gift is bestowed upon a person for his own sanctification and salvation, it is said to be a grace in the usual sense of the term. There are three kinds of grace understood in the latter sense: uncreated grace, created or sanctifying grace, and actual grace. Uncreated grace refers to the abiding presence of the holy Trinity in the souls of the just. (The just are the righteous, the friends of God. Justification is the transition from a state of sin or aversion from God to a state of sanctifying grace or friendship with God.) Created or sanctifying grace is a created sharing in the life of God Himself. It is something permanent by its nature. Uncreated grace and created grace are inseparable. Actual grace is a transient help of God enlightening the mind and strengthening the will to do good and avoid evil.

The Teaching of the Church

With respect to *uncreated* grace, the Church teaches that God—Father, Son, and Holy Spirit—dwells in the soul of the just as in a temple.[1] However, this divine presence in the just differs from the presence of God which beatifies the blessed in heaven.[2] The dwelling of the Trinity of divine persons in man is attributed in a special way to the Holy Spirit.[3] The effect of the Spirit is to give life.[4]

The Council of Trent (1547) spoke of *created* or *sanctifying* grace in its decree on justification. According to the council, infants are justified instantaneously by the sacrament of baptism; but an adult must ordinarily prepare himself for justification by acts of faith, sorrow, and love. God justifies the sinner in the sacrament of baptism by forgiving his sins and infusing sanctifying grace with the virtues and gifts that accompany it. One who is justified becomes a son of God and heir of heaven. It is possible to advance in the state of grace by keeping the commandments and by good works which gain merit for eternal life. Grace is gratuitous and supernatural. It is lost by every mortal sin; but it can be recovered by repentance and the sacrament of penance.[5]

With respect to *actual* grace, the Church teaches that man can perform good works without grace.[6] Still, it is grace that elevates man's good works to the supernatural order.[7] It is grace that brings a man to justification,[8] without, however, robbing him of his freedom.[9] Under the influence of grace, an individual must prepare himself for justification,[10] but faith alone is not sufficient for justification.[11] Actual grace is necessary to avoid mortal sin for a long time.[12] To persevere to the end requires a special grace.[13] God grants everyone the grace he needs to keep the commandments,[14] but not to avoid all venial sins.[15]

In several passages, the Second Vatican Council referred to these traditional doctrines. According to the council, the cross of Christ is the fountain from which every grace flows. Grace works unseen in all men of good will. Under the impulse of divine grace man is disposed to acknowledge the word of God; but it is necessary for the faithful to cooperate with grace. Everyone must administer to others the grace that he has received. The liturgy is a source of grace. The saints are perfected by the grace of God. In summary: "When the Son had accomplished His Father's work on earth, the Holy Spirit was sent on Pentecost day to sanctify the Church forever. . . . He is the Spirit of life, a fountain of water springing up to life eternal. Through Him the Father gives life to men who are dead from sin. . . . The Spirit dwells in the Church and in the hearts of the faithful as in a temple. He prays in them and bears witness to the fact that they are adopted sons. The Spirit guides the Church in the way of all truth and unites her in fellowship and service. He equips and directs her with charismatic gifts and adorns her with fruits of His grace. By the power of the Gospel He makes the Church grow, perpetually renews her, and leads her to perfect union with her spouse. The Spirit and the bride both say to the Lord Jesus, 'Come!' "[16]

Grace in the Bible

In the Old Testament, Yahweh is recognized as a "God of tenderness and grace, slow to anger and rich in kindness and fidelity" (Ex 34:6). God manifests His grace—His kindness and fidelity—by showing favor (Heb *hanan*) to all creatures (Si 1:8), but especially to Israel. The most striking sign of God's grace was His election of Israel (Dt 7:7-8). Yet, God showed favor to Israel in other ways too: by granting prosperity (Gn 33:11), by delivering Israel from its enemies (2 K 13:23), and by accepting sacrifice (Ml 1:9). God's favor was absolutely gratuitous (Ex 33:19). The effect of God's favor to men is a blessing (which may be called a grace in a derived sense).

In the New Testament, the Greek word, *charis*, or grace, is used in a variety of ways. It occurs frequently in the introduction and final greetings of the epistles (Rm 1:7; 1 Cor 16:23; etc.) usually in conjunction with peace. It represents all that one Christian could wish for another. Very frequently, grace designates the saving will of God manifested in Jesus Christ and brought to fruition in men. The grace of God has appeared in Jesus Christ, offering salvation to all (Tt 2:11). Grace is the free favor manifested by God towards man (Ac 15:11). It is a commission given by God to a human agent (Rm 1:5). It is the totality by which men are made righteous (Rm 3:24). The surpassing grace of God is within the Christian (2 Cor 9:14). Christians are to grow in the grace and knowledge of Jesus Christ (2 P 3:18). In these passages, grace is something given gratuitously to the Christian as the beneficiary of God's saving will. Paul emphasizes the opposition between grace and works (Rm 11:6; Gal 2:21; etc.). Grace is the principle of Christian life and action. It fructifies in good works (1 Cor 8:1). It enables Paul to resist temptations (2 Cor 12:9). It is something dynamic (Ep 3:7-9).

Of course, the idea of grace is not confined to the use of *charis* in the New Testament. Wherever the New Testament speaks of God's intervention in the world out of sheer love and His manifestation in the person and work of Jesus, there is the idea of grace. In the Synoptic Gospels, this idea is bound up with the advent of the kingdom of God which is offered to all upon the condition of repentance. In John's Gospel, the idea of grace is reflected in the remarks of Jesus about a new birth from on high, a new life, and a new divine presence in the soul of the believer, a life and a presence nurtured by the Eucharist.

The Greek word, *charisma*, or charism, signifies a free favor or gift (Rm 5:15-16 etc.) or a divinely conferred endowment which enables its receiver to perform some office or function in the Church (Rm 12:6; Ep 4:11). It is evident from the New Testament and from the literature of the post-apostolic age that certain charism were elements of the birth of the Church which did not endure once it had been firmly established.

The Development of the Doctrine of Grace

The characteristic teaching of the Greek Fathers about grace at the beginning of Christianity may be found in the writings of Irenaeus (died c. 200). Irenaeus emphasized the doctrine of human divinization: the Son of God became man so that man might become the son of God.[17] The Christian possesses the Holy Spirit and is united to Him. The Spirit makes a man perfect and spiritual.[18] Man's divinization results in true liberty.[19]

Among the Latin Fathers, Tertullian (died c. 225) was the first to think of grace as a divine energy working in the soul; but he insisted that it did not destroy responsibility for one's actions. Augustine (d. 430), however, was the great doctor of grace for the western Church. He developed his theology of grace especially in controversy with the British theologian and exegete, Pelagius. Pelagius held that Adam's sin was not transmitted to his descendants by generation. The descendants of Adam sin by following his bad example; but they do have the natural capacity to avoid sin and achieve the beatific vision. Grace makes it easier for them to do this, but it is not absolutely necessary.

Augustine saw matters differently. The whole human race suffers the consequences of Adam's sin to which individuals add the guilt of their personal sins.[21] Only the grace of Christ can raise human beings from this evil state. The external preaching of the Gospel must be accompanied by the internal operation of God's grace if a person is to be converted from sin. Prevenient grace, that is to say, grace antecedent to conversion, is a free gift of God.[22] The remission of sins and the grace of justification are received in baptism. The grace of Christ makes the baptized person an adopted son or daughter of God and the temple of the Holy Spirit.[23] Even after man's conversion, the divine energy must cooperate with him if he is to persevere in good works.[24] If a person dies in justice and charity, he will receive eternal life as recompense for his merits. Perseverance to the end, however, cannot be merited. One must pray for it.[25] The distinction between efficacious and sufficient grace stems from Augustine. The former is followed by its proper effect, while the latter, though adequate, is not. Ultimately, the effect depends upon God's choice.[26]

In general, the Second Council of Orange (529) accepted Augustine's teaching on grace. The Council taught that God initiates the movement of the individual toward salvation, that His grace is necessary for every salutary action, that, nonetheless, an adult must play his part.[27]

Thomas Aquinas (d. 1274) synthesized and developed the patristic doctrine of grace by employing the philosophy of Aristotle. In His goodness, God established a supernatural end, the vision of the divine essence, for the human race. God has elevated the nature and faculties of human beings by grace and the virtues so that there is a proportion between human activity and the supernatural end toward which it must tend.[28] The grace of God has the character of an habitual gift; but it also heals and moves the soul of man to act.[29] In virtue of habitual (sanctifying) grace and the capacity for knowing and loving God which it supplies, God is not only present in the soul but dwells in it as in a temple.[30] Through grace one becomes an adopted son of God. This adoption is the work of the whole Trinity.[31] The grace that one receives is derived from the glorified humanity of Christ. Grace was conferred upon Christ "as upon a certain universal principle in the class of those having grace."[32]

The Reformers adhered to Augustinianism as they understood it. Martin Luther (1483-1546) rejected the idea of grace as an infused quality. Grace is rather the gracious condescension of God to man which is given in Christ. Luther also rejected every kind of work-righteousness. Man is justified by faith alone, that is to say, by confidence in the sufficiency of Christ's death on Calvary to atone for sin. Even though man always remains the bearer of his corrupt nature and can only sin, God declares him just by a kind of forensic justification. The justified sinner, however, cannot *merit* heaven.[33] In opposition to the Reformers, the Council of Trent set forth the Catholic idea of grace.

In the Catholic Church there were two serious disputes about grace in the post-Tridentine period. One was the dispute between the Thomists and Molinists about the efficacy of grace and human freedom. The Thomists, under the leadership of D. Banez, O.P. (1538-1604), spoke of a "physical premotion" on the part of God which produces in man both the human act and its freedom. The Molinists, under the leadership of F. de Molina, S.J. (1535-1600), denied physical premotion. Rather, they said, God, by His "middle knowledge," knows what man *would* do in any concrete situation with a general and indifferent movement from God. When God brings about a particular concrete situation, He knows beforehand what man will do without prejudice to human freedom. Both the Thomists and Molinists theories were recognized as orthodox by Paul V in 1607.[34] The other dispute was the Jansenist controversy which arose out of the posthumous publication in 1640 of the *Augustinus* written by C. Jansen, bishop of Ypres (d. 1638). Jansen held that just men do not have the capacity or the grace to observe all the commandments of God, that grace is irresistible. Innocent X rejected these ideas in 1653.[35] The system of Baius (1513-89) is often considered an anticipation of Jansenism. Among other things, Baius denied the supernatural and gratuitous character of grace. This error was rejected by Pius V in 1567.[36]

The Lutheran conception of grace and justification continued to prevail among many Protestants of the 19th and 20th centuries; but there were divergencies. With Luther, F. Schleiermacher (1768-1834) rejected the idea of grace as an infused quality; rather, to be in the state of grace is to live in fellowship with Christ. If men continue in this state, impulses flow from Him to them until they find that He has become the source of their activity. A. Ritschl (1822-89) held that grace is the disposition of God the Father to cleanse and reconcile sinners to Himself. S. Kierkegaard (1813-55) held that grace was God in action, seeking to win the soul for His own. God's action was manifest especially in Christ. If Christ lives in the Christian, the Christian becomes the channel of His life to the world. For K. Barth (1886-1966) grace meant that men are enabled to live as followers of Christ by the power of Christ living in them. For R. Bultmann (1884-1976) grace was not a special quality of God. It was rather an event, namely, the act of God in Christ. This event becomes present to the hearer through the preaching of the Word. By this event God places within the grasp of the sinner his lost possibility of authentic being. Authentic being means the being from which man has fallen away through sin. Such grace is an act of forgiveness.[37]

In general, there is agreement among Catholics and Orthodox about the doctrine of grace. The Orthodox recognize the necessity, freedom, and universality of grace without asserting its irresistibility. The Orthodox view the conditions and terms of justification much as Catholics do. They see grace as a participation of God. Nature appears as an imperfect image of God and grace perfectly realizes this image.[38]

Contemporary Catholic studies of grace are marked by a return to the sources, the historical perspective, consciousness of doctrinal and theological development, and spiritual and pastoral concerns. Along with adherence to the traditional stance on grace and justification, there is continuing study of the divine indwelling. Some explain it in terms of efficient causality—God's causality of created grace makes Him present in a new way in man. Others explain the divine indwelling by saying that grace affords a new capacity to take possession of God through knowledge and love. Moreover, theologians are studying the personal relationship between God and the soul entailed by the divine indwelling. Is this relationship common to the whole Trinity and *appropriated* to the Holy Spirit? Or is this relationship proper in some way to each divine person? Catholic theologians are also studying the Christological and ecclesiological dimensions of grace and inquiring into the consciousness and psychology of grace.[39]

Some Clarifications

Repeatedly in the preceding pages grace has been described as supernatural—something above and beyond the natural. To understand what is supernatural one must understand what is natural. Something is *natural* to a being in several ways: either it is a part of its essence (as the soul is part of man's essence), or it flows from the essence (as the intellect does in man), or it is required for the activity of its essential powers (as food is required by man), or it is merited by action within the capacity of those powers (as the worker merits his wage). Hence, that is *supernatural* which is *not* part of a being's essence, does *not* flow from its essence, is *not* required for the activity of its essential powers, and is *not* merited by action within the capacity of those powers. Grace is supernatural to man; it is entirely gratuitous.

A natural order is a situation in which a creature is offered a merely natural end (for man, a discursive knowledge of God) and suitable means to that end. (For man, it is reason and other natural means.) Actually, there never has been a merely natural order for man. A supernatural order is a situation in which a creature is offered a supernatural end (such as the beatific vision) and suitable means to that end (such as grace and revelation).

It is necessary to distinguish between natural and supernatural virtues. The virtues modify the faculties of the soul and enable man to live rightly. The *natural* virtues are acquired by the repetition of good acts. The fundamental natural virtues are prudence, justice, fortitude, and temperance. The *supernatural* virtues are qualities infused by God into the faculties of the soul. They accompany the infusion of sanctifying grace. Corresponding to the natural moral virtues mentioned above are the supernatural moral virtues infused by God. The latter perfect and elevate the corresponding natural virtues. However, the principal infused virtues are the theological virtues which have God for their object. They are faith, hope, and charity. When grace and charity are infused into the soul, the gifts of the Holy Spirit are also infused. They render the soul docile to the impulse of the Holy Spirit.

Can human beings be absolutely certain that they have the grace of God? The Council of Trent denied that they can have such certitude because of their weakness and indisposition.[40] Nevertheless, there are certain signs which afford a measure of probability about the presence of grace in the soul. These signs include a delight in the things of God, contempt for what is sinful in the world, and the testimony of a good conscience which is unaware of any mortal sin.[41]

Sanctifying grace renders the good works of the just man meritorious. Sacred Scripture speaks of the reward which these works merit: God repays the just man with eternal life for doing right (Rm 2:6-7) and He judges each one justly on the basis of his actions (1 P 1:17). Hence, the Council of Trent held that justified individuals can merit an increase of sanctifying grace and eternal life.[42] Of course, merit is based on the free gift of God, that is to say, grace, so that God, the just judge, rewards and crowns His own gift.

Footnotes

1. DS 3330, 3814-15.
2. DS 3331, 3815.
3. *TCC* nos. 718, 833; DS 1913, 3329-3331, 3814.
4. *TCC* no. 831.
5. *TCC* nos. 709-770.
6. *TCC* nos. 775-789, 795-804.
7. *TCC* nos. 688-702, 738-740.
8. *TCC* nos. 691-701, 714, 738-740.
9. *TCC* nos. 714, 741, 791, 793, 805-807.
10. *TCC* nos. 714-715, 741-746.
11. *TCC* nos. 722-723, 726, 746, 749-751.
12. *TCC* nos. 680-682, 689.
13. *TCC* nos. 729-730, 753, 759.
14. *TCC* nos. 365, 702, 725, 755, 777, 790.
15. *TCC* nos. 683-685, 725, 760.
16. *Lumen Gentium* no. 4.

17. *Against Hereresies* 3, 19, 1.
18. *Against Heresies* 5, 6, 1; 5, 8, 1-2; 5, 9, 2.
19. *Against Heresies* 4, 4, 1.
20. *Against Marcion* 2, 9.
21. *The Grace of Christ and Original Sin* 2, 14; 2, 44-46.
22. *The Predestination of the Saints* 2, 5; 3, 7f.
23. *Against Faustus* 3, 3. *On the Psalms* 49, 2. Tractate 110 on the Gospel of John. *On the Trinity* 4, 20, 28-29; 15, 18, 32.
24. *On the Spirit and the Letter* 30, 32. *The Predestination of the Saints* 8, 13. *The Grace of Christ* 18, 19-22.
25. *On the Gift of Perseverance* 6, 10, 14, 35.
26. *On the Merits and Remission of Sins* 2, 31. *On Rebuke and Grace* 12, 33-39.
27. *TCC* nos. 696-702.
28. *ST* 1a.12.4; 1a2ae.65.3; 110.4.
29. *ST* 1a2ae.109.9.
30. *ST* 1a.43.3.
31. *ST* 3a.23.1-2.
32. *ST* 3a.7.9.
33. Cf. H. Hermelink, *Grace in the Theology of the Reformers* in *The Doctrine of Grace*, ed. W.T. Whitley, London, 1931, SCM Press, 176-208. Also, *Luther, Martin* in the *ODCC* 848; H. Kerr, *A Compend of Luther's Theology*, Philadelphia, 1966, The Westminster Press, 98-106.
34. Cf. *Banezianism* and *Molinism* in *TD* 45, 290-291. *See* also *Grace* in the *NCE* 6, 664-665.
35. *TCC* nos. 790-794.
36. *TCC* nos. 207-210.
37. *See* E. Fortman, S.J., *op. cit.* 294-332.
38. *Ibid.* 333-352.
39. *Ibid.* 353-395.
40. *TCC* no. 723.
41. *ST* 1a2ae.112.5.
42. *TCC* nos. 734-736.

Chapter 10

THE CATHOLIC CHURCH
ITS SELF-IMAGE

Bibliography: W. Abbott, S.J. (ed.) *The Documents of Vatican II*, New York, 1966, Corpus Books; L. Bouyer, *The Liturgy Revived*, Notre Dame, 1964, Univ. of Notre Dame Press; G. Barauna (ed.), *La Chiesa del Vaticano II*, Firenze, 1965; H. Vorgrimler, S.J. (ed.), *Commentary on the Documents of Vatican II*, New York, 1967, Herder and Herder; C. Hollis, *The Achievements of Vatican II*, New York, 1966, Hawthorn Books; B. Leeming, S.J., *The Vatican Council and Christian Unity*, London, 1966, Darton, Longman & Todd; C. O'Donnell (ed.), *The Church in the World*, Milwaukee, 1967, Bruce Publishing Co.; K. McNamara (ed.), *The Constitution on the Church*, Chicago, 1968, Franciscan Herald Press; J. Deretz, A. Nocent (comp.), *Dictionary of the Council*, Washington, 1968, Corpus Books; H. Küng, *The Church*, New York, 1967, Sheed and Ward; L.-J. Suenens, *Coresponsibility in the Church*, New York, 1968, Herder and Herder; M. Schmaus, *Dogma: The Church*, New York, 1972, Sheed and Ward; R. Latourelle, S.J., *Christ and the Church*, Staten Island, 1972, Alba House; J. Maritain, *On the Church of Christ*, Notre Dame, 1973, University of Notre Dame Press; A. Dulles, S.J., *Models of the Church*, Garden City, 1974, Doubleday & Co.; G. Berkouwer, *The Church*, Grand Rapids, 1976, W.B. Eerdmans Publishing Co. (a Protestant work); Paul VI, *Evangelization in the Modern World*, Washington, 1975, U.S. Catholic Conference; J. Macquarrie, *Principles of Christian Theology*, New York, 1977, 2nd ed., Charles Scribner's Sons, 386-446 (an Anglican work).

In a sense, the Catholic Church is the extension of Christ in space and time. The Catholic Church is a group of persons committed to God through Jesus Christ. It is charged with preaching the good news of the kingdom of God as Jesus preached it. The group possesses the visible leadership of Peter and the apostles and their successors. It has a rite of initiation, baptism, and a communal meal, the Eucharist. It is the new people of God rejoicing in the forgiveness of sins and the abiding presence of the Holy Spirit. The mission of the Church extends to all persons in accordance with a universal need.

This chapter deals with the self-image of the Catholic Church, that is, its conception of itself and its mission. The Second Vatican Council has given us one of the most recent, extensive, and authoritative expressions of the Church's self-image. What follows in this chapter is a summary of certain pivotal documents published by the council.

The Church (Lumen Gentium)

The Mystery of the Church. The Church is a mystery because it is an essentially transcendent, supernatural entity. The origin of the Church lies in the will of the heavenly Father. The Father sent His Son into the world to give mankind a share in His divine life. The work of the Holy Spirit is to complete the work of Christ through the Church. The Church is described in the Bible by many metaphors. It is a sheepfold; God is the shepherd. It is a building; Christ is the cornerstone. It is our mother, the spouse of Christ. The Church is an exile journeying in a foreign land. The Church is the body of Christ. Christ communicates life to the members of His body, each of whom performs a different function in the Church.

Christ did not establish two churches, that is, a visible assembly and a spiritual community separate from each other. No, He established only one Church in which a divine and human element come together. The Church can be compared to the incarnate Son of God in whom a divine and a human nature are united in one person. This Church subsists in the Catholic Church which is governed by the successor of Peter, the Pope, and the bishops in communion with him. Still, other Churches share to some degree in the elements of truth and sanctification entrusted to the Church of Christ. Like its master and founder, the Church is called to a life of poverty and self-denial.

The People of God. Originally, God made a covenant with the ancient people of Israel. He made a new covenant with Jew and Gentile alike through the shedding of Christ's blood. This new people of God has Christ for its head and is called the Church of Christ. The new *people of God* shares in Christ's priestly office. It exercises its priesthood through the administration and reception of the sacraments and the practice of the virtues. The *people of God* also shares in Christ's prophetic office by bearing witness to Him. The entire body of the faithful cannot err in matters of faith and morals. To this priestly and prophetic office the Spirit of God freely grants a variety of gifts or charisms.

All persons are called to belong to the *new people of God, the Church.* In fact, all persons are already related to the Church in some way. Catholics are fully incorporated in the Church because of their visible union with it; but if they do not persevere in charity, they cannot be saved. Non-Catholic Christians are linked to the Church because they have certain elements of truth and sanctification which have been entrusted to the Church. These are the Bible, several sacraments, the life of grace, and others. Non-Christians too are linked to the Church in somewhat the same way. They can be saved if they strive to lead a good life with the grace of God. The purpose of the Church's missionary activity is to bring non-Christians a richer and more assured salvation. No one, however, who recognizes the divine origin of the Catholic Church and rejects it can be saved. Such a person is guilty of grave sin.

The Hierarchical Structure of the Church. The Lord Jesus chose twelve men to be with Him and to preach the kingdom of God. The twelve formed a kind of college or fixed group which He placed under the apostle Peter. Jesus sent them first to the nation of Israel and then to all nations so that all might become His disciples. For this reason, the apostles provided for successors to continue and consolidate their work. By divine institution bishops are the successors of the apostles, and the Pope is the successor of Peter as the head of the apostolic college.

Through the bishops Christ continues to teach, sanctify, and lead the members of the Church. Bishops act in the person of Christ because they have received the sacrament of orders, the imposition of hands and the words of consecration. The sacrament of orders confers the grace of the Holy Spirit and a sacred character. The Pope and the bishops form an episcopal college. Membership in the college is established by episcopal ordination and communion with the head and members of the college. The Pope is the head of the college. He has full, supreme, and universal authority over the Church. With its head the episcopal college also has supreme and universal authority over the Church. It exercises this authority in an ecumenical council and in other ways. Just as the Pope is the visible principle of unity in the universal Church, so the individual bishop is the visible principle of unity in the particular Church entrusted to him. The variety of local Churches living in harmony with one another is a luminous sign of the catholicity of the undivided Church.

As successors of the apostles, bishops have a mission from the Lord, a mission to serve. A bishop serves his people by preaching the Gospel, celebrating the liturgy, and governing. As preachers of the Gospel, bishops speak in the name of Christ; and the faithful are to give religious assent to their teaching. While the individual bishop is not infallible, the college of bishops can speak infallibly on questions of faith and morals just as the Pope can. At the core of the Church's existence is the Eucharist which the bishop offers or causes to be offered. The bishop sanctifies the faithful through the regular celebration of the sacraments all of which he regulates by his authority. Finally, bishops govern the particular Churches under their jurisdiction. In virtue of their pastoral authority, they have the sacred right and duty to make laws for their subjects, pass judgment on them, and direct the order of worship and the apostolate.

Priests are the close associates of the bishop. They represent him in the local congregations. Consequently, they too must preach the Gospel, administer the sacraments, and lead the faithful. Priests make the universal Church visible in their own locality. In close cooperation with the bishop and his priests, deacons are called to serve the *people of God* in the ministry of the liturgy, the word, and charity.

The Laity. What Vatican II had to say about the *people of God* in a foregoing section applies equally to the laity, religious, and clergy. Lay people have been dedicated the mission of the Church by baptism and confirmation. They seek the kingdom of God by their involvement in material and secular affairs. They are immersed in family, social, and business life; they practice the trades and professions. In this way they carry out the plan of God for the world. They make the Church present and active in those situations accessible to them alone. The laity share in the priesthood of Christ by their sacrificial lives and especially by their participation in the Holy Eucharist. They share in the prophetic office of Christ by giving witness to Him and living the Gospel in the world. They share in the kingly office of Christ by bringing all things, including themselves, into subjection to the Father. The faithful are encouraged to recognize the meaning and value of creation. By their technical skill and cultural endowments they can assist all human beings to benefit from created goods. By striving for a just social order they can prepare the field of the world for the seed of the Gospel.

Lay persons are members of both the Church and human society. Both make different, though complementary, demands upon them. The temporal sphere is governed by its own principles; but it is not withdrawn from God's dominion.

The laity will cooperate with their pastors as the pastors carry out their responsibility to teach and minister. Reciprocally, pastors will be responsive to the natural ability, training, experience, and supernatural gifts of the laity. The Church rightly expects rich results from this exchange.

The Call of the Whole Church to Holiness. The Church is unfailingly holy. It is the bride of Christ; it is the body of Christ; the Holy Spirit abides with the Church. In baptism the followers of Christ become sons of God and sharers in the divine nature. They become holy. Yet holiness can be intensified. All Christians are called to the fullness of Christian life and the perfection of love. Holiness is intensified when Christians live as befits holy people, when they conform themselves to the will of the heavenly Father. The will of the heavenly Father makes different demands upon individuals. The ministers of the Church are expected to serve the people of God. This service should be the principal means of their sanctification. Married couples sanctify themselves by generous love for one another and their children. Widows and single persons grow in holiness by fulfilling their responsibilities. Laborers are joined with Christ who was a carpenter. Those who suffer poverty, sickness, and persecution are united with the suffering Christ who called them blessed. Christians can grow daily in holiness in and through the conditions, duties, and circumstances of their lives if they accept everything from the hand of God.

Holiness means loving God above all things and loving others because of God. Love is nurtured by listening to the word of God, the reception of the sacraments, prayer, self-denial, fraternal charity, and the practice of the virtues and evangelical counsels. The latter were recommended by Jesus to His disciples. They are celibacy, poverty, and chastity.

Religious. In His mercy, the Lord has blessed the Church with religious families such as the Franciscans, Dominicans, and Sisters of Charity. The members of these families devote themselves to particular apostolates. Religious draw their members from both the laity and clergy. They undertake to observe the evangelical counsels according to a manner of life approved by the Church. Observing the counsels, religious are freed from certain worldly cares hindering the exercise of charity. The life of religious reflects the pilgrim status of the Church in the world and the fruits of Christ's redemption. It points to the demands and glory of the kingdom of God.

It is the duty of the hierarchy to regulate the practice of the evangelical counsels since the hierarchy is responsible for the spiritual welfare of the faithful. The hierarchy accepts and approves the rules of religious life presented by saintly men and women such as St. Ignatius and St. Elizabeth Ann Seton. A spirit of cooperation between the hierarchy and religious families is necessary for the success of the apostolate.

The Church regards the profession of the counsels as beneficial to human development. The counsels purify the heart and free the spirit. They conform the Christian to Christ and to His mother Mary. The lives of many holy men and women testify to the truth of these statements.

Eschatology. This unusual word refers to the last time when history will come to a close and God's kingdom will be definitively established. We pray for the kingdom in the Lord's prayer when we say: "Thy kingdom come." Actually, the kingdom is already present among us in a hidden way, as Jesus taught (Mk 1:15; Mt 3:2); but it will be manifested clearly and decisively only when Jesus returns at the end. The pilgrim Church on earth is oriented towards this final reality. Even though Christians are already the Sons of God, they are still exiled from the Lord in the present life. They await the final day with intense anticipation.

There is a bond between the blessed in heaven, the faithful on earth, and those who are being purified in purgatory. The blessed in heaven are more closely united to Christ; they intercede for the faithful on earth; they encourage those who remain behind by their example. The faithful on earth venerate the blessed in heaven; they invoke their intercession; they follow their example. Some of the faithful who have passed away are being purified from their sins. From the earliest days of the Christian religion the Church has always offered supplications to God for these individuals. "It is a holy and wholesome thought to pray for the dead that they may be loosed from their sins" (2 M 12:46).

The Blessed Virgin Mary and the Church. Our heavenly Father solicited and received the consent of Mary regarding the incarnation of His divine Son. She is truly the mother of God and the mother of the redeemer. Mary conceived the Son of God through the power of the Holy Spirit and remained a virgin throughout her life. She was accorded all those privileges consistent with her divine maternity—freedom from original and personal sin, the fullness of grace, and bodily assumption into heaven at the end of her life.

Mary is not only the mother of God, but also the mother of men in the order of grace. Although she was totally dependent upon her divine Son, she cooperated with Him in the redemption of the human race, in the restoration of mankind to the life of grace. This cooperation justifies her title as the mother of men in the order of grace. Just as the members of the Church share in the priesthood of Christ, so Mary shared in the mediation of Christ. This sharing was not demanded by the nature of things; rather, it was a free arrangement of God's providence.

As a mother and a virgin, Mary is a type of the Church. The Church too is a mother because she begets children through preaching and baptism. The Church is a virgin because she keeps with virginal purity an entire faith, a firm hope, and a sincere charity. Mary is an example of that maternal love that ought to animate the Church in its apostolate.

The Church venerates Mary because she is the mother of God and our mother. Veneration of Mary leads one to love her and imitate her virtues. The veneration of the Church for Mary has taken various forms according to the circumstances of time and place and the ingenuity of the faithful. In this way, the prophetic words of Mary have been verified: "All generations will call me blessed because He that is mighty has done great things for me" (Lk 1:49). The veneration given by the Church to Mary differs radically from the worship given by the Church to her divine Son. Despite her privileges, Mary remains within the realm of creatures. The Church vigorously encourages devotion to Mary. It is the recognition and approbation of God's work in and through her. Glorified in body and soul in heaven, Mary is a sign of hope and solace to the people of God during its sojourn on earth.

The Church Today (Gaudium et Spes)

In another document beginning with the Latin words, *Gaudium et Spes*, the Second Vatican Council dealt with the mission of the Church to the modern world.

The Present Situation. At the outset, the concil described the human situation in the modern world. Change is characteristic of the present age. Education has been profoundly shaped by the mathematical, natural, and behavioral sciences. Technology is transforming the world. The human race has passed from a rather static conception of the world to a more dynamic, evolutionary one. Society is becoming increasingly industrial and urban. New and more efficient means of communication are being employed. Traditional values are being questioned. Growing numbers of people are abandoning the practice of religion. Populations are expanding. There is a cry for social justice. Women are seeking equality with men. There are drastic imbalances between nations.

The Dignity of the Human Person. The Council reaffirmed the dignity of human beings in the midst of all the changes. Human beings are created after the image of God. They are capable of knowing and loving their creator. They are the masters of all other earthly creatures. Though made of body and soul, they are one. They have a law written in their hearts by God. They are free and only in freedom can they pursue goodness. They are called to communion with God. It is the incarnate Son of God who fully reveals human beings to themselves.

The Community of Mankind. Human beings are becoming more dependent upon each other. Modern technical advances are responsible for this dependence. As a matter of fact, all men and women constitute one family. Individuals develop and prosper through their relationships with others; but they can also suffer grave harm from an evil social order. Human dignity requires that all men and women have whatever is necessary for living a truly productive life.

Since all human beings have been created after the image of God, since they have the same nature, since they have been redeemed by Christ and share the same opportunity for a blessed immortality, they are basically equal. It would be unrealistic, of course, to overlook the great physical, intellectual, and moral differences that distinguish individuals. Nevertheless, with respect to the fundamental rights of the person, every type of discrimination whether social or cultural, whether based on sex, race, color, social condition, language or religion, is to be overcome and eradicated as contrary to God's intent. Therefore, although rightful differences exist among human beings, the equal dignity of persons demands that a more humane and just condition of life be brought about. Excessive economic and social differences among men violate the dignity of the human person.

No one may content himself with a purely individualistic morality. The obligations of justice and love are fulfilled only if each person contributes to the common good according to his ability and the needs of others. Freedom acquires new strength when individuals take on the many demands of human partnership and commit themselves to the service of the human community.

Man's Activity throughout the World. The human race has been commanded by the creator to subject the earth and all it contains to itself. By its labor the human race implements the plan of its creator. The Church does not regard the marvelous accomplishments of human activity as opposed to the works of God. These accomplishments are the fulfillment of God's plan. To the extent that human activity contributes to the genuine good of the human race and enables men and women as individuals and members of society to attain their purpose in life, to that extent it is good and praiseworthy.

In a sense, human activity which is concerned with the things of this world is autonomous. The things of this world are regulated by their own principles which man must discover and utilize. The Church has no fear that the discovery of these principles will be harmful to religion, for both the world and religion emanate from the same God. On the other hand, no human activity is totally autonomous in the sense that it may proceed without any reference whatsoever to the creator. The creature though may never be totally divorced from the creator.

The Role of the Church in the Modern World. The foregoing remarks about the dignity of the human person, about the human community and the meaning of human activity, lay the foundation for the relationship of the Church with the world. The purpose of the Church can be fully realized only in the future world; but the Church acts as a leaven in this world. The Church reveals God to man and teaches him the meaning of his existence. The Church upholds human dignity and freedom by preaching the Gospel of Christ. Without ties to any political or social system, the universal or catholic Church can signify and effect human solidarity. The Church is aware of the distance between the Gospel and the failings of Christians; and she encourages Christians to struggle against them. Conversely, if society is in debt to the Church, the Church is in debt to society. The progress of society benefits the Church too.

In the remaining part of *Gaudium et Spes* which deals with the role of the Church in the contemporary world, Vatican II singled out a number of subjects for particular consideration. These subjects are marriage and the family, human culture, the social, economic and political dimensions of modern life, and the advancement of peace. The council examined each of these subjects in the light of the Gospel and human experience. However, these subjects are taken up elsewhere in this volume.

Ecumenism (Unitatis Redintegratio)

The restoration of unity among Christians was one of the principal objectives of Vatican II. The ecumenical movement, as it is called, is aimed at removing the divisions among Christians. It is only through the Catholic Church which is led by Peter and his successors, the Popes, that one can benefit fully from the means of salvation. Non-Catholic Christians are not blessed with that unity which Jesus Christ bestowed on His Church. All are invited to share this unity which is to be found in the Catholic Church. Nevertheless, those who are members of separated Churches but believe in Christ and have been baptized are in communion with the Catholic Church even though this communion is imperfect.

An important means of promoting the ecumenical movement is dialogue. Dialogue enables experts from separated Churches to explain the teaching of their communion in greater depth. When Catholics engage in dialogue with non-Catholics, they should present the Catholic faith without equivocation, remembering though that there is a hierarchy of truths. Another means of promoting the ecumenical movement is the renewal of the Catholic Church by greater fidelity to her own calling. There can be no ecumenism worthy of the name without a change of heart on the part of Catholics. Change of heart and holiness of life along with public and private prayer for the unity of Christians is the soul of the ecumenical movement. Cooperation in a social apostolate can bring Catholics and non-Catholics together.

The ecumenical activity which the Second Vatican Council recommended must take into consideration two major divisions that now rend Christendom—the division between the Catholic Church and the Eastern Orthodox Churches and the division between the Catholic Church and the Christian Churches and communities of the West. These divisions, of course, did not arise at the same time and for the same reasons.

The Catholic Church and the Eastern Orthodox Churches have much in common—a liturgical worship of which the Holy Eucharist is the center, warm devotion to the Mother of God, true sacraments, apostolic succession, and a monastic tradition. To be sure, the Catholic Church and the Eastern Orthodox Churches follow their own laws and customs; but these need not be sacrificed in the interest of unity. What is required is unity in essential matters. The Catholic Church and the Christian Churches and communities of the West also have much in common— confession of Jesus as Lord and sole mediator between God and man, reverence for the Bible, the celebration of baptism and the Lord's Supper, and other forms of public and private prayer. Unquestionably, there are serious differences between Catholics and Protestants; but their common acceptance of the Bible offers a possibility for ecumenical dialogue.

The dialogue between Christians is subject to certain dangers such as superficiality and imprudent zeal. Another danger is the possibility of raising needless obstacles by preconceived judgments. Despite these dangers and notwithstanding the serious differences that divide Christians, they will not be dismayed in their quest for unity. They will be encouraged by the prayer of Jesus "that all may be one."

Missions (Ad Gentes)

At the beginning of its statement on missions, Vatican II recalled certain principles which it had enunciated in *Lumen Gentium*. To share His life with mankind, the Father sent His divine Son into the world. What the Lord preached and accomplished for the salvation of mankind must be spread abroad and published to the ends of the earth. Christ established the Church for this purpose.

The missionary activity of the Church is to be distinguished from the pastoral and ecumenical activity of the Church. The pastoral activity of the Church is directed to the needs of the faithful. The ecumenical activity of the Church is directed to the restoration of Christian unity. The missionary activity of the Church is aimed at those people or groups who do not yet believe in Christ. It seeks to preach the Gospel and establish the Church among them. The members of the Church are impelled to carry on missionary activity out of love for God by which they desire to share with all men the spiritual goods of both this life and the life to come. All men stand in need of Christ, their model, their mentor, their liberator, their savior, and their source of life.

To accomplish the enormous missionary task confronting the Church, the Church relies heavily upon those Catholics who live in mission lands. They can give testimony to the truth by the example of their lives, by associating themselves with the common struggle against poverty, disease and ignorance, and by identifying themselves with the people among whom they live. Missionaries are the vanguard of the Church's missionary activity. The missionaries in the field are entitled to the support of the entire Church, for evangelization is the duty of every member of the Church according to his position and capacity.

Religious Freedom (Dignitatis Humanae)

Religious Freedom has to do with immunity from coercion in civil society. It has nothing to do with the moral obligation of human beings to embrace the truth and the Church of Christ. Vatican II declared that the human person has a right to religious freedom. This freedom means that all men are to be free from coercion on the part of individuals or groups. No one is to be forced to act in a manner contrary to his own beliefs. The right to religious freedom is based on the dignity of the human person. Because human persons are endowed with reason and free will and are, therefore, responsible moral agents, they have the obligation to seek and embrace the truth, especially religious truth within a given framework.

Individuals also have a right to religious freedom when they act together. It is natural for individuals to band together to give expression to their religious convictions. Hence, religious communities rightfully claim freedom to worship the Supreme Being publicly, to select and train their own ministers, to erect buildings for religious purposes, to give public witness to their beliefs, and to establish educational, cultural, charitable, and social organizations.

Religious freedom, however, is not unlimited. In the exercise of their rights, individuals and groups are bound by the moral law to respect both the rights of others and the common good. Men and women are to deal with others justly and civilly. Society has a right to defend itself against abuses committed on the pretext of religious freedom.

The Church claims freedom for itself. The freedom of the Church is the basic principle regulating its relationship to the State. The Church claims freedom to preach the Gospel to every creature. The Church also claims freedom for its members to live in society in accordance with the precepts of the Christian faith.

Chapter 11

THE DEVELOPMENT OF ECCLESIOLOGY AND AN APOLOGETIC FOR CATHOLICISM

Bibliography: R. Schnackenburg, *The Church in the New Testament*, New York, 1965, Herder and Herder; J. McKenzie, *Church* in *DB* 133-136; P. Ternant, *Church*, in *DBT* 72-78; J. O'Rourke, *Church, I (In the Bible)* in *NCE* 3, 678-683; Y. Congar, O.P., *L'Eglise de saint Augustin à l'époque modern*, Paris, 1970, Les Éditions du Cerf; E. Gratsch, *Where Peter Is*, Staten Island, 1976, Alba House; J. Kelly, *Early Christian Doctrines*, New York, 1959, Harper & Row; Y. Congar, O.P., *L'Ecclésiologie du haut-Moyen Age*, Paris, 1968, Les Editions du Cerf; B. Tierney, *The Crisis of Church and State 1050-1300*, Englewood Cliffs, 1964, Prentice-Hall, Inc.; B. Tierney, *Foundations of the Conciliar Theory*, Cambridge, 1955, Cambridge U. Press; T. Tappert (ed.), *Selected Writings of Martin Luther*, Philadelphia, 1967, Fortress Press; J. Calvin, *Institutes of the Christian Religion*, Philadelphia, 1960, The Westminster Press; M. Nedoncelle, *L'Ecclésiologie au XIXe siècle*, Paris, 1960, Les Editions du Cerf; T. Ware, *The Orthodox Church*, Baltimore, 1963, Pengui Books; U. Valeske, *Votum Ecclesiae*, Munchen, 1962, Claudius Verlag; W. Abbott (ed.), *The Documents of Vatican II*, New York, 1966, America Press.

For the apologetic: G. Thils, *Les Notes de L'Eglise*, Gembloux, 1937; R. Knox, *The Belief of Catholics*, Garden City, 1958, Doubleday & Co.; P. Santi, *La Chiesa Cattolica*, Torino, 1960, Societa Editrice Internazionale; Y. Congar, O.P., *L'Eglise, une, sainte, catholique et apostolique*, Paris, 1970, Editions du Cerf; E. Gratsch, *The Credentials of Catholicism*, Washington, 1976, Univ. Press of America; K. Rahner, S.J., *Foundations of Christian Faith*, New York, 1978, The Seabury Press, 322-401.

This chapter is concerned with two main topics, the development of ecclesiology (or theology of the Church) and an apologetic for Catholicism. The self-image of the Catholic Church described in the preceding chapter developed over the course of twenty centuries. The present chapter gives an overview of this development. An overview of this nature will clarify details of the Church's self-image. The present chapter also offers an apologetic for Catholicism, that is, reasons for the conviction of Catholics that Christ founded and sustains the Catholic Church. These two topics are treated separately. First, the overview.

The New Testament

The New Testament was written in Greek. The Greek word for Church, *ekklesia*, meant originally an assembly of citizens in a self-governing city. The word, *ekklesia*, was used in the Septuagint, a pre-Christian Greek version of the Jewish Scriptures, to render the Hebrew word, *kahal*, which designated the religious assembly of the Israelites. The word, *ekklesia*, is used in the New Testament to designate all those who believe in Christ. It was first applied to the local community of Christians at Jerusalem. The fact that the Christians applied the word, *ekklesia* or church, to themselves implied that they regarded themselves as the legitimate successors of the Israelite community, the new and true Israel.

Initially, the distinction between the Christian Church and the Jewish synagogue was not clearly evident. Even after the death and resurrection of Jesus, those who believed in Him continued to worship in the temple and observe the prescriptions of the Jewish law. The break came later with the admission of large numbers of Gentiles to the Christian communities. It was decided that the Gentiles did not ave to adopt Judaism to become Christians (Ac 15; Gal; Rm). The result was a split between Church and synagogue.

It is possible to distinguish three groups of writings in the New Testament: the Synoptic Gospels together with the Acts of the Apostles, the Pauline epistles, and the Johannine writings. We shall consider each group in turn for information about the Church.

The Synoptic Gospels and Acts. The word, *ekklesia* or church, appears only three times in the Synoptic Gospels: once in Mt 16:18 and twice in Mt 18:17; but the reality of the Church is evident throughout the

Gospels. The central theme of Jesus' message was the kingdom of God. Jesus gathered followers around Himself in order to attach them to His person and send them forth to preach His message. These were to win other followers for Jesus (Mt 28:19; Mk 16:15). The followers of Jesus constituted the Church. The Synoptic Gospels also indicate the peculiar position of Peter in the apostolic Church (Mk 3:16; Mt 1:18; Lk 22:32).

Each of the evangelists presents his own view of the Church. Mark, though, does not sketch the proportions of the Church as boldly as Matthew and Luke do. Matthew sees the Church as the new, the true Israel. After Christ, God's people, the Church, are no longer an ethnic, national entity, but a nation "that will yield a rich harvest" (Mt 21:43). This nation is made up of Christian believers both Jewish and Gentile. No longer is the Church bound by Jewish Law but by the law of Christ promulgated in the sermon on the mount. Matthew envisions the universal mission of the Church (28:19). He recognizes authority within the Church to enforce discipline (18:17). He is conscious of the Lord's abiding presence with the community (28:20).

In his two works, the Gospel and Acts, Luke distinguishes three great periods of sacred history. The first period was that of Israel under the Law and the prophets; the second, that of Jesus at the "mid-point of time;" and the third, that of the Church (H. Conzelmann). Luke portrays Christianity as a religious faith open to all (Ac 1:8; 10:34). He speaks of the gift of the Spirit to the community on Pentecost (Ac 2). He notes the command of Jesus to celebrate the Eucharist (Lk 22:19). He warns that the age of the Church is a time of temptation and persecution (Lk 22:31; Ac 14:22). He mentions the organization of the Church with bishops, presbyters, and deacons (Ac 15; 20:6). He makes it clear that admission to the Church is gained by acceptance of Christ, repentance, and baptism (Ac 2-3).

The Pauline Epistles. Paul uses the word, *ekklesia*, frequently. Generally, it signifies the local Church—at Thessalonica, for example; but in Ephesians and Colossians it designates the worldwide assembly of Christians. Paul is the first to work out the theology of the Church. He speaks of it as the body of Christ. Christ is the "head of the Church, which is His body, the fullness of Him who fills the universe in all its parts" (Ep 1:22). This fullness is communicated by Christ to the members of the Church. The members of the Church may be compared to the members of a human body. Just as the members of the human body—the eye, ear, foot—have different functions which serve the whole body, so the members of the Church have different functions which serve the whole Church (1 Cor 12:12-31; Rm 12:4-5). The unity of the one body is symbolized by the one bread of the Eucharist (1 Cor 10:17).

Paul thinks of the Church as the bride of Christ when he calls upon husbands to love their wives as Christ loves the Church. Christ has sacrificed Himself for the Church and sanctified it through baptism, He continued to cherish the Church as His own body. The Church in turn is subject to Christ as a dutiful wife is subject to her husband (Ep 5:21-23). For Paul, the Church is also a building or a temple: "You are God's building . . . As a wise builder I laid the foundation, and another builds thereon. No one can ever lay any other real foundation, than that one we already have—Jesus Christ . , . Do you not know that you are the temple of God and that the Spirit of God dwells in you?" (1 Cor 3:9-16). The Church of the living God is the house of God, the pillar and bulwark of truth (1 Tm 3:15). God has provided the Church with different offices (apostles, prophets, teachers, miracle-workers) and charisms (healing, helpfulness, government, and tongues—1 Cor 12:28).

Paul thinks of the Church as a pilgrim in this world. As "saints" and "chosen ones" (Rm 8:27-28), Christians have been taken out of the world and separated from "those outside" (1 Th 4:12; 1 Cor 5:12; Col 4:53. Christians are obliged "to be blameless and guileless, children of God without blemish in the midst of a depraved and perverse reneration" (Ph 2:15). As the people of God upon earth, they have here no lasting city but seek a future one (Heb 13:14). Their citizenship is in heaven (Ph 3:20). The Gospel is foolishness to the world (1 Cor 1:18).

The titles which Paul gives to Christians—"saints," "chosen ones," and others such as "those called to be a holy people" and "Church of God" (1 Cor 1:2)—are drawn from the Old Testament. They indicate that for Paul the Church has succeeded to the covenant promises in place of Israel which has decided to refuse its Messiah.

The Gospel of John and the Apocalypse. In John's Gospel, Jesus employs the metaphor of a flock to describe the Church. God is the owner of the sheep who has entrusted them to Jesus. Jesus knows and loves the sheep and lays down His life for them. He gives eternal life to the sheep who follow Him. There are many sheep who do not belong to His fold.

He must lead them so that all men will become one flock under one shepherd (Jn 10:1-18). In the last chapter of John's Gospel, Jesus commits His flock to Peter as its shepherd (Jn 21:15-17). Jesus also speaks of Himself and the Church in terms of a vine and its branches. Jesus is the true vine which the Father cultivates. His disciples are the branches and by their union with Him they become fruitful (Jn 15:1-8). The metaphors that Jesus employs explain why He calls the Church so insistently to unity. The Church is drawn into the communion between Father and Son. The love of the Father for the Son also embraces those who are in communion with the Son and unites them.

While the word, *ekklesia*, is not found in the Gospel of John, it is used in the Apocalypse to refer to particular Churches. The Apocalypse was intended primarily to confirm the faith of the contemporary Church. The Church is the new Israel symbolized by the 144,000 "marked with a seal" in chapter 7. In chapter 12, the woman adorned with the sun, the moon, and the stars, symbolizes God's people in the Old and New Testaments. God's people in the Old Testament gave birth to the Messiah. This people has become the new Israel, the Church, which suffers persecution from the dragon or forces of evil. In chapter 19, John envisions the Church as the bride of the Lamb to express the close union between Christ and the Church. This symbol is enhanced by the symbol of the New Jerusalem in chapter 21. The Apocalypse inculcates the close association between the afflicted Church on earth and the triumphant Church in heaven.

These passages reflect the idea of the Church proposed at the beginning of the preceding chapter. The Church comprises the followers of Jesus. There is a spiritual union between Jesus and His followers which a later theology will call mystical. The mission of the Church is to preach the good news of the Gospel to all nations. The Church is the new, the true Israel, the heir of the covenant promises. It admits new members by baptism and celebrates a communal meal, the Eucharist. It is an organized community with offices of distinct rank.

The Fathers

In general, the Fathers of the Church are the ancient writers who are witnesses to, and teachers of, the faith of the early Church. They pored over the Bible and readily saw references to, or likenesses of, the Church in its pages. They analyzed the Biblical images of the Church such as the body of Christ and His bride,[1] flock, vineyard, and heavenly Jerusalem. They compared the Church to the fishing nets of the apostles, the bark of Peter, the moon, a dove, and the seamless robe of Christ. They saw a likeness between the Church and Biblical personages such as Eve,[2] Rahab, Mary Magdalene, and Mary the mother of Jesus. In the seafaring Mediterranean world, the Fathers loved to compare the Church to a ship: the world is the sea; Christ is the pilot; the cross is the mast; the Holy Spirit is the wind in the sails; the commandments are the anchors; and paradise is the port.[3] These images convey less an ontology of the Church than a pattern of Christian conduct: they tell us not so much what the Church is in itself, but rather how Christians are to act.

The Fathers were influenced in varying degrees by Platonism. According to Plato (427?-347 B.C.), there are two worlds: the unchanging world of forms or ideas which have objective existence and the sensible changing world in which we live. Sensible realities reflect the order of heaven. Some Fathers thought that men encounter the heavenly world in the Church, especially in its sacraments and ministers.

The Fathers differed among themselves about the possibility of salvation. Gregory of Nyssa (d. 394) believed that all human beings would finally be saved in Christ.[4] Cyprian (d. 258) held that no one could be saved outside the Church just as no one could be saved outside the ark in the days of Noah.[5] Augustine (d. 430) adopted a more moderate position, admitting the possibility of salvation for heretics in good faith.[6]

The so-called "monarchical" bishops established themselves during the patristic period. The leaders of the early Christian communities were known sometimes as bishops, sometimes as presbyters or elders. These administered the community under the supervision of the founding apostle. Probably one of the bishops was elected to succeed the founding apostle when he passed away. This bishop functioned as the sole, supreme religious leader of the community, that is, as a monarchical bishop. The title, bishop, was reserved to him. Apparently, some Churches were always led by monarchical bishops while the office soon prevailed everywhere. The martyr, Ignatius of Antioch, who died under the emperor Trajan (98-117) is one of the earliest witnesses to the position of the bishop in the Church.[7]

While the bishops were recognized as the successors of the apostles, the bishop of Rome claimed to be the successor of Peter, the prince of the apostles, and the visible head of the Church. This claim was presented and recognized less explicitly at the beginning and more explicitly with the passage of time. The Popes appealed to Mt 16:18-19 ("You are Peter, a rock, and upon this rock I will build my Church") to support their contention that Christ built His Church upon Peter who lived on in his successors, the Popes. They claimed a primacy of doctrinal authority and jurisdiction in their capacity as head of the Church. With Pope Leo the Great the theology of the papacy achieved considerable maturity.[8] The papal claim did not go entirely unchallenged. For example, Cyprian, the African bishop and martyr (d. 258), refused to recognize any other bishop as his juridical superior.[9]

At the end of the 5th century Pope Gelasius I (429-496) formulated a principle governing the relationship between the Church and the State. Two powers, he wrote, rule the world, the sacred authority of the Popes and the royal power of kings. While kings are supreme in human affairs, they must submit to those in charge of spiritual affairs.[10] In the following centuries this principle was invoked by both sides in disputes between the Pope and the secular power.

The Middle Ages

The Middle Ages are considered to be the period of European history from about 500 to about 1500. This period of Church history extends from the close of the patristic era to the beginning of the Protestant Reformation. The Middle Ages are notable for the practical implementation of papal authority in the life of the Church. In order to resist the interference of the secular power in ecclesiastical affairs and to reform the Church, the Popes intervened more often and more directly in the affairs of local Churches. For example, they began to appoint archbishops and bishops. Frequently, they issued "decretals" for the direction of others. Decretals are papal letters giving an authoritative decision on a point of canon law. Innocent I (401-417) issued the first authentic decretals. These dealt with such matters as clerical continence, the sacraments, conjugal fidelity, and the canon of Scripture. One of the most famous collections of decretals is Gratian's *Decretum* (c. 1140-41).[11] Gratian's collection contained both decretals and the canons of Church councils. It became the standard text in the schools of law as well as an essential tool of the courts. It had the effect of providing a juridical basis for the centralization of authority and jurisdiction in the hands of the Popes.

The Middle Ages saw the beginning of the lamentable division between the Catholic and the Eastern Orthodox Churches. There were several causes of the division: different traditions, the difficulty of communication, national pride, scandals in the West, and Greek contempt for Latin ignorance and barbarity. In 863, Nicholas I, the bishop of Rome, excommunicated Photius, the bishop of Constantinople because of irregularities in the election of the latter to his see. In reply, Photius sent a letter to the bishops of the East in which he bitterly denounced the Latins on various grounds. Subsequently, Rome and Constantinople were reconciled and lived in union for two centuries, although contact between the two sees diminished. In the 11th century, Michael Cerularius, the patriarch of Constantinople, renewed Photius' denunciation of the West. After a complicated series of events, papal legates excommunicated Michael at Constantinople in 1054. In turn, Michael excommunicated the legates. Happily, in 1965, Pope Paul VI and Athenagoras I, patriarch of Constantinople, expressed publicly their regret for the events of 1054 and their desire to withdraw the sentences of excommunication.[12] However, the division between East and West persists.

The dominant conception of the Church during the 12th and 13th centuries—the golden age of Scholasticism—was the idea of the Church as the body of Christ. There were two main reasons for this prominence: greater devotion to the humanity of Christ and the influence of Augustine upon the Scholastics. The Church as the body of Christ is a prominent theme in Augustine's writings. Thomas Aquinas is representative of the Scholastics in this regard. For Aquinas, the whole Church is said to be one mystical body by reason of its similarity to the natural body of a man. Just as the members of a human body have different functions, so the members of the Church have different functions. Christ is said to be the head of the Church because—as the Scholastics thought—His function in the Church is similar to the function of the head with respect to the body.[13] To complete the image, Aquinas spoke of the Holy Spirit as the soul of the Church because the Spirit is the principle of the Church's life.[14] For Aquinas, the sacrament of ecclesiastical unity was the Holy Eucharist, the body and blood of Christ. Because the faithful are one with

Christ through the Eucharist, the effect of the Eucharist is to unite the faithful among themselves.[15]

Medieval theologians and canonists recognized the Church as infallible. They were agreed that the Church as a whole could not err in matters of faith and morals. A general council over which the Pope, the head of the Church, necessarily presided, was infallible. There was a general feeling that a Pope could lape into heresy and, as a result, cease to be head and member of the Church. However, theologians and canonists were confident that divine providence would always prevent the Church as a whole from being led astray.

The major concerns of the 14th and 15th centuries were Church-State relations and conciliarism. At the beginning of the 14th century Boniface VIII (1294-1303) claimed the right to "establish the earthly power and judge it."[16] The reason was that the spiritual power is necessarily superior to the temporal power. On the other hand, France was unwilling to admit any papal claim of political supremacy; and Germany denied the Pope the right to ratify the election of the emperor. In temporal affairs, it was held, the civil authority is supreme. In *The Defender of Peace* (1324) Marsilio of Padua asserted that the papal claim to the plenitude of authority disrupted the orderly functioning of the State. William of Ockham (1285-134'), an English Franciscan, took the same position.

Conciliarism is the false theory which asserts that a general council constitutes the supreme authority in the Church, the Pope being subject to such a council. The difficulties of the time, especially the Great Schism, secured wide acceptance of the theory. During the Great Schism (1378-1417) there were rival claimants to the papacy. Some felt that the only solution to the problem was to convoke a general council which should decide among them. A general council, they said, represented the whole Church and was superior to individuals in the Church including the Pope. However, others pointed out that the Pope is the vicar of Christ, the head of the Church; hence, he is superior to a general council. The theory of conciliarism was rejected by the Council of Florence (1438-45) and the Fifth Lateran Council (1512-17), the 17th and 18th ecumenical councils respectively.

The Modern Age

This period of Church history extends from the Reformation to the present day. The Reformation began in the 16th century when Martin Luther (1483-1546) ejected some Catholic doctrines and practices and established the Lutheran Church. Luther spoke of two Churches, an invisible and a visible one. The first, which is natural, essential, real and true one, he called a spiritual, inner Christendom. The other, which is man-made and external, he called a bodily, external Christendom. He compared the Churches to the soul and body in man.[18]

For John Calvin (1509-64), the father of the non-Lutheran Reformed Churches, the Church was composed of those who were predestined to eternal life by God. Therefore, the Church was essentially invisible since predestination is known only to God. Nevertheless, by a judgment of charity, Calvin regarded as members of the Church those who by confession, example, and participation in the sacraments profess God and Christ.[19]

The Thirty-Nine Articles of Religion drawn up by the English bishops in 1562 and approved by Queen Elizabeth in 1571 defined the dogmatic position of the Church of England at the time of the Reformation. The nineteenth article offered a definition of the Church. It said in part: "The visible Church of Christ is a congregation of faithful men, in which the pure Word of God is preached, and the Sacraments be duly administered according to Christ's ordinance, in all those things that of necessity are requisite to the same." The article is somewhat ambiguous. Is acceptance or rejection by the Church the test of Christian doctrine and the proper administration of the sacraments or are Christian doctrine and the proper administration of the sacrments the test of the Church?

The Catholic response to the ecclesiological questions raised by the Reformers came from St. Robert Bellarmine (1542-1621). Bellarmine was intent on defending the visible structures of the Church because the Reformers rejected them. According to Bellarmine, Christ is the head of the universal Church which includes the Church militant on earth, the Church suffering in purgatory, and the Church triumphant in heaven. The Church on earth is governed by an individual, the Pope, the successor of Peter. As an ecclesiastical monarchy, the Church reflects the reign of God over the universe and the sovereignty of Christ over the entire Church. The Church on earth "is the congregation of persons bound together by profession of the same Christian faith and participation in the same sacraments under the government of legitimate pastors and especially of the one vicar of Christ on earth, the Roman Pontiff.''[20] Hence, membership in the Church is not based on predestination, grace and charity. Moreover, the Church is a ''congregation of persons which is just as visible and tangible as a group of the Roman people or the kingdom of France or the republic of Venice.''[21] The profession of the same faith, the reception of the same sacraments, and the recognition of the same pastors entail such visibility. This visible Church cannot err; that is, what all the faithful believe and all the bishops teach as a matter of faith is necessarily true and actually a matter of faith.[22]

The 17th century is notable for the development of Gallicanism. The term designates a number of theories sustained for the most part in the French or Gallican Church and in the theological schools of that country. These theories tended to restrict papal authority in favor of the authority of the king (political Gallicanism) or the bishops (episcopal Gallicanism). The classical statement of Gallicanism was formulated in four articles by Bossuet, the bishop of Meaux, in 1682. The First Vatican Council (1869-70) was particularly sensitive to the questions raised by Gallicanism. Febronianism and Josephinism appeared in Germany and Austria respectiely. They were transplanted forms of Gallicanism.

Two ecclesiological currents emerged during the 19th century. One current was ultramontanism. This current pressed for greater recognition of papal authority. It was represented in France by J. de Maistre (d. 1821) and F. La Mennais (d. 1854), in Italy by M. Cappellari (later Pope Gregory XVI), and in Ireland and England by W. Ward (d. 1882) and H. Manning (d. 1892) respectively. The Jesuit professors at the Gregorian University in Rome—J. Perrone (d. 1876), C. Passaglia (d. 1887), J. Franzelin (d. 1886), C. Schrader (d. 1875)—also waged a vigorous defense of papal prerogatives. The ultramontanist movement tended to resist both Gallican and liberal tendencies in the Church. It also prepared the way for the First Vatican Council (1869-70) which solemnly defined papal primacy and infallibility.

The other ecclesiological current of the 19th century viewed the Church as a communion with an inner life of its own. European romanticism of the early 19th century reawakened an interest in the past and an awareness of human solidarity. In this way it encouraged German Catholic theologians to undertake a study of the Scriptural and patristic sources of the past. It stimulated them to study the Church as a fellowship animated by the Spirit of Christ. J. Möhler (1796-1838) of Tübingen, Germany, was the most influential member of this group.[23]

Pope Leo XIII (1878-1903) clarified a number of ecclesiological questions: the Christian constitution of States (*Immortale Dei*, 1885), Church unity (*Statis Cognitum*, 1896), the Holy Spirit and the Church (*Divinum Illum*, 1897) and the Holy Eucharist, the sacrament of Church unity (*Mirae Caritatis*, 1902).

The problem of modernism troubled the Church at the end of the 19th and the beginning of the 20th centuries. Modernism is the name given to a conglomeration of ideas having to do with Biblical criticism and the philosophy of religion. These ideas were sustained by some Catholic thinkers in France, England, and Italy who wished to bring Catholic teaching abreast of the times. Among the most prominent modernists was Alfred Loisy, a French priest, whose book, (Eng. tr.) *The Gospel and the Church* (1902), was placed on the Index of Forbidden Books. The ideas of the modernists were condemned in the Roman documents, *Lamentabili* (1907) and *Pascendi* (1907).[24]

During the first half of the 20th century there was a burst of theological activity much of which centered on the Church. Bellarmine's emphasis upon the visible side of the Church had been widely sustained up to this time; but many theologians believed that the invisible, communitarian, and "mysterious" side of the Church deserved greater attention. Pope Pius XII's encyclical *Mystici Corporis* (1943) studied the Church as the mystical body of Christ. The image of the Church as the people of God and the sacrament of salvation regained prominence. Y. Congar, K. Rahner, R. Guardini, L. Cerfaux, H. de Lubac, J. Murray, G. Thils, M. Schmaus and others made notable contributions to a greater understanding of the Church. The ecumenical movement—the effort to heal the divisions among Christians—gained strength.

Pope John XXIII (1958-63) summoned the Second Vatican Council (1962-65) to renew the Church and thereby further the cause of Christian unity. He died before the council had completed its work; but his successor, Paul VI (1963-78) gave the council warm support. The council fostered a more active and intelligent participation in the liturgy on the part of the laity. It encouraged a wider use of the Bible among Catholics. It gave vigorous support to the ecumenical movement. It engendered in Catholics a new opennes to the world. It explained and implemented the idea of collegiality and dialogue among the members of the Church. It adopted a positive attitude toward the religious values of non-Catholic Churches and religions; but it continued to stress the obligatory character of Catholicism.

Since Vatican II certain theologians of Latin America—G. Gutiérrez, J. Segundo, S.J., C. Torres, H. Assmann, G. Arroyo, S.J., and others—have elaborated "theologies of liberation." They wish to liberate their continent from ignorance, hunger, misery, and oppression. They compare their struggle for liberation to the exodus of the Jewish people from Egypt. They cite a number of reasons for the plight of Latin Americans: sin, egoism, and built-in structural injustices. The mission of the Church in South America, they say, is to liberate the oppressed millions. The Church, the body of Christ, includes all those who have committed themselves to this struggle. Some theologians of liberation analyze the situation in Marxist terms by pointing to class-struggle and encouraging it as a means of achieving a classless society.[26]

An Apologetic for Catholicism

At the beginning of this chapter, two main points were proposed for discussion, namely, the development of ecclesiology and an apologetic for Catholicism. Having completed the overview of the development of ecclesiology, we now take up the apologetic. The purpose of the apologetic is to offer reasons for the conviction of Catholics that Christ founded and sustains the Catholic Church. Both the First and Second Vatican Councils expressed this conviction repeatedly.[27] An apologetic for Catholicism is necessary in view of the conflicting claims of Christian Churches and denominations to represent the Church of Christ.

How is the Church of Christ to be identified? Quite commonly non-Catholic Christians will point to the faithful preaching of the Gospel and the correct administration of the sacraments in their Churches as signs of Christ's Church among them. This answer presents a grave difficulty for Catholic theologians. Surely, Catholic theologians say, the Church of Christ preaches the Gospel faithfully and administers the sacraments correctly. But how is the average person going to apply this criterion? Presumably by testing the faith and practice of the various Christian Churches in the light of the New Testament. Yet such a test seems to be beyond the capacity of the average person. It is quite difficult to distill the essential elements of the Gospel from the New Testament. Catholic theologians are wont to say that it is not the faithful preaching of the Gospel which verifies the Church; rather, it is the Church which verifies the faithful preaching of the Gospel.

Therefore, in this section we shall apply different criteria. Traditionally Catholics have employed three criteria among others to demonstrate the divine origin of the Catholic Church and its foundation by Christ. These three criteria are the continuation of the Petrine office in the Catholic Church, the catholic unity of the Catholic Church, and the enduring continuity of the Catholic Church throughout the centuries. The first two criteria are easily recognized as signs of Christ's Church in the New Testament and as characteristic of the Catholic Church. The third criterion is an historical fact whose significance will be discussed. By the application of these criteria we shall attempt to show that the Catholic Church is the Church of Christ.

The discussion that follows supposes a particular conception of the Church, that is, that it is both invisible and visible in different ways. The Church of Christ is a group of believers or persons who have committed themselves to God through Christ. This commitment, being both intellectual and volitional, is essentially invisible. Yet Christ enjoined certain visible actions upon believers designed to initiate and sustain this commitment. These actions include preaching the Gospel, baptism, celebrating the Holy Eucharist, and performing the works of mercy. In this sense the Church is visible. On the basis of these actions one can single out the Church of Christ.

The Petrine Office. One reason for the belief of Catholics that Christ founded and sustains the Catholic Church is the continuation of the Petrine office in the Catholic Church. In other words, Christ made the apostle Peter the leader of those who believed in Him. Christ provided for successors to Peter in his capacity as leader of the Church, so that where Peter and his successors are, there is the Church of Christ. The Pope, the bishop of Rome, is the successor of Peter as the leader of the Church. Hence, those believers in Christ—Catholics—who recognize the leadership of the bishop of Rome constitute the Church of Christ. What follows is an explanation of this line of argumentation.

The New Testament indicates that Christ made Peter the leader of His Church. Christ changed his name from Simon to Peter (Mk 3:16; Lk 6:14;

Mt 16:18; Jn 1:42). In the Bible a change of name meant that a person was to fill an important position (cf. Gn 17:5; 32:28; 35:9-10). The name Peter means "rock." Peter was the rock or foundation upon which Christ built His Church (Mt 16:18). Further, Christ gave Peter the keys of the kingdom of heaven (Mt 16:19) and commissioned him to feed His flock, the Church (Jn 21:15-17). The image of the keys and the image of feeding the flock are Biblical symbols signifying authority (cf. Is 22:21-22; Rv 1:18; 2 S 5:2; Ez 34:23). As the foundation of the Church, Peter was to have authority over the Church. The supposition that Christ made Peter the leader of His Church explains well the prominence of Peter in the Gospels. He is mentioned much more frequently than any other disciple.[28]

What is more, Christ provided for successors to Peter in his capacity as leader of the Church. The permanence of the Petrine office is bound up with the permanence of the Church of which it is the foundation. However, the Church is a permanent institution since Jesus sent His representatives who are the Church to preach the Gospel to all nations until the end of time (Mt 28:19-20; Mk 16:15-16). The missionary mandate of Jesus is consistent with His universal point of view (Mt 8:11; 25:31-46; Mk 10:45; 14:24; Lk *passim*). The Church must necessarily be a permanent institution if it is to reach all for whom the Gospel is intended.

The permanence of the Church supposes the permanence of its foundation. The Petrine office of leadership is the foundation of the Church; hence, it is a permanent structure of the Church. Peter was the foundation of the Church precisely and insofar as he was intrusted with a position of leadership and authority not shared by others. He can remain the foundation of the Church only if his position is handed down to other individuals. By the will of Christ who gave him the name, Cephas or Peter or "Rock" was to be stable, permanent and enduring. The name demands continuity and succession.

The Pope, the bishop of Rome, is the successor of Peter as the leader of the Church. The Pope is the only individual who claims and exercises the office intrusted to Peter by Christ. By itself this fact identifies the Pope as the successor of Peter. The will of Christ for the Church cannot be frustrated in this regard. The connection between Peter and the Pope is explained most easily by the fact that Peter lived and died in Rome. The leader of the Roman Church, the bishop, succeeded to Peter's office.

Therefore, those believers—Catholics—who recognize the religious leadership of the Pope constitute the Church of Christ.

Catholic Unity. A second reason for the belief of Catholics that Christ founded and sustains the Catholic Church is its catholic unity. The idea is this: the Church of Christ is characterized by unity and catholicity. The creed drawn up by the Council of Constantinople (381) speaks of the unity and catholicity of the Church of Christ. This creed is still recited by many Christians at Sunday worship. However, the Catholic Church is truly remarkable among all other Christian bodies for unity and catholicity. Therefore, the Catholic Church is the Church of Christ.

The word "catholic" means "universal" and it can be understood in several ways. Here the Church of Christ is said to be catholic in the sense that it has a conspicuous number of members throughout the world. The Church of Christ is catholic in this sense for reasons given earlier in another context. That is to say, Jesus sent His representatives, the Church, to preach the Gospel to all nations until the end of time. He promised His abiding assistance as the Church carried out its mission (Mt 28:19-20). Jesus foresaw the success of the mission by anticipating the catholicity of the Church (Mt 8:11; 24:14; Ac 1:8). The Church must be catholic because it plays a vital role in implementing the universal mediatorship of Jesus. All of which is to say that the Church of Christ has a conspicuous number of members throughout the world.

The Church of Christ is not only catholic, but it is also unified. In this case, unity means that the members of the Church agree upon the essential elements of the Christian faith without schismatical separation from each other. The matter could not be otherwise. Catholicity entails unity. The Church could not be universal if it were not one. Moreover, the Church is to bring the message of Jesus to every generation. Yet Jesus could not have intrusted His message to a divided Church, for He recognized the disastrous consequences of disunity for any enterprise (Mt 12:25; cf. Mk 3:24-25). Jesus prayed earnestly for unity among His followers so that the world might recognize Him as sent by His Father (Jn 17:20-21). Jesus promised to assist His followers to preach *His* message and not a defective copy of it (Mt 28:18-20). All this means that the Church is unified in its profession of the Christian faith. This means too that the Church of Christ cannot consist of two Christian bodies— Baptists and Catholics, for example—who disagree about the essential elements of the Christian faith.

The Catholic Church is truly remarkable among all other Christian Churches and communities for unity and catholicity. Catholics are united in the profession of the same faith. They recognize the Bible as God's word to mankind; they accept the same creeds as succinct expressions of the Biblical word; they look to the Pope and the bishops in communion with him for the authentic interpretation of the word of God. The Catholic Church is catholic in the sense that it has a conspicuous number of members throughout the world. In fact, the Catholic Church is uniquely catholic because the number of Catholics greatly exceeds the number of other Christians. The other Christian bodies approach only remotely the universal diffusion of the Catholic Church.[29] Hence, Catholics see in the catholic unity of their Church evidence that it is Christ's Church.

The Enduring Continuity of the Catholic Church. Under this heading we are concerned with the Church as a moral miracle. This means that the age-old existence of the Catholic Church reflects the extraordinary intervention of God on behalf of His Church. The Catholic Church is itself a sign that it comes from God and teaches His message.

The statements in the preceding paragraph rest upon a number of facts. The Catholic Church has remained substantially the same for almost twenty centuries. It continues to recognize the same Scriptures, the same creeds, the same rites of worship, the same social authority embodied in the Pope and the bishops in communion with him. The Catholic Church has maintained its identity over a wide, even universal, geographical area and among persons of highly diverse national and cultural backgrounds. It has done so in the face of enormous obstacles: the severe demands of the Christian message it preaches, the weakness of human nature, and the disruptive force of racial and social differences, persecution, and conflicting philosophies.

What is the significance of these facts? The answer is this: it is the fate of human societies having a very large number of members to change, fragment, and disappear with the passage of time. History testifies to the appearance and dissolution of countless political institutions, religious sects, and social organizations. Human societies suffer this fate because they are subject more or less to the same disruptive forces which challenge the Church. Yet the Catholic Church has not disappeared with the passage of the centuries. Indeed it remains "not in decay, not a mere antique, but full of life and youthful vigor,'' as the Protestant historian Macaulay wrote.[30] One must conclude that the Catholic Church is not sustained by human resources but by the extraordinary or miraculous help of God. The words of Gamaliel are apropos: the works of men are overthrown while the work of God endures (Ac 5:38-39). The Catholic Church is itself a sign that it comes from God. As a work of God it claims a divine mission and a divine message.

Karl Rahner, S.J., proposed another argument in support of the truth of the Catholic Church. The Church of Christ, he argued, is a visible and historical entity in view of God's claim upon the whole man who is a social and historical being. The closer the concrete historical connection between one's own Church and the original Christian Church, the greater is the presumption that one's Church is the Church of Christ. The historical continuity of the Catholic Church with the original Christian Church is clearer than that of any other Christian Church. The Pope and the bishops demonstrate this continuity.[31]

Footnotes

1. Second Epistle of Clement 14.
2. Methodius, *On Virginity* 3, 8.
3. Hippolytus of Rome, *On Christ and Antichrist* 59.
4. *The Great Catechism* 26.
5. *On the Unity of the Church* 6.
6. Letter 43, 1.
7. Letters to the Magnesians 6, Trallians 6-7, Smyrneans 8.
8. Sermon 3, 2-4. *PL* 54, 145-147; Letter 10, 1.
9. *CSEL* 3, 1, 436.
10. DS 347.
11. A Latin text can be found in Migne *PL* 187.
12. *AAS* 58 (1966) 20-21.
13. *ST* 3a.8.1.
14. *Explanation of the Apostles Creed* 9.
15. *ST* 3a.73.4.
16. *Unam Sanctam* (1302). *CT* no. 154.
17. *CT* 164; DS 1445.
18. *The Papacy at Rome*, Works of Martin Luther, Philadelphia, 1915-32, vol. 1, 355f.
19. *Institutes of the Christian Religion* 4, 1, 7-9.
20. *Controv. Generalis de Conciliis et Ecclesia* 3, 2.
21. *Ibid.*
22. *Ibid.* 3, 14.
23. *Symbolik* 1832.
24. DS 3401-3466; 3475-3500.
25. Cf. M.D. Koster, O.P., *Ekklesiologie im Werden*, Paderborn, 1940; O. Semmelroth, S.J., *Die Kirche als Ursakrament*, Frankfurt, 1953.
26. The litterature is immense, but *see* G. Gutierrez, *A Theology of Liberation*, Maryknoll, 1973, Orbis Books; and J. Segundo, *Liberation Theology*, Maryknoll, 1976, Orbis Books.
27. Vatican I, *Pastor Aeternus, TCC* nos. 370-388; Vatican II, *passim*; cf., e.g., *Lumen Gentium* no. 8 or ch. 3.
28. In a sense the other apostles too are the foundation of the Church (Ep 2:20), but they are built on Peter.
29. One may verify this fact by consulting any table of religious statistics—in the Encyclopedia Britannica, for example.
30. T.B. Macaulay, *The Miscellaneous Works, Critical and Historical Essays*, New York, 4, 366-67.
31. K. Rahner, S.J., *op. cit.* 346-369.

Chapter 12

THE CHURCH'S SACRAMENTS
GENERAL CONSIDERATIONS

Bibliography: B. Leeming, S.J., *Principles of Sacramental Theology* (2 ed.) Westminster, 1960, Newman Press; A.G. Martimort, *The Signs of the New Covenant*, Collegeville, 1963. Authorized transl. from the French; K. Rahner, S.J., *The Church and the Sacraments*, New York, 1963, Herder & Herder. Transl. by W. O'Hara; E. Schillebeeckx, O.P., *Christ the Sacrament of the Encounter with God*, New York, 1963, Sheed and Ward. Transl. by P. Barrett, O.P.; *ST* 3a.60-65.

The Second Vatican Council declared that "the wonderful works of God among the people of the Old Testament were but a prelude to the work of Christ the Lord in redeeming mankind and giving perfect glory to God. He achieved His task principally by the paschal mystery of His blessed passion, resurrection from the dead, and glorious ascension, whereby dying, He destroyed our death, and rising, He restored our life. For it was from the side of Christ as He slept the sleep of death upon the cross that there came forth the wondrous sacrament of the whole Church. Accordingly, just as Christ was sent by the Father, so also He sent the apostles, filled with the Holy Spirit. This He did so that, by preaching the gospel to every creature, they might proclaim that the Son of God, by His death and resurrection, had freed us from the power of Satan and from death, and brought us into the kingdom of His Father. His purpose also was that they might accomplish the work of salvation which they had proclaimed, by means of sacrifice and sacraments, around which the entire liturgical life revolves."[1]

These liturgical sacraments, seven in number, of which the chief is the eucharistic sacrifice, are the sacraments of the Church. In celebrating them, the Church achieves her own identity as the mystical body of Christ. These sacraments, then, are the signs which point to the Church as the object signified. The traditional definition of a sacrament of the Church was stated by the *Baltimore Catechism* in this way: a sacrament is an outward sign instituted by Christ to give grace."[2] The sacraments have also been called the "visible forms of invisible grace."[3] Until the time of Vatican II, it was customary to refer to the Church's sacraments as simply "the sacraments;" but the council has reminded us that sacramentality has a wider significance. Christ our Lord Himself is the primary visible form of invisible grace. For in Christ God reconciles the world to Himself (2 Cor 5:19). He has spoken His Word to the world in visible form. The Son of God has taken flesh and dwelt among us. The incarnation of the divine Word is, therefore, the fundamental sacrament of our redemption. We have traditionally used the word "mystery" for this, reserving the term "sacrament" for the Church's sacraments. But mystery is merely the Greek form of the word sacrament. So, the mystery of the incarnation can properly be called sacrament. The sacred mysteries of Christ Himself are the foundation stones for the efficacy of the Church's sacraments. By His saving deeds Jesus Christ merited the efficacy that He wanted the Church's sacraments to have. And as He was lifted up from the earth on the cross, He poured out from His sacred side the saving blood and water, twin symbols of the mystical life by which the Church comes to birth and is sustained in her Christ-life. The whole efficacy of the Church's sacramental system is rooted in the mysteries, or sacraments, of Christ Himself, of which the holy cross stands as the central, one might say, crucial, point. His atoning death struck the rock of the new Horeb, and from that source flowed out the flood of grace that makes the Church a holy people of God.

The twentieth-century person cannot, however, stand literally at the foot of the cross; for barriers of time and space set limits. It is in the holy rites that these limits are transcended, and that people of all times and places are enabled to have a real share in the Christ-event. In liturgy the mysteries of Christ are renewed; not repeated, not done all over again, but renewed in a mystical way that is proper to sacramental action. The Second Vatican Council says: "The renewal in the Eucharist of the covenant between the Lord and man draws the faithful into the compelling love of Christ and sets them on fire. From the liturgy, therefore, and especially from the Eucharist, as from a fountain, grace is poured forth upon us."[4] The grace of the liturgical life of the Church owes itself to Christ as fountainhead. This is basically what we mean when we say that the Church's sacraments were "instituted" by Christ.

The Sacraments in the New Testament

To say that the Church's sacraments were instituted by Christ is tantamount to saying that these sacraments have a basis in sacred scripture. How one searches the scriptures for the sacraments will depend upon how one understands the word "institute." A false path of inquiry leads one to look for an inaugural address in our Savior's mouth for each of the seven. And where the pages of the New Testament yield no such declaration, one may be tempted to deny the biblical warrant for the sacrament in question. This approach is chiefly responsible for the shrinking number of the sacraments in the writings of some of the leading figures of the Reformation in the sixteenth century. When we say that Christ instituted the sacraments, we are not asserting that He gave a speech of institution, but rather that He gave to these holy rites the efficacy that we claim for them.

Jesus manifested His mind more often by deeds and parables than by explanatory discourses. The Presbyterian theologian, D.M. Baillie (1887-1954) wrote: "The question of the dominical institution of the sacraments is a little like the question of whether and when and in what sense Jesus 'founded' the Christian Church. . . . These become almost unreal questions when we realize that what really founded the Church (or rather reconstituted the ancient people of God as the New Israel in the Christian Church) was the *whole* episode of what God did in Christ, in His life and words and works, His cross, His resurrection and ascension, and the gift of the Spirit at Pentecost—the whole of that mighty work of God. And is not the same thing true in some sense of the origin of the sacraments? If so, then the question of their 'dominical' origin does not in the deepest sense depend on a few isolated texts."[5] On the other hand, it would be an all too simplistic approach to the sacraments in scripture, if one were to say that the sacraments of the Church are merely "arbitrary symbols chosen from time to time against the background of a sacramental universe."[6] Baillie insisted that "they are something more. It has always been regarded as being of their essence that they go straight back historically to the episode of the incarnation, to the words and works of Jesus Christ in the days of His flesh."[7] The magisterial authority of the Church cannot claim any right to alter the essence of the Church's sacraments, nor to institute new sacraments, nor to abolish any of the seven in its possession. Not even the apostles had this power, according to Thomas Aquinas (1225-74). "Just as the apostles could not institute another Church," he wrote, "neither could they hand on another faith nor institute other sacraments. The Church rather is said to be formed by those sacraments which flowed from the side of Christ as He hung upon the cross."[8] The fact that the number of the Church's sacraments is fixed at seven in Catholic teaching means that these sacraments depend upon the positive will of our Savior in a determined manner that does not allow for essential change by Church authority at any level. Otherwise the number could vary.

Why did our Savior institute seven sacraments for His Church? To answer this question we must acknowledge the richness of the life of divine grace that we have from God, and thus perceive the need for a variety of divine gifts. One sacrament alone would not have encompassed the richness of divine life that our Lord wished to share with us. Moreover, Jesus was a Jew whose personal religious heritage was endowed with a variety of sacred ritual. In giving form to His Church, Jesus of Nazareth drew upon His religious heritage, giving to the sacred symbols of His people a richer and eschatological significance. Henceforth, the rites already to be found in religious use would have a new meaning for the New Israel that came to birth from the Savior's sacred heart. The tradition of the Church has always recognized that the sacramental rites themselves are rooted in the very words and deeds of the historical Jesus. For this reason Christians are led to reject the so-called relevant appeals for "trans-culturalism" in the Church's sacred signs. Perhaps a good argument can be made for substituting beer for wine in certain cultures, and rice for bread in others, when the Eucharist is celebrated. If Christianity had been born of some trans-cultural myth, open to a multi-national flexibility, such changes might be cogently argued. But Christianity is an historical religion. The mind of the Founder is the mind of a real Jew who lived in the Near East almost two thousand years ago. The stamp of His time, His Jewishness, His human will shows; the Church that he founded will bear this stamp even as it spreads to the utmost corners of the earth. His authority to institute a Church and its sacraments derived from His divinity; but it was in His human state that He taught His disciples, worked His signs, and fulfilled His paschal mysteries.

The Age of the Church Fathers

During the period of the Greco-Roman Empire which is the period of the Church Fathers, there were no systematic treatises on the Church's sacraments. Among other reasons was the fact that the Fathers did not know of the sevenfold number. Although the Council of Trent in 1547 would solemnly define that the sacraments instituted by our Lord Jesus Christ are seven, no more, no less,[9] this listing of the sacraments, so familiar to Catholics today, comes only from the middle of the twelfth century. Nevertheless, the seven sacraments existed in the Church from the very beginning; the fact that they had not been counted and categorized did not inhibit their use nor their power to make people holy. And to the Fathers of the Church we owe a great debt for much of the theological understanding of these sacraments which even today is central to our grasp of their meaning.

A sacrament is said to have been instituted "to give grace," according to the simple definition of the catechism. The Fathers understood this truth. They looked upon the sacred rites as true encounters with the Lord. They viewed the material elements used in the sacred rites as transformed by the touch of Christ and the Holy Spirit, so that these transformed elements might, in their turn, impart to those whom they touched the life and vigor of the divine persons. Thus we read in the third *Mystagogial Catechesis* attributed to S. Cyril of Jerusalem (c. 315-386): "Beware of supposing that this ointment is mere ointment. Just as after the invocation of the Holy Spirit the Eucharistic bread is no longer ordinary bread, but the body of Christ, so this holy oil, in conjunction with the invocation, is no longer simple or common oil, but becomes the gracious gift of Christ and the Holy Spirit, producing the advent of His deity. With this ointment your forehead and sense organs are sacramentally anointed, in such wise that while your body is anointed with the visible oil, your soul is sanctified by the holy, quickening Spirit.''[10] Thus Cyril saw the holy oil as bringing to those anointed the very presence of the godhead. And the belief that the Eucharistic elements were transformed to become the very body and blood of Christ laid the foundations for the doctrine of transubstantiation that would reach formulation in the early Middle Ages.

Although these holy rites of the Christian Church were seen by the Fathers as conveying to the recipients the gift of God, they were never regarded as magical rites. Magic assumes that the god in whom one believes can be somehow controlled by the use of rites. The believer in religious magic is convinced that the correct performance of a rite will oblige the god to give his gifts. The gifts are in fact not true gifts, because they are given under duress, not freely. The Christian Fathers, on the contrary, saw Christ and the Holy Spirit as initiators of the sacred actions, and human celebrants of the rites as ministers or agents of the Lord, fully subject to His power and dominion. The God whom Christians worship is no numen who grudgingly gives up his gifts to those who enslave him by magical rites; He is rather a loving Lord who generously bestows His graces upon those who respond to His all to become His sons and daughters. This response itself plays an important role in the sanctification of those who take part in the divine liturgical rites. The rites do not dispense grace after the manner of an automat; they achieve different effects in different persons, for each recipient comes to the celebration with a different disposition. The Fathers often warned their people that they could expect God's favor from the holy rites only if they came to them rightly disposed. Cyril of Jerusalem, addressing the catechumens preparing for baptism, said: "If there is any man here who thinks of tempting God's grace, he deceives himself and knows not its power. . . . The recipients of this spiritual and saving seal must have the proper disposition. For as the pen or the dart requires the hand of the user, so grace also demands believers."[11] The Fathers, on the other hand, did not see those dispositions as a "human work" putting limits on the work of God. Rather they saw the dispositions themselves as the work of the Holy Spirit, by whose inspiration Christians would pray, fast, and give alms so as to come worthily to the holy mysteries.

The emphasis which the Fathers laid upon the interior spiritual aspect of the liturgical life of their people led them to an understanding of sacramental life that was wider than actual ritual participation. While asserting unequivocally that the sacramental life is necessary for incorporation into the body of Christ, and hence for salvation, they came to understand very early that one can be "born again" of the Spirit even without water, if one sheds one's blood in holy martyrdom for the holy name. This same crown and palm of martyrdom they saw as fulfilling the Lord's command to "eat my flesh and drink my blood" (Jn 6:54-56) in a spiritual manner that involved no bread or wine. The close bond of love between our Lord and one who had laid down life itself for Him transcended the need for material sacraments. This is the reason why martyrdom has often been called "baptism of blood."

From this understanding of the possibility of sharing the divine life apart from the actual sacraments, the Fathers moved to the notion that one may share the divine gifts by reason of a desire for the sacraments in which those gifts are properly given, even before one actually receives the sacraments. A sincere catechumen, therefore could have "baptism of desire" during the catechumenate, while still looking forward to the actual liturgical baptism itself. In fact, Augustine (354-430) does not hesitate to praise a good catechumen as being closer to Christ than one who had been baptized liturgically but whose life was unreformed. "The centurion Cornelius while unbaptized was better than Simon Magus who had been baptized," he wrote. "The former was filled with the Holy Spirit prior to his baptism, while the latter after baptism remained puffed up with an unclean spirit."[12] And Ambrose (339-397) told those who mourned the unbaptized Valentinian not to fret. "Did he not have the grace which he longed for? Did he not receive what he had asked for? Yes, he did, because he asked for it," Ambrose said, for he had intended to be baptized in the near future.[13]

Nevertheless, the Fathers did not confuse these "substitute" sacraments with the real thing. Even though they recognized that one might have the divine gift of grace apart from the use of the rites, they also knew that one is not *liturgically* baptized, anointed, or communicated except in the actual sacramental rites. So there was never any thought among them of denying the rite of water to those who had exhibited a holiness of life before baptism at the font. Nor did the spiritual eating of the Lord's body preclude the sacramental eating. Rather, the Fathers consistently urged their people to both. "Become what you have eaten!" That is, they told their people to become in conduct like unto the Christ whom they had received in the holy mystery.

Thus, if asked about the necessity of the sacraments for salvation, the Fathers would have resoundingly answered that they are necessary for salvation. They did in fact assert this regarding the three sacraments of initiation. Since the fundamental necessity of divine birth belongs to baptism rather than to confirmation, later writers in the Church said that confirmation is not so necessary for salvation as baptism is. But since the Fathers did not separate the two sacraments into two liturgies given at different ages in the life of the Christian, as we do for children, they would not have been able to appreciate this distinction. It is true, however, that the fundamental necessity of a new birth in Christ occurs at baptism, and hence confirmation, the fulfillment of baptism does not have the same degree of necessity. It is, however, a grave error to assert that confirmation is an optional sacrament to be ignored at the pleasure of those who have little interest in liturgical life. It is a sacrament that we are bound to receive in due time when the opportunity is there for it. This position of the Church's canon law is in full accord with the attitude of the Fathers.[14] A similar relationship exists between the two sacraments of reconciliation and healing. For those who sin gravely after liturgically entering the Church through the baptismal font, the sacrament of reconciliation or penance is as necessary as baptism is for those not yet liturgially initiated. Since the sacrament of the anointing of the sick is a kind of perfection of penance, it does not have the same degree of necessity as penance does for such a person's salvation. Nevertheless, that sacrament is likewise intended by our Savior for persons who are eligible for it because of their condition or illness. Hence, the Church's law has once again spoken of an obligation to receive this sacrament: "Though this sacrament is not in itself a necessary means of salvation, nobody may neglect it."[15] Finally, the two sacraments of vocation, orders and matrimony, are intended only for those who feel called to these vocations. They are given personal freedom to seek out their place in life and to ask for these sacraments according to their preference and conscience. The necessity of these two sacraments, therefore, is restricted to those who enter upon these vocations. These sacraments are, nonetheless, necessary for the Church as a whole.

So, while the Fathers handed on a tradition of the necessity of the sacraments, which found expression in the statement of the Council of Trent: "All true justification either begins through the sacraments, or once begun increases through them, or when lost is regained through them,"[16] they also understood that sacramental sharing in the mystery of Christ was not totally fenced in by the liturgical rites. Martyrdom and a desire for union with Christ are also portals of entry into Christ's divine life. Yet, while they do bring to such a well disposed person the life of grace, they do not bring that person the liturgical reality itself. And one who has baptism of desire or Eucharist of desire will, by that very fact, seek to find God's will and to draw near to the liturgical reality itself when opportunity allows. For no one can claim to desire something and not seek it. One always finds a lost article in the last place one looks; after it is found, the desire to look ceases. And if the article is not really desired, there will be no serious search for it to begin with. Thus, a "sacrament in desire" really is not a substitute for the real thing; it is rather the beginning of an action that will terminate, please God, in the liturgical rite itself. What we traditionally call "spiritual communion" is nothing other than an expressed desire for the sacrament itself. And it is plain to see that one who *always* makes "spiritual" communions, showing no interest in receiving the sacrament, really isn't making any communion at all, sacramental or spiritual.

While the sacraments themselves insert us liturgically into the mystery of Christ and His Church, they point to the spiritual reality, the divine life of grace, as their true goal. So it is the grace of the sacrament that bestows value upon the sacrament itself. Receiving the sacraments validly but unworthily will not bring a person to everlasting life. The Fathers knew this very well. And as they thought about people who did in fact misuse the sacraments, they were puzzled by the notion that one could on the one hand receive a true sacrament of the Church, while at the same time they were attached to attitudes of grievous sin. Some earlier Fathers, especially in Roman Africa, like Cyprian of Carthage (d. 258), asserted that those who baptized in schism from the true Church, did not really baptize at all. Their waters were polluted by schism and error, and the Spirit was absent from them. The Roman Church opposed this view, but was not able to offer any sound theological refutation to the position of Cyprian. It is to Augustine that we owe the theological development that made it understandable for us to say that one can indeed receive a valid sacrament while at the same time receiving no gift of divine life.

The issue arose over the question of rebaptism. Donatists, in schism from the Catholic Church in Africa, were rebaptizing any person who left the Catholic Church to join them, even though these people had been previously baptized as Catholics. On the other hand, Augustine followed the Roman tradition, and did not rebaptize those who left the Donatists to become Catholics. And he developed the theological justification for his mode of action. Working from the earlier patristic notion that those who receive Christian initiation are "sealed" by Christ, Augustine developed the theology of the *sacramental character*. Ephrem (c. 306-373), for instance, had said that "the Holy Spirit by means of the oil impresses His seal upon His flock."[17] Augustine taught that the validly conferred sacrament effects, not only the grace of the sacrament as its final reality, but also an intermediary reality, which, while being a divine gift, is nonetheless not the kind of grace that makes one pleasing to God, namely, sanctifying grace. So, if one is unworthily baptized owing to an attachment to sin or schism, the sacrament will be valid as to the intermediary reality, but no sanctifying grace will be given to that unworthy recipient. Later, when such an unworthy person is moved to repentance, it is necessary to admit such a one to the mystery of reconciliation; for the baptismal seal or "character" is already there and, coming to life, will at last be the cause of sanctifying grace and spiritual newness of life. No baptism is called for, because the previous valid rite has left its seal, which only needs to "revive" to bring about the effect of baptismal grace.[18]

This intermediary reality was later called *res-et-sacramentum* by theologians, as they applied it not only to the three sacraments which give a character in the strict sense and therefore cannot be repeated, but also to the other sacraments of the Church, especially the anointing of the sick and matrimony. While these two sacraments are repeatable, they are not without some permanence. The intermediate reality was called *res*, for like grace itself, it is an effect of the sacramental rite. But like that rite, it is a cause of the final effect, grace, and therefore shares in the nature of *sacramentum*, albeit an invisible one. To put this term, *res-et-sacramentum*, into English, we prefer to use the translation, *liturgical reality*. It is the immediate effect of the liturgical action; it cannot be present in one who has the sacrament only in desire. Yet, its liturgical nature points to its power to effect the reality which the liturgy symbolizes, namely, the grace proper to the sacrament. Others have translated this term differently; for example, symbolic reality,[19] or ecclesial effect.[20]

The Fathers, finally, were aware that, although the ultimate grace of each sacrament is a share in the very life of God, this grace is as complex as life itself. The grace of justification is not a kind of liquid which has seven faucets to add to its mass an undifferentiated grace. Each sacrament brings its own proper grace. That is why Christian initiation itself comprises three major steps of sacramental action: baptism for new birth, confirmation for a share in Christ's spiritual anointing, and holy communion for a share in the banquet table of divine life. Each sacrament has its own grace, its own mode of inserting us into the mytery of Christ. Thus the Church celebrates, not one, but seven sacraments wherein she finds her identity.

Post-patristic Developments

When the Fathers defined a sacrament as the sign of a sacred reality, they had a definition so vague that it fit not only the sacraments instituted by our Lord, but likewise the auxiliary and imitative rites of ecclesiastical origin, which today we call sacramentals. The definition, "visible form of invisible grace," from the early Middle Ages, was more picturesque, but not much more exact. But by the middle of the twelfth century, the search for a definition had made progress to the point where Peter Lombard (c. 1100-60) put forth a definition with such precision, that it encompassed the seven sacraments known to us, and excluded the many rites we call sacramentals. "For a sacrament, strictly speaking, is a sign of divine grace and the visible form of invisible grace in such a manner, that it begets its image and is its cause," wrote Peter Lombard.[21] The observation that the sacraments *cause* in the Church the holy things that they signify gave the Lombard's definition a special value, and in fact, looked at the sacraments as true *symbols* in the ritual or liturgical order. It would be naive to think that the development of a proper definition was the sole cause for the emergence around 1140 of the sevenfold number of the Church's sacraments. Concurrent with this search for definition was the growing appreciation of the sacramental tradition in the Church, and a realization that the seven rites singled out by Peter Lombard were actually of special value and regarded as coming from apostolic tradition. In fact, the unknown author of the *Summa Sententiarum*, a contemporary of Peter Lombard, also lists the seven rites as the sacraments of the Church. And the Eastern Churches, already separated from the West since 1054, developed also a theology with the same seven mysteries or sacraments. Since then, the main current of reducing the number has flowed out of the Reformation's tradition. These writers felt that only baptism and the Eucharist have warrant in the New Testament. It is true that the New Testament gives much more prominence to these rites of initiation than to the other sacraments. But since those writings are largely concerned with new converts and prospective converts, this emphasis should not surprise us, nor lead us to downgrade the other rites.

The "visible form" of the sacrament is the outward sign. It consists of matter, form, and minister. The Fathers had used prayers along with gestures and even material elements for giving the sacraments from earliest times. The naming of the "visible" part of the rite "matter," and the "audible" part "form" derives from an analogy with Aristotelian cosmology, and the terminology was introduced into sacramental theology by William of Auxerre (d. 1231). The form gives the specific meaning to a sacred action. The imposition of hands, for instance, could signify ordination, priestly blessing, or penitential absolution. The form will make it clear which it is. The form is a prayer. It is a *biblical* prayer. Hence, it must always be rooted in the Scriptures. It is not a theological statement; it is God's word compendially applied to this particular sacramental action.

Matter and form alone do not make a sacramental sign; there must also be a minister. Whether the minister needs ordination will depend upon the sacrament in question. Lay people can administer baptism and matrimony. The minister is not a robot. In order to be a valid minister, he must act humanly. This means that, in confecting a sacramental action, he must not only perform the rite, but also must have the intention of doing what the Church does. He is presumed to have such an intention, unless in his heart he makes a contrary intention. Then that hypocrisy renders his action invalid, not merely illicit. The intention is an act of the will, whereby the minister freely posits the sacred act. The intention is not necessarily absent, even though the minister has lost the faith or all love for Christ and the Church; it is still possible to intend what the

Church does. Sometimes the context of the action tells everyone that the minister does not intend to do a liturgical act; for example, a priest who offers a "demonstration mass" does not actually consecrate the elements, and a person who baptizes another in a theatrical play does not really baptize that person.

Peter of Poitiers (d. 1205) is behind two Latin expressions that became widely used after the council of Trent. To stress the fact that sacramental grace is the work of Christ and the Spirit, and therefore not dependent upon human power, he spoke of the sacraments as giving their grace *ex opere operato* to those who received them rightly. The dispositions of the human agents involved in sacramental acts were said to bring grace *ex opere operante*. (Soon the writers changed this latter expression to *ex opere operantis*.) He was trying to show that the sacramental act could be considered from two points of view: passively, or in itself, and actively, or from the point of view of the human agents. Since the Council of Trent wanted to point out that the sacraments confer their grace in virtue of their divine origin, and not merely because of human trust in them, the Fathers of the council used this expression *ex opere operato* to assert their position. Thus, a piece of jargon from the medieval schools found a place of honor in post-tridentine catechisms. Thomas Aquinas, incidentally, dropped these expressions from his sacramental treatises in his theological *Summa*, preferring to use a fine Latin style free of academic jargon.

Footnotes

1. *Sacrosanctum Concilium*, Liturgy, nos. 5-6.
2. Quest. 304.
3. E.g., by Berengar of Tours and Peter Lombard.
4. *Sacrosanctum Concilium*, no. 10.
5. *The Theology of the Sacraments*, New York, 1957, Scribner's, 59-60.
6. *Ibid.* 55.
7. *Ibid.* 55.
8. *ST* 3a.64.2.ad 3.
9. *TCC* no. 413.
10. *Mystag. Catech.* 3, 3.

11. *Catech.* 1, 3.
12. *On Baptism* 4, 21, 28.
13. *De obitu Valentiniani consolatio* 51.
14. *CIC* c. 787.
15. *CIC* c. 944.
16. *TCC* no. 412.
17. *Hymns on the Oil and the Olive* 4.
18. *See*, e.g., Augustine, *On Baptism* 1, 12, 18, and *Against the Letter of Parmenianus* 2, 18, 29.
19. Leeming, *op. cit.* 251.
20. Schillebeeckx, *op. cit.* 174-176.
21. *Sententiae* 4, d.1, c.4.

Chapter 13

THE INDIVIDUAL SACRAMENTS

Bibliography: *The Rites of the Catholic Church*, New York, 1976, Pueblo Publ. Co.; B. Neunheuser, O.S.B., *Baptism and Confirmation*, New York, 1964, Herder & Herder; A. George, S.M., and others, *Baptism in the New Testament*, Baltimore, 1964, Helicon; M. Bohen, O.S.U., *The Mystery of Confirmation*, New York, 1963, Herder & Herder; Murphy Center for Liturgical Research, *Made, not Born*, Notre Dame, 1976, UND Press; J. Delorme and others, *The Eucharist in the New Testament*, Baltimore, 1964, Helicon; J. Powers, S.J., *Eucharistic Theology*, New York, 1972, Herder & Herder; O. Casel, O.S.B., *The Mystery of Christian Worship*, Westminster, 1962, Newman Press. Transl. by I.T. Hale; E. Mascall, *Corpus Christi*, London, 1965, Longmans; B. Poschmann, *Penance and the Anointing of the Sick*, New York, 1964, Herder & Herder. Transl. by F. Courtney, S.J.; B. Haering, *Shalom: Peace*, Garden City, 1969, Doubleday Image; J. Mohler, S.J., *The Origin and Evolution of the Priesthood*, Staten Island, 1970, Alba House; E. Schillebeeckx, O.P., *Marriage: Human Reality and Saving Mystery*, New York, 1965, Sheed & Ward. Transl. by N.D. Smith; E. McDonagh (ed.), *The Meaning of Christian Marriage*, Staten Island, 1963, Alba House; *ST* 3a.66-90 & Suppl. 1-68.

Since the middle of the twelfth century, seven sacraments of the Church have been enumerated, namely, baptism, confirmation, holy Eucharist, penance (reconciliation), extreme unction (anointing of the sick), holy orders, and matrimony. This list was recognized as arising out of apostolic tradition, and not from arbitrary choices by Church leaders or theologians. The Council of Trent in 1547 canonized this list of the Church's sacraments in its seventh session.[1]

Christian Initiation

"Jesus came from Nazareth in Galilee and was baptized in the Jordan by John. Immediately on coming up out of the water He saw the sky rent in two and the Spirit descending on Him like a dove. Then a voice came from the heavens: You are my beloved Son. On You my favor rests (Mk 1:9-11). This is the mystery of the Lord's epiphany and in this mystical event He instituted the Church's sacraments of baptism and confirmation.[2] The Head of the Church was baptized and anointed with the Spirit, so that the members of the Church might, by a mystical baptism and anointing, share the grace that flows down from the Head. He came to Jordan as Messiah-king[3] and Servant of the Lord, the suffering Ebed-Adonai.[4]

Because Jesus personally was baptized with water, the Church has always considered water as essential to the rite of initiation; and because of the theophany of the Holy Trinity that marked this mystery at Jordan, the Church has always insisted upon a prayer-formula that is trinitarian. An early formula for baptism is found even in the gospel itself; for in Mt 28:19-20 we read a formulated baptismal rite in the mouth of our Lord: "Go therefore and make disciples of all nations, baptizing them in the name of the Father and of the Son and of the Holy Spirit, teaching them to observe all that I have commanded you." Variations on this formulation have marked the baptismal rites of the Church from then until the present day, in spite of actual differences in formulas between East and West. Although Jesus was baptized in the Jordan, His mystic contact with those waters hallowed *all* the waters of the earth. And so water as such, a simple element of human experience, became the door to the Church. Before the incarnate Son of God touched Jordan in His baptism, those waters were saving waters by way of biblical type,[5] but henceforth all waters enjoyed the fulfillment of the Lord's promises. "He bathed in the river Jordan and, after imparting the fragrance of His Godhead to the waters, came up from them,"[6] wrote Cyril of Jerusalem. Yet, there remained after His baptism in Jordan a fulfillment of the *paschal* mysteries of Christ to be accomplished before the Church could come to birth and begin to benefit from these saving waters of initiation into the life of Christ. For the Spirit was not yet given, until Jesus had been glorified (Jn 7:39). His passion, death and resurrection, ascension, and the sending of the Spirit from the Father—these paschal mysteries— would give meaning and effectiveness to the Church's rites. Jesus Himself was conscious of this fulfillment to which He had committed Himself by accepting the baptism of Jordan. He spoke of His passion, His exodus (Lk 9:31), as His *baptism yet to be* (Lk 12:50) and also as a *cup* which He must drink, a Eucharistic reference (Mk 10:35-40). In John's catechesis, Jesus was "lifted up" (Jn 3:14; 8:28; 12:32) on the cross itself, and from the pierced side of the Crucified came forth the Church's sacraments as blood and water, the gift of the Spirit whom the waters of chapters 4 and 7 symbolize. In Luke's catechesis, Jesus was lifted up (Lk 24:51; Ac 1:9) at His ascension, and from His place at the Father's side sent the Spirit upon the Church on the day of Pentecost. Thus, the Church celebrates two birthdays. One is the johannine Good Friday; the other is the lucan Pentecost. In either case, the catechesis is the same. Christ has merited the grace of our sacramental life in His passion, and in His glorification has sent the Spirit upon the Church to be its life principle. The visible form of this invisible grace is the liturgy of the Church. And the water rite imitates the Jordan event in both matter and form.

But Christ did not receive from John the Baptist an anointing with material oil or balm. The liturgy states that the divine Son "was baptized by John and anointed with the Spirit."[7] This anointing, however, came directly in the theophany, as the dove descended upon our Savior. The Fathers speak of two anointings of Christ: the first was in the incarnation itself; the second was at Jordan. Cyril of Jerusalem, acknowledging that neither anointing was a material one, says that Christ, fulfilling the image of the royal personage in Psalm 45, was anointed with the oil of gladness. He adds that "Christ was anointed with a mystical oil of gladness; that is, with the Holy Spirit, called oil of gladness, because He is the cause of spiritual gladness."[8] Cyril then applies this to our confirmation: "So, you, being anointed with ointment, have become partakers and fellows of Christ."[9] We should recall that in Greek Christ means "anointed." This anointing with the Spirit, which corresponds to confirmation, was so important to Cyril that he is ready to call "Christians" in the proper sense only those who have received it.[10] In spite of this, we cannot forget that in

Acts 8 and 15 the apostles gave the Spirit, not with ointment, but by the imposition of hands.

Several considerations emerge from this. First, confirmation is an integral part of Christian initiation. It is not merely a solemn renewal of baptism. Nor is it a kind of bar mitzvah for those baptized in infancy. The proper grace of confirmation is strength in the Spirit. The sacrament imprints a character, making it, like baptism itself, unrepeatable once it has been validly received. This strength had been represented catecheti-cally by metaphors like these: baptism makes us citizens, confirmation makes us soldiers; baptism gives us new birth, confirmation gives us growth to spiritual adulthood. This latter metaphor should not be used as a basis for delaying confirmation till one is an adult in body. After all, an elderly convert can be spiritually a newborn child of God in baptism. Bodily age is the basis of the metaphor, not of the rule of sacramental participation. In fact, an infant in danger of death should be confirmed no matter how young; for "it is of the greatest importance that the initiation of every baptized Christian be completed by the sacraments of confirma-tion and the Eucharist."[11] And adult converts should be confirmed, if not by the bishop, then by the priest who receives them into the Church, so that their first holy communion will *follow* confirmation.

While confirmation should sacramentally precede the first holy com-munion of children who were baptized in infancy,[12] many bishops prefer to delay confirmation to the time of adolescence for pastoral reasons, thus putting this sacrament after the first holy communion.

A second consideration concerns the sign of confirmation. Since our Lord was not anointed with visible oil, the Church has felt free to confer this gift of the Spirit by a variety of signs: imposition of hands as in the Acts of the Apostles, the oil of chrism as at Jerusalem in Cyril's time, or both. This gives us a kind of rule for how free the Church can be in regard to sacramental signs. When our Lord Himself did not set the sign by His example, the apostles freely adapted biblical signs to the sacramental purposes, and left room for other signs to be similarly adapted. We have such an instance with confirmation.

A third consideration is the necessity of the liturgy of Christian initiation. Cyril said that people are not properly Christian before these paschal rites are shared by them. The *liturgical reality* of both baptism and confirmation is a "character," an indelible seal of Christ and the

Spirit. While baptism alone suffices to put us through the door of the Church, baptism is intrinsically oriented to confirmation. This second sacrament is not optional in any sense. We are expected to receive it in due time to complete our initiation. The lack of the liturgical reality of confirmation does not invalidate other sacraments, as the lack of baptism's liturgical reality does. But one is not made the liturgical image of Christ, if one is not *liturgically* anointed with the Spirit in this holy rite.

Many Churches of the Reformation tradition reject confirmation as unnecessary. They see clearly the call for baptism in Jesus' conversation with Nicodemus (Jn 3:5). But they are convinced that confirmation is not warranted in the New Testament, and even assert that it was invented to enhance the power of the bishops. This attitude is no doubt fed by the picture of a bishop imposing himself upon older children, insisting that they renew their baptismal vows before him. But the tradition that we have seen in this study does not support this picture. While the bishop is the ''original'' minister of confirmation, his sacramental role in confirmation is shared in many instances with presbyters. It is still commendable, however, for converts to enter the Church at the bishop's celebration; and then they are confirmed by him on the very occasion of their baptism.

Another dispute among Christians concerns the method of baptism. Should the candidates be immersed, or simply have water poured or sprinkled upon the head? While certain evangelical Churches hold out for immersion only, many Christians recognize the validity of the other forms. Catholics may be baptized by immersion or infusion. This second method is widely used because of its practicality. Sprinkling is generally avoided because of the danger that too little water will be used to constitute a true baptism.

Yet another dispute among Christians is the question of infant baptism. The Church's canon law calls for it.[13] Most Christian Churches are open to it, even if they do not insist on it. Some Churches, particularly those which insist on immersion as the only form, hold for ''believers' '' baptism alone as acceptable. They argue that one should profess his faith personally and ask for baptism. Tertullian of Carthage (c. 160-c. 220) in the third century lent them support. In reply, those who favor infant baptism offer two observations. First, it is necessary to admit that Christ can call us to His fellowship at any time, even before we have the use of reason. Our personal faith is not a "work" that begets salvation by human means. Salvation is a gift of God; hence, it requires nothing but acceptance. Second, it must be acknowledged that Jesus loved little children (Mk 10:13-16) and embraced and blessed them. Are these to be held outside the kingdom of God until they reach an age when they can recite a creed? Is it logical to close the liturgical door against a person who expects to grow up as a Christian?

To grow up a Christian! That is crucial. We do not baptize infants indiscriminately. The sign that Christ is in fact calling this particular infant to baptism lies in the context of a promise that the child will grow up to be a Christian. When parents give reason to believe that they will not raise the child in the faith, then the Church's minister should discourage them from presenting the child to the Kingdom of Light at the font, only to present that child to the Kingdom of Darkness in the formative years to follow.

And what is required for "acceptance" of Christ's call? Need one have the conscious intention of receiving baptism? We know that one cannot validly be the minister of a sacrament without a conscious, free intention to do what the Church does. To receive a sacrament validly, one must relate to it *in accord with one's ability to do so*. So, an adult who has the use of reason cannot be validly baptized unless he or she wants to be. But a child under the age of reason can be validly baptized without such a will act, because it is not in the ability of such a child to make a will act. This is the point that Schillebeeckx makes in his book, *Christ the Sacrament of the Encounter with God*.[15] It was the underlying principle of Pope Pius X's argument in *Quam singulari*[16] that children should be admitted to holy communion when they can learn the catechesis "in keeping with their ability." This same principle also argues that, as their ability to learn increases with age, they are to be taught in greater depth the truths of faith and conduct to which their infant baptism committed them.

While the children of Christians should be raised as Christians, and never need to undergo a conversion from unbelief to belief in Christ, there are those who must indeed come to Christ by the path of conversion, if they are to come to Him at all. These are the converts, in the strict sense of the term. While converts in the earliest days of the Church were baptized quickly upon their profession of faith, there soon developed a catechumenate, in which the prospective Christians were instructed, tested in their sincerity and desire, and initiated step by step into the holy mysteries. Hippolytus (c. 170-c. 235) tells of a three-year catechumenate. The catechumenate died out toward the close of the patristic age, as infant baptism overshadowed the adult rites of initiation. The liturgical renewal has again given us this beautiful form for leading converts to faith and sharing in the Christian community, as a renewed liturgical usage in nine steps. A study of the rite itself and of the essays in the book, *Made, not Born*, will provide valuable insights into this long needed rite for converts to Christ.

The culmination of Christian initiation is the sacrament of the Eucharist. It is received, not once in life, but on numerous occasions. It is, so to speak, the extension of our baptism-confirmation into our Christian days. In the Eucharist, our initiation becomes repeatable, renewable.

The Holy Eucharist

The Eucharistic sacrifice is Calvary renewed. In the Mass Christ's passion, and indeed His entire paschal mystery, is made present anew for the Church of today. It is not a re-crucifying of Christ, but a mystical representation. "Christ's crucifixion was real, His burial was real, and His resurrection was real; and all these He has freely made ours, that by sharing His sufferings in a *symbolic enactment* we may really and truly gain salvation. . . . Christ felt the pain: and on me without pain or labor, through the fellowship of His pain, He freely bestows salvation."[17] Attempts at explaining just how the Mass is truly a sacrifice have been varied and of diverse worth. E.L. Mascall gives a panorama of such attempts in his book, *Corpus Christi.*[18]

Since the divinely instituted sacraments effect what they signify, the Eucharistic celebration effects a change in the elements of bread and wine. "Once the consecration takes place this bread will be the body of Christ and this wine will be His blood. This happens in Christ's name and by His grace. Even though it looks as it did before, its value is not what it was before. Had you eaten it before, you would have had food for the stomach; but after the consecration it provides food for the soul."[19] Out of the eleventh-century controversy, in which Berengar of Tours (c. 999-1088) denied the Eucharistic real presence, came the terminology for expressing theologically this wondrous change in the elements. Transubstantiation means that the substance, or underlying reality, of the bread and wine are by divine power converted into the very body and blood of Christ. Visually and chemically they remain unchanged; the sign value of these table elements is preserved. Yet one eats and drinks, not bread and wine, but the flesh and blood of our Savior (Jn 6:53). The bishops at Trent in 1551 canonized this term as suitable for expressing the wondrous mystery.[20] Since the mid-twentieth century, some theologians, especially in Holland, have searched for newer notion to express the mystery, since they felt that transubstantiation was too bound up with the philosophy of Scholasticism. Pope Paul VI (1897-1978) in the encyclical *Mysterium Fidei*[21] stated: "When transubstantiation has taken place, the appearances of bread and wine acquire, beyond doubt, a new meaning and a new finality. They are no longer ordinary bread and ordinary drink, but the symbol of a sacred thing and the symbol of spiritual nourishment. But if they acquire a new significance and a new finality, it is because they contain a new 'reality' which we justly call *ontological*."[22] So, he said that "transignification" and "transfinalization" are rooted in transubstantiation. They are useful terms, but not really substitutes for the other. Joseph Powers (b. 1926) gives a good history of the development of these ideas in his book, *Eucharistic Theology*.[23]

Each celebration of the Mass, by ancient tradition and practice, opens with a liturgy of the word, wherein Christians are nourished with readings and explanations of the word of God in holy Scripture. Then follows the properly Eucharistic rite, whose Eucharistic prayer enshrines the words of institution, spoken by our Lord at the Last Supper as He took bread and called it His body, took wine and called it His blood. The New Testament relates the account of the supper in four writings: the three synoptic Gospels (Mt 26:26-30; Mk 14:22-26; Lk 22:14-20) and Paul's account in 1 Cor 11:23-26. Although the different accounts represent slightly different traditions, they agree in essence that Jesus gave His disciples His flesh and blood as food and drink under the symbols of bread and wine. By "doing this for a memorial of Him" we become partakers in His life-giving Spirit and are nourished unto a future resurrection. This is the doctrine that John teaches us pointedly in chapter 6 of his Gospel. Our resurrected glory will be, therefore, a Eucharistic glory. "This holy bread is super-essential in the sense of being ordained for the essence of the soul. Not of this bread is it said that it 'passes into the stomach and so is discharged into the drain' (Mt 15:17); no; it is absorbed into your whole system to the benefit of both soul and body.''[24] This holy food is the fountainhead of that grace of healing which is the proper grace of two other sacraments. Our bodies are "vivified by His immortal flesh, and in some degree participate His immortality," said Calvin (1509-1564). The sacramental grace of the Eucharist is, then, a nourishment in the Spirit for the individual recipients, and for the Church as a community, a bond of unity and peace in the charity of Christ. That is why schism so profoundly contradicts the Eucharist; and fidelity to the Eucharistic symbolism requires that inter-communion across lines of schism be allowed only where the persons involved are not personally responsible for the schism, and where those persons have a need for the Eucharistic nourishment. The "liturgical reality" of the Eucharist is the very body and blood of Christ, made present by the consecratory act of the priest or priests celebrating Mass. Christ, the high priest of the new covenant, is the chief priest under whose initiative the ordained priests act as celebrants. He who changed water into wine at the Cana epiphany (Jn 2:1-11) now changes wine into His life-giving blood by the power of the Spirit in each holy Mass.

Having once entered liturgically through the door of the Church by baptism, confirmation, and our first communion, we are invited to share this sacrament often, even daily, if we are also willing to form our lives on the pattern of Christ's life, whose mystical body is formed of His communicants. Thus, we must examine ourselves, lest we eat and drink unworthily unto condemnation (1 Cor 11:27-32). Our communions must lead us to make progress in the life given us in baptism. If necessary, we must prepare for our holy communion by a good confession. We are commanded in Church law to receive but once a year; yet we have a command to attend Mass weekly. No Mass is truly fruitful if it lacks at least a spiritual communion. So, the annual communion is a legal minimum; spiritual writers urge us to receive holy communion, not just spiritually, but sacramentally as well as spiritually, as frequently as we can in accord with our readiness to put the gift of grace into practice in our lives. Finally, this holy sacrament is a "last" sacrament. It is the third of our sacraments of initiation, and it continues as a companion during all the days of our lives as Christians. At the approach of death, our Lord in this sacrament wishes to be our "viaticum," our companion on the way to the next world. The priest or deacon who attends us at death will give us this holy sacrament as viaticum. And if it should be that we cannot receive sacramentally in that hour, our spiritual communion will suffice, reviving our past sacramental communions unto this special grace of final perseverance.

Sacraments of Healing

"It is fitting that one who has received the baptismal remission of sins should sin no more," wrote Clement of Alexandria[26] (c. 150-c. 215). Clement knew and all of us know that this ideal is not achieved, except by our Lord and our Lady. Sins great and small are the warp and woof of our life, even after we have been enlightened in baptism, sealed with the Spirit, and tasted the greatness of the Lord. Just as bodily illnesses require doctors and medicines, so our life in Christ has need of spiritual healing. This is supplied in the sacrament of penance, or reconciliation, and the anointing of the sick, also called extreme unction. In them Christ is our healer.

Some of the signs that Jesus worked during His public life were prophetic signs of the Church's mystical life, like the multiplication of the loaves. Many of His signs, however, were works of healing the sick and even raising the dead. In His healing ministry Jesus exercised His power over the Kingdom of Darkness, whence comes sin and death, sickness and ill fortune. Victorious already over Satan in the temptations (Mt 4:1-11), He hastened to the ultimate victory on the cross. If the positive side of His redeeming work was life and grace, the negative side was remission of sin and release from sin's domain—sickness and death. We live in the pilgrim Church, already redeemed in Christ, but still struggling onward as Christ's members put on Christ and experience failures in that endeavor. The mystical body of Christ is still building; and until all is consummated in the eschaton, the Kingdom of Darkness will bid for our allegiance. It will have temporary successes with the saved; and for those who are not among the predestined, that kingdom will prove attractive enough for full allegiance.

The healing hand of Jesus, in the person of an ordained priest, is extended to us in our sins and in our sickness. To lift us up from post-baptismal sins, he offers us penance. Penance is the virtue whereby the sinner turns away from past evil deeds and attitudes and seeks reconciliation with God. This reconciliation, made visible as a sacrament, is at once a vessel of restored gracious life for the penitent, and of healing for the Church as a whole; for if one member suffers the blight of sin, the whole body suffers. This virtue of penance undergirds the sacrament; without it there cannot be valid sacrament nor forgiveness of sins. Contrition for sin, a strong hatred for one's evil past and a profound detestation of sin, is the central act of the penitent who seeks reconciliation. To confess sins without sorrow for them is merely to catalogue them, not to be freed from them. When the sins are brought to the sacramental forum by the penitent, the confessor assigns a satisfaction, also called by the name "penance," which is a sacred sign of a change of heart. One has done *evil* by sinning; now one is assigned some token *good* to do. This satisfaction, though it be a simple good work or prayer, is a vital part of the sacrament. To reject it is to render the sacrament invalid.

Contrition is said to be "perfect" when animated by the virtue of charity. At the conscious level it will manifest itself in sorrow arising out of the motive of love for God. Such contrition, by definition, justifies the sinner even prior to sacramental reconciliation. But this is in fact a case of a sacrament *in desire*; and one must still use the sacrament for the *liturgical reality* of reconciliation. "Imperfect" contrition though it arises from faith and hope, does not become informed by charity until the power of Christ's mysteries effects this change during the absolution given by the priest during the sacrament of reconciliation. At the level of conscious motives, this imperfect contrition or "attribution" arises from fear of God's wrath or the fires of hell: motives of faith, but not of charity or *agape*.

Sins are to be confessed by the penitent to a priest, who is authorized to hear confessions because he is canonically approved with "faculties" for this purpose. Serious sins are to be confessed by kind, and the number of times committed. Venial sins, being optional matter for this sacrament, may be confessed as the penitent sees need to do so. The sacrament does reconcile us to God more closely, even in respect to these lesser sins. And the confession of them can be a powerful spiritual aid toward growth in the Christ-life.

When the confessor is satisfied that the penitent has elicited true repentance and purpose of amendment, as far as he can judge, he assigns the satisfaction and gives absolution. This prayer of the priest is the sacramental form of this rite. The matter is made up of the penitent's acts of sorrow, confession and acceptance of the satisfaction.

Along with baptism, this sacrament is often called a sacrament of the *dead*; for it achieves its most profound effect in those who are spiritually dead in sin. The other sacraments are called sacraments of the *living*; for their normal mode of effectiveness is to increase the life of grace, rather than to inaugurate it from nil. Catholics are to receive this sacrament at least annually. They must also receive it before holy communion if they are conscious of a serious sin not yet confessed and absolved. This consciousness of sin is not a real proof that they have in fact lost God's life of grace, for we cannot ever know for certain the state of our souls.[27] But the law binds us in accord with out conscious level of self-examination. And we consciously reach out for our Lord's saving hand, as Peter did when sinking in the water.

As sin besets the pilgrim Church, so does illness and death. The apostle James wrote: "Is there anyone sick among you? Let him call for the elders of the Church, and let them pray over him and anoint him in the name of the Lord. This prayer, made in faith, will save the sick man. The Lord will restore his health, and if he has committed any sins, they will be forgiven" (Jm 5:13-15).[28] Here one sees the bond between the two sacraments of healing. This one is a kind of crown upon the life of penance and struggle against sin. It repels illness. The anointed receive divine aid toward recovery; not a substitute for the doctor, but aid at a more profound, mystical level. It also prepares those who are, in God's plan, to die of their illness for the glory of the life to come. Sin itself and the ravages of past sins are put under the healing hand of our Savior. The recipient of this sacrament of the anointing of the sick is given fellowship with Christ as the Suffering Servant. In His body He bore our sins upon the cross, a man of sorrows and acquainted with grief (*see* Is 53:4-5). In His mystical body, Christ still suffers in us when we suffer. "If we realize that our sufferings are preparing us for eternal life in glory, then they will seem short and even easy to bear."[29] So, those who experience serious illness or injury, including serious debility from old age, should receive this sacrament from a priest, especially from their own pastor. The sacrament is not meant to raise the dead; so the dead are not anointed. Jesus' power to raise the dead did not pass into the Church's sacraments.

The proper effect of this sacrament is a special consecration of one's illness to Christ, giving fellowship in His suffering and the touch of His healing hand. This liturgical reality of the sacrament becomes the font of the many special graces that we surely need in time of illness. The revised rite for this sacrament and for the general pastoral care of the sick was promulgated by Pope Paul VI on November 30, 1972.

Sacraments of Vocation

Like wild olive branches, Christians have been grafted onto the True Vine (Jn 15) by the three sacraments of initiation; they have wounds of both body and soul healed through the two sacraments of healing. These five sacraments, then, are offered to *all* the followers of Christ. There remain two sacraments that are intended only for *some* of the faithful: holy orders and matrimony. These are sacraments of vocation.

In the mystical body of Christ, "all the faithful are made a holy and kingly priesthood, they offer spiritual sacrifices to God through Jesus Christ, and they proclaim the virtues of Him who has called them out of darkness into His admirable light" (1 P 2:5, 9).[30] Yet, there is a special ministerial priesthood entrusted only to divinely called persons, and which is confereed on them by a special sacrament. "Though they differ essentially and not only in degree," said Vatican II, "the common priesthood of the faithful and the ministerial or hierarchical priesthood are nonetheless interrelated. Each of them in its own special way is a participation in the one priesthood of Christ. The ministerial priest, by the sacred power he enjoys, teaches and rules the priestly people; acting in the person of Christ, he effects the Eucharistic sacrifice and offers it to God in the name of all the people. But the faithful, in virtue of their royal priesthood, join in the offering of the Holy Eucharist. They exercise that priesthood too by the reception of the sacraments, prayer and thanksgiving, the witness of a holy life, self-denial and active charity."[31]

The outward sign of this sacrament consists of a bishop as the only valid minister of orders, the imposition of hands as the matter, and the consecratory prayer proper to each ordination as the form. This moreover is not a single sacrament, but it has a threefold office to confer on different recipients. The hierarchical priesthood consists of bishops and presbyters; and a third order, that of deacons, completes the traditional picture of holy orders. Lesser orders, once in the Church but again abolished, shared some of the functions of these three orders, and were received, not by the imposition of hands, but by the handing over of a symbol of their office. Today there are two ministries, readers and acolytes but these are *lay* ministries and not orders.[32]

Bishops hold the fullness of priesthood by their sacred ordination, and together with their brethren in the episcopal order, form the hierarchy of jurisdiction in the Church. The chief bishop of this hierarchy is the bishop of Rome, who, by reason of holding that apostolic see, is the successor to Peter, prince of the apostles, the rock upon whom our Savior built His Church (Mt 16:18). The other bishops rule various dioceses and missions throughout the Christian world; some of these bishops serve as auxiliaries to those who have the care of a diocese or mission. The bishops are the teachers and shepherds of their Churches, and to them is entrusted the conferring of the sacrament of holy orders, and, as original ministers, the sacrament of confirmation. Presbyters may replace bishops in this latter role.

Presbyters are priests of second order. The purpose for which "priests are consecrated by God through the ministry of the bishop is that, being made sharers by special title in the priesthood of Christ, they might act as His ministers by performing sacred functions. In the liturgy they continue to carry on His priestly office by the action of His Spirit. . . Especially by the celebration of Mass they offer sacramentally the sacrifice of Christ. But in the administration of all the sacraments . . . priests are bound together hierarchically with the bishop by various titles; and so in a certain way they make him present in every congregation."[33]

Pope Paul VI in 1972 gave papal norms for the restored diaconate in the Church. Although priesthood candidates pass through the diaconate by long tradition, the deacon who would receive that order as a terminal ordination was authorized by the Second Vatican Council.[34] Ancient Christian writers described the deacon "as the bishop's ear, mouth, heart and soul. The deacon is at the disposal of the bishop in order that he may serve the whole people of God and take care of the sick and the poor; he is correctly and rightly called one who shows love for orphans, for the devout and for the widowed, one who is fervent in spirit, one who shows love for what is good. Furthermore, he is entrusted with the mission of taking the holy Eucharist to the sick confined to their homes, of conferring baptism, and of attending to preaching the word of God with the express will of the bishop."[35] Deacons and presbyters receive their canonical call to ordination from their proper bishops or competent religious superiors. Bishops receive their canonical call, in the present discipline, from the bishop of Rome.

The 1970's raised a new issue: should the call to ordination be given only to men, or also to women? The acceptance of women into the priesthood by the American Episcopal Church, a Church that has a tradition of priestly ministry, has added impetus to the movement among Roman Catholics to open up ordination to women. Much rhetoric is offered by people on both sides of the issue. The Orthodox Church does not encourage any such movement among its members. The real issue to be decided is in fact this fundamental issue: "Was it Christ's will that only men be called to the ordained ministry as a matter of principle?" If the answer is "Yes," then women cannot be validly ordained, even if one chooses to ignore canon law. If the answer is "No," then the magisterium of the Church could change canon law and allow women to be ordained to the priesthood. Those who oppose the ordination of women in principle feel that the tradition of excluding them derives from the mind of Christ. Their opponents think that the tradition is simply a relic of past ages when women were expected to defer to men. Archbishop Joseph Bernardin (b. 1928), speaking for the American hierarchy, said at a news conference in November, 1975, that the Church "has consistently taught and understood that it was Christ's will that only men were called to the priesthood."[36] Yet, he did not rule out further study of the question by theologians, provided that they take into account this constant tradition of ordaining only men, and realize that final decisions belong to the Church's legitimate magisterium.

One cannot say *a priori* that our Lord could not have intended that only men be called; this must be learned from the fonts of revelation. In the second of the sacraments of vocation, we find both sexes called to share it, and sexuality is the central feature of that sacrament. The union of a man and a woman in marriage has been called by our Savior to the level and dignity of a sacrament of His Church.

Christ is the head of His body, the Church. As such He is the bridegroom to whom the Church is united in a most intimate union. The letter to the Ephesians (5:22-33) shows that the marriage of two Christians is the sacred sign of this union of Christ and the Church. Marriage in

Christ is the visible form of the invisible grace that makes each Christian home into a mirror of the Church. The Church became joined to Christ in His twofold anointing with the Spirit. In the incarnation humanity was wedded to the godhead, never again to separate. In Jesus' baptism, the bride herself was purified in the bath because her head was the hallower of the waters, and He received the Spirit in her name. Each husband is to love his wife just as he loves himself, and the wife is to respect her husband. Thus the apostolic author gives the husband the place of eminence in the home, since he is the mirror of Christ as head of the Church. But in commanding him to love his wife with a love also modeled on Christ's love for the Church, the apostolic author raises womanhood to a new dignity in Christianity. The wife is a true *partner* in marriage, whose rights are violated by any infidelity of her husband. Such men are "adulterers;" and men no longer have any right to divorce their wives in the new covenant. The age of harems is over with the birth of the Church and her spiritual marriage to Christ. "What God has joined together, man must not separate" (Mt 19:6). In a home filled with Christ's love, the wife's subjection implies no servitude or debasement; her model is the Church.

Christian marriage, mirroring the permanent union of Christ with the Church, takes on the strength of the union it symbolizes. Thus, *permanence* in marriage is the result of its sacramentality. Man and wife are wedded until the death of one of them dissolves the marriage bond.

Closely allied to this property of permanence is the property of *oneness*. One man is wedded to one woman. There is no room for harems or mistresses, nor male counterparts. Conjugal fidelity is demanded by the nature of marriage and the mind of Christ. To enter marriage with intentions otherwise is to render the attempted marriage null and void.   The marital partnership of a man and woman is by nature oriented toward the begetting of children. New life is the fruitfulness of marriage. It is true that this fruitfulness is sometimes absent. Sterility of one partner does not necessarily invalidate marriage. Even a virginal marriage, if agreed upon by both partners, can be a valid one. Yet it must be possible for the partners to be sexually active in a human way. Impotence excludes one from marrying. And homosexual marriages are, by their very nature, invalid, since the fundamental nature of sex demands the male-female union.

"Husband and wife, through the mutual gift of themselves, which is specific and exclusive to them alone, develop that union of two persons in which they perfect one another, cooperating with God in the generation and rearing of new lives. The marriage of those who have been baptized is, in addition, invested with the dignity of a sacramental sign of grace for it represents the union of Christ and His Church."[37] Moreover, "responsible parenthood requires that husband and wife, keeping a right order of priorities, recognize their own duties toward God, themselves, their families and human society. From this it follows that they are not free to act as they choose in the service of transmitting life, as if it were wholly up to them to decide what is the right course to follow. On the contrary, they are bound to ensure that what they do corresponds to the will of God the creator. The very nature of marriage and its use makes His will clear, while the constant teaching of the Church spells it out."[38]

Not all are called to the married state. Some are called to single life, either in consecrated chastity or celibacy, or in a choice prompted by other worthy motives. To those who receive the divinely initiated call to marriage in Christ a truly beautiful life's work is given. In their mutual unselfish love they mirror Christ's love for the Church. Their children, if it be in God's providence that they come to be, are an affirmation that nature and nature's God intend that there be a tomorrow. The city of God will continue in these little ones who are destined to grow up, instructed and nourished on the divine word, in the Christian home. This vision of the future looks ultimately to the day when sacrament shall cease, and the Lord will come in glory to consummate His work in the final eschaton.

Footnotes

1. *TCC* no. 413.
2. Epiphany consists of three mysteries: the magi, the baptism of Christ, and the Cana miracle.
3. Ps 2:7.
4. Is 42:1.
5. Joshua (Jos 3:14-17), Elijah and Elisha (2 K 2:8, 14), Naaman's cure (2 K 5:14).
6. *Mystag. Catech.* 3, 1.
7. Prayer for blessing baptismal water.

8. *Mystag. Catech.* 3, 2.
9. *Ibid.*
10. *Ibid.* 5.
11. Rite of confirmation, no. 52.
12. *See* Bohen, *op. cit.* 140-145.
13. *CIC* c. 770; Rite of baptism for children, no. 8.
14. *On Baptism* 18.
15. *Op. cit.* 107-112.
16. *AAS* 2 (1910) 577.
17. Cyril of Jerusalem, *Mystag. Catech.* 2, 5 (emphasis added).
18. Chs. 5-6.
19. Augustine, *Sermo Guelf.* 7.
20. *TCC* no. 487.
21. *AAS* 57 (1965) 753-774.
22. *See* O'Neill, *New Approaches to the Eucharist*, Staten Island, 1967, Alba House, 110-111.
23. Ch. 4.
24. Cyril of Jerusalem, *Mystag. Catech.* 5, 15.
25. *Institutes* 4, 24, 43.
26. *Carpets* 2, 13.
27. *TCC* 723.
28. Translation as given in the Ritual.
29. Rite of anointing, no. 2.
30. *Presby. Ordinis* Priests, no. 2.
31. *Lumen Gentium* no. 10.
32. *Ministeria Quaedam AAS* 64 (1972) 529-534.
33. *Presby. Ordinis* no. 5.
34. *Lumen Gentium* no. 29.
35. *Ad Pascendum.*
36. Cincinnati *Catholic Telegraph*, Nov. 28, 1975.
37. Paul VI, *Humanae Vitae* no. 8.
38. *Ibid.* no. 10.

Chapter 14

ESCHATOLOGY

Bibliography: E. Schillebeeckx, O.P. (ed.), *Concilium* 1/5 (1969) Burns & Oates; E. Fortman, S.J., *Everlasting Life after Death*, Staten Island, 1977, Alba House; H. Schwartz, *On the Way to the Future*, Minneapolis, 1972, Augusburg; *ST* Suppl. 69-99 and *Compendium* 1.149-184; C.H. Dodd, *The Parables of the Kingdom*, first publ. 1935, rev. ed. New York, 1961, Scribners; R. Bultmann, *Theology of the New Testament* first publ. 1948-53 in German, Engl. ed., New York, 1951-55, Scribners. Trans. by K. Grobel; J. Jeremias, *The Parables of Jesus*, New York, 1963, Scribners. Trans. by S. Hooke.

Eschatology is the study of the last things. This discipline is as old as theology itself, although the term "eschatology" is more recent. The Fathers of the Church were concerned about the consummation of the Christian era as well as the goal of the individual Christian beyond death. They saw salvation in Christ as being far more than a kind of betterment of life on earth. In its profound implications salvation meant life without end and eternal life worth living. Because such a life becomes possible by reason of the mighty acts of God in His Christ, Christians are sustained in their quest for everlasting happiness by the virtue of hope. And therefore the treatise on eschatology is often called a treatise on the *Christian hope*. The manuals of theology that were written in Latin called this treatise *De novissimis*, which is really Latin for eschatology.

Traditional Eschatology

In this section we shall consider traditional eschatology, which is mainly *futuristic* eschatology. This frame of mind looks to the future for the great day of the Lord, in which the last events of the present age will occur. For the individual person, death is the personal eschaton, and traditional eschatology also has addressed the question of what happens when a human being dies. Moreover, the placing of this treatise right after the one on the sacraments of the Church is also traditional. The Second Vatican Council, using the traditional, futuristic frame of mind, speaks of the earthly liturgy as the foretaste of our hope of glory. "In the earthly liturgy we take part in a foretaste of that heavenly liturgy which is celebrated in the holy city of Jerusalem toward which we journey as pilgrims, where Christ is sitting at the right hand of God, minister of the holies and of the true tabernacle. With all the warriors of the heavenly army we sing a hymn of glory to the Lord. Venerating the memory of the saints, we hope for some part and fellowship with them. We eagerly await the Savior, our Lord Jesus Christ, until He, our life, shall appear and we too will appear with Him in glory."[1]

Traditional eschatology is wont to list *four last things* for each individual person: death, judgment, heaven or hell. Death is a visible and undeniable reality in human existence. "Although the mystery of death utterly beggars the imagination, the Church, taught by divine revelation, teaches that man has been created by God in view of a blessed destiny beyond the reach of earthly misery. Moreover, the Christian faith teaches that bodily death from which man would have been immune had he not sinned will be vanquished when man, who was ruined by his own doing, is restored to wholeness by an almighty and merciful Savior. For God has called man and still calls him so that with his entire being he might be joined to Him in sharing forever a divine life free from all corruption. Christ won this victory when he rose to life, for by His death He freed man from death. Hence, to every thoughtful man a solidly established faith provides the answer to his anxiety about the future. At the same time faith gives him the power to be united in Christ with his loved ones who have already been snatched by death. Faith arouses the hope that they have found true life with God."[2]

The council Fathers spoke in the foregoing quotation about "an almighty and merciful Savior." The Christian virtue of *hope* is rooted in these two attributes of God. For, we could not hope for salvation if God were not merciful; without God's good will we are left unaided. But more important still is the might of God. For if God wanted to save us but were unable to do so, we would always risk being lost. But since God is almighty, we cannot be snatched from His hand, not by the devil nor by any other force of evil. Thus the firmness of our hope is frequently represented in art by an anchor. Aquinas (1225-74) affirms this truth, saying: "A cause does not fail in keeping proper control over its own effect, unless it suffers from some deficiency. But there is no deficiency of knowledge in God, for all things are open to His eyes (Heb 4:13). God is not lacking in power, for the hand of the Lord is not shortened so that He cannot save (Is 59:1). Neither is God lacking in good will, for the Lord is good to them who hope in Him, and to the soul that seeks for Him (Lm 3:25). And therefore the hope that one places in God does not bring confusion upon one who hopes (Rm 5:5)."[3]

Yet, solid though this anchor of hope may be, we must still work out our salvation in fear and trembling, and not neglect to pray for ourselves nor to seek the fonts of divine grace. Hell is a real threat to our happiness. Augustine (354-430) wrote that "the one thing which we may by no means believe is that bodies in hell will be such that they will be unaffected by any pains inflicted by fire."[4] Augustine spoke of the *bodies* of those in hell, because he believed that the damned would also rise at the final judgment, but to ultimate condemnation in both body and soul. This belief has been generally proposed in traditional eschatology.

The eschatology of the Fathers developed slowly, and often the Fathers were not so good in guiding the Church in this matter as they were in other matters of faith. Some of the early Fathers, much influenced by the writings of Origen of Alexandria (c. 185-c. 253), taught mistaken notions of the after-life. Some, like Origen, were too literally impressed by the apocalyptic language of *Revelation* and some of the pseudepigraphal apocalypses. Understanding the numerical symbols there too literally, they postulated a period of a thousand years in which the earth would be visibly ruled by the saints, even with Christ Himself as leader, before the consummation of the age. This mistaken view is called *chiliasm* or *millenialism*. Another view, also stemming from Origen, was the *universalism* of salvation. Traditional catechesis teaches that Christ's redemption extends to all people, but it adds that some will fail to benefit by it and be forever lost. While Origen believed in the existence of hell, he saw hell as temporary, and thought that even the damned would eventually be purified of their evil and come to union with God. Chiliasm and universalism have repeatedly cropped up in Christian thought over the course of history, and even today there are some groups that put their trust in these theories. They are found today, however, chiefly among Christian sects, and are generally excluded from main-line Christian thought. Professor Hans Schwarz has put these ideas among the "blind alleys" in eschatology that lead to no suitable theological conclusions.[5]

The Fathers, moreover, were rather vague in their grasp of the status of a person between death and the general judgment when the Lord comes again to judge the quick and the dead. Augustine wrote: "During the time moreover which intervenes between a man's death and the final resurrection, the soul dwells in a hidden retreat, where it enjoys rest or suffers affliction just in proportion to the merit it has earned by the life which it led on earth."[6] A hidden retreat is surely vague. But Augustine is clear on the point that people do experience reward or punishment in this period after death. They are not in a state of suspended animation until the second coming. But the resurrection of the body, in Augustine's thought, is necessary before one can come to one's essential reward or punishment. Later theologians modified this stance by claimng that after death the soul is judged in the *particular judgment*, and assigned its place among the saved or the damned. The blessedness of those who see God in the beatific vision is not essentially, but only accidentally, to be increased by the resurrection of the body. The same is true in its own way of those who are lost. While this view of the particular judgment was to reach dogmatic definition in the constitution of Benedict XII (d. 1342) in 1336, the question of the relation of the resurrection to the happiness of the departed is still an open one. The importance of our resurrection was stressed by Aquinas in the fact that he opens his consideration of eschatology in the *Summa theologica* with this issue.[7] And in his *Compendium* he taught that separation of soul and body is not natural; it happens to us because we have upset nature by sin, and therefore death has come upon us; but we shall in the eschaton receive our nature restored in the resurrection.[8]

The solemn constitution of Benedict XII in 1336, *Benedictus Deus*, put to rest by its papal authority the view that those who have died are in some sort of waiting room until the general resurrection takes place. His definition declared that those who die are "soon" judged and assigned to heaven or to hell, according to their state. Moreover, this constitution upholds the doctrine of *purgatory*, by declaring that those who are worth of the vision of God, but who are in need of some purification, will undergo such purification before entering the beatific vision of God.[9] This doctrine would find further dogmatic affirmation in the councils, like Florence and Trent.[10] This doctrine has not found acceptance among many Christians not in union with Rome. Professor Schwarz (b. 1939) has put purgatory among the "blind alleys" in eschatology, along with chiliasm and universalism.[11] The position of this modern Lutheran is, therefore, in accord with Luther (1483-1546) himself who rejected purgatory along with the doctrine of indulgences. The Greek Church, while not acknowledging purgatory as such, does hold memorial liturgies for the departed. Purgatory is often pictured as a temporary hell, with fire and torments similar to those of the damned. Purgatorial suffering is indeed true suffering, but we know almost nothing about its nature from the fonts of divine revelation.

An issue related to purgatory is *limbo*. The limbo of which we speak is the *limbo of children*, not the *limbo of the fathers*. This latter limbo ceased to be when our Savior ascended into heaven, and opened heaven's gates to the righteous. Before His ascension, all those who were among the saved, including Abraham, Isaac, Jacob, and the patriarchs, were excluded from the vision of God because of the power of sin, which took its origin in Adam. In His descent into Sheol (that is, the place of these holy persons, called "hell" in the creed), Christ broke the bonds of sin and death by virtue of His cross, and brought the joy of deliverance to these righteous ones, who had benefited in their days on earth by His grace anticipated.

The limbo of children refers to the everlasting lot of those who die without being justified by Christ, but also without any personal sin. Such are those who have not attained the use of reason, and who are not brought to the waters of baptism. The Decree for the Greeks at the Council of Florence in 1439 stated in part: "The souls of those who depart this life in actual mortal sin or in only the original sin, soon go down to hell, where they are punished with diverse sufferings."[12] This stated the matter in Augustinian language. Augustine had no doctrine of limbo; the infants who did not get baptized were therefore not predestined to glory. And hell was the place for all who did not rise up from the *massa damnata* through the power of Christ. The medieval theologians, however, argued that, since these unbaptized infants did not positively turn toward evil, it should be said that they suffer no positive punishments for evil deeds. They would, nevertheless, be deprived of the vision of God because of their unregenerate condition. Many such theologians even felt that these persons would not be made to grieve over the loss of the beatific vision, but would enjoy a "natural" happiness in their special state. This was what they meant when they spoke of limbo. The doctrine of the Council of Florence does not really condemn their view, since the statement of the council admits a diversity in the lot of those who go down to hell. Limbo, then, has long been taught as a "merciful" theological explanation of what happens to unbaptized infants.

Since the middle of the twentieth century, this doctrine has been considered by a number of writers as outdated and not really very merciful. Various attempts have been made to argue that such persons might actually have a path to Christ and His grace not known to us.[13] While theological discussion legitimately takes place, catechists are to continue to urge parents to provide for the divine life of baptismal grace for their children in accord with the traditional practice of the Church.[14]

As biblical studies began to emphasize the Hebraic nature of the written word of God, certain writers began to feel uneasy with the notion of "souls of the departed." They argued that the division of the human being into body and soul was a derivative of Greek philosophy, whose thinkers viewed human beings as a composite of *psyche-soma*. The Hebrew mentality, they argued, did not make room for a separated soul, no longer joined to the fleshly body. Thus, we encountered articles like this one in 1969: "Should we de-mythologize the separated soul?"[15] While this concern is surely worthy of theological investigation, one cannot lose sight of the teachings put forth by the magisterium about the state of those who have died, or who will die, before the second coming of Christ. Moreover, if we are to have our proper *identity* in the resurrection, then there must be a continuity between what we are now and what we shall be then. Perhaps this doctrine can be stated in better terms, and perhaps biblical theologians will find those better terms. But the terms must not render void the tradition.

Jesus used manifold parables to describe the kingdom of heaven both in its earthly and its glorified reality. The Second Vatican Council, after recalling that the Eucharist on earth is the foretaste of the heavenly banquet, described our faith in the consummation of the plan of God in Christ in these words: "Deformed by sin, the shape of this world is passing away; but we are taught that God is preparing a new dwelling place and a new earth where justice will abide. . . . After we have obeyed the Lord and in His spirit nurtured on earth the values of human dignity, brotherhood and freedom, and indeed all the good fruits of our nature and enterprise, we shall find them again, freed from stain, burnished and transfigured, when Christ hands over to the Father a kingdom eternal and universal, a kingdom of truth and life, of holiness and grace, of justice, love and peace. That kingdom is already present on this earth in mystery. When the Lord returns it will be brought into full flower."[16]

While our citizenship is in heaven and our eyes are fixed on the things that are above, we are told by the Fathers of the council not to walk with our heads in the clouds. "The expectation of a new earth must not weaken but rather stimulate our concern for cultivating this one, for it is here that the body of a new human family grows, a body which even now is able to foreshadow in some way the age which is to come. Hence, while earthly progress must be carefully distinguished from the growth of Christ's kingdom, such progress is of vital concern to the kingdom of God to the extent that it contributes to the better ordering of human society."[17]

Non-Traditional Eschatology

We can only indicate in the briefest way some of the main non-traditional explanations of eschatology. Further studies may be undertaken in the sources recommended.

Schweitzer's Eschatology. The beginning of the twentieth century brought with it one of the earliest of the non-traditional eschatologies. Albert Schweitzer (1875-1965), who was to achieve world renown, not only as a theologian, but also as an expert on Johann S. Bach (1685-1750) and as a missionary in Africa, put forth a theory that Jesus of Nazareth never intended to found a lasting Church. His intent was to proclaim a short-term movement with its own interim ethical code, that was to reach consummation in the imminent eschaton. Because He was mistaken in this belief, the Church, made up of His followers, had to adjust itself to the facts of life and form a community, which could not rely on the Gospel for its norm of conduct, since Jesus would have spoken differently had He known that the eschaton was not imminent. This position of Schweitzer's was in contradiction to that of many of the liberals of the Ritschlian school. The liberals had launched their quest for the "historical" Jesus, hoping to find behind the Christ of faith in the Gospels the true Jesus as He really was before the earthly Church transformed Him. They worked from a number of presuppositions, one of which was that Jesus would not have spoken in the grand style of apocalyptic literature. The vision of His coming on the clouds of heaven was added by the early Church. Jesus in His historical reality would have delivered His message about the fatherhood of God and the brotherhood of mankind, with its distinctive ethical norms. They sought to strip the image of Jesus of these so-called accretions, as one strips a piece of fruit of its pulp, to reveal the pit that lies hidden thereunder. The Catholic Modernist, Alfred Loisy (1857-1940), warned them that they were not stripping a fruit to expose the pit; they were peeling an onion, which would yield layer after layer, until this process should reveal, not a pit, but absolutely nothing! Schweitzer's own contention was, in short, that the liberals who were engaged in the quest for the historical Jesus had erred gravely in assuming that Jesus would have been alien to the eschatological statements in the Gospels. Rather, He would surely have been at home with those expressions; for He was a Jew of the first century, and His thought would have been that of a man of that era. From there, Schweitzer built his own theory about Jesus' eschatological expectations of an imminent eschaton, and the way in which that idea affected His teaching and conduct. Because Schweitzer *affirmed* the eschatological mind of Jesus, in opposition to the liberals who denied it, his eschatology gets the name of "consistent" or "thoroughgoing" eschatology.[18]

Non-Futuristic Eschatology. The "realized eschatology" of C.H. Dodd (1884-1973) is one of the best known of those systems that place the eschaton, not in some future age, but in the present time. According to Dodd, the final age of the world came in Jesus. His mysteries were the eschatological event. Dodd argued chiefly from the parables in which Jesus described the kingdom of heaven. In them Dodd saw the kingdom depicted as existing in the here and now. Hence, the title of his book, *Parables of the Kingdom.*[19]

Joachim Jeremias (b. 1900) reacting favorably to Dodd's general thought, has written a work on *The Parable of Jesus* which modifies Dodd's realized eschatology. It recognizes the presence of the eschatological kingdom in the present, but looks yet to the future for the final consummation. The kingdom is already here, but not yet consummated. His eschatology may be termed "inaugurated eschatology."

Still other writers, like Rudolph Bultmann (1884-1976), saw the eschaton in terms of one's own *authentic existence* in Christ. This kind of eschatology, based upon the philosophical underpinnings of Heidegger's existentialism, transforms eschatology into a kind of "finality" in the order of purpose and existence, rather than in the order of time.[20]

In conclusion of this discussion of non-traditional eschatologies, we must say that, while these theories have some positive values to contribute to the attitude that we Christians are to have toward the present age of the kingdom of God, they cannot fully supplant the traditional, futuristic eschatology. "Christian theology cannot exist without a future goal of history," wrote Professor Schwarz.[21] When we realize that the present Church is the pilgrim Church, and that the promise of resurrection and final victory over death and the power of hell remain unfulfilled, we cannot do otherwise than agree with this observation, and look ahead to the glorious day of Christ's coming for the second and final judgment.

Footnotes

1. *Sacrosanctum Concilium*, Liturgy, no. 8.
2. *Gaudium et Spes*, The Church Today, no. 18.
3. *Compendium* 2, 4.
4. *The City of God* 21, 9.
5. *Op. cit.* 143-155.
6. *Enchiridion* 10, 9.
7. Suppl. 69.
8. *Compendium* 1, 151-152.
9. *TCC* nos. 818-822.
10. DS nos. 1304, 1820.
11. *Op. cit.* 137-143.
12. DS no. 1304.

13. *See* G. Dyer, *Limbo: Unsettled Question*, New York, 1964, Sheed & Ward.
14. *See* Pope Pius XII, *Address to Midwives*, Oct. 29, 1951, no. 19; *see* also *CIC* c. 770.
15. J.M. Gonzalez-Ruiz, *Concilium* 5/1 (1969) 43-49.
16. *Gaudium et Spes* no. 39.
17. *Ibid.*
18. *See* Schweitzer's *Quest of the Historical Jesus* and H. Schwarz, *op. cit.* 79-83.
19. *See* also H. Schwarz, *op. cit.* 90-93.
20. *See* also H. Schwarz, *op. cit.* 83-88.
21. H. Schwarz, *op. cit.* 88.

PART 2
THE RESPONSE

MORAL THEOLOGY

INTRODUCTION

Part 1 of this book was concerned with God's call to the human race. The one and triune God created men and women to know Him, love Him and serve Him in this life and to be happy with Him forever in heaven. God calls men and women to share in a created way in the life of the Father, Son and Holy Spirit, a life that is lived already on this earth, but one that can be realized perfectly only in heaven. The friendship between God and man was interrupted by the rebellion of the parent of the human race against his Maker, a rebellion that is continued by Adam's sons and daughters. God intervened in human history to win the rebels back to Himself. He sent His only Son into the world as a sacrificial victim. The Son proclaimed the Father's forgiveness and called sinful human beings to conversion. He established the Church to continue the proclamation and designated the sacraments as channels of divine life. To those who respond to the call delivered by His Son and His Church God promises a kingdom. In that kingdom we hope to be filled completely by the glory of God as He wipes away every tear from our eyes, when we shall see Him just as He is and when we shall be like Him for all eternity and praise Him unceasingly through Christ our Lord.[1] Rebirth in water and the Holy Spirit engenders a new kind of life which is lived through Christ and in Christ and is crowned by admission into the everlasting kingdom of God.[2]

A clear conception of the goal of life is vitally important, for it determines how one lives. One who believes that God calls human beings to eternal hapiness will obviously live differently than one who believes that death is the end of existence, that the present life affords the only opportunity for happiness.

Thomas Aquinas (1225-74) presented the study of moral teaching as the study of man as the image of God.[3] Having studied God, the divine exemplar of man, Thomas turned to man, the image of God. Man is the image of God insofar as he is an intellectual being and has dominion over his actions. We may conclude that the life to which God calls man consists in a life that will perfect the divine image in man. In other words, as human beings respond to God's call, the divine image in them grows more perfect. Human beings most perfectly reflect the image of God by the practice of charity. This idea refers to the fact that God *is* love (Jn 4:8). Human beings cannot actually reflect God by *being* love, but they can reflect God's image by *living* a life of love.

The fact that God calls human beings to fellowship with Him and eternal happiness implies that they have the capacity to respond to the divine invitation. Aquinas stated that adults achieve the possession of God through good works, that is, through a life of charity.[4] This is also the clear teaching of Sacred Scripture and the Church. In the comprehensive sense it is correct to say that God's call to man is a call to a life of charity. Hence, there is a need of good works if men and women are to achieve their happiness. These good works are human acts. Consequently, it is necessary to study human acts in order to know which ones lead to happiness and which ones do not.[5] Part 2 of this book is concerned with human acts, with a person's response—positive or negative—to God's call. These human acts are considered first in general and then in particular.

Whereas Part 1 of this book was concerned with dogmatic theology, Part 2 is concerned with moral theology. Moral theology deals with the goal of life and the means to achieve it. Moral theology takes a general view of these means including freedom, responsibility, conscience, law and virtue; and it is concerned with the details of day-to-day living, that is, with the application of general principles to particular, concrete decisions and intentions. As part of theology, moral theology is the study of God who is the goal of life and calls men and women to a virtuous life. Moral theology uses the theological tools of revelation and reason. Therefore, moral theology is not the same as faith, which accepts the revealed truths of God by an act of belief; nor is it the same as moral philosophy which attempts to describe the norms of human conduct on the basis of reason alone. Moral theology uses both revelation and reason.

The infallible teaching authority of the Church extends to matters of faith and morals. According to the Second Vatican Council, the Pope can teach infallibly in his capacity as the supreme teacher of the faithful. The bishops can teach infallibly when they are gathered in an ecumenical council or even when they are dispersed throughout the world but reach a consensus about a revealed doctrine or a teaching inextricably bound up with a revealed doctrine.[6] Generally, the bishops teach morality infallibly as they are dispersed throughout the world. In this way, for example, they teach the specific demands of the Ten Commandments, such as the prohibition of blasphemy, adultery, and theft. The teaching of the bishops is known from their provincial councils, pastoral letters and catechisms, and from the writings of theologians which they have approved.[7]

A History of Moral Theology

Bibliography: T. Slater, S.J., *A Short History of Moral Theology*, New York, 1909, Benziger; *NCE, Moral Theology, History of*, 9, 1117-1123; F. Murphy, *Moral Teaching in the Primitive Church*, New York, 1968, Paulist Press; B. Häring, C.SS.R., *The Law of Christ*, Paramus, 1966, The Newman Press, 1, 3-33; T. O'Connell, *Principles for a Catholic Morality*, New York, 1978, The Seabury Press, 10-19. *See* also *Notes on Moral Theology* appearing regularly in *TS* for contemporary trends.

The Bible approaches ethical questions from several standpoints. The Old Testament spoke of God's *covenant* with His people whereby Yahweh imposed certain duties on the Israelites and in turn promised to be their God (Jr 24:7; Ezr 11:20). Jesus established a new covenant by shedding His blood (Mt 26; Mk 14; Lk 22; 1 Cor 11). The central theme of Jesus' preaching was the *kingdom of God*, a kingdom of joy, life, and light (Mt 25:21; Mk 9:42; Lk 16:8). The kingdom is essentially a gift of God; but it also entails personal responsibility—basically, repentance and belief (Mk 1:15). *Repentance* signifies a total transformation of one's being, total conformity to the will of the Father (Mt 7:21-23), and the cessation of sinful acts so that one becomes a new creature. Jesus gathered disciples around Himself. *Discipleship* means willingness to abandon father and mother, son and daughter, and to take up one's cross and lose one's life in following Jesus (Mt 10:37-38; Lk 14:26-27), In the Sermon on the Mount, Jesus appears as a new Moses. He came to fulfill the *law*, not to abolish it (Mt 5:17-19); but He internalizes it. The great commandment of the law is *love*—love of God above all else and love of neighbor as oneself (Dt 6:5; Mt 22:34-40; etc.).

The disciples of Jesus continued His preaching; indeed, Jesus became the object of their preaching. They explained the significance of Jesus' life, death, and resurrection from human salvation. Paul, especially, answered the questions and dealt with the problems of converts to Christianity who had to live in the midst of pagan neighbors.

During the patristic period, the Apostolic Fathers of the first and early second centuries—Clement of Rome, Ignatius of Antioch, Polycarp, and others—wrote moral treatises dealing with such practical matters as the imitation of Christ and one's obligations to family and society. The Apologists of the second century—Justin Martyr, Irenaeus, and others—attacked pagan superstition and immorality and defended the Christian way of life. Irenaeus was concerned with human freedom. Man is free, he wrote, because he was created in the image of God; but his eternal existence depends upon his moral conduct.[8] Irenaeus seemed to think that the soul was not immortal independently of its moral conduct.[9] The Latin and Greek Fathers of the third century, including Tertullian, Cyprian, Hippolytus, Clement of Alexandria, and Origen, analyzed Christian conduct as an expression of the image of God and the imitation of Christ. They specified the obligations of Christians as patience, fasting, almsgiving, justice, and so on. Some believe that the first systematic exposition of Christian moral teaching is to be found in Clement's two works, *The Tutor*, and *The Stromata (Carpets)*.[10] The third book of Origen's *The First Principles* is a discussion of free will and responsibility and gives an outline of moral theology.

The Eastern Fathers of the fourth century stressed the divinization of man through cooperation with the Holy Spirit. Basil, Gregory of Nyssa, and John Chrysostom spoke about the practical duties of the laity, monks, and priests. In the West about the same time, Ambrose wrote his *De officiis* for the clergy of Milan. It is modelled on Cicero's *De officiis* and is one of the first comprehensive presentations of Christian ethics. Augustine of Hippo is perhaps the greatest moral theologian of all. He did not compose a systematic treatise on moral theology, but he did write about all those subjects of fundamental importance to the study, namely, grace, law, freedom, love, and works. In addition, he dealt with such specific subjects as marriage, riches, virginity, and lying. Pope Gregory the Great (590-604), with his books, *Liber regulae pastoralis, Moralis in Job*, and *Dialogi*, influenced Christian ethical thought for centuries afterwards. Finally, the *Expositio* of John Damascene (675-749), the last of the great Fathers, was important in the medieval period for its dogmatic and moral teaching.

The period from 600 to 1200 was not a particularly creative one for moral theology. The "penitentials" spread from Ireland and the British Isles throughout a large part of Europe. The penitentials were lists of sins together with the appropriate penances to be imposed by confessors. One must study the sermons and decrees of Popes, councils, and bishops for a more comprehensive view of the moral theology of the period.

In the twelfth and thirteenth centuries there was a revival of learning through he rise of the great European universities. The canonists—among them, Gratian, the author of the famous *Decretum* (1140)—dealt with such practical matters as laws and contracts, sins, marriage, and the theology of penance. Peter Lombard's *Book of Sentences* (completed 1157-58) was a synthesis of dogmatic and moral theology and became the textbook of the theological schools for four centuries. The Franciscan school—Alexander of Hales, Bonaventure, and Duns Scotus—affirmed the primacy of the will and charity in moral theology. Thomas Aquinas devoted the second part of his theological synthesis, the *Summa Theologica*, to moral theology. Thomas understood moral theology to be the science which directs human beings to their final end and teaches them how to enhance the divine image in themselves and conform themselves to Christ, our way to God.

In the fourteenth century, William of Ockham stressed the unique value of the individual; but he understood good and evil to be totally dependent upon the divine will—good is good and evil is evil only because God wills it so. In the sixteenth century, there was a revival of Thomistic studies with the Dominicans, Cajetan, de Vitoria, and Banez, and the Jesuits, Vasquez and Suarez. The study of justice and the rights of nations was cultivated. The norms of the Council of Trent (1545-63) for the sacrament of penance spurred the composition of manuals devoted to casuistry for the benefit of confessors. This was a development of profound significance. Moral theology was more clearly distinguished from dogmatic theology and, in a certain sense, began to assume an independent existence.

In the seventeenth and eighteenth centuries, there were sharp disputes about laxism, probabilism, probabiliorism, and rigorism. These are reflex principles used to solve cases of conscience. The Church condemned both the laxist and rigorist positions. Among the greatest moral theologians of the period were the Carmelites of Salamanca who composed the *Cursus Theologiae Moralis* (1665-1724) and Alphonso Liguori (1696-1787) whose work, *Theologia Moralis* (1948) went through more than seventy editions. The Church regards the opinions of the saint as practically reliable.[11] In the nineteenth century, Austrian and German theologians, such as John Sailer and John Hirscher, strove once more for a synthesis of dogmatic and moral theology. They reexamined the biblical basis of moral theology and treated it not only as a science for confessors but also as a call to Christian perfection.[12]

Contemporary moral theologians are concerned with a variety of matters. Many of these matters are objects of perennial concern; but many of them have come to the fore because the human race to a greater extent than ever before is living in a society which is industrial, urban, scientific, medically-advanced, politically-sophisticated, and international. Among the subjects studied by contemporary moral theologians one may mention (without any logical order): secularization and pluralism, the encyclical *Humanae vitae*, the family, peace and war, morality and the competence of the magisterium, political protest, genetic engineering, conscientious objection, pacifism, abortion, sterilization, artificial insemination, norms and consequences, the behavioral sciences, divorce and remarriage, theology and liberation, homosexuality, death and dying, premarital sexual relations, the socio-political role of the Church, natural law, pluralism in moral theology, the transplantation of organs, bioethics, human rights, social justice, the rights of conscience, public policy, and the principle of double effect.[13]

To further the progress of moral theology, the Second Vatican Council made this recommendation: "Let the theological disciplines be renewed through a more living contact with the mystery of Christ and the history of salvation. Special care must be given to the development of moral theology. Its scientific exposition, nourished more on the teaching of the Bible, should shed light on the loftiness of the calling of the faithful in Christ and the obligation that is theirs of bearing fruit in charity for the life of the world.''[14]

Footnotes

1. See *The Sacramentary*, New York, 1974, Catholic Book Publ. Co.; Euch. Prayer 3, comm. for a deceased person.
2. *Ibid.*, Mass for the Conferral of Baptism, 830-831.
3. *ST* 1a2ae. Prol.
4. *ST* 1a2ae.5.7.
5. *ST* 1a2ae.6. Introd.
6. *Lumen Gentium* no. 25.
7. For contrary opinion *see* T. O'Connell, *Principles for a Catholic Morality*, New York, 1978, The Seabury Press, 95-96.
8. *Against Heresies* 5, 9, 1.
9. *Ibid.* 2, 34, 3.
10. B. Häring, *op. cit.* 6.
11. DS 2725-2727.
12. J. Sailer, *Handbuch der christlichen Moral* 1817; J. Hirsher, *Die christliche Moral* 1835.
13. *See* the subjects treated during the last decade in the ''Notes on Moral Theology'' published regularly in *TS*.
14. *Optatam Totius* no. 16.

Chapter 15

HUMAN ACTS

Bibliography: *DB, Work*, 941-942; *DBT, Responsibility* 491-492; *JBC,* see the index for *Works*; R. Schnackenburg, *Moral Teaching of the New Testament*, New York, 1965, Herder and Herder; K. Schelkle, *Theology of the New Testament, Morality*, Collegeville, 1973, The Liturgical Press, 3; J. Houlden, *Ethics and the New Testament*, Baltimore, 1973, Penguin Books; *ST* 1a2ae.6-48; F. Connell, C.SS.R., *Outlines of Moral Theology*, Milwaukee, 1958, Bruce Publ. Co., 13-26; J. Ford, S.J., and G. Kelly, S.J., *Contemporary Moral Theology*, Westminster, 1962, The Newman Press, 1; *NCE, Human Act*, 7, 206-209; B. Häring, C.SS.R., *The Law of Christ*, Paramus, 1966, The Newman Press, 1; *Idem, Free and Faithful in Christ*, New York, 1978, Seabury, 1; F. Böckle, *Fundamental Concepts of Moral Theology*, New York, 1968, Paulist Press, 29-44; *Idem, Fundamentalmoral*, Munich, 1977, Kösel; J. Schaller, *Our Emotions and the Moral Act*, Staten Island, 1968, Alba House; J. Fuchs, S.J., *Human Values and Christian Morality*, Dublin, 1970, Gill and Macmillan; C. Curran, *Themes in Fundamental Moral Theology*, Notre Dame, 1977, Univ. of Notre Dame Press; T. O'Connell, *Principles for a Catholic Morality*, New York, 1978, Seabury, 45-66; G. McCool (ed.), *A Rahner Reader*, New York, 1975, The Seabury Press, 245-270.

Men and women respond to God's call and achieve their eternal destiny by acting in a truly human way. A distinctively *human act* is one that is performed with knowledge and freedom, one for which a person is responsible. It is to be distinguished from an *act of man* which is performed without knowledge and freedom, an act such as sleepwalking or digestion.

The Teaching of the Church

Human freedom means that a person is responsible for his or her actions.[1] Human beings are required to obey the commandments of God because they have free will.[2] A deadly necessity would prevail i one were to deny the imputability of human acts and the existence of reward and punishment.[3] Even in the state of fallen nature a person remains free[4] and he or she is capable of performing naturally good works[5] without sinning mortally or venially.[6] To be sure, more than freedom alone is required for a good work.[7]

No one is good except through participation in the goodness of God.[8] A sin which is opposed to right reason is also an offense against God.[9] The Church has rejected the opinions of certain theologians known as "laxists"[10] as well as those of certain "rigorists" who require a supernatural motive for every morally good act.[11] Violence excuses a person from sin;[12] but fear does not make an act involuntary and take away reward and punishment.[13]

The Church also teaches that a work (natural or supernatural) becomes good by reason of its object and circumstances.[14] Those circumstances which change the moral species of an act must be declared in confession.[15] The end does not justify the means.[16] The external act has moral significance and is imputable.[17]

The Second Vatican Council had much to say about human responsibility and the dreedom which it presupposes. According to the council, "There is an increasing number of men and women who are conscious that they themselves are the authors and artisans of the culture of their community. . . . There is a similar growth in the sense of independence and responsibility. . . . We are witnesses of the birth of a new humanism, one in which man is defined first of all by his responsibility to his brothers and to history."[18] "A sense of the dignity of the human person has been impressing itself more and more deeply on the consciousness of our contemporaries. The demand is increasingly made that humans should act on their own judgment, enjoying and making use of a responsible freedom. . . . This demand for freedom in human society chiefly regards the quest for values proper to the human spirit."[19]

Sacred Scripture

One can pursue the biblical teaching about human activity by investigating such themes as "works," "liberty," "responsibility," and "reward."

Works. Sometimes the New Testament views the works of men and women (in the sense of deeds) with deep pessimism. They are deeds of darkness (Rm 13:12; Ep 5:11), deeds of the flesh (Gal 5:19), wicked deeds (Jn 3:19). Even the works of the law do not justify a person; only faith in Jesus Christ does (Rm 3:28; Gal 2:16). However, once a person has been justified, then he or she must perform the works of a Christian. The works of a Christian include the practice of good deeds (Gal 5:6; Jm 2:14-17) with purity of intention (Mt 5:16), the fulfillment of the two primary commandments (Mt 22:36-40), employing one's talents profitably (Mt 25:14-30), and building up the Church, the body of Christ (1 Cor 1:9; 15:58; Rm 14:20; Ph 1:6).

Liberty. The Bible gives no definition of liberty; but it does suppose that human beings are able to respond to God by a free choice. They are responsible for what they do. God's grace and man's free obedience are necessary for salvation. In the Old Testament liberty meant to be a free person rather than a slave. It also meant to be free of foreign domination. Some circles among the Israelites considered the monarchy to be a restriction upon their traditional freedom (1 S 8:11-18).

In the New Testament, the idea of liberty is to be found almost exclusively in the Pauline and Johannine writings. "Christ freed us for liberty" (Gal 5:1). The liberty for which Christ freed us is freedom from sin (Rm 6:18-23; Jn 8:31-36), freedom from death, the inevitable companion of sin (1 Cor 15:56-57), freedom from concupiscence (Rm 7:3-25), and freedom from the Jewish Law (Rm 7:3-6; Gal 4:21-31). No longer do the bonds of sin, death, concupiscence, and the Law impede the believer who is guided by the spirit (Gal 5:18). Led by the Spirit of God, believers are sons of God who have not received a spirit of slavery but a spirit of adoption (Rm 8:14-15). They live under a new law, the law of love. But liberty is not license that gives free rein to the flesh. Christians are to place themselves at one another's service (Gal 5:13-14). Paul made himself the slave of all (1 Cor 9:19); in this, however, he imitated Christ (1 Cor 11:1), the servant of all. In the Christian community all enjoy equal freedom through baptism (1 Cor 12:13). All are equally free in

Christ so that Christians are not distinguished by national, social, or racial characteristics (Gal 3:28). However, Christian freedom is not an excuse to foment revolution. Paul urged Christians to be content with their lot and to recognize legitimate authority (1 Cor 7:17-25). Still, the principle of freedom enunciated by Paul had political and social consequences of the highest order.

Responsibility.[20] The Bible holds human beings responsible for their actions. While God is good and creation is good, sin and death entered the world through one man (Rm 5:12). Man is partly but really responsible for the evil that is in the world. The Jewish Law made the Israelites conscious of their responsibility to God. It was a pedagogue given by God (Gal 3:24) instructing them what to do and what not to do. It confronted the Israelites with a choice for or against God. The pagans were confronted with the same responsible choice, for the demands of the law were written "in their hearts" (Rm 2:15). The prophets of Israel held prince and people responsible for the good or evil they had done. In effect, Nathan said to David, "Because you have done a wicked thing, the sword will not depart from your house" (1 S 12:10). Ezekiel wrote: "The virtuous man will be credited with his virtue; and the wicked man, with his wickedness" (Ezk 18:20). Israel had been exiled, the prophets said, because it had failed in its responsibility to God.

The confession of sins in the Bible is a confession of human guilt and an exoneration of God who is just: "Yours, Lord, the justice; ours the shame" (Dn 9:7). The prayer of repentance restates the conviction of Genesis that God is good and the sinner is responsible for evil. The first three chapters of Romans describe the depravity of the pagan world. It was the evil will of the pagan world that provoked the divine anger and abandonment. However, the Gospel revealed the justice of God (Rm 1:17). The Gospel is concerned with Jesus. Through Jesus, God offers man the gift of faith by which he can be saved. The sinner can achieve faith only through repentance and the realization of his responsibility.

Reward. The idea of reward and its antithesis, punishment, is prominent in the Bible. God is an equitable master: He does not fail to give each one what is due him (1 S 26:23; Pr 12:14; Is 59:18; etc.). God approves or disapproves the work of His servants. There is a conception of collective responsibility in the Bible. Each person is responsible for his own actions; yet, these actions have significance for the whole group. The obvious example of solidarity in punishment is the story of Adam's fall in Genesis 3; and the obvious example of solidarity in reward is the common participtaion in the salvific death and resurrection of Christ (Rm 5:15). Still, each person is responsible at every moment for his own destiny: if he is virtuous, he shall surely live; but if he is wicked, he shall surely die (Ex 18). Jesus and His apostles sustained the traditional teaching of Israel about reward and punishment. The believer will receive a reward for his works (Mt 16:27; Mk 9:41; etc.). At the last judgment, the Son of Man will sit on His throne. He will assign each one to heaven or hell according to his works (Mt 25:11-46).

The nature of the reward or punishment was clarified in the Bible only gradually. According to the Old Testament, at least for the most part, reward and punishment were confined to this life and ceased with death. A definitive teaching about retribution in the next life, while intimated in certain books of the Old Testament, came only with Christ.

Theological Reflection

A. The Essence and Division of Human Acts. Here we are concerned with those actions for which a person is responsible—those which proceed from reason and free will. The act of the will follows upon the recognition of a value by the intellect; for example, the intellect recognizes the value of jogging and so the will commands the act. The will is able to choose among created values precisely because they are limited; that is, they have both a good and a bad side. Thus, the will is able to choose among the various forms of exercise because they all have their advantages and disadvantages.

Elicited human actions are completed in the will itself. An act of love for God is an elicited human act. *Commanded* human actions originate in the will and are completed by another human faculty. Jogging is a commanded human act. Some human actions are internal while others are external. An *internal* human act, such as an act of the intellect or will, involves only the person's spiritual nature. An *external* human act, such as eating or writing, involves a person's bodily organs functioning under the direction of the will. An external human act is always a commanded act. An internal human act can either be elicited (if it proceeds immediately from the will) or commanded (such as an act of faith emanating from the intellect at the command of the will). The internal human act especially is the bearer of responsibility. Decision rests with it.

A human act is a voluntary act; that is, it is elicited or commanded by the will. In contrast to what is voluntary (the *voluntarium*), there is that which is merely wished (the *volitum*) but not effected by the will. If someone helps my friend when I cannot, the help that is given is wished but not voluntary on my part. A further distinction: something can be fully or imperfectly voluntary. It is *fully* voluntary if it follows upon clear reflection and full consent of the will. It is *imperfectly* voluntary if either reflection or consent is partially lacking. Thus, an injury inflicted on another may be perfectly or imperfectly voluntary according to the degree of reflection and consent involved. A final distinction of great importance: something can be directly or indirectly voluntary. Something is *directly* voluntary when it is intended immediately and for itself; for example, a theft is directly voluntary for a thief. Something is *indirectly* voluntary (or voluntary in cause) when one foresees it without intending it as a side effect of what is directly voluntary. An accident caused by a drunken driver is indirectly voluntary on his part if he foresaw it while he was still sober. This distinction is of great importance for the evaluation of actions which have a twofold effect, one that is good and one that is evil. The discussion of this point will be taken up later.

B. Impediments to Human Activity. Impediments to human activity are those factors which eliminate or diminish a person's responsibility for what he or she does. They do so by excluding or limiting one's knowledge and freedom in acting. Aquinas listed four classical impediments to human activity—force, fear, passion and ignorance.[21] The first two originate outside a person; the other two, from within.

Force is the external violence which compels a person to do something to which he or she is opposed internally. An exterior act performed against one's will is not a human act. A rapist uses force upon his victim. A person can be forced to drink an excessive amount of intoxicating liquor. In neither case is the victim responsible for what happens. What happens is involuntary on the victim's part.

Fear arises from the threat of an impending future evil. If the fear is so great that it deprives a person of the capacity to think clearly and make a free decision, then he or she is not responsible for what happens. In her fear, a woman may go so far as to kill a potential rapist without realizing what she is doing. Ordinarily, however, fear only diminishes knowledge and freedom without eliminating responsibility for one's actions. If I have the capacity to resist pressure and do not use it, then I am morally responsible. For example, I am not allowed to renounce my allegiance to Christ even under the threat of persecution. One other thing must be said: it is a principle recognized by ecclesiastical authorities that fear excuses a person from observing the positive laws of the Church.

Technically, a *passion* is something common to human beings and other animals. It is human (in men and women) to the extent that it is under the control of reason and free will.[22] Often, the term, passion, refers to an intense feeling or emotion such as anger, hatred, envy, and sexual desire. It is not likely that a passion can be so intense as to absolve a person of responsibility completely; but it can diminish it.

Ignorance, in the technical sense, is a lack of knowledge which a person should have. A lawyer who is ignorant of the law is ignorant in the technical sense, but not so if he or she knows nothing about medicine. Ignorance is *inculpable* if it cannot be dispelled despite one's god will. Obviously, inculpable or invincible ignorance renders an act involuntary, for one cannot be held responsible for what is inculpably unknown. A motorist who strikes down a child running into the street between parked cars is inculpably ingorant of the child's presence and is not responsible for injuring the child. Ignorance is *culpable*, however, if it could have been dispelled in the circumstances. A confessor who gives the wrong advice to a penitent is responsible for the mischief that follows. To be sure, his responsibility is diminished to some degree by his lack of knowledge. From a moral standpoint inadvertence is equivalent to ignorance.

Of course, there are other factors too which influence responsibility—one's personality, acquired habits, prejudices, and degree of mental health. Personality, in this context, is the total of an individual's behavioral and emotional characteristics. Behavioral psychology emphasizes the role of learning in personality development. Psychoanalysis emphasizes unconscious levels of motivation and stresses the importance of early childhood experiences in determining mature personality. Habits are acquired by the frequent repetition of certain acts. Habits lend facility to the performance of these acts whether they be good or evil. Prejudice is a preconceived judgment or opinion. It leads one to judge or act without just grounds or sufficient knowledge. Thus it can create an irrational state of hostility toward an individual or group. Finally, neurotic and psychotic states, obsessions, and feelings of guilt impair one's mental health. Insofar as these factors limit awareness and freedom, they limit truly human activity and responsibility.

C. The Morality of Human Acts. Human conduct is marked by freedom. To the extent that human beings freely conform to the order established by God, they act rightly; to the extent that they do not, they act wrongly. The order established by God is the norm of human conduct. Morality is the transcendental relationship of a human act to the divine order. A transcecendental relationship is one that is inherent in the act itself. The relationship can be one of conformity or disconformity to the norm. Against this background, a thing is good or bad when it acts in accordance with, or contrary to, its God-given nature. An apple tree is a good apple tree when it produces apples; it is a bad apple tree when it does not. A person is a good person or a bad person when he or she acts in accordance with, or contrary to, human nature and God's purposes for it. Of course, the norm of human conduct is human nature considered not only in itself, but also in its essential relationship to its origin and its environment. Man does well when he reverences every being in its essence, when he "allows to every being its authentic form of realization."[23] Goodness, then, is something more than having a good intention. It is something grounded in being itself.

The created order established by God has been freely willed by Him. Out of an infinite number of possibilities, He has freely chosen the one that exists. When I freely submit to this order, when I act in accordance with the essence of the things chosen by God, I am obedient to the personal God. When I do what is good, I do the will of God and express my love for Him.

Those who analyze morality in this way speak of the nature of God as the *remote* norm of morality. It is the efficient cause and prototype of human nature which is the *proximate* norm of morality. Whatever is in conformity with human nature is necessarily in conformity with the divine nature.

According to the conception of morality explained in the preceding paragraphs, some actions are good or bad by their very nature. These are commanded because they are good and forbidden because they are bad. By their very nature, reverence for one's parents is a good act while adultery is a bad act. However, there are other actions which are good because they are commanded and bad because they are forbidden. These are actions which are commanded or forbidden by positive legislation whether the legislator be divine or human. The observance of a specific speed limit by a motorist is a good act because it has been commanded by a civil authority. Smuggling is a bad act because it has been forbidden by a civil authority. Some ethicists (known as positivists) maintain that *all* actions are good or bad simply because they have been sanctioned or forbidden by a human legislator. According to this idea, no actions are right or wrong in themselves. Theoretically, any action which is forbidden at one moment could be sanctioned at another moment by a competent human legislator.

D. The Sources of Morality. In this section we continue the discussion begun in the preceding section. Morality means the conformity or nonconformity of a human action to its norm. The norm of human action is the order established by God together with human nature which reflects that order. To determine whether an individual human action is or is not conformable to the norm of morality, one must consider three elements (or sources of morality): the object of the act, its circumstances, and the intention of the agent.

By the *object* of the act we mean that to which the act naturally tends before all else. For example, the object of eating is to sustain life; the object of stealing is to take what belongs to another. If the object conforms to the norm of morality (as in the case of eating), the object is good; if it does not conform to the norm of morality (as in the case of stealing), it is evil. If the object implies neither conformity nor nonconformity to the norm of morality, it is said to be indifferent without being good or evil. For example, it is a matter of indifference whether a man wears a pair of black shoes or a pair of brown shoes. The morality of such an act is then determined by the circumstances that surround it and the intention of the agent.

The *circumstances* give an added moral dimension to an action already morally specified by its object. The circumstances of an action may be determined by the answers to such questions as, Who did this? Where? By what means? When? Why? To what extent? How much? For example, the gravity of a theft is increased when a large, rather than a small, amount is stolen. Such a circumstance can change a venial to a mortal sin if the amount stolen is sufficiently large although the act remains a sin of theft. Such a circumstance is said to alter the *theological* species of the sin. But some circumstances alter the *moral* species of the sin by violating still another virtue or commandment. For example, an unmarried person who commits adultery with a married person sins against both chastity and justice. The Council of Trent (1545-63) obliged sinners who approached the sacrament of penance to confess those circumstances which change the species of a sin. Only then can the confessor really know how the penitent has sinned.

Actually, the *intention* of the agent is one of the circumstances of a human act, but it is singled out because it has a very important bearing upon such an act. The intention of the agent is the reason he or she acts. The intention of the agent (the *finis operantis*) may coincide with the object of the act (the *finis operis*) or it may not. For instance, I may eat simply to sustain my strength or I may eat simply to pass the time of day even though I do not need the food.

To be truly good, a human act must be good in every respect[24]—in its object, circumstances, and purpose. In other words, any failure or defect vitiates the moral goodness of an action. The reason is that moral goodness consists in meeting a norm and the norm must be met in every respect. Thus, doctors and lawyers who do not meet all the standards of the medical and legal professions are not good doctors and lawyers. It follows from what has been said that a good intention does not justify a bad means. I may not murder in order to help a friend. Furthermore, an evil intention vitiates an otherwise good act. If I help a poor person out of pride, my act ceases to be a good act (Mt 6:1-4).

Commonly theologians teach that every human act is either good or bad. Even though the object of the act (the *finis operis*) may be morally indifferent, such as the act of walking, the intention of the agent (the *finis operantis*) will be either good or bad; and this will make the act good or bad.

Situation Ethics and Moral Absolutes. This subject is related to the discussion about the sources of morality. Situation ethics is a system of thought which denies the absoluteness of moral principles. There are many variations of this system, some of which are atheistic, although many Christians teach and practice some form of situation ethics. Sometimes this system is called "The New Morality" or "Existential Morality.'' Some forms of situation etchics deny that there are any universal principles of morality. Others admit the existence of universal principles but allow for exceptional cases in which one is not bound to follow the principles. Others admit only one universal principle: ''Do the loving thing.'' The basis of situation ethics is an exaggeration of the importance of circumstances and intention in determining the morality of a human act.

Unquestionably, circumstances and intention must be taken into account in assessing the morality of an act. However, Catholic moral teaching objects to situation ethics because it does not admit that some actions are always good and some are always evil. Situation ethics is prepared to admit that certain acts which are generally ''evil'' may in some circumstances, particularly because of a good intention, become good. Situation ethics does not say merely that a person is excused from subjective culpability because of a good intention, but that the evil act becomes in reality a good one.

In contrast to this idea, the Catholic bishop of the United States stated: ''The Christian must know that there are moral values which are absolute and never to be disregarded or violated by anyone in any situation. Fidelity to them may require heroism of the sort which we see in the lives of the saints and the deaths of the martyrs.''[25] The reason for the permanence of these values is that there is something constant about human nature and about the call which God addresses to all men and women to serve Him in certain determined ways. As a result, there are moral values which are permanent and the moral norms which flow from these values are also permanently valid.

Some, like Karl Barth, the Swiss theologian, deny the existence of moral absolutes on the grounds of God's sovereign will and absolute freedom. Obedience to God, they say, can transform an evil deed into a good one. They point especially to God's demand for the sacrifice of the innocent Isaac (Gn 22). Such a position seems to be similar to that of William of Ockham in the fourteenth century who held that good is good and evil is evil only because God wills it so. In other words, God Himself is bound by no norm and can make conflicting demands upon individuals. However, according to the view of morality taken in these pages, God is bound by His own nature so that He cannot act arbitrarily in making demands upon His creatures. The chapter in Genesis which deals with the sacrifice of Isaac is really a condemnation of human sacrifice (Eichrodt). Aquinas taught that the ten commandemtns are moral absolutes, although he was prepared to say that legitimate authority must determine in certain instances whether this or that is murder or theft or adultery or not.[26] Häring maintains that everyone, except certain extremists, recognizes instances of moral absolutes, for example, the prohibition against blasphemy, rape, sexual promiscuity, cruel punishment of children, and torture.[27]

Fundamental Option. Many modern authors approach the matter of morality and intention from the viewpoint of what is called the "fundamental option" in one's life. This refers to the ultimate or basic determination which a person makes concerning his or her life, namely, the gift or refusal of self in love to God. The basic self-determination (fundamental option) should not be thought of as a separate act by which one directs his or her life toward God or away from Him. The direction of life takes place *in* the acts one performs because we live in and by our actions. "The various free moral acts are accordingly a constitutive element of self-realization in basic freedom, but at the same time they are also—at least in themselves—a sign of this realization."[28] One's motive or option is discernible from the way one actually *lives*. One must not get the idea that the acceptance or adoption of a fundamental option sets one in a rigid pattern from which it is impossible to depart.

A *Declaration on Sexual Ethics* issued by the Sacred Congregation for the Teaching of the Faith in 1975 also understood the fundamental option to be that which ultimately determines a person's moral disposition. The declaration notes that the fundamental option can be completely changed by particular acts, especially when the groundwork for a change has been prepared by previous and more superficial acts.[29] Hence, a single act of adultery can change one's fundamental option; but it often happens that lesser infidelities have prepared the way. It is difficult to say whether or not a person can change his or her fundamental option frequently or easily. A person who has been guilty of adultery might repent immediately. It must be noted further that each act of adultery following upon an initial act which determined one's fundamental option has the character of a mortal sin which must be declared in confession. Each sin is a serious reaffirmation of one's definite stance against God.

E. Actions and Their Effects. In this chapter we are concerned with human actions. A human act is one that is performed with knowledge and freedom, one for which a person is responsible. To what degree, however, is a person responsible for the *effects* of his or her actions? It must be said, first of all, that an individual is totally responsible for the *directly-willed* effects of an action. Thus, an arsonist who sets fire to a house with the intention of killing the inhabitants is also a murderer. Secondly, an individual is responsible for the *indirectly-willed* effects of an action in certain circumstances. An arsonist is a murderer even if he wished only to burn down a house without intending to kill the inhabitants, provided, of course, that he knew they were inside the building. He could and should have avoided the death of his victims. A third conclusion: under certain conditions an individual may perform an act which has a double effect—one good and one evil; otherwise, human life would be unbearable. Thus, a surgeon may remove a pregnant woman's cancerous womb even though the operation means the death of the fetus. The surgical act has a twofold effect—the curing of the mother and the death of the child. Such an act is permissible because four conditions are met: 1) The action is morally good or at least morally indifferent by its nature. (The removal of a cancerous womb is a morally good act.) 2) The bad effect is only permitted; it is not willed in itself. 3) The bad effect is not the means of achieving the good effect. We may not do evil in order to do good. (The death of the child is not the means of saving the mother's life.) 4) Finally, there is a sufficient reason to compensate for the evil effect. (The life of the mother compensates for the death of the child.)

F. The Merit of Human Acs. According to the Scriptures, God repays each one for what he has done—eternal life to those who do right and wrath to those who are disobedient (Rm 2:6). Or as 1 Peter (1:17) puts it: The Father judges each one justly on the basis of his actions. Merit is the quality of a good work which renders it worthy of a reward. A naturally good work deserves a natural reward while a supernaturally good work deserves a supernatural reward. A supernaturally good work is one performed by a person who has been born again through God's grace given in Jesus Christ. Such a work, according to the Council of Trent,[30] merits an increase of grace and eternal life. Christ merited rebirth and divine life for others. On the basis of His merits, we are able to merit for ourselves by our good actions.

Footnotes

1. DS 3245.
2. DS 227, 245.
3. DS 283.
4. DS 1555.
5. DS 1557.
6. DS 1575.
7. DS 725.
8. DS 240.
9. DS 2291.
10. DS 2101-2167.
11. DS 1925, 1934-38, 2307-2313, 2444-2459.
12. DS 2715, 2758, 3634, 3718.
13. DS 1678, 1705, 2070, etc.
14. DS 1962.
15. DS 1681, 1707.
16. DS 815, 1254, 1998, 3684.
17. DS 733, 739, 966-969, 2240.
18. *Gaudium et Spes* no. 55.
19. *Dignitatis Humanae* no. 1.
20. *See DBT, Responsibility* 491-492.
21. *ST* 1a2ae.6.
22. *ST* 1a2ae.6. Introd.
23. J. Pieper. Quoted by Böckle, *op. cit.* 36.
24. *Bonum ex integra cause, malum ex quocumque defectu*: Good when whole, evil whenever defective.
25. NCCB *Basic Teachings for Catholic Religious Education*, Washington, 1973, U.S.C.C., no. 17.
26. *ST* 1a2ae.100.8c et ad 3.
27. B. Häring, *Free and Faithful in Christ* 364.
28. J. Fuchs, *op. cit.* 99.
29. No. 10.
30. *TCC* no. 769.

Chapter 16

LAW

Bibliography: *DB, Law*, 495-501; *DBT, Law*, 301-308; *NCE, Law*, 8, 545-565; *JBC, Law, (see* the index); J. McKenzie, *The Power and the Wisdom*, Milwaukee, 1965, The Bruce Publ. Co., 213-232; *ST* 1a2ae.90-108; W. Farrell, O.P., *A Companion to the Summa*, New York, 1938, Sheed & Ward, 2, 365-389; F. Connell, *Outlines of Moral Theology*, Milwaukee, 1958, The Bruce Publ. Co., 27-37; J. Fuchs, S.J., *Natural Law*, New York, 1965, Sheed & Ward; B. Häring, C.SS.R., *The Law of Christ*, Paramus, 1966, The Newman Press, 1, 227-285; *Idem, Free and Faithful in Christ*, New York, 1978, The Seabury Press, 1. 302-377; F. Böckle, *Fundamental Concepts of Moral Theology*, New York, 1967, The Paulist Press, 45-67; C. Curran, *Themes in Fundamental Moral Theology*, Notre Dame, 1977, Univ. of Notre Dame Press, 27-98; T. O'Connell, *Principles for a Catholic Morality*, New York, 1978, The Seabury Press, 117-195.

Morality consists in the conformity or noncomformity of a human action to the norm of conduct. The ultimate or remote norm of conduct is the nature of God and the order established by Him. The proximate norm of human conduct is human nature which has been created and redeemed by God. These norms confront, and are made known to, human beings in terms of moral law and conscience. The former is said to be the *objective* norm of conduct; the latter, the *subjective* norm. In this chapter we are concerned with moral law; in the next one, with conscience.

The Teaching of the Church

Eternal law is the eternal plan of the creator.[1] This law is the foundation of human laws dealing with matters that are good or evil by their very nature.[2] Eternal law is the principle of all right.[3] Natural law is the eternal law of God inscribed in the hearts of men. Natural law commands what is right and forbids what is wrong.[4] It is a reality and can be known.[5] The principal rights of human beings derive their validity from the natural law.[6] These rights are enumerated in Pope John XXIII's *Pacem in Terris*.[7] Naturalism obscures the idea of right.[8] The Church has rejected the ideas that moral laws do not need the divine law for their foundation,[9] that the state is the source and origin of all rights,[10] that the will of the people is the supreme law.[11] Human law plays the same role in society that natural law plays in the lives of individuals. Human law in the proper sense refers to the ordinances of civil authority regulating matters not immediately determined by natural law.[12] Christ is not only a redeemer, but He is also a legislator.[13] Ecclesiastical and civil authority comes immediately from God.[14]

According to the Second Vatican Council, "the highest norm of human life is the divine law—eternal, objective, and universal—whereby God orders, directs, and governs the entire universe and all the ways of the human community by a plan conceived in wisdom and love. Man has been made to participate in this law with the result that, under the gentile disposition of divine providence, he can come to perceive ever more fully the truth that is unchanging. . . . On his part, man perceives and acknowledges the imperative of the divine law through the mediation of conscience. In all his activity a man is bound to follow his conscience in order that he may come to God, the end and purpose of life."[15] The Council also encouraged obedience to just civil laws.[16]

Sacred Scripture

Old Testament. The Laws of the Israelites were contained mostly in collections, sometimes called "codes." Possibly the earliest collection is the decalogue found in Ex 20 and Dt 5. According to Hebrew tradition, God gave these commandments to Moses on Mt. Sinai. The Code of the Covenant (Ex 20:22-23:33) contains additional laws about the ownership of slaves and property. The Yahwist ritual decalogue of Ex 34:17-27 has to do with images, festivals, and offerings. The Deuteronomic Code (Dt

12-26) is a detailed exposition of the customary law of the Israelites. It is hortatory rather than imperative. The Holiness Code of Lv 17-26 contains no civil or criminal laws but is entirely religious and cultic. Finally, the Priestly Code is to be found in various places of the Pentateuch. It too is a collection of cultic-ritual laws.

According to the Hebrew mind, these collections of laws manifested the will of Yahweh for His people as mediated by Moses. The *Torah* or law was closely connected with the covenant. Yahweh elected Israel as His chosen people, and He joined certain promises to His election. If the Israelites were to be the beneficiaries of these promises, they had to obey the law given through Moses. The law was inextricably bound up with the covenant. The law was a sacred obligation. The fate of society and the individual was thought to be determined by their attitude toward the law. The priests were, *ex officio*, the custodians and specialists of the Torah. Indeed, the word, Torah, probably signifies the law as the revelation of Yahweh given through the priests. The prophets recognized the authority of the Torah and rebuked the people when they violated it (Ho 4:6; Ezk 22:26). After the exile, the Jews placed the Torah at the center of their life. The law was considered to be wisdom and to contain all knowledge, divine and human. The Pharisees developed an oral law to make the violation of the written law more difficult. Still, the prophets anticipated a new covenant and a new law (Jr 31:31-33). Men's hearts would be changed and they would finally come to obey the laws and ordinances of God (Ezk 36:26-27).

New Testament. According to the Synoptic Gospels, Jesus Himself observed the Torah or written law, although He rejected the oral law of the Pharisees (Mt 15; Mk 7). Jesus had come to fulfill the law and not to abolish it; and whoever fulfills and teaches the commandments of the law shall be great in the kingdom of God (Mt 5:17-20). One is saved by keeping the commandments of the decalogue (Mt 19:16-19; Mk 10:17-19; Lk 18:18-20). Jesus emphasized the significance of one's interior disposition (Mt 5:27-28); and He reduced all the commandments of the law to the twofold commandment of love (Mt 22:34-40; Mk 12:28-34; Lk 10:25-28).

In His various pronouncements upon the law, Jesus appeared as a new legislator, a new Moses, one greater than Moses. He did not hesitate to restate the law: "You have heard the commandment given to your fathers

. . . however, what I say to you is . . ." (Mt 5:21-48). Jesus is the lord of the Sabbath (Mt 12:8; Mk 2:28; Lk 6:5). The Father acknowledges those whom Jesus confesses (Mt 10:32-33; Lk 12:8-9). As a son of the kingdom Jesus was exempt from paying the temple tax (Mt 17:34-36). Hence, Jesus recognized the law as the revelation of the Father's will; but He Himself constituted a new and more perfect revelation of the Father, a fullness that hitherto had not been achieved, one that would not be surpassed.

The apostolic community continued to obey the Jewish law. However, the admission of the Gentiles to the Christian community raised an important question. Were they to be bound by the Mosaic law? A plenary council at Jerusalem, with the support of Paul, Peter, and James, finally affirmed the freedom of the converts from the law.

Paul taught that a person is justified by faith in Jesus Christ and not by the works of the law (Gal 2:16; Rm 3:28). This means that the ritual practices of Judaism were futile and that a person cannot merit his or her own justification. What then was the purpose of the law in the plan of salvation? It gave a knowledge of what is good, but not the strength to do it (Rm 7:16-18). It impressed upon the Jews their absolute need of the Savior. Once the Savior had come, the people no longer needed the law as a pedagogue (Gal 3:25). Still, the whole law continues to find its fulfillment in the great commandment of love (Gal 5:14). What about the Gentiles who were without the Mosaic law? Even so, they were not without a law written on their hearts, and they will be judged in accordance with that law (Rm 2:14-16). God's eternal power and divinity were made known to the Gentiles by the things He has made (Rm 1:32).

The epistle to the Hebrews speaks of the law especially in a cultic-ritual sense. This law was a shadow of the good things to come, but without power to perfect those who worshiped under it (10:1). The epistle of James is concerned entirely with Christian conduct. For James, the Gospel is a new law, a perfect law of liberty (1:25). One must obey the whole law which is reduced to the single precept of love (2:8-11). For John, law refers to the Mosaic law (Jn 1:17, 45; etc.). Keeping the commandments of God revealed by Jesus is a sign of true love (Jn 14:21). One commandment is supreme—that of fraternal love (Jn 13:34; 15:12) which flows from the love of God (1 Jn 4:21).

Theological Reflection

A. The Nature of Law. A law is a dictate of reason directed toward the common good; it stems from, and has been promulgated by, a competent legislator in the community. Hence, a law is an exercise of good sense by a legislator who obliges a community to do such and such a thing. The purpose of a law is to secure the good of the society in which it prevails. A law that is harmful to society is not really a law at all. A law differs from a precept because the latter is intended for the benefit of an individual or a few. A law stems from a competent legislator whether authority is vested in an individual (such as a mayor) or in a group (such as a legislature). Of course, a law must be promulgated so that those subject to the law can know of its existence. The manner of promulgation—for example, in an official publication or in a newspaper—is left up to the legislator.

B. The Eternal Law. When a builder constructs a house, he works according to a definite plan. From many possible plans he has chosen one which he executes. Those who help the builder in the construction of the house try to implement his plan as faithfully as possible. The eternal law of God is similar to the plan of a builder. Aquinas defined the eternal law of God as "the plan of divine wisdom insofar as it directs all activity and all change toward a final end."[17] When God created the universe, He worked according to a plan. He executes the plan with a definite purpose in mind. God's plan established goals for His creatures and the means to achieve them. The plan God chose to implement was only one among innumerable possibilities. He chose one definite order of existence and obligation. The determination of God to create and act according to a definite plan was eternal, although it is executed in time.

Creatures carry out the eternal law of God, His plan for creation, in different ways. Irrational creatures carry it out necessarily, guided as they are by natural forces. Rational creatures are expected to carry out the eternal law voluntarily. All the other laws binding rational creatures must conform to the eternal law of God. From this law they derive their binding force. The eternal law of God guarantees the ultimate triumph of goodness—if not always in the present world, at least at the end of history.

C. The Natural Law. Thomas Aquinas defined the natural law as the participation of the rational creature in the eternal law.[18] The natural law, therefore, is God's eternal law as it governs human beings. As an intelligent agent, God created human nature for a definite purpose. He endowed that nature with a natural tendency toward the goal He established for it, and He provided it with faculties necessary to achieve it. When men and women act in accordance with human nature and its inherent characteristics and propensities, they act in accordance with the natural law and the eternal law of God: they act rightly. When they do not act in such a manner, they act wrongly.

Rational creatures are not constrained to obey the natural law as brute animals are constrained to obey the law of their nature. Rational creatures are responsible agents; they must make provision for themselves and others; they share actively in forging their own destiny; they must answer to God for their lives. The natural law is a mandate which they must carry out in full and free responsibility. They have a duty to act in a manner corresponding to their nature. They can evade this duty even though they have a moral obligation to fulfill it. The natural law is promulgated through the light of reason. In this sense, rational creatures have a law written on their hearts and they will be judged in accordance with that law (Rm 2:15).

We can distinguish various precepts of the natural law. There are precepts of the most general nature, such as "Good must be done; evil must be avoided." In this case, good means that which is in accordance with human nature, while evil means that which is not. These precepts are self-evident and every human being understands them immediately. From these first and fundamental precepts follow, by way of conlusion, other secondary precepts of the natural law which are restated in the ten commandments. Normally, every mature individual knows that it is wrong to steal, to murder, and to commit adultery. However, it could happen that a person is invincibly ignorant of these secondary precepts for a time. Such ignorance might be the result of a faulty education or other social influences. Finally, there are other precepts of the natural law which are still more remote, but nonetheless direct, conclusions from the primary and secondary precepts. The prohibition of fornication in every circumstance is such a precept. So too is the prohibition of suicide. A person could be invincibly ignorant of these remote precepts all his life. The more removed the conclusion, the greater the danger of error. One of the purposes of divine revelation and the ecclesiastical magisterium is to afford a person a good grasp of ethical precepts of the natural order which might otherwise prove elusive. One cannot contravene the precepts of the natural law, even in an invincibly ignorant manner, without paying a penalty in some way.

Those who understand the natural law in the sense of the preceding paragraphs speak of its unchanging, permanently valid moral dictates. The law flows from the very principles of human nature itself; and human nature does not change even though its existential situation can and does change. Such principles as the dignity of the individual, the brotherhood of men, human dependence upon God, the necessity of living in accordance with God's plan for the world, and others, are permanently and universally valid. Such principles to be sure are quite general in nature, and it is up to the theologian and ethicist to apply them to the human situation in the concrete. What constitutes a violation of human dignity in the present century? What obligations does the brotherhood of men impose upon the developed countries with respect to the underdeveloped countries? Only informed reflection based upon the unchanging principles of the natural law can answer these and other questions like them. Sometimes, Catholic moral theologians disagree among themselves about the application (though not about the existence) of these universal principles.

In some cases, the expression of the natural law—even by the Almighty in the promulgation of the ten commandments—needs analysis and interpretation. For example, the precept which forbids killing does not forbid the killing of animals; rather, it forbids the direct killing of an innocent person.

D. The Divine Positive Law. This is the law which was directly and supernaturally revealed by God. As the epistle to the Hebrews remarks, "God at sundry times and in diverse manners spoke in times past to the fathers through the prophets. Last of all in these days He has spoken to us through His Son Jesus" (Heb 1:1-2). Speaking to His people through the law, the prophets, and His Son Jesus, God manifested His will for His subjects. In some instances, He reaffirmed the prescriptions of the natural law in order to clarify and certify them for all. Thus, He gave the ten commandments to the Israelites through Moses. In other instances, He communicated the decisions of the divine will relative to the circumstances in which human salvation was, and is, to be worked out. These decisions, particularly, constitute the divine positive law in the strict sense.

Under the Old Testament, the Israelites were governed by the divine law mediated through Moses and incorporated into the Pentateuch. This was the Torah, "the law of Moses." This law flowed from the covenant between Yahweh and the twelve tribes of Israel. The law contained moral, cultic, and social prescriptions. It was intended to preserve the knowledge of the true God among the people and to prepare them for the coming of the Messiah. With the coming of the Messiah, the cultic and social prescriptions of the law were no longer necessary and lost their validity. The moral prescriptions, however, were restated and reinforced by Christ. Under the New Testament, Jesus came to fulfill the law and not to abolish it. Jesus was "the new Moses" and the sermon on the mount was "the new Torah." Jesus imposed certain new obligations on the human race—to accept His word as the word of the Father, to enter His Church, and to approach His sacraments. But this new law is accompanied by the grace of the Holy Spirit imparted through faith in Jesus Christ (Rm 3:27; 8:2). The new law is able to free individuals from sin and death.

E. Civil Law. A civil law is an ordinance of reason promulgated by public authority for the common good. A civil law aims at the common good of the society in which it prevails and not at the good of a few individuals only. The purpose of civil laws is to bring order into society so that the majority of citizens can benefit. One can easily imagine the chaos if, for example, there were no traffic laws. Civil authorities can pass laws which bind citizens in conscience, since civil authorities are the representatives of God Himself (Rm 13:1).

Civil laws clarify the content of the natural law with respect to concrete, sociological, and historical conditions. Civil laws can penalize the violation of the natural law by imposing, for example, a penalty for theft. Civil laws can apply the natural law to concrete situations by specifying, for example, the rights of property owners. Finally, civil laws can add new prescriptions to the natural law when, for instance, they specify the form of wills.

The Second Vatican Council noted that "there are those who profess grand and rather noble sentiments; nevertheless, in reality they live as if they cared nothing for the needs of society. Many in various places even make light of social laws and precepts. They do not hesitate to resort to various frauds and deceptions in avoiding just taxes or other debts to society. Others think little of certain norms of social life, for example, those designed for the protection of health or laws establishing speed limits. They do not avert to the fact that by such indifference they imperil their own life and that of others."[19]

Some theologians speak of purely penal laws. Such laws, they say, do not bind in conscience unconditionally; rather, they leave one a choice—either to observe the law or to pay the penalty for violating it. There is no sin for the violation of the law as long as one is prepared to pay the penalty upon conviction. Other theologians deny the existence of penal laws. All laws, they hold, bind in conscience. If a law is just—if it is reasonable and serves the common good, then there is a moral obligation to obey it.

F. Ecclesiastical Law. Christ gave His Church the authority to make laws. This authority is sometimes described as the power to bind and loose. This authority is exercised by the Pope and ecumenical councils on behalf of the universal Church and by the bishops on behalf of their dioceses. The Code of Canon Law, which was promulgated in 1918 by Pope Benedict XV, contains the laws of the Holy See. Some of these laws have been revised by succeeding Popes and the Second Vatican Council (1962-65). The Second Vatican Council reaffirmed all that the First Vatican Council (1869-70) had to say about the authority of the Pope to make laws for the universal Church.[20] At the same time, the council stated that "bishops, as vicars and ambassadors of Christ, govern the particular Churches entrusted to them by their counsel, exhortations, example, and even by their authority and sacred power. . . . This power, which they personally exercise in Christ's name, is proper, ordinary, and immediate. . . . In virtue of this power, bishops have the sacred right and duty before the Lord to make laws for their subjects, to pass judgment on them, and to moderate everything pertaining to the ordering of worship and the apostolate."[21]

The authority of the Church to make laws extends only to baptized persons. Only by baptism does one enter the Church and become subject to its laws. The Church can only preach the Gospel to unbaptized persons without legislating for them. The Church can legislate for baptized persons in such a way that they are bound by a serious obligation. For example, Catholics are bound by a serious obligation to observe the more important laws of the Church about marriage. Those who violate the laws of the Church in a serious matter not only commit a serious sin, but they can also incur a penalty such as excommunication and suspension.

G. Cessation of Legal Obligation. A law ceases to oblige *permanently* when it is repealed or changed by the legislator or when it becomes unjust or impossible to observe. A law ceases to oblige *temporarily* for three reasons—because of moral impossibility, dispensation, and epikeia. Moral impossibility excuses a person from observance of a law. A person is morally incapable of observing a law when observance of the law would involve grave inconvenience for the individual or someone else. Thus, a worker is morally incapable of fasting when he does heavy physical labor. However, the more important the law, the greater must be the difficulty which excuses from it.

A person is excused from observance of a law by a dispensation. A dispensation is a relaxation of the law given by a competent authority for a good reason in a particular case. A pastor has the authority to dispense individuals and families from the obligation of attending Mass on Sundays.[22] The reason need not be so great as to excuse them; otherwise, they would not need a dispensation. Finally, a person is excused from observance of the law through epikeia. Aquinas defined epikeia as the virtue "which leads one to disregard the letter of the law and carry out what the concept of justice and the common good demands."[23] The legislator simply cannot envision every single case to which his law might literally apply. In a few cases, the literal application of the law might be harmful. For example, the law requires property to be restored to its owner. To restore a knife to a demented person, however, while faithful to the law in a literal sense, would be harmful to the person himself and to others. Epikeia excuses from the literal application of the law to achieve a greater good. Of course, the exercise of epikeia requires prudence.

With these remarks, we conclude our exposition of law as the objective norm of human conduct. Law is not something abstract and impersonal; rather, it is the expression of God's will for human beings. Obedience to law is obedience to God.

Footnotes

1. DS 3247, 3973.
2. DS 3248, 3781, 3973.
3. DS 3249.
4. DS 3247 (3272), 3780, 3956.
5. DS 2302, 3131-33, 3150, etc.
6. DS 3970.
7. DS 3857, 3970.
8. DS 2890.
9. DS 2956-2964.
10. DS 2939.
11. DS 2890.
12. DS 3248.
13. DS 1571.
14. DS 3151, 3170.
15. *Dignitatis Humanae* no. 3.
16. *Christus Dominus* no. 19.
17. *ST* 1a2ae.93.1.
18. *ST* 1a2ae.91.2: *Participatio legis aeternae in rationali creatura.*
19. *Gaudium et Spes* no. 30.
20. *Lumen Gentium* no. 18.
21. *Ibid.* no. 27.
22. *CIC* c. 1245.1.
23. *ST* 2a2ae.120.1.

Chapter 17

CONSCIENCE

Bibliography: *DBT, Conscience*, 90-92; *DB, Conscience*, 147; *NCE, Conscience*, 4, 196-205; *JBC, Conscience (see* the index); *TD, Conscience*, 95-96; *ST* 1a.79.13; 1a2ae.19.5-6; F. Connell, C.SS.R., *Outlines of Moral Theology*, Milwaukee, 1958, Bruce Publ. Co., 38-48; J. Ford, S.J., and G. Kelly, S.J., *Contemporary Moral Theology*, Westminster, 1962, The Newman Press, chs. 7-8; B. Häring, C.SS.R., *The Law and Christ*, Paramus, 1966, The Newman Press, 1, 135-189; *Idem, Free and Faithful in Christ*, New York, 1978, The Seabury Press, 1, 224-300; F. Böckle, *Fundamental Concepts of Moral Theology*, New York, 1967, Paulist Press, 67-78; W. Bier, S.J. (ed.), *Conscience: Its Freedom and Limitations*, New York, 1971, Fordham Univ. Press; J. Deedy, *What a Modern Catholic Believes about Conscience, Freedom and Authority*, Chicago, 1972, Thomas More Press; J. Donnelly and L. Lyons (editors), *Conscience*, Staten Island, 1973, Alba House; C. Curran, *Themes in Fundamental Moral Theology*, Notre Dame, 1977, U. of N.D. Press, 191-231; T. O'Connell, *Principles for a Catholic Morality*, New York, 1978, The Seabury Press, 83-97.

Law is the *objective* norm of human conduct. It is the expression of God's will for human beings. In a sense, it is something outside the individual. Law furnishes general information about the morality of various actions. On the other hand, conscience is the *subjective* norm of human conduct. It is a reality within the moral agent. It applies the general principles of morality to personal conduct and furnishes information about the morality of individual actions.

The Teaching of the Church

The function of conscience is to manifest what is in keeping with the moral order and to enjoin its observance.[1] Conscience applies an objective law to a particular situation.[2] A situational ethic which decides on the basis of personal intuition and not on the basis of objective laws must be rejected.[3] The systems of rigorism and laxism must also be rejected;[4] but the systems of probabilism and probabiliorism may be sustained.[5] One may follow the authority of St. Alphonse Liguori on morality without denying the legitimacy of other opinions too.[6]

The Second Vatican Council had much to say about conscience: "In the depths of his conscience, man detects a law which he does not impose on himself, one which holds him to obedience. Always summoning him to love good and avoid evil, the voice of conscience, when necessary, speaks to his heart more specifically: Do this, shun that. For man has in his heart a law written by God. To obey it is the very dignity of man; according to it he will be judged.

"Conscience is the most secret core and sanctuary of a man. There he is alone with God whose voice echoes in His depths. In a wonderful manner conscience reveals that law which is fulfilled by the love of God and neighbor. In fidelity to conscience, Christians are joined with the rest of men in the search for truth and for the genuine solution to the numerous problems which arise in the life of individuals from social relationships. Hence, the more right conscience prevails, the more persons and groups turn aside from blind choice and strive to be guided by the objective norms of morality. Conscience frequently errs from invincible ignorance without losing its dignity. The same cannot be said for a man who cares but little for truth and goodness, or for a conscience which gradually grows practically sightless as a result of habitual sin."[7]

Especially in its declaration on religious freedom, Vatican II clarified its mind on conscience: "Man perceives and acknowledges the imperatives of the divine law through the mediation of conscience. In all his activity a man is bound to follow his conscience in order that he may come to God, the end and purpose of life. It follows that he is not to be forced to act in a manner contrary to his conscience. Nor on the other hand is he to be restrained from acting in accordance with his conscience, especially in matters religious."[8] "God calls men to serve Him in spirit and truth; hence, they are bound in conscience, but they stand under no compulsion."[9] "The Christian faithful, in common with all other men, possess the civil right not to be hindered in leading their lives in accordance with their consciences."[10] "In the formation of their consciences, the Christian faithful ought carefully to attend to the sacred and certain doctrine of the Church. For the Church is, by the will of Christ, the teacher of the truth."[11]

Sacred Scripture

There is no single Hebrew word which expresses the idea of conscience. The Greek word, *syneidesis*, which means conscience, appears in the Old Testament only in the book of Wisdom (17:11), a book much influenced by Hellenistic ideas. There it means the internal admission of wickedness. Still, the idea of a judgment assessing the morality of a concrete situation is found in the Old Testament. This judgment may be attributed to the heart, the Hebrew word which most nearly expresses the idea of conscience. The book of Genesis (3:7-11) describes the remorse of conscience which Adam and Eve experienced after they had disobeyed God. David realized that he had sinned grievously by counting the people (2 S 24:10). In the midst of his trials, Job's heart did not reproach him for any of his actions (Jb 27:6).

The Greek word for conscience, *syneidesis*, is not found in the Gospels at all; but Paul uses it frequently. Apparently, Paul borrowed the word from the religious language of the time—probably from Stoicism. For the Stoics, conscience was the ultimate and autonomous judge of one's own acts. It conferred a kind of independence upon the sage. Paul used the word to express the reflex and autonomous judgment that the Bible attributes to the heart. Paul's conscience testified that he had fulfilled his apostolate with purity of intention (2 Cor 1:12; Ac 23:1; 24:16). What the Law was for the Jews, conscience was for the pagans (Rm 2:15). Christians should submit to civil authorities not only to escape punishment but also for the sake of conscience (Rm 13:5). Whoever acts against his conscience, even when it is erroneous commits sin (Rm 14:14, 23). Sometimes, the "weak" conscience of a brother may compel me to forego the otherwise legitimate exercise of my freedom (1 Cor 8:1-10). The judgment of conscience is always subject to that of God (1 Cor 4:4). Love springs from a pure heart, a good conscience, and sincere faith (1 Tm 1:5). Some have made shipwreck of their faith by rejecting the guidance of conscience (1 Tm 1:19). Men with seared consciences have forbidden marriage and required abstinence from foods (1 Tm 4:2). The minds and consciences of defiled unbelievers, for whom nothing is clean, are tainted (Tt 1:15).

The epistle to the Hebrews normally uses the word, conscience, in a sacrificial context. The sacrifices of the Old Testament were not able to purify the conscience of the worshipper, that is, to remove the sense of guilt (9:9; 10:2). In contrast, the blood of Christ purifies our consciences from dead works to worship the living God (9:14). This purification takes place at baptism (10:22).

Theological Reflection

A. The Nature of Conscience. In the view of Aquinas, conscience is the application of knowledge to act.[12] Therefore, conscience is primarily an act of reason, the faculty of knowledge. Others, notably the Scotists, place the essence of conscience in the will act. In neither view, however, is the other faculty excluded from the process of arriving at moral judgments. It is a matter of emphasis, not exclusion. Conscience is sometimes described as a faculty rather than an act. This usage is acceptable if it is understood to signify the functioning of the intellect and will in a particular area (morality) and not as an entirely distinct faculty.

Here we are concerned with conscience in its strictest sense, that is, as a judgment that a certain act is good or evil and therefore should be performed or omitted. Moreover, we are concerned especially with the judgment which *precedes* the act, called the *antecedent* conscience. This judgment is to be distinguished from the judgment which *follows* the act. The latter is called the *consequent* conscience. The consequent conscience is concerned with the morality of past actions. It is the act known as the examination of conscience.

In its strictest sense, therefore, conscience is not moral science which is an habitual knowledge of right and wrong. Nor is it an habitual attitude toward moral conduct, although we do use the term sometimes in this sense. For instance, we speak of a delicate conscience or a lax conscience or a scrupulous conscience. Rather, in this context, conscience is understood to be an act of judgment about the morality of an action which one is contemplating for the future.

B. Following One's Conscience. Before we discuss the necessity of following one's conscience, it is necessary to make several distinctions. A judgment of conscience is *true* when it conforms to what is objectively right. It is *erroneous* when it does not. Thus, a conscience which judges abortion to be immoral is a true conscience. A conscience which judges abortion to be permissible is an erroneous conscience. A conscience errs because of false principles or incorrect reasoning. If the error cannot be overcome, it is invincible; otherwise, it is vincible. A judgment of conscience is *certain* if a person has no doubt about the correctness of his judgment. It is *doubtful* if a person is unsure about the correctness of his judgment. A doubt may arise because the person is unsure about the facts of a particular situation (a doubt of fact). For example, a hunter may be unsure whether he saw a human being or an animal move in the distance. Or a doubt may arise because a person is unsure about the provisions of the law in question (a doubt of law). Thus, a hunter may not know all the provisions of the law about hunting. Finally, a judgment of conscience may *command* or *prohibit* or *permit* or *advise* a particular course of action.

With these distinctions in mind, we can now draw some conclusions about the necessity of following one's conscience. A person is obliged to follow his conscience when it is both *true* and *certain*. Such a decision of conscience is in agreement with the objective norm of conduct and it excludes all fear of error about acting rightly. A person is obliged to follow his conscience when it is both *invincibly erroneous* and *certain*. Everyone must do what he or she regards, to the best of their knowledge, as the good. This firm but erroneous judgment is the reality known as "good faith." The failure to make the required effort to know what one should know convicts the individual of ignorance which is culpable and vincible, the condition known as "bad faith." The agent is responsible for the evil actions which flow from such a condition. To recall the words of Vatican II: "Conscience frequently errs from invincible ignorance without losing its dignity. The same cannot be said for a man who cares but little for truth and goodness, or for a conscience which gradually grows practically sightless as a result of habitual sin."[13]

The most important thing to remember about conscience is the idea that it is an echo of the voice of God. Its function is to *manifest* the correct norm of action; it does not *establish* the norm. Therefore, it is always dependent on the voice of God speaking to us; it is not autonomous. This idea is especially important today with the emphasis on conscience as the guide of one's life. Vatican II presents conscience in this light. Everyone's effort, then, must be directed toward learning the will of God in his or her regard. This process is known as the "formation" of conscience. "Forming" one's conscience includes *in*forming it intellectually and developing the nonintellectual virtues which are required for an upright life.

Still another principle is applicable to following one's conscience; namely, it is never permissible to act with a *doubtful* conscience or with a conscience that is *vincibly erroneous*. In practice, a vincible erroneous conscience is the same as a doubtful conscience. To act with a doubtful conscience is tantamount to willing the evil that may be present. He who acts despite the serious warning of his conscience is prepared to sin. Hence, one must make an effort to arrive at a judgment of conscience which is both true and certain. But this conclusion gives rise to a practical problem. What is one to do when he cannot reach certitude that his decision is correct and yet he cannot refrain from acting?

If possible, an individual must seek a *direct* solution to his problem by a study or a further study of the problem and its relevant factors. This includes consultation with others and the study of approved authors. The important factor here is to understand the reasons given for the positions taken.

If a direct solution is impossible, an individual may invoke the "reflex" principles generally accepted by people. These principles are called "reflex" because they do not offer a direct solution; but by reflection on them, one may arrive at the practical certitude that is required for a conscientious judgment free of practical doubt.

Here are some examples of reflex principles:

1. A doubtful law does not bind.
2. In doubt one must favor the one who has presumption in his favor.
3. In doubt the one in possession must be favored.
4. A crime is not presumed but must be proven.
5. In doubt the accused must be favored.
6. In doubt presumption stands for the superior.
7. In doubt judgment should be made on the basis of what usually happens.
8. In doubt the validity of an act is to be upheld.

9. In doubt favors should be extended and burdens restricted.

10. In doubt the minimum obligation is to be imposed.[14]

These principles are simply presumptions growing out of the thought and practice of people over a long period of time. As presumptions, they are accepted as true and as starting-points in the solution of problems. As presumptions, they yield to proof of the contrary. For example, the objective of the prosecution in a criminal trial is to convict the accused. If evidence of guilt cannot be produced, the fifth principle listed above must be invoked. This is the principle of innocence on which the courts rely.

There is a biblical example which involved the use of reflex principles. Solomon had to decide which of two women was the mother of a baby whom both women claimed. One woman had the baby in her possession (the third principle listed above). The other woman manifested a mother's love by pleading for the infant's life (the seventh principle). In this case, Solomon decided that the third principle was inapplicable and awarded the baby to the rightful mother (1 K 3:16-28).

In some exceptional cases we must always follow the safer course even though the application of the reflex principles might suggest a different one. When the validity of a sacrament is threatened or when there is danger of serious harm either to myself or someone else, then I must choose the safer course. For example, a hunter may not shoot at an object which might be a human being even though it is likely to be an animal. The hunter may not shoot after appealing, for example, to the seventh reflex principle.

C. Moral Systems.[15] The so-called moral systems of interest to us are probabilism, equiprobabilism, and probabiliorism. They are concerned with the reflex principle: "A doubtful law does not bind;" that is, with the dividing line between binding law and personal freedom in moral matters. According to probabilism, one may follow an opinion favoring personal liberty as long as there are sound reasons supporting that opinion—even though the reasons supporting the obligation of the law are stronger. A doubtful law, probabilists say, does not bind. Equiprobabilism holds that a person may follow an opinion favoring personal liberty as long as the reasons supporting it are at least as strong as those which support the obligation of the law. It is true, equiprobabilists say, that a doubtful law does not bind; but they add that the probabilist exposes himself excessively to error when he acts in favor of liberty even on the basis of reasons which are less probable than those which favor the law. According to probabiliorism, a person may choose freedom only if the opinion in favor of freedom is the more probable one. Only in this way does an individual have the assurance of doing the right thing in a greater number of cases in the long run.

All three of these systems are accepted by the Church as worthy of Christians. None of them tries to evade one's real obligations. "The entire controversy about moral systems is bedeviled with misunderstanding. It has not always been borne in mind that the concept of *good* extends beyond what is laid down by law. And the moral systems do not deal with freedom to do evil, but with freedom from a doubtfully binding law, so that one may seek a real good in free ventures and with a sense of responsibility."[16]

D. Freedom to Follow One's Conscience. "Freedom of conscience" is an abstraction. Actually, a *person* is free to follow his or her conscience. This statement means that an individual, in following his or her conscience, ought to be free from coercion by other human beings, free from unjust penalties, and free to seek perfection or fulfillment, both natural and supernatural.

At the same time, everyone has a duty toward the true religion and toward the one Church of Christ. This duty—to seek the truth and to embrace it—obliges the human conscience.[17] Where is freedom if one has a duty? Freedom lies in the capacity to carry out the duty in a responsible, human manner. Freedom, therefore, exists in relation to other human beings; duty exists in relation to God and the call which He gives and the demands which He makes. God calls us to serve Him freely, rationally, and humanly; but He does not intend or expect us to ignore His call. His call is a true summons which makes demands on us. Acting according to one's conscience is not only a good thing, but a real obligation. The person who acts against conscience has gone astray.

Three conclusions follow from these considerations: 1) A person is bound to follow his or her conscience in order that he or she may come to God by following the commandments of the divine law. 2) As a consequence, no one is to be hindered by other human beings from acting in accordance with one's conscience. Freedom to follow one's conscience is restricted, however, by the rights of others and the just requirements of public order. 3) No one is to be forced by other human beings to act in a manner contrary to his or her conscience. These conclusions are based on the teaching of Vatican II that in the realm of conscience men and women stand alone before God.[17]

E. Habitual Dispositions of Conscience. Although in its strictest sense the term, conscience, refers to an act of judgment, the term is also used to designate an habitual attitude toward moral conduct. A *delicate* conscience is alert to the moral quality of an action and to the subtle differences between good and evil. For example, a delicate conscience will detect the difference between a witty and an offensive remark. A *lax* conscience is insensitive to a moral obligation in a particular area. For instance, a worker may regularly engage in petty thievery from his employer without realizing he is being unjust. One who is insensitive to a moral obligation in a particular area may be quite conscientious otherwise. A lax conscience is overcome by fidelity to one's religious duties and better instruction. A *scrupulous* conscience exaggerates the gravity of sin or sees sin where it does not exist. Thus, a scrupulous person may judge his thoughts to be sinful when in reality they are only a temptation. A scrupulous conscience is overcome by prayer to the Holy Spirit for guidance and complete and literal obedience to one's confessor. Finally, theologians speak of a *perplexed* conscience. A person with a perplexed conscience fears that she will commit a sin whether she acts or not. For example, a wife who is caring for a sick husband on Sunday, may fear that she will sin in any event—either by failing to attend Mass or by failing to take care of her husband. A person who acts with a completely perplexed conscience commits no sin no matter what she does, even though she may think that she is sinning.

Footnotes

1. DS 3956.
2. DS 3918.
3. DS 3918-3921.
4. DS 2303, 2105-2165.
5. DS 2175-2177.
6. DS 2725-2727.
7. *Gaudium et Spes* no. 16.
8. *Dignitatis Humanae* no. 3.
9. *Ibid*. no. 11.
10. *Ibid*. no. 13.
11. *Ibid*. no. 14.
12. *ST* 1a.79.13.
13. *Gaudium et Spes* no. 16.
14. *See* D. Prümmer, O.P., *Manuale Theologiae Moralis*, Barcelona, 1946, Editorial Herder, 1, 218.
15. Actually, the term, moral systems, is a misnomer in this case. The moral systems in question deal with a relatively small portion of morality only.
16. F. Böckle, *op. cit.* 77-78.
17. Vatican II, *Dignitatis Humanae* no. 1.
18. *Gaudium et Spes* no. 16.

Chapter 18

SIN

Bibliography: *DB, Sin*, 817-821; *DBT, Sin*, 550-557; *NCE, Sin*, 13, 234-248; *JBC, Sin, (see* the index); A. Gelin, *Sin in the Bible*, New York, 1965, Desclee; K. Schelkle, *Theology of the New Testament, (3 Morality)*, Collegeville, 1973, The Liturgical Press; E. Maly, *Sin*, Dayton, 1973, Pflaum/Standard; *ST* 1a2ae.71-89; W. Farrell, O.P., *A Companion to the Summa*, New York, 1938, Sheed and Ward, 2, 255-361; F. Connell, C.SS.R., *Outlines of Moral Theology*, Milwaukee, 1958, Bruce Publ. Co., 49-56; P. Riga, *Sin and Penance*, Milwaukee, 1962, Bruce Publ. Co.; P. Schoonenberg, *Man and Sin*, Notre Dame, 1965, Univ. of N.D. Press; B. Häring, *The Law of Christ*, Paramus, 1966, The Newman Press, 1, 339-384; *Idem, Free and Faithful in Christ*, New York, 1978, The Seabury Press, 1, 378-470; F. Böckle, *Fundamental Concepts of Moral Theology*, New York, 1967, Paulist Press, 83-110; P. Delhaye, *Pastoral Treatment of Sin*, New York, 1968, Desclee; G. Berkouwer, *Sin*, Grand Rapids, 1971, Eerdmans (a non-Catholic work); K. Menninger, *Whatever Became of Sin?* New York, 1973, Hawthorn Books; C. Curran, *Themes in Fundamental Moral Theology*, Notre Dame, 1977, Univ. of N.D. Press; T. O'Connell, *Principles for a Catholic Morality*, New York, 1978, The Seabury Press, 67-82.

Here we are concerned with personal sin which is the voluntary act of an individual who transgresses the law of God. Personal sin is to be distinguished from original sin which is the state into which all human beings are born. It is a state of alienation from God which is the result of the fall of Adam, the first of men, their ancestor and head. Our treatment of personal sin in this place is not concerned with the analysis of individual sins but with the considerations that apply to all sins. Much of the material in this chapter is an application of the previous material dealing with human acts in general.

The study of the Christian life consists of a description of the ideal life in Christ and with Christ. The Christian life must be directed to the growth and perfection of the image of God in man. The image of God in man is effected by those human acts which also bring him to eternal happiness. Unfortunately, some human acts do not bring man to eternal happiness. They prevent the attainment of happiness because they destroy life in Christ which is an absolute necessity for the fulfillment of the goal of life. This loss of life in Christ or sin is the subject with which the present chapter deals. It would be simply unrealistic to study human life without facing the fact of sin.

There is another consideration. The incarnation of Christ and His redemptive work cannot be understood unless one has an idea of that from which Christ redeemed the human race. Christ redeemed the human race from sin. Only after one understands the reality of sin can he or she appreciate more fully the significance of Christ's life, death, and resurrection.

The Teaching of the Church

Sin is a turning away from God,[1] an offense against God,[2] a free transgression of the law of God,[3] and the sinner is an enemy of God.[4]

There is a difference between mortal and venial sins.[5] The effect of mortal sin is enmity with God,[6] the loss of sanctifying grace[7] and eternal blessedness,[8] exclusion from the kingdom of God,[9] subjection to the devil,[10] eternal damnation and hell.[11] Not every mortal sin does away with faith.[12]

Venial sin is such that even holy men and women succumb to it in this life.[13] Apart from a special privilege, a person cannot avoid venial sins throughout life.[14] A person can always say truly that he or she is a sinner.[15] Venial sin does not take away sanctifying grace,[16] but a cleansing may be necessary after death.[17] The Church has condemned the idea that no sin is venial by nature, that every sin merits eternal damnation.[18]

. Only the will of the person sinning is the cause of sin.[19] God is not the cause of sin;[20] nor does God demand the impossible.[21] The devil is the cause of sin insofar as he is the tempter.[22] One must flee the occasions of sin and resist temptations.[23]

Christ is the source of the remission of sins through His passion;[24] but the Church is the mediator of the forgiveness of sins.[25] Baptism has been given for the remission of sins prior to baptism.[26] Penance has been given for the remission of sins committed after baptism.[27] Even before the reception of the sacrament of penance perfect contrition effects the forgiveness of sins; however, it must include the desire for the sacrament.[28] Venial sins can be forgiven in many ways besides confession.[29] The Eucharist is recommended as an antidote.[30] There is no such thing as a purely philosophical sin.[31]

Writing about sin, the Second Vatican Council taught: "Although he was made by God in a state of holiness, from the very onset of his history man abused his liberty, at the urging of the Evil One. Man set himself against God and sought to attain his goal apart from God. Although he knew God, he did not glorify Him as God; but his senseless mind was darkened and he served the creature rather than the creator. What divine revelation makes known to us agrees with experience. Examining his heart, man finds that he has inclinations toward evil too and is engulfed by manifold ills which cannot come from his good creator. Often refusing to acknowledge God as his beginning, man has disrupted also his proper relationship to his own ultimate goal as well as his whole relationship toward himself and others and all created things."[32]

Subsequently, a statement on sexual ethics published by the Sacred Congregation for the Doctrine of the Faith spoke about sin and the fundamental option: "It is precisely the fundamental option which is the last resort defines a person's moral disposition. But it can be completely changed by particular acts, especially when, as often happens, these have been prepared for by previous more superficial acts. Whatever the case, it is wrong to say that particular acts are not enough to constitute mortal sin. According to the Church's teaching, mortal sin, which is opposed to God, does not consist only in formal and direct resistance to the commandment of charity. It is equally to be found in this opposition to authentic love which is included in every deliberate transgression, in serious matters, of each of the moral laws.

"Christ Himself has indicated the double commandment of love as the basis of the moral life. But on this commandment depends the whole

Law and the prophets also. It therefore includes the other particular precepts. . . . A person therefore sins mortally not only when his action comes from direct contempt for love of God and neighbor, but also when he consciously and freely, for whatever reason, chooses something which is seriously disordered. For in this choice, as has been said above, there is already included contempt for the divine commandment: the person turns himself away from God and loses charity."[33]

Sacred Scripture

Old Testament. The idea of sin is found on almost every page of the Old Testament. It is commonly described in terms which are borrowed from human relationships. Sin is missing the mark, a failure to attain a goal. It is an ommission, a breach of the covenant, an iniquity, a corruption of the person, a rebellion, an insult to Yahweh, an injustice, an abomination, a lie, and a folly.

The cause of sin is the failure to take God into account (Ho 4:1, 6). Sin arises out of an evil heart (Jr 7:24). The Old Testament holds man fully responsible for his sinful actions. It knows no psychological grounds for mitigating human responsibility. The Old Testament does not answer the question how sin could enter a world governed by Yahweh's saving power. The parents of the human race sinned because they wished "to be like gods knowing both good and evil" (Gn 3:5). Like God, they wished to decide between good and evil. They wanted something which was not theirs. After that initial sin, all mortals came to lead depraved lives (Gn 4-11).

The principal effect of sin is death (Gn 3; Ezk 18:4). The Old Testament teaches that sin brings curse and disaster. According to the prophets, the fall of Israel is the necessary consequence of national guilt. Still, the Old Testament offers hope. The eventual defeat of sin and evil was foreseen (Gn 3:15). Already in the book of Genesis good was at work among the families of Noah and Abraham. Through Abraham all the nations of the earth would be blessed (Gn 12:2-3). God Himself seeks the dispersed sheep (Ezk 34). Man returns to God by renouncing his own will and submitting to God.

After the fall of the kingdoms of Israel and Judah, sin came to mean primarily an offense against the law. The Gentiles were sinners because they did not observe the law. The devil makes his appearance as the tempter in this period (Ws 2:24). He will reappear in the New Testament.

New Testament. The New Testament uses the Greek words *hamartia* and *hamartema* to designate the reality of sin. Sin is conceived as an act, a state or condition, and a power. Jesus is recognized as the conqueror of sin.

In the Synoptic Gospels, Jesus exercises a ministry among sinners, for He has come to call sinners and not the just (Mk 2:17). Jesus acknowledges that wicked deeds come from the heart (Mk 7:21). The parable of the prodigal son teaches that sin is an offense against God, that pardon is possible only with the return of the sinner to God (Lk 15:17-32). Jesus shed His blood, the blood of the covenant, on behalf of many for the forgiveness of sins (Mt 26:28). There is joy in heaven at the return of the sinner (Lk 15:7, 10).

In the Johannine writings, the malice of sin is explicitly stated. The sinner loves the darkness rather than the light for fear that his wicked deeds will be exposed (Jn 3:19-20). Everyone who lives in sin is a slave of sin (Jn 8:34) and the slave of the devil (1 Jn 3:8-10). Sin is lawlessness (1 Jn 3:4), wrongdoing (1 Jn 5:17), the lust of the flesh, the lust of the eyes, and the pride of life (1 Jn 2:16). In these passages, sin often signifies a state or condition which is the result of a sinful act. John also recognizes the satanic power behind the sinful acts of an individual (Jn 8:34; 1 Jn 3:8-10). For John, Jesus is the conqueror of sin. He is without sin Himself (Jn 8:46; 1 Jn 3:5). He is the lamb who takes away the sin of the world (Jn 1:29). He is an offering for the sins of all (1 Jn 2:2; 4:10).

The writings of Paul, especially the first part of Romans, contain a relatively full theology of sin. In several places Paul draws up lists of sins. Those who do such things—fornicators, idolaters, adulterers, sodomites, thieves, misers, drunkards, slanderers, and others—will not inherit the kingdom of heaven (1 Cor 6:9-10; Gal 5:19-21; etc.). Indeed, sin is the human condition. Both Jew and Greek are under the dominion of sin; all men have sinned and do not attain to the glory of God (Rm 2:1-3:31). Sin reigns as a power throughout the world. Sin was introduced into the world by Adam's disobedience and entered into all men (Rm 5:12-19). The wages of sin is death (Rm 6:23); and the universality of death proves that all men are sinners (Rm 5:12). Sin enslaves man so that he is unable to do what is right even when he wishes (Rm 7:15-25).

However, Paul holds out hope. If solidarity with Adam has involved the human race in sin and death, a superior solidarity with Christ has brought it acquittal and life (Rm 5:15-19). Justified by faith and baptism, the Christian has put on Christ (Gal 3:27-28). If anyone is in Christ, he is a new creation (2 Cor 5:17). He is no longer in the flesh, but in the spirit (Rm 8:9).

Theological Reflection

A. The Nature of Sin. Sin is an offense against God, a voluntary transgression of the law of God. Even a voluntary transgression of a human law is a sin because the law of God is the basis of all human legislation. To commit a sin it is not necessary for a person to be conscious of offending God. Rational creatures have a duty to act in a manner corresponding to their nature. If a person acts at variance with his or her nature, he or she sins whether the individual thinks of God or not. Hence, the Church has rejected the idea of a philosophical sin. In other words, there is no such thing as an act which is at variance with human nature and right reason without being an offense against God—even in one who is ignorant of God.

The element which formally renders an act sinful is the turning away from God involved in it. Sin is a rebellion against God. The rebellion is constituted and manifested by the sinful acts directed to this or that particular object. A sinful human being wishes to be independent of God—to decide for himself what is good and evil. In this light, the term, sin, refers primarily to mortal sin and only analogously to venial sin.

An imperfection is not the same thing as a sin. An imperfection is sometimes described as the omission of an act which is not obligatory but a matter of counsel. Understood in this sense, an imperfection is certainly not a sin, since what is counseled is left to the free choice of the person acting. Nor can an imperfection be equated with venial sin. To speak of "indeliberate" venial sin as an imperfection is a confusion of terms, since a truly indeliberate act is outside the realm of morality. Actually, an imperfection is the omission of a good or better act; for example, failing to attend Mass on a weekday or giving only five dollars to the poor when one might have given ten. Such an imperfection is not sinful because one is not always obliged to do the better thing, although one is always obliged to do the good thing. In conformity with the principle that every act is either good or bad, one must hold that even the so-called "imperfect'' or ''less perfect'' act is good. The distinction is the same as that between ''good'' and ''better,'' not that between ''good'' and ''bad.''

An act becomes sinful if it fulfills three conditions. 1) The act itself must be disordered; that is, it must fail to measure up in some respect to the standards of human conduct. 2) The agent must perceive that the act is disordered or defective. This perception is intellectual. 3) Finally, the agent must consent to act in this disordered manner. Consent is the act of the will. If one of these three conditions is not fulfilled, the act loses its sinful character.

We have already distinguished *original* sin from *personal* sin. The former is the state of alienation from God into which all are born as the result of Adam's sin. The latter is the voluntary act of an individual who transgresses the law of God. A *personal* sin may be *actual* or *habitual*. An *actual* sin is the sinful human act itself. *Habitual* sin is the sinful condition which is the result of the act. An *actual* sin is a sin of *commission* if it violates a negative precept such as the divine precept against theft. An *actual* sin is a sin of *omission* if it violates a positive precept such as the ecclesiastical precept to fast at appointed times. An actual sin can be committed in one's heart or by word and deed. A sin is *material* when a person does something objectively wrong without realizing it. A sin is *formal* when advertence and consent are present. Finally, a sin is *mortal* when it causes spiritual death by depriving an individual of divine life. It is *venial* when it diminishes the fervor of love. Later we shall return to the distinctions between mortal and venial sin.

Where human beings are presented with absolute good, that is, God, they are not free. The blessed in heaven who see and love God as He is in Himself are constrained by the force of their nature to join themselves to Him. During their pilgrimage on earth, however, human beings are not confronted by the absolute good so as to be bound by it. They see only the reflection of it in the particular goods to which they can be indifferent. They can pick and choose among these particular goods, sometimes making sinful choices in opposition to the call of God. Thus the possibility of sin.

B. The Distinction of Sins. Sins can be distinguished *specifically* and *numerically*. This distinction has an important bearing upon the sacrament of penance, since penitents are required by divine law to confess their mortal sins according to species and number.[34]

According to Aquinas, sins are distinguished *specifically* by the objects toward which they tend by their very nature. This tendency determines the objective morality of sins and places them in various species. Thus, murder is specifically distinct from theft, because murder takes away a person's life, while theft takes away his goods. The species of the sin arises from the object sought and not from the rejection of God which is present in every sin.[35] Other theologians, such as Duns Scotus (d. 1308), hold that sins are distinguished specifically insofar as they are opposed to different virtues. Thus, a sin of disobedience differs specifically from sin of intemperance. Still other theologians, such as Gabriel Vasquez (d. 1604), distinguish sins on the basis of their opposition to different precepts. Thus, a sin against the fourth commandment of the decalogue differs specifically from a sin against the sixth. These norms for distinguishing sins specifically do not seem to be opposed to each other. Aquinas' norm seems to be more fundamental while the other norms seem to be more proximate ones.[36]

Other principles govern the *numerical* distinction of sins. Sins are multiplied numerically as often as they are distinguished specifically. An adulterer commits two specifically distinct sins and two numerically distinct sins by one act of adultery since he violates both chastity and justice. Sins are obviously multiplied in number each time a sinful act is repeated. Each time a robber robs a bank he commits a numerically distinct sin. Authors do not agree about the answer to the question whether sins are multiplied numerically if *one* act is directed to several objects. It seems that if each of these objects is an entity in itself, if, for example, one crime injures several persons, then most authors consider this a case of numerical multiplication. If, however, one object is subordinate to another, then most authors consider the total act performed as *one* sinful action. Thus, all the preparations made by a robber who plans to rob a bank constitute one sin with the actual robbery.

C. Internal Sins. Internal sins are those which are committed in one's heart and do not appear externally. Jesus was speaking about an internal sin when He taught that anyone who looks lustfully at a woman has already committed adultery with her in his heart (Mt 5:28). Distinguishing between internal sins, theologians are wont to speak about morose delectation (*delectatio morosa*), sinful complacency (*gaudium peccaminosum*), and evil desire (*desiderium pravum*). The first concerns the *present*; the second, the *past*; and the third, the *future*. It should be noted that only an act of the will can be sinful and not an act of the intellect. In other words, to think about something evil is not in itself sinful. Thinking about evil may be necessary in some case when, for example, one examines his conscience. But thinking about evil can also be an occasion of sin when, for example, one dwells on sensual thoughts. Sin enters when, in effect, a person approves the evil contemplated.

Morose delectation is taking sinful satisfaction in the thought and imagination of evil without actually desiring it. For example, a person is guilty of morose delectation if he is pleased by the thought of harming another. Sinful complacency means approval of a sinful action committed by oneself or another in the past. For example, if a person says to himself, "John injured Tom in the past and I am glad he did," that person is guilty of sinful complacency in the evil deed. Finally, an evil desire is the wish and intention to do something evil in the future. Jesus spoke about the malice of an evil desire (Mt 5:28). The criminal who intends to rob a bank but holds back when he sees a guard is already guilty of robbery in the eyes of God even though he does not go through with the crime. In all three cases—morose delectation, sinful complacency, and evil desires, the thought and the deed do not differ essentially as far as malice is concerned. The absence of the deed does not remove the sin of the perverse will. An individual may take satisfaction in a good effect which follows upon something evil. Thus, a wife may take satisfaction in the fact that she is no longer physically abused by an alcoholic husband who drank himself to death.

D. Mortal and Venial Sin. The distinction between mortal and venial sin has to do with the "theological species" of sin. Here we are dealing with the gravity of sins. The idea that sins are not equal in gravity refers not only to the distinction between mortal and venial sin, but also to the distinction in gravity among mortal sins.

Mortal sin destroys the life of grace; it is spiritual death; and it is punished with eternal damnation in hell. Venial sin does not destroy the life of grace; but it incurs temporal punishment. When one sins mortally, he turns away from God; God is no longer the goal of his life. There is a radical opposition between the mortally sinful act and the love of God. When one sins venially, he does not turn away from God; God remains his goal; but he takes a kind of detour on the road to God. Mortal sin is sin in the full and proper sense of the word. Venial sin is sin only in an analogical sense.

Before one is guilty of mortal sin, three conditions must be verified: 1) The matter must be grave. There must be a situation in which one's fundamental loyalty to God is at stake. The gravity of the matter can be recognized from Holy Scripture, the teaching of the Church, and common sense. All three sources, for example, tell us that taking a human life is a very serious matter. 2) There must be sufficient reflection on the part of the intellect; that is, the agent must be clearly aware of the gravely evil action he is contemplating. And 3) there must be full consent of the will to the seriously evil action. If the matter involved is not seriously sinful, then the sinful action can only be venial. If reflection and consent are only imperfect, even where grave matter is involved, the sin is necessarily venial. The chief danger of venial sin, however, is that it makes us less fervent in the service of God and disposes us to mortal sin.

E. The Causes of Sin. In his discussion of the causes of sin, Aquinas recalls that the will is the principal faculty in the performance of any human act, good or bad, that the intellect directs the will, that the passions influence, but do not control, human acts.[37] Only the will of the sinner is the cause of sin; but the will is the subject to temptation from without and within.

God is not the cause of sin, although He is the cause of the act which is sinful. Human failure is responsible for the disorder of a sinful act.

The Scriptures depict the work of Christ as the overthrow of the power of Satan. The devil tries to lead people into sin. The devil can only tempt human beings; but he cannot force anyone to sin. Not even the angelic power of the devil can infringe upon human freedom. However, not every temptation comes from the devil.

The "world" is not the cause of sin because it too cannot force the will to act wrongfully. But the world can tempt us to sin; it can be an occasion of sin. Here we are thinking of those persons, places, and things which can lead us into sin. We are bound to avoid the proximate occasions of sin—those which constitute a grave danger. If we cannot avoid a proximate occasion of sin, then we must take steps to lessen the danger. The more remote occasions of sin simply cannot be avoided; they are part of life.

The devil and the world tempt us from without; but concupiscence tempts us from within. Concupiscence means an inclination to evil within the human person. It is "the lust of the flesh, the lust of the eyes, and the pride of life" (1 Jn 2:16). Concupiscence has to do with carnal desires, worldly ambitions, selfish aims, a spirit of acquisitiveness, the attraction to material values, and worldly ostentation. All these things can flare up within the human breast and constitute a temptation to sin.

Sometimes, people despair of resisting certain temptations to sin. They should remember, however, that God permits no one to be tempted beyond his strength to resist. An excellent means of avoiding sin is to avoid entirely those persons, places and things that lead us into sin. The regular use of the sacrament of penance is also a great help. Temptations are not meant for our ruin, but for our good. They are meant to strengthen the nerve and the sinew of our minds and hearts and souls. They are the test which enables us to emerge the stronger for the fight.

Christ calls sinners to conversion. Conversion means turning away from sin and back to God. It signifies total conformity to the will of the heavenly Father, the cessation of sinful acts, and a revolution in one's point of view and desires so that one becomes a new creature. However, the subject of conversion is dealt with at greater length in connection with the sacrament of penance.

Footnotes

1. DS 1525.
2. DS 3891.
3. DS 2291.
4. DS 1528.
5. DS 795, 1537, 1680, 3381, etc.
6. DS 1680.
7. DS 1544.
8. DS 1705.
9. DS 835.
10. DS 1521.
11. DS 1002.
12. DS 1544, 1578.
13. DS 1537, 1680.

14. DS 1573.
15. DS 228-230.
16. DS 1680.
17. DS 838.
18. DS 1920.
19. DS 1515, 1950, 1966.
20. DS 1556.
21. DS 1536, 1568.
22. DS 800, 1694.
23. DS 2161-2163, 2192, 2241, 2253.
24. DS 485, 1523, etc.
25. DS 348, 349, 684, etc.
26. DS 1514, 1672, etc.
27. DS 1680, 1701, etc.
28. DS 1677, 1971.
29. DS 1680.
30. DS 1638, 3375.
31. DS 2291.
32. *Gaudium et Spes* no. 13.
33. Dec. 29, 1975. U.S.C.C., Washington, 1976, no. 10.
34. DS 1679-1680.
35. *ST* 1a2ae.72.1; 72.6.ad 2.
36. Sins are specifically distinct too if they are opposed to the same virtue in different ways, that is, by excess of defect.
37. *ST* 1a2ae.75-84.

Chapter 19

THE VIRTUES IN GENERAL

Bibliography: *DBT, Virtues and Vices,* 637-638; *JBC, Virtues (see* the index); *NCE, Virtue,* 14, 704-709; K. Schelkle, *Theology of the New Testament (3 Morality),* Collegeville, 1973, The Liturgical Press, 207-212; *ST* 1a2ae.49-70; W. Farrell, O.P., *A Companion to the Summa,* New York, 1938, Sheed & Ward, 147-254; P. Lumbreras, O.P., *De habitibus et virtutibus in communi,* Romae, 1950; R. Coerver, C.M., *The Quality of Facility in the Moral Virtues,* Washington, 1946, Catholic University of America; F. Connell, C.SS.R., *Outlines of Moral Theology,* Milwaukee, 1958, The Bruce Publ. Co., 57-62; B. Häring, C.SS.R., *The Law of Christ,* Paramus, 1966, The Newman Press, 1, 485-496; *Idem, Free and Faithful in Christ,* New York, 1978, The Seabury Press, 1, 193-208; J-P. Schaller, *Our Emotions and the Moral Act,* Staten Island, 1968, Alba House, ch. 4.

Aquinas approached the study of the Christian life from the viewpoint of man's powers (*potentiae*) which produce the good works necessary for salvation. These powers are modified by intrinsic principles called habits. Habits are characterized by a certain measure of permanence or stability. When habits are directed to moral good, they are known as virtues. Aristotle defined a virtue as that which makes both a person and what he does good. There are supernatural and natural virtues. The former can be present only by infusion, since they are the free gift of God and are necessarily connected with the presence of sanctifying grace. The latter virtues, on the other hand, can be either tendencies toward certain virtues which one has by temperament or inheritance, or the virtues which are acquired by practice, that is, by repeated actions. We shall also consider the gifts of the Holy Spirit in this chapter because they too are good habits, wholly supernatural, which are infused by God.

The Teaching of the Church

The Church has asserted the existence of natural virtues.[1] It has condemned the rejection of the supernatural virtues in favor of the natural virtues,[2] and also the idea that the exercise of the virtues is an imperfection.[3] The Church teaches that God is chiefly worshipped by acts of faith, hope, and charity.[4]

The Second Vatican Council commended certain virtues to priests, namely, goodness of heart, sincerity, strength and constancy of mind, the zealous pursuit of justice, and affability.[5] For the creation of a new humanity, the council called for the cultivation of the moral and social virtues.[6] It is through the sacraments and the exercise of the virtues that the Church functions as a priestly community.[7] Dedication to God's service should move religious men and women to practice the virtues, especially, humility, obedience, courage, and chastity.[8] The laity should hold in high esteem the virtues relating to social behavior, namely, honesty, justice, sincerity, kindness, and courage.[9] The apostolate of the laity is carried on through faith, hope, and charity which the Holy Spirit diffuses in the hearts of all members of the Church.[10]

Sacred Scripture

The Old Testament knows many virtues and vices, but there is no Hebrew word which expresses the general concept of virtue. The Septuagint, the Greek version of the Old Testament, uses the word *arete* to signify the concept of virtue. In the book of Wisdom the word signifies the religious-moral conduct of the pious (4:1; 5:13) and the four cardinal virtues (8:7). The general concept of virtue is also found in the books of the Maccabees (2 M 10:28; 15:12) in the sense of valor or constancy. The New Testament uses the word *arete* to signify not only a gracious act of God (1 P 2:9; 2 P 1:13), but also virtue and uprightness (Ph 4:8; 2 P 1:5).

The Bible contains lists of virtues and vices which at the outset are only catalogs of concrete lapses and individual deeds; for example, the decalogue (Ex 20:2-17; Dt 5:6-21). Isaiah (11:2) gives a list of virtues which is the source for the traditional names of the gifts of the Holy Spirit, namely, wisdom, understanding, counsel, and so on. We have already referred to the list of the four cardinal virtues in the book of Wisdom which also contains a list of vices (14:22-29). The latter lists show the influence of Greek ethics.

The New Testament offers numerous catalogs of virtues. Paul, for example, speaks of his own resolution, fidelity, patience, love, and endurance in persecution and suffering (2 Tm 3:10. *See* also Gal 5:22; Col 3:12-14; Ph 4; etc.). These virtues are not so much the product of human endeavor as they are the fruit of the Spirit and the gift of God. The New Testament also contains tables of vices. Thus, Paul writes that the vices of the pagans include malice, greed, ill will, envy, murder, bickering, deceit, and craftiness (Rm 1:29-31. *See* also 1 Cor 6:9-10; 2 Cor 12:20; etc.). These catalogs reflect both Jewish and Greek influences.

One may say that for the Old Testament the virtuous man is the one who seeks God with his whole heart in obedience to the divine will. The fundamental vice is to follow other gods (Dt 6:14) and to be unfaithful to the covenant. According to the psalms, the heart of the virtuous man is full of the law of God (Ps 1:2; 37:31), while the foolish or evil man says in his heart that there is no God (Ps 14:1). For both the Old and the New Testaments, virtue springs from the heart which is full of love (Dt 6:5; 10:16; Mk 12:30). So too from the heart spring the vices that make a man impure (Mt 15:19-20). It is necessary that he should be recreated with a renewed spirit in order for his heart to become pure (Ps 51:12). Christ revealed to His disciples the role of the Spirit in this interior renovation (Jn 14:26; 16:31).

Theological Reflection

A. Virtues. A virtue is a habit or a permanent disposition which inclines a person to do good and avoid evil. Or, to quote Aristotle again, a virtue is that which makes both a person and what he does good. Earlier we spoke of the importance of action in the assimilation of men and women to God; hence, the importance of virtues, since they are directed to action. It is especially through the virtue of charity that human beings are assimilated to God. For this reason, charity is called the queen of the virtues. Charity is the virtue by which we love God above all things for His own sake, and our neighbor as ourselves for the love of God.

Aquinas made a distinction between entitative and operative habits.[11]

An entitative habit, such as bodily health, inheres in, and modifies, the substance of a being. An operative habit inheres in, and modifies, a faculty. Some operative habits, such as facility in speaking a language, are morally indifferent. Some operative habits, such as greed and gluttony, are morally bad and are called vices. Some operative habits are morally good, and these are the virtues. Some virtues are acquired; others are infused by God. The former are the natural virtues; the latter, the supernatural virtues.

B. The Natural Virtues. The natural moral virtues are acquired and strengthened by one's own actions. For example, a person acquires and strengthens the natural virtue of truthfulness by repeatedly telling the truth. The practice of the natural virtues reflects the demands of the natural law. The natural virtues impart facility and pleasure in the corresponding action. So the person with the virtue of truthfulness finds it easy and pleasurable to tell the truth. Even a sinner may have certain natural virtues. Thus, a person may be perfectly honest even though he is a drunkard. Still, the moral virtues are connected in such a way that the existence of one frequently demands the existence of another. Hence, the lack of one virtue can militate against the existence of another. One who is intemperate, for example, may find it impossible to be honest.

All the natural moral virtues can be reduced to the cardinal virtues. These are prudence, justice, fortitude, and temperance. They are called cardinal virtues (Latin, *cardo*, hinge) because all the other virtues can be arranged or classified under them. Prudence is in the intellect and it enables the individual to recognize his moral duty and the means to accomplish it. Justice resides in the will and it inclines a person to render everyone his due. Fortitude is in the irascible appetite, and it enables a person to stand firm against the hardships of this life, especially, the fear of death. Temperance resides in the concupiscible appetite and enables a person to keep his passions and emotions under the control of reason.

All the other moral virtues can be classified or arranged under the cardinal virtues. Thus, those virtues which are required for the practice of a cardinal virtue are called the *integral* parts of the cardinal virtue. For example, caution and circuminspection are integral parts of the virtue of prudence. Those virtues which are related to the cardinal virtue as species to genus are called the *subjective* parts of that virtue. Thus, legal justice, or social justice, and commutative justice, which prevails among individuals, are subjective parts of the cardinal virtue of justice. Finally, those virtues which possess some of the characteristics of the cardinal virtue, but not all of them, are called *potential* parts of the virtue. The virtues of humility and meekness, for instance, are potential parts of the virtue of temperance.

It is said that *Virtus in medio stat* which means that virtue consists in the golden mean. In other words, a virtuous action measures up to the norm prescribed by reason. The action which is not virtuous fails to measure up to the norm either by excess or defect. Thus, the temperate person eats what is necessary to sustain life, whereas the intemperate person eats either too much or too little. In this sense, virtue consists in the golden mean. Where justice is concerned, the golden mean designates not only the norm dictated by reason, but also that equality in material terms—neither more nor less—which is due someone else.

C. The Supernatural Virtues. These are infused by God together with sanctifying grace. Even baptized infants have all the supernatural virtues. God is the author of the supernatural virtues, although He does employ such instruments as the sacraments to communicate them. The supernatural virtues modify and elevate the faculties of human beings so that they are able to act in a supernatural manner, that is, in a manner proportionate to their supernatural destiny. The supernatural virtues take deeper root in the human faculties with the intensification of sanctifying grace. All these virtues (with the exception of faith and hope) are lost through mortal sin; but they are not diminished or expelled by venial sin. Faith is lost only by a mortal sin opposed directly to this virtue. Hope is lost only by a mortal sin opposed directly to this virtue or by a sin that expelled faith.

In this context, one notices a parallel between the natural and supernatural orders. In the natural order, an individual has a principle of life, the soul. With the natural concurrence of God, the soul can act through its faculties and natural virtues in a naturally good way. For example, a man who has sinned grievously by gross injustice can still act in a naturally good way by caring for his family. Analogously in the supernatural order, an individual has a principle of life, sanctifying grace. With the supernatural concurrence of God or actual grace, the soul vivified by sanctifying grace can act through its faculties and the supernatural virtues in a supernaturally good way.

A natural virtue imparts ease and pleasure to the corresponding action. However, this is not the case with a supernatural virtue. A supernatural virtue supernaturalizes the activity of a human faculty without necessarily rendering it easy or pleasant. Hence, a person who has led a sinful life for a long time does not necessarily find it easy and pleasant to live a good life even after he has repented of his sins and recovered grace and the supernatural virtues.

We distinguish the *material* and *formal* objects of a supernatural virtue. The material object of a virtue is that with which the virtue is concerned. Thus, the material object of faith (viewed as a virtue in the intellect) is the truths revealed by God. The formal object is the motive which prompts the faculty to act as it does with respect to the material object. For example, the formal object of faith is the authority of God's revelation. This authority moves the intellect to accept the truths of revelation even though they lack that evidence which usually determines the assent of the intellect.

D. Different Kinds of Supernatural Virtues. Paul speaks of three virtues that abide in the present life and are therefore greater than the transitory spiritual gifts. These three are faith, hope, and charity; and the greatest of these is charity (1 Cor 13:13). Theologians call these virtues the *theological* virtues (from the Greek, *theos*, God) because they understand them to have God for their immediate object. The object of faith is God as the supreme truth. The object of hope is God as *our* supreme good. The object of charity is God insofar as He is good in Himself.

In addition to the theological virtues there are also infused *moral* virtues. These are communicated by God along with sanctifying grace. They perfect and elevate the corresponding natural virtue. They are concerned with the means by which we achieve our supernatural destiny in God. They have the same names as the natural moral virtues, although they are totally distinct from them. Whereas the natural moral virtues are directed by reason, the supernatural moral virtues are directed by faith. With the natural virtues, the supernatural virtues reside in the faculties of the human person.

Besides the theological virtues and the infused moral virtues, there are also *gifts of the Holy Spirit*. These too are infused along with sanctifying grace. According to Aquinas, the gifts are habitual dispositions by which we become docile to the influence of the Holy Spirit. They are distinct from the virtues. The virtues are intrinsic principles of activity while the gifts are dispositions that open us to the external impulse of the Holy Spirit.[12] Louis Billot, S.J. (1846-1931) compared the virtues to the motors of a ship and the gifts to sails unfurled to receive the movement of the wind. Commonly, Catholics recognize seven gifts of the Holy Spirit: wisdom, understanding, counsel, fortitude, knowledge, piety, and fear of the Lord. This enumeration is based upon the text of Isaiah (11:2) in the Septuagint. The *fruits* of the Holy Spirit are human actions which flow from the gifts of the Holy Spirit. They are called fruits because they are effects of the gifts and afford us a certain delight as we accomplish them.[13] The twelve fruits of the Holy Spirit are charity, joy, peace, patience, benignity, goodness, long-suffering, mildness, faith, modesty, continency, and chastity (*see* Gal 5:22-23). The *beatitudes* are also effects of the gifts. Matthew enumerates eight (Mt 5:3-10); Luke, four (Lk 6:20-22). They are called beatitudes because in a particular way they bring us happiness (beatitude means happiness) both on earth and in heaven.[14]

As far as we can judge, the blessed in heaven will retain the virtues and the gifts. Along with sanctifying grace they elevate the human person for immediate fellowship with God. However, faith and hope will disappear. Faith will give way to vision, and hope to possession. Some of the virtues will be exercised to an intense degree—love, for example. But some of the virtues will not be exercised. For example, we shall no longer practice fortitude because we shall no longer fear death.

E. Moral Education. This type of education endeavors to teach children and adolescents, youths and adults, how to lead virtuous lives. It seeks to make the Catholic faith a vital, conscious and active force in their thinking and acting.[15] Therefore, moral education is directed toward behavior. Faith, however, must be the basis of behavior; and the instruction given by moral educators should be based on Sacred Scripture, tradition, liturgy and the teaching authority and life of the Church. In this way, the belief of the Church provides a sound basis for virtuous living. With respect to the teaching authority of the Church, the Second Vatican Council taught: Catholics "must always be governed by a conscience dutifully conformed to the divine law itself. They should be submissive to the teaching authority of the Church which authentically interprets the divine law in the light of the Gospel."[16] But teachers must be concerned not only for the cognitive side of moral education but also for the affective and attitudinal sides. In other words, they should strive not only to illumine the mind but also to influence the heart.

Those engaged in the moral education of others ought not to forget that faith is a free response to the grace of the revealing God.[17] They will help their students to form their consciences as fairly and honestly as they can. Obviously, the selection of material as well as the pedagogical method employed by the teacher must be suited to the character, ability, age, and circumstances of the students. Psychologists have noted how individuals are motivated differently at various stages of their psychological development. Acting for a reward, they should come to act out of conviction.

Teachers will attempt to inculcate the social implications of the Gospel. We cannot lead virtuous lives if we do not fulfill our social obligations to others, especially, the poor, the deprived, the endangered, and the oppressed. The biblical revival in the Catholic Church will encourage teachers to seek and explain the roots of Catholic moral teaching in the Bible. Teachers will impress upon students the need to continue their moral and religious education throughout their lives. Learners should be able to verbalize their faith by familiarity with the apostles' creed, the ten commandments, the beatitudes, and other doctrinal expressions. Thus, they will know clearly what they are committed to. Even young people should memorize these doctrinal summaries. Increased understanding will come as they mature. Liturgical participation is also an essential part of a program of moral education. ''The liturgy is the summit toward which the activity of the Church is directed. . . . It is the font from which all her power flows.''[18]

Footnotes

1. DS 1916, 1925, 1936-38, etc.
2. DS 3343-45.
3. DS 896, 2231, 2368.
4. DS 2188.
5. *Prebyterorum Ordinis* no. 3.
6. *Gaudium et Spes* no. 30.
7. *Lumen Gentium* no. 11.
8. *Perfectae Caritatis* no. 5.
9. *Apostolorum Acutositatem* no. 4.
10. *Ibid.* no. 3.
11. *ST* 1a2ae.49.
12. *ST* 1a2ae.68.
13. *ST* 1a2ae.70.
14. *ST* 1a2ae.69.
15. *Christus Dominus* no. 14.
16. *Gaudium et Spes* no. 50.
17. *General Catechetical Directory* no. 3.
18. *Sacrosanctum Concilium* no. 10.

Chapter 20

RESPONSIBILITY TO GOD

Bibliography: *DB, Faith,* 267-271, *Hope,* 368-369, *Love,* 520-523, *Prayer,* 686-688, *Vow,* 916, *Divination,* 200-201, *Magic,* 534-536; *DBT, Faith,* 158-163, *Hope,* 239-243, *Love,* 322-327, *Worship,* 680-683, *Prayer,* 445-449, *Magic,* 327-328, *Blasphemy* 47, *Sabbath,* 511-512; *NCE, Faith,* 5, 792-805, *Hope,* 7, 133-144, *Love,* 8, 1039-1045, *Charity,* 3, 464-470, *Worship* 14, 1030-1034, *Religion, Virtue of,* 12, 270-271, *Sunday,* and *Sunday and Holyday Observance,* 13, 797-799; *ST* 2a2ae.1-46, 81-100; W. Farrell, O.P., *A Companion to the Summa,* 3, 1-138, 247-300; F. Connell, C.SS.R., *Outlines of Moral Theology,* Milwaukee, 1958, The Bruce Publ. Co., 65-98, 142-154; B. Häring, C.SS.R., *The Law of Christ,* Westminster, 1967, The Newman Press, 2, 15-346; Vatican II, *Sacrosanctum Concilium,* Constitution on the Sacred Liturgy; C. Peschke, S.V.D., *Christian Ethics,* Alcester and Dublin, 1978, C. Goodliffe Neale, vol. 2.

In the preceding chapters of Part 2 we were concerned with the general principles of moral theology. With the present chapter we begin to apply these principles to particular, concrete decisions and intentions. We begin to focus upon the details of day-to-day living. We shall discuss these details in terms of human responsibility, that is, as an appropriate or inappropriate response to God's call for which the human person is liable. In this chapter, we shall take up the theological virtues, faith, hope, and charity, which have God for their immediate object, and also the virtue of religion which is directed toward the worship of God. In the following chapters, we shall deal with those moral virtues and actions which have oneself and others for their immediate object. This arrangement corresponds to the commandments of the decalogue. The first three commandments speak of a person's responsibility to God; the last seven, of his responsibility to himself and his neighbor.

Faith, Hope, and Charity in the Bible

Faith. In the Old Testament, the Hebrew word which lies at the basis of the New Testament *pistis* and *pisteuein* is *'aman.* "Believe" and "faith" in our English Bibles translate the Greek *pisteuein* and *pistis.* In the Old Testament, the man of faith, one who believes, is a member of the community which was established by the covenant on Mt. Sinai. Faith is the manner of existence of the man who is committed to God, who says "Amen" to God (Weiser), who looks to God for guidance out of trust born of a living recollection of God's leadership in the past (Buber).

Different shades of meaning are attached to the terms "faith" and "believe" in the Old Testament. For example, Is 7:9: Faith and existence are identical. Heb 2:4: The believer is the man who displays the truth of God in his own life. Gn 15:6, Nb 20:12, Ps 78:22: Faith is trust in God's promises. Ezk 14:31, 19:9: To believe in God is to take Him seriously. Is 28:16: Faith is a total reliance upon Jahweh. In Is 43:10 and Ps 27:13 faith and belief are taken in an intellectual sense, and in Ws 12:2, belief signifies fidelity to the Law.

In the New Testament, faith (or belief) signifies the right response of the individual to God who has revealed Himself through His Son, Jesus Christ. But again there are different shades of meaning. In the Synoptic Gospels, faith (or belief) signifies such things as belief in the Second Coming (Mk 13:21), belief in miracles (Mk 2:5), trust in God (Mk 11:22), and confidence in the power and willingness of Jesus to work a miracle (Mt 9:28). For Paul, a man is justified by faith in Jesus Christ (Rm 3:22). Faith comes from the hearing of the word (Rm 10:14-21). Faith is a gift (Ep 2:8; Ph 1:29). To have faith is to know God (Gal 4:9). Faith is hope for salvation and life (Rm 6:8). Faith excludes boasting (Rm 3:27). For John, faith takes the place of Jewish "works" (Jn 6:28-29). Faith is a personal belief in Jesus (Jn 2:11; 3:16). The works of Jesus lead to faith in Him (Jn 14:10-11; 5:36). John wrote his Gospel to beget faith (Jn 19:35; 20:31).

Hope. Yahweh was the hope of Israel under the Old Testament (Jr

14:8; 17:13). One must hope in Yahweh even when He "hides His face" (Is 8:17), that is, withdraws His favor. The reason for hope is that Yahweh is faithful to His promises; and His mighty deeds in the past testify to His power to help. The object of the hope of the patriarchs in the Pentateuch was that of descendants in great numbers and the possession of the land promised to them (Gn 17:8; Ex 3:8; etc.). The destruction of the kingdom of Israel in 721 B.C. and of the kingdom of Judah in 587 B.C. dealt a severe blow to the hopes of God's people. But the prophets rekindled those hopes in a different way. Jeremiah spoke of a new covenant which God would write upon the hearts of His people (31:31; 32:38-41). Ezekiel promised that God would remember His covenant with Israel (Ezk 16:59-63). God would give His people a new heart and a new spirit (Ezk 36:25-28). However, Israel's hope did not extend beyond the grave. Those who go down into the pit do not await God's kindness (Is 38:18); and when a man dies he is not roused out of his sleep (Jb 14:21). Only at the very end of the period was there a hint of personal survival (Ws 5:5; 2 M 12:46).

In the New Testament, the doctrine of hope is developed especially in the Pauline writings. Abraham is the model of hope for he "hoped against hope" (Rm 4:18). The Christian is saved through hope whose object is not seen (Rm 8:24). Hope is the fruit of proved virtue and patient endurance (Rm 5:4). There are in the end three things that last—faith, hope, and charity (1 Cor 13:13). The object of hope is glory (Col 1:27) and the resurrection (1 Cor 15:19). Hope distinguishes the Christian from the Gentiles who are without hope, especially, for life after death (Ep 2:12; 1 Th 4:13). Hope is a firm anchor which extends beyond the veil (Heb 6:19). The believer should be prepared to give the inquirer a reason for his hope (1 P 3:15).

Charity (Love). The term, love (Heb. *'ahab* and its cognates), is used in the Old Testament much as it is used in English. In general, it signifies a voluntary attachment (good or evil) to things and persons. The person may be one's wife, son, friend, neighbor, or master. Love is the sentiment which Yahweh has for Israel (Ho 11:1). It is the band by which He draws His people to Himself (Ho 11:4); but He will withdraw His love because of their wicked deeds (Ho 9:15). The idea of love is prominent in the book of Deuteronomy. The selection of the Israelites as the people of God was a matter of free choice and love on the part of the Lord (Dt

7:6-8). Out of love the Lord led the Israelites out of Egypt (Dt 4:37; 7:8). He will love and bless and multiply them (Dt 7:13). In turn, the Israelites are commanded in the decalogue to love the Lord their God (Ex 20:6; Dt 5:10). They are commanded to love Him with all their heart, and with all their soul, and with all their strength (Dt 6:5). They are to love the Lord and heed His statutes, decrees, and commandments (Dt 11:1). Other passages in the Old Testament speak of the connection between love and observance of God's commandments (Dn 9:4; Ne 1:15).

The Greek language uses three words and their cognates to designate the word, love; namely, *eros, philia,* and *agape*. In the New Testament, one does not find the word, *eros*, which signifies sexual desire. One does find, however, the word, *philia*, which in profane Greek signifies primarily the love of friends, and *agape*, which was probably chosen to signify the Christian idea of love. The word, charity, is often used to translate the word, *agape*. In the Synoptic Gospels, Jesus identifies the great commandment of the law as love of God and neighbor (Mt 22:34-40; Mk 12:28-34; Lk 10:25-28). One's neighbor is even the person from whom one feels alienated (Lk 10:29-37). Jesus' command is to love even one's enemies (Mt 5:43-48). The love of God must be exclusive, suffering no rival (Mt 6:24; Lk 16:13) and the disciples' love of Jesus must be greater than their love for parents or children (Mt 10:37).

According to Paul, the love of God has been poured into our hearts by the Holy Spirit (Rm 5:5). God has proved His love for us in that Christ died for us while we were still sinners (Rm 5:8). No trial or creature can separate us from the love of Christ (Rm 8:35-39). Husbands should love their wives as Christ loves the Church (Ep 5:25). All things work together for good to those who love God (Rm 8:28). All the other commandments are summed up in the commandment to love neighbor as self (Rm 13:8-10; Gal 5:13-14). Paul teaches that Chritians live in an atmosphere of love—of God for men and of men for God and neighbor. Love builds the Christian community (1 Cor 8:1). Love is the foundation and root of the Christian life (Ep 3:17). Love binds all the virtues together (Col 3:14). Love is the way which surpasses all others; it is the most excellent of all the gifts which are of no value without it; and it remains even after faith and hope disappear (1 Cor 13:1-13)).

Love is a prominent theme in the Johannine writings. Out of love the Father has adopted us as His children (1 Jn 3:1). Jesus showed His love for His own to the very end (Jn 13:1). He laid down His life for them (1 Jn 3:16). The one who is without love has known nothing of God, for God is love (1 Jn 4:8, 16). Love is demonstrated by keeping the commandments of God and Jesus (Jn 14:15, 21, 23). The new commandment of Jesus is to love one another (Jn 13:34; 15:17). As the Father has loved Jesus, so Jesus loved the disciples (Jn 15:9). The Father and the Son abide with one who loves Jesus (Jn 14:21, 23). Out of love God sent His Son into the world to be our savior. Whoever believes in Him has eternal life (Jn 3:16-17). Through love for one another we can be certain that God dwells in us and brings His love to perfection (1 Jn 4:7-21). In these writings, therefore, love is a mutual, all-embracing, unifying force.

Faith, Hope, and Charity in Theology

Faith. While the Bible ascribes various shades of meaning to the word, faith, the magisterium uses the term in a specific and technical sense. According to the First Vatican Council, faith is the assent of the intellect, under the influence of grace, to a truth revealed by God, not because we understand it, but because God, who can neither deceive nor be deceived, has revealed it.[1] Thus, Catholics accept the mystery of the three persons in the one God on faith; that is, they accept it, not because they understand it, but because God has revealed it. What God has revealed has been communicated to us especially through His divine Son, Jesus Christ (Heb 1:1-2), who has been accredited to us by His extraordinary deeds.[2] This teaching of the First Vatican Council has been reaffirmed by the Second Vatican Council.[3]

Faith resides in the intellect as a virtue and as an act. But the will also concurs in the act of faith because the truths to which the intellect assents lack that evidence which usually determines the assent of the intellect. The intervention of the will is necessary to move the intellect to adhere to the revealed truth. Hence, "the act of faith is of its very nature a free act. Man redeemed by Christ the Savior, and through Christ Jesus called to be God's adopted son, cannot give his adherence to God revealing Himself unless the Father draw him to offer to God the reasonable and free submission of faith."[4] Because faith rests on the authority of God revealing and not on the intrinsic evidence of truth, it is obscure; but it is nonetheless firm and certain. Furthermore, both in its beginning and its development, faith is always the effect of God's grace.[5]

The First Vatican Council defined the object of faith: "By divine and Catholic faith we must believe everything that is contained in the word of God, whether it is found in the Bible or has been handed down, and that is proposed by the Church as divinely revealed either by a solemn decree or by her ordinary and universal magisterium."[6] The same council defined the necessity of faith: Without faith it is impossible to please God (Heb 11:6).[7] At least the virtue of faith is necessary for infants while adults must orient their lives toward God by acts of faith.

The Second Vatican Council added further clarifications. Every disciple of Christ has the obligation of spreading the faith according to his ability.[8] Bishops are the preachers of the faith par excellence. They preach the faith that Catholics must believe and put into practice.[9] One of the principal aims of Christian education is to make the baptized person more conscious of the gift of faith.[10] The Spirit sustains the sense of faith among God's people.[11] Faith penetrates the believer's entire life.[12] Before men can come to the liturgy they must be called to faith and conversion.[13] The Christian way of life among non-Catholic Christians is nourished by their faith in Christ.[14]

Hope. Consideration has already been given to the virtue of hope in chapter 14 which is concerned with eschatology or the last things. Hope is the virtue by which we firmly trust that God, who is all-powerful and faithful to His promises, will in His mercy give us eternal happiness and the means to attain it. In chapter 14 it was noted that Christians hope for some part and fellowship with the saints in heavenly glory, that hope is rooted in the mercy and power of God who is able to save us, that the firmness of our hope is frequently represented in art by an anchor, that solid though this anchor of hope may be, we must still work out our salvation in fear and trembling in view of human willfulness. At least the virtue of hope, acquired through baptism, is necessary for infants while acts of hope are necessary for adults since they cannot direct their lives toward God and eternal happiness without hoping for it. To despair of salvation as well as to presume to gain it without personal effort is to sin against hope. Both as a virtue and as an act hope resides in the will. As faith gives way to vision, so hope gives way to possession in the after-life.

Charity. This is the greatest of the theological virtues (1 Cor 13:13). By it we love God above all things for His own sake, and our neighbor as ourselves for the love of God. Charity is the fulfillment of the great commandment of the Christian religion. As a theological virtue, charity loves God for His own sake, and ourselves and others because we participate in the goodness of God. Charity is not interested love (*amor concupiscentiae*), but the love of friends for each other (*amor benevolentiae*), a love which is not self-seeking, but rests in the goodness of the Beloved. Charity is the root and form of all the other virtues, because it has for its object the ultimate end, God in Himself, to whom it directs all supernatural activity with a continual influence, either latent or manifest. Charity means dedication to God and neighbor and a well-ordered concern for oneself. To have charity is to make God the center of our lives and to keep His commandments. Charity is the benevolence which God has for human beings.

Charity is love; it resides in the will both as a virtue and as an act. It is infused and increased with sanctifying grace. It is not diminished by venial sin, but it is lost by mortal sin. Charity remains even in the after-life when we shall love God whom we possess. Aquinas distinguished three degrees of charity—that of *beginners* who seek to detach themselves from sin, that of the *proficient* who are striving to perfect themselves, and that of the *perfect* who are united to God in a remarkable way even in this life.[15] Charity includes even our enemies. It obliges us to employ the ordinary means to preserve health and life. Charity is willing to renounce any created good out of love for God. Charity impels us to assist our brother and sister who find themselves in spiritual and temporal necessity; hence, the duty of fraternal correction and contributing to the poor. Charity forbids us to cooperate in the sins of others; but it does not forbid us to perform actions which others will abuse provided we have sufficient reason for doing so. Hatred, envy, sloth, and scandal are sins against charity. Scandal is an action which is either evil or has the appearance of evil and can be the occasion of another's sin.

Worship in the Scriptures

Christians have always seen themselves united with Christ; "through Him they give worship to the eternal Father."[16] The word, worship, means to ascribe supreme value to God. Sometimes worship is equated with the virtue of religion which means to render God the honor due Him. However, the word, religion, causes some confusion because it has other common meanings.[17]

The Catholic Church believes that "God chose to reveal Himself and to make known to us the hidden purpose of His will (Ep 1:19) by which through Christ, the Word made flesh, man has access to the Father in the Holy Spirit and comes to share in the divine nature" (Ep 2:18; 2P 1:4).[18] This revelation invites a response. "Therefore all the disciples of Christ, persevering in prayer and praising God (Ac 2:42-27), should present themselves as a living sacrifice, holy and pleasing to God" (Rm 12:1).[19] Christians respond to God's revealed love by uniting with Christ to offer worship to the eternal Father.[20]

In the Old Testament, the many references to worship reveal certain characteristics. The sole object of worship is Yahweh, a personal God, who cannot be represented by any image (Ex 20:2-5; Dt 5:2-10). Worship of other gods, sorcery, magic, divination, human sacrifices, and worship of the dead were all condemned. Worship itself was characterized by such cultural institutions as the ark of the covenant, a priesthood, various kinds of sacrifices, and a calendar of annual religious feasts.

Whenever God makes His glory and majesty known He invites a response: "Give glory to My name" (Ml 2:2; Jr 13:16; Is 42:8-12). The response of worship was rooted in the right inward disposition, especially the love of God (Dt 6:4-9; 10:12; 11:13). The prophets stressed the futility of ritual worship that lacked the proper interior disposition (Am 5:21-24; Jr 7:21-26; Mi 6:6-8). "What care I for the number of your sacrifices? says the Lord. I have had enough of whole-burnt rams and fat of fatlings; in the blood of calves, lambs, and goats I find no pleasure. . . . Wash yourselves clean! Put away misdeeds from before my eyes; cease doing evil, learn to do good. Make justice your aim; redress the wronged, hear the orphan's plea, defend the widow" (Is 1:11, 16-17).

In the New Testament, Jesus and His disciples practiced the traditional forms of Jewish worship (Mt 4:23; 26:17-19; Mk 6:2; Jn 2:13-14). Jesus Himself taught the command of the decalogue: "You shall worship the Lord your God and Him only shall you serve" (Mt 4:10). Jesus taught us to pray (Mt 6:7-13) and prayed Himself both publicly and privately. Following the prophetic tradition He demanded worship "in spirit and truth" (Jn 4:23). External cult without interior sentiments is worthless. "If you are offering your gift at the altar, and there remember that your brother has something against you, leave your gift there before the altar

and go; first be reconciled to your brother and then come offer your gift''
(Mt 5:23-24).

The New Testament also strongly emphasizes Jesus as the object of
worship. Jesus Himself prayed: "Father, give me glory at your side, a
glory which I had with you before the world began" (Jn 17:5). The early
Church understood Jesus to receive glory equal to the Father. "To the
One seated on the throne, and to the Lamb, be praise and honor, glory and
might, forever and ever!" (Rv 5:13). The fullness of God's love will
come when Christ returns in His glory (Rm 8:18-25). The power to
participate in the glory of God comes from the Holy Spirit: "All of us,
gazing on the Lord's glory with unveiled faces, are being transformed
from glory to glory into his very image by the Lord who is the Spirit" (2
Cor 3:18).

After Pentecost the apostles continued to observe Jewish rituals (Ac
2:46; 21:26), but they also began to honor Jesus (Jn 5:23; Ph 2:9-11). The
reenactment of the Last Supper was the center of the new worship (Mk
14:22-24; 1 Cor 11:17-34). The "breaking of the bread" was held on the
first day of the week instead of the sabbath (Ac 2:42; 1 Cor 16:2) to
commemorate the resurrection. Besides the Eucharist, other new Christian institutions, such as baptism, anointing of the sick, and the imposition of hands, were introduced (Ac 1:5; Jm 5:14-16; Ac 6:6; 8:17).

Forms of Worship

Prayer. The Gospels tell us that Jesus prayed often (Mt 14:23; 26:36;
26:42-44; Mk 1:35). Jesus' prayer reflects a childlike confidence in His
Father. His confidence in the absolute goodness of God was imitated by
His disciples. Moreover, closeness to Christ actually enables the Christian to pray. "The proof that you are sons is the fact that God has sent
forth into our hearts the spirit of His Son which cries out 'Abba!
Father!' " (Gal 4:6).

Since the time of the Apostolic Fathers prayer has been defined as
"speaking to God." Jesus' prayer in the garden of Gethsemane illustrates
this definition of prayer (Lk 22:41-44). Such a concept of prayer shows
that God has a personal concern for man and is moved by his prayers.
John Damascene (died c. 750) defined prayer as "raising the soul to
God." This concept stresses man's desire to unite himself with the
absolute holiness of God. Hence, mere mental reflection about God

would not be prayer.

The content of prayer may center on adoring God, thanking Him for favors received, asking His help, or expressing sorrow for our sins. All these purposes for praying give honor to God and none should be neglected. Traditionally, prayers of adoration and thanksgiving have been considered more perfect acts of worship in that they are more directed to the glorification of God.

Prayer in the Christian tradition has also been directed to the Blessed Mother, the angels, and saints because the glory of God has been manifested in them in a special way. God alone is to be adored; angels and saints are venerated for "the example in their way of life, fellowship in their communion, and aid in their intercession."[21] Special veneration is given the Virgin Mary, Mother of the Son of God, who, because of this sublime grace, "far surpasses all other creatures, both in heaven and on earth."[22]

The forms of prayer are commonly divided into interior or exterior, individual or common, formal or informal, liturgical or non-liturgical. All are good and serve different purposes. Interior prayer is the encounter of the heart with God and is usually called meditation or contemplation. Exterior prayer expresses itself in words and rituals and takes into account the fact that man is both body and soul. Common prayer recognizes that man is not only an individual, but a member of society, and needs the support of others and is responsible to others. "Where two or three are gathered in my name, there I am in their midst" (Mt 18:20). Informal prayer is commonly referred to "as talking with God in our own words" while formal prayer makes use of the wealth of religious experience of past generations. Liturgical prayer is the "full, public worship performed by the mystical body of Jesus Christ, that is, by the Head and His members."[23] The Mass, sacraments, sacramentals, and the divine office are examples of liturgical prayer. "The liturgy is the outstanding means by which the faithful can express in their lives and manifest to others the mystery of Christ and the real nature of the Church."[24]

In any prayer the one praying should have certain dispositions, namely, attention, reverence, and trust. Attention is the actual awareness of the mind to the content of prayer or the presence of God. The person wants to lift his mind and heart to God. Involuntary distraction cannot be avoided and should not be a cause of anxiety. In long oral prayers it is not necessary to be attentive to each sentence as long as the attention is directed to God in a general way. Reverence is a basic attitude which acknowledges the complete otherness of God and our complete dependence on Him. Trust means our confidence in the goodness of God and that He will hear our prayers.

Sacraments. Vatican II teaches that "the purpose of the sacraments is to sanctify men, to build up the body of Christ, and, finally, to give worship to God."[25] Sacraments are the heart of liturgical worship by which "the sanctification of man is manifested by signs perceptible to the senses and is effected in a way which is proper to each of these signs; in the liturgy full, public worship is performed by the mystical body of Christ."[26] In the past the emphasis of the sacraments was on God's imparting grace to man. Since Vatican II more emphasis has been given to the sacraments as the outstanding acts of common worship.

Certain dispositions are necessary if the reception of the sacraments is to be fruitful. Above all the recipient must have faith in God and Jesus Christ whom He sent.[27] The person must intend to receive the sacraments because God does not force His grace on anyone. The reception of the sacraments can be seen as a personal encounter with Christ. A distinction is made between baptism and penance which give the divine life of grace to those separated from God through sin, and the other sacraments which demand that the recipient be in the state of grace for a worthy reception.

Related to the sacraments which were instituted by Christ are the sacramentals instituted by the Church. The sacramentals "are sacred signs which bear a resemblance to the sacraments: they signify effects, particularly of a spiritual kind, which are obtained through the Church's intercession."[28] They dispose us to receive more fully the grace of the sacraments and to render various occasions in life more holy. Sacramentals are part of the Church's mission of sanctifying all things: the material order, time and space, and man.

Sunday Observance. From the earliest times "the Lord's Day" (Rv 1:10) has been a day of special prayer in memory of the resurrection of Jesus (Ac 20:7). The custom of Christians on Sunday to hear the word of God and to partake of the Eucharistic meal is recorded in the *Didache* (c. 100), by Ignatius of Antioch (d. 107), and by Justin Martyr (d. 160). Vatican II reiterated the importance of Sunday. "By an apostolic tradition which took its origin from the very day of Christ's resurrection, the

Church celebrates the paschal mystery every eighth day; with good reason, then, this bears the name of the Lord's day or the day of the Lord. For on this day Christ's faithful should come together into one place so that, hearing the word of God and taking part in the Eucharist, they may call to mind the passion, the resurrection, and the glorification of the Lord Jesus, and thank God who 'has begotten us again, through the resurrection of Jesus Christ from the dead, unto a living hope.' "[29]

The heart of the Sunday worship is the Mass which Jesus instituted at the Last Supper on the night before He died. "He did this in order to perpetuate the sacrifice of the cross throughout the centuries until He should come again, and so to entrust to His beloved spouse, the Church, a memorial of His death and resurrection: a sacrament of love, a sign of unity, a bond of charity, a paschal banquet in which Christ is consumed, the mind is filled with grace, and a pledge of future glory is given to us."[30] Since the richness of the Lord's powers and mercies are too great to be absorbed on a given Sunday, the Church assigns different readings from the Scriptures for each Sunday, so that the various events of Christ's life and saving work are recalled throughout the year.[31]

Special mention must be made of the community nature of Sunday worship to counteract a certain individualistic approach to Sunday observance in the past in which the faithful attended Mass as "silent spectators."[32] The reforms in the ritual of the Mass have stressed the fullest participation. "Therefore, the liturgical life of the parish and its relationship to the bishop must be fostered in the thinking and practice of both laity and clergy; efforts must also be made to encourage a sense of community within the parish, above all in the common celebration of the Sunday Mass."[33] Canon 1248 of the Code of Canon Law obliges Catholics to attend a holy Mass and to observe a sacred rest on Sundays and holydays of obligation. This law is understandable both in the light of man's natural duty to worship God and in the light of the place of the Mass in Christian tradition.

Sunday as a day of rest continued the long tradition of the Sabbath rest of the Old Testament. Vatican II reaffirmed this tradition. "The Lord's Day is the original feast day, and it should be proposed to the piety of the faithful and taught to them in such a way that it may become in fact a day of joy and of freedom from work."[34] Sunday rest, then, should provide an unhurried time for reflection and development of the interior life. It should provide a break from the routine of the work-a-day world to allow cultivation of higher values including the strengthening of family and community bonds.

These principles should be kept in mind in trying to define what work is forbidden on Sunday. Both the changing American culture as well as the needs of the individual are important factors to be considered. In general, those works and activities are to be omitted which are incompatible with the requirement of common worship or which deprive one of being renewed in body and spirit.

Vows. A brief mention should be made of vows as a form of worship. A person takes a vow by making a special promise to God to perform a specific act (e.g., to make a pilgrimage or to give an alms) or to live in a particular state of life (e.g., as a nun). Vows differ from promises made to God in that a vow involves a sin if it is broken. The serious nature of a vow demands sufficient thought, deliberation, and preparation. A vow is private when the person makes it with God alone. A vow is public when it includes a special responsibility to the Christian community and is recognized as such by Church authorities. Vatican II sees the vowed life as an act of supreme love committing a person to the honor and service of God under a new title. "The consecration gains in perfection since by virtue of firmer and steadier bonds it serves as a better symbol of the unbreakable link between Christ and His spouse, the Church."[35]

Sins against True Worship of God. The Scriptures are strong in their condemnation of the worship of false gods (idolatry). "I the Lord, am your God, who brought you out of the land of Egypt, that place of slavery. You shall not have other gods besides me. You shall not carve idols for yourselves in the shape of anything in the sky above or on the earth below or in the waters beneath the earth; you shall not bow down before them or worship them" (Ex 20:2-5; *see* also 1 Cor 10:14; 1 Jn 5:21; Rv 21:8). Closer to our age of wealth and materialism is the idolatry denounced in the New Testament of making money and pleasure ultimate values (Mt 6:24; Ep 5:5; Ph 3:19; Col 3:5).

It is a sin to dishonor the name of God. Reverence for the name of God is widely mentioned in the Bible because to honor God's name is to honor Him. In the New Testament the name of Jesus is also to be revered and adored (Ph 2:9-11). Paul makes it clear that Christians must act so that Jesus' name is glorified. "We pray for you always that our God may make you worthy of his call, and fulfill by his power every honest intention and work of faith. In this way the name of our Lord Jesus may be glorified in you and you in him, in accord with the gracious gift of our God and of our Lord Jesus Christ'' (2 Th 1:11-12).

Blasphemy, which is intentionally insulting God or denying His goodness, is always seriously wrong. Profanity is a disrespectful use of God's name, usually in thoughtlessness or in anger. In profanity the person doesn't intend to insult God and so the offense is not as serious. "Cursing" and "swearing" have various meanings. They could be used to mean blasphemy or profanity. And they are often used to signify vulgar or "barnyard" language. In the latter case they are more a problem of etiquette than of morality.

Sins against true worship include superstition (including magic), divination and vain observance, and lack of reverence for God's name and for persons and things especially related to God. Superstition in the strict sense is the inappropriate attempt to make God depend on man's actions. It is inspired by the idea that man can manipulate God by special prayers or rituals. Sometimes it is difficult to judge in this matter—what may be a superstitious practice for one person may be a deeply religious action for another. In superstition the person at least attributes the power to God as the source of all power. In magic a person believes he can manipulate certain supra-human forces by means of special prayers and rituals. Superstition and magic are not practices limited to more primitive cultures. We might think how often we hear of the number 13, horoscopes, black cats, and good luck charms. If these go beyond the joking stage to be taken seriously, then they are an affront to the true worship of God.

Divination is the attempt to predict the future or to obtain occult knowledge by certain kinds of actions. Common forms of divination are astrology, communication with the dead (spiritualism), card and tea leaf reading, and palm reading. Each divination must be judged separately, for all conjectures about the future are not superstition, especially if some, however remote, scientific explanation can be offered. Certainly if one appealed to the devil in order to know the future, his act would be idolatry. Divination is wrong if the diviner believes he is guided by occult powers operative in the world. ''Even though the diviner does not accept his own claims to occult power but perpetrates a hoax and exploits the superstitious credulity of others, he is guilty of superstition and violation of fraternal love, for he seduces them and cooperates in their superstition."[36]

Honor for God also implies reverence for consecrated persons, places, and things. Reverence for consecrated persons means that certain people (e.g., priests and religious) are signs of God's presence among men and accordingly are to be respected for the sake of God. An injury inflicted on a consecrated person (e.g., striking a bishop) is called a personal sacrilege. Places set aside for the worship of God are to be shown reverence (e.g., respect for a church building). Material things used exclusively in divine cult are to be shown reverence. The Blessed Sacrament by its nature is the most holy thing; and to receive it unworthily or to profane it deliberately is the gravest form of sacrilege. Bibles, sacred vessels, holy oils, relics, and crucifixes are all sacred things that must be shown proper respect. The more exclusively the object is ordered to divine cult, the greater is the respect to be shown.

A special offense against holy things is simony which is the buying and selling of spiritual things such as blessings, sacraments, indulgences, prayers, and ecclesiastical offices.

Footnotes

1. *TCC* no. 35.
2. Vatican I, *TCC* no. 36.
3. *Dei Verbum* nos. 4-5.
4. Vatican II, *Dignitatis Humanae* no. 10.
5. Second Council of Orange (529), *TCC* no. 698.
6. *TCC* no. 38.
7. *TCC* no. 39.
8. *Lumen Gentium* no. 17.
9. *Ibid*. no. 25.
10. *Gravissimum Educationis* no. 2.
11. *Lumen Gentium* no. 12.
12. *Gaudium et Spes* no. 21.
13. *Sacrosanctum Concilium* no. 9.
14. *Unitatis Redintegratio* no. 23.

15. *ST* 2a2ae.24.9.
16. *Sacrosanctum Concilium* no. 7.
17. Häring, *op. cit.* 2, 119-120.
18. *Dei Verbum* no. 2.
19. *Lumen Gentium* no. 10.
20. *Sacrosanctum Concilium* no. 7.
21. *Lumen Gentium* no. 51.
22. *Ibid.* no. 53.
23. *Sacrosanctum Concilium* no. 7.
24. *Ibid.* no. 2.
25. *Ibid.* no. 59.
26. *Ibid.* no. 7.
27. *Ibid.* no. 9.
28. *Ibid.* no. 60.
29. *Ibid.* no. 106.
30. *Ibid.* no. 47.
31. *Ibid.* no. 102.
32. *Ibid.* no. 48.
33. *Ibid.* no. 42.
34. *Sacrosanctum Concilium* no. 106.
35. *Lumen Gentium* no. 44.
36. Häring, *op. cit.* 226-227.

Chapter 21

RESPONSIBILITY FOR TRUTH, FIDELITY, HONOR, AND JUSTICE

Bibliography: Church documents: Leo XIII, *Rerum Novarum*, 1891. Engl. transl. in *Rerum Novarum*, New York, 1939, Paulist Press; Pius XI, *Quadragesimo Anno*, 1931, Engl. transl. in *The Social Order*, London, 1960, Catholic Truth Society; John XXIII, *Mater et Magistra*, 1961. Engl. transl. in *The Gospel of Peace and Justice*, Maryknoll, 1976, Orbis Books; John XXIII, *Pacem in Terris*, 1963, *ibid.*; Vatican II, *Gaudium et Spes*, The Pastoral Constitution on the Church in the Modern World, 1965. Engl. transl. in Abbott-Gallagher, *The Documents of Vatican II*, New York, 1966, The America Press; Paul VI, *Populorum Progresio*, 1968. Engl. transl. in *The Gospel of Peace and Justice*, Maryknoll, 1976, Orbis Books; Paul VI, *Octogesima Adveniens*, 1971, *ibid.*; Roman Synod of Bishops, *Justice in the World*, 1971, *ibid.*; John Paul II, *Redemptor Hominis*, 1979. Engl. transl. in *The Pope Speaks*, vol. 2, no. 2, 1979. Other writings: *DB*; B. Häring, C.SS.R., *The Law of Christ*, Cork, 1963, The Mercier Press, vol. 3; J. Clavez and J. Perrin, *The Church and Social Justice*, London, 1961, Burns and Oates; O. von Nell-Bruening, *Christian Social Doctrine*, in *SM*, 6; P. Pavan, *Papal Social Thought* in *NCE* 13; C. Peschke, S.V.D., *Christian Ethics*, Dublin, 1978, C. Goodliffe Neale, vol. 2.

Truth, fidelity, and honor have to do with those interior values which enable people to live in peace and harmony with each other. Truthfulness is the virtue that inclines one to speak only the truth, that is, what one believes to be in conformity with reality. This social virtue is necessary if there is to be trust among peoples. Closely allied to truthfulness is fidelity which inclines one to stick to his convictions and promises. Honor is the virtue that inclines us to give the esteem due another because of his position in the community or because of his true value.

Truth and Fidelity in the Scriptures

In the Old Testament, the word for truth is *emeth* which is best translated as faithfulness. When *emeth* is said of God, it means that He is faithful and trustworthy; and He is especially faithful to His covenant (Dt 7:9; Ne 9:35; Ps 71:22; Is 49:7). When *emeth* is said of man, it generally means that he is loyal to God's covenant and law (Zc 8:3; 1 K 2:4; Tb 4:6; Si 29:9). Jeremiah uses *emeth* in a narrower sense to signify the conformity of what is said to reality. The Lord expects men to be faithful (*emeth*) to their words (Jr 23:28). Not to speak the truth is iniquity (Jr 9:5).

It is truth in the narrower sense that we are interested in here. The Old Testament clearly condemns the lie (Ex 20:16; Lv 19:11; Jr 9:3-9). Yet in some places the Old Testament seems to condone falsehood for a good purpose. We can see it in the story of Abraham (Gn 12:11 ff), Isaac (Gn 26:7-11), Jacob (Gn 27:18ff), David (1 S 20:6ff) and Judith (Jdt 10:12ff).

In the New Testament truth is a word rich with different meanings. It can signify fidelity to God (Rm 3:3-7). It can signify sound doctrine (1 Tm 1:10 ff). It can mean the revelation of God in Christ (Jn 1:17). In the narrow sense of conformity of speech to reality, Paul says: "Put away falsehood; let everyone speak the truth with his neighbor, for we are members of one another" (Ep 4:25). The New Testament is more strict against lying. "Do not lie to one another" (Col 3:9). The devil is the father of lies (Jn 8:44). The "yes" and "no" of Jesus' disciples must be so reliable that they do not need an oath (Mt 5:37).

The Lie

The teaching of the Fathers on lying was dominated by Augustine who, relying on the Scriptures, taught that a lie was intrinsically evil, that is, forbidden in all circumstances. He defined a lie as a false statement with the intention to deceive. Aquinas accepted the teaching of Augustine, although he saw the evil of lying to be essentially against the natural meaning of speech intended by God. Although the lie was against nature, theologians held that it was not grave matter unless it caused great harm to another.

To understand a lie as intrinsically evil, as always forbidden, creates practical problems when one is asked an awkward question or a question that the inquirer has no right to ask. "Do you like the dress I made?" "Is that student on drugs?" "Is Mr. Jones the man who took the money?" Questions like these have traditionally called for evasive answers. We are more inclined to say that the dress is interesting or different rather than hurt the women's feelings by saying that it is the worst dress we have ever seen. Or we might say that we haven't heard that the student was on drugs. We mean that we haven't heard it for you to know, since you have no right to know and the student's name must be protected.

Theologians have justified this evasive language calling it mental reservation. Mental reservation means veiled speech in which the words used have a secondary meaning intended by the speaker which an astute listener would understand. If the secondary meaning of the words is so restricted that an astute listener could not fathom the real meaning, the mental reservation is the same as a lie. So, to say, "The boss is not in," is generally accepted to mean that he is not available to you right now. This would be a broad mental reservation. But to say, "I didn't take the money," meaning that I took the bag (and the money happened to be inside) would be a strict mental reservation which is equivalent to a lie.

Mental reservation is a way to keep from hurting someone's feelings out of charity or to protect someone out of justice without telling a lie which is never permitted. Clearly, it has its drawbacks. Some see it as a mental gymnastics unworthy of a Christian. Others see it as not too helpful if the listener is really astute and the speaker is trying to protect the rights of a third party. A rather dramatic and true case cited by Father Häring concerns the mother superior of a convent in wartime Germany who wished to protect Jewish children from the Gestapo. Was she permitted to "lie" to save the lives of these innocent children? The most common traditional answer was "No," because it is never permitted to do something intrinsically evil even for the purpose of saving lives.

To deal with such cases, some theologians distinguish a lie from false speech. A lie would be false speech which violates the listener's right to know the truth. But if the inquirer has no right to know the truth, as in the case of the Gestapo hunting for Jewish children, false speech is morally justified. By distinguishing a lie from false speech, this view would see truthfulness in speech as a very important value but not the highest value. This view would justify the mother superior's false speech to save the lives of Jewish children. The proponents of this second view would argue that a reasonable person would accept hearing false speech in such a rare situation. It must be kept in mind that these theologians are speaking of a very rare cases.

The difficulty with this second view is that it conflicts with the traditional understanding of a lie as intrinsically evil. Moreoever, there is the danger that the rare, exceptional case may become more common and people may lost confidence in the word of another.

Oaths

Because people at times want to be assured of the truthfulness of an important statement, they have the speaker invoke God as witness to the truthfulness of the statement. This calling on the name of God to witness the truth of a statement or promise is called an oath. There are many examples in the Old Testament (Dt 6:13; Lv 19:12; Ps 24:4 ff; Si 23:9-11). In the New Testament Jesus seems to forbid oaths (Mt 5:34-37), although this is not generally understood literally. It is rather seen as a call to perfection or the description of a reborn society in which there is no need for oaths, because no one ever lies. Paul often took an oath (Rm 1:9; 2 Cor 1:18; Gal 1:20; 1 Th 2:5).

In practice, the Christian tradition has always accepted oaths under three conditions: truthfulness, moral soundness, and sufficient reason. Clearly, it would be seriously wrong to invoke God's name to support a lie (perjury) or for immoral purposes. One should not invoke God's name for a frivolous reason. A promissory oath, cr an oath enforcing a promise, would cease to bind if circumstances changed so that the results would be an obstacle to a greater good or if the results were contrary to the original intention.

The Promise

A promise is a free offer by which one binds himself to do something for another. The obligation is one of being true to one's word or, simply, one of fidelity. One does not normally bind oneself under grave obligation. If failing to keep a promise would cause great harm to another, one would be gravely bound to his promise. There are several reasons for which just one of the parties could terminate the promise: unforeseen, harmful circumstances, renunciation of the promise by the recipient, or impossibility of carrying out the promise. Also it would cease if a circumstance would arise in view of which the promisor would never have made the promise had he foreseen it.

Secrets

A secret is a hidden fact which one may not divulge. Generally secrets are divided into three kinds: natural, promised, and the committed secret. A natural secret is one which by its very nature requires the knower not to reveal it in order to protect another. Thus, we keep secret our knowledge that our neighbor has some moral fault or a prison record or a mental illness. A promised secret is based on one's word not to reveal what has been entrusted. "Promise me you won't tell . . .," would be the common expression of this secret. The committed or entrusted secret is based on justice arising out of a professional relationship. Doctors, counselors, lawyers, and ministers are often given secret knowledge because of their position. This is the most serious kind of secret because its violation most hurts the common good.

The obligation to keep a secret ceases in three cases: if the one being protected wants the secret known; if the secret becomes public knowledge by other means; or if a sufficient reason justifies its revelation. This latter case is a catch-all that is often hard to determine. For example, a doctor may be required by law (for the common good) to reveal certain committed secrets such as gunshot wounds or venereal disease. Revelation of natural secrets about public officials is generally accepted since these people serve the public. Even here, the more serious the secret, the more serious the reason needed to reveal it. In the rare case of revealing a committed secret, special care must be taken of the long-range results. Few reasons would ever justify the public's loss of confidence in counselors, doctors, and ministers. No reason would justify the breaking of the seal of confession.

Honor

Honor is the high estimation and external respect we give to someone based on that person's self-worth or place in the community. The duty to honor is found in the Scriptures. One of the ten commandments obliges us to honor our father and mother (Ex 20:12). Paul tells us to pay "respect and honor to everyone who deserves them" (Rm 13:7) and that we are not only to love each other but to anticipate each other in showing honor (Rm 12:10). Fitting honor for oneself is praiseworthy (Pr 22:1; Si 41:12). Paul is anxious to protect his good name (1 Cor 1 Cor 10:32 ff; Ac 24:16; 2 Cor 1:12). To dishonor someone receives the highest condemnation (Mt 5:22; Mt 7:1; 1 Cor 6:10; Jm 2:2-6).

The highest honor, of course, is given to God; and we show this honor to God by both internal and external acts of respect. Next, we show honor to people who reflect God's goodness. Thus, the mother of God and the saints receive special honor. Honor is also given to a person, such as the president of a country, because of his position. Honor is given to persons who develop their natural talents. Honor is given to oneself. The phrase, "a person of honor," means one who recognizes his own self-worth and, accordingly, is true and faithful to his own convictions. In its most basic form honor is due every person because he is made in the image of God. This honor is due to all persons irregardless of moral achievements or failures.

Contumely is the unjust dishonoring of someone in his presence. Contumelious treatment includes the mocking of a representative of that person or of his picture or hanging him in effigy. The evil consists in depriving the person of the honor due him. Again the words of Jesus are very strong: "What I say to you is: everyone who grows angry with his brother shall be liable to judgment; any man who uses abusive language toward his brother shall be answerable to the Sanhedrin, and if he holds him in contempt he risks the fires of Gehenna" (Mt 5:22). Detraction is the making public some true but hidden fault of another without sufficient reason. Everyone has the right to his good name. However, this right to a good name is conditioned by the good of society. So sometimes secret faults have to be revealed. Accordingly, a person seeking an important public office is scrutinized to see if he is a worthy candidate. Hidden faults relating to his ability to carry out the duties of office should be revealed.

Calumny is the willful attribution of evil defects to another which one knows to be false. Calumny thus has the added malice of a lie. This is commonly called slander. The Scriptures speak very harshly about slander (Lv 19:16; Rm 1:29ff; 2 Tm 3:3). One can cooperate in the defamation of another merely by listening to the defamer. Sometimes it is difficult to avoid the one defaming. However, to elicit talebearing or slander is the moral equivalent of speaking it. Where possible, the defamer is to be rebuked. Parents have the responsibility to warn their children against gossip, talebearing, and, above all, slander.

Justice in the Scriptures

Justice is generally understood as rendering to another his due. But the concept is so basic to the moral life that, like love, it has many meanings. In the Old Testament righteousness and judgment are used to express justice. A righteous weight is one that is exact (Dt 25:15; Lv 19:36). Judges should not show partiality but justice (Lv 19:15). The good king loves righteousness (Ps 45:8). Justice is seen as the implementation of the rights of others (Ex 23:6-8). The prophets railed against injustice always seeing it as an offense against God (Am 5:11-15; Is 5:22 ff; Jr 22:13-18). The just man is one who serves God (Ml 3:18) and is faithful to the Law (Gn 18:19), upright and blameless (Gn 18:23-32; Ws 1:1).

In the New Testament the concept of justice is even more complex. The man of good moral conduct is righteous (Mk 2:17; Mt 5:45; Lk 20:20). One is to seek first the kingdom of God and its righteousness (Mt 6:33). The righteousness of Jesus' followers is to surpass that of the scribes and Pharisees (Mt 5:20). The Christian is righteous as Jesus is righteous (1 Jn 3:7). Righteousness is specified as love of one's brother (1 Jn 3:10). "The way of justice" means to live according to God's command (Mt 21:22; 2 P 2:21). The just man lives an upright life (Mt 1:19; 13:17; Lk 1:6; 2:25).

In the theology of Paul, righteousness comes not by observing the Law but by faith in Jesus (Rm 1:17; 3:28). We are made righteous or justified through God's grace by the redemption of Jesus (Rm 5:18). The kingdom of God is justice, peace, and the joy that is given by the Holy Spirit (Rm 14:17). It was Paul's wish that Christians "be found rich in the harvest of justice which Jesus Christ has ripened in you to the glory and praise of God" (Ph 1:11). Perfect justice always eludes us; it remains an object to be hoped for in the Spirit (Gal 5:5).

Notion of Justice

Justice is so basic to moral living that its concept is hard to pin down especially in concrete cases. Justice is giving each one what is his by right. It is a social norm in that it guides the actions of people in their dealings with each other. That an action is just means that it is good and should be done. Not to do justice is to do evil. Moreover, there is an objectivity about justice which means that justice for one person implies justice for another. In other words, what is sauce for the goose is sauce for the gander.

While there is agreement in Catholic theology that justice is the firm and constant will to give everyone his due, this description is too vague to determine what justice is in a concrete case. Traditionally, justice has been divided into commutative, distributive, and legal or general justice. Pius XI added the term, social justice. But even these terms are highly controverted among Catholic authors, especially, the terms, legal and social justice.

Of all these terms the easiest to understand is commutative justice which inclines one to render that which is his to the point of arithmetic equality. For example, if you agree to work for me for three dollars an hour and I pay you three dollars for every hour you work, justice is done as it is understood from a commutative point of view. However, this example shows the problem of establishing justice. If you are a family man who cannot support your family on three dollars an hour, something is unjust about the situation even though you were paid exactly as agreed. Nor would I be considered a just man if I said: "I paid you exactly as you agreed. On your way if you don't like it. There are many others who want to take your place. I violate no law because three dollars an hour is not below the minimum wage established by law." Aquinas foresaw this difficulty, and he subordinated particular justice and its concrete applications to general justice which regulates conduct with respect to the common good. In other words, a particular application of justice is unjust if it violates the common good. In the case cited, the common good is violated in that the wage agreed upon is not a living wage.

Another kind of particular application of justice is distributive justice which inclines the rulers of a society (community, family) to distribute the goods and burdens of that society according to the merits and capabilities of the members. Unlike commutative justice, there is no strict arithmetic equality, but a geometric proportionality. Distributive justice distributes the burdens of a society according to one's capabilities. For example, in our society a rich man pays proportionally more taxes than a poor man. Only healthy men are drafted. The blind and the aged are given special tax breaks. Again, for a particular incident of distributive justice to be truly just, it must be in accord with general justice which regulates the common good. Naturally, in a given case there is often a difference of opinion as to what is the common good.

General justice was called legal justice by Thomas Aquinas, because divine and natural law (not man-made or positive law) has for its function the direction of action to the common good.[1] General justice is concerned with the objective norm governing our social relationships toward the common good while commutative and distributive justice are the subjective expressions of this norm. That is to say, we don't do specific acts of general justice but always acts of particular justice, whether commutative or distributive. All the requirements of general justice are resolved into rights and duties, either of the individual toward another individual (commutative justice) or of the social authority to the subjects of that authority (distributive justice).

With the rise of nation states in the 16th and 17th centuries, Francis de Vitoria (d. 1546) and Hugo Grotius (d. 1645), the fathers of international law, strove to protect people, especially, in small, neutral countries, by guaranteeing their rights in positive law. They reinforced with positive law basic rights that they believed were ultimately based on divine and natural law. Later on, some thinkers came to believe that the people had rights only if they were stated in man-made (positive) laws. By the beginning of the 20th century, theologians were using the term, legal justice, to mean positive or man-made laws. This, of course, was a complete reversal of the position of Aquinas. Because of the misuse of the term, legal justice, Pius XI in 1931 used the term social justice to indicate conformity with the common good, especially in the economic area. There is still debate today ovec the precise meaning of the term. Some see it as a virtue that regulates the structure of society. Others see it to be the same as Aquinas' general justice. Either way, the important element is that individual acts of justice (commutative and distributive) must be rooted in some higher justice that seeks the dignity of the person in the common good.

The Basis of Justice

The Catholic tradition has consistently rooted justice in human rights which, in turn, flow from the dignity of the person. The oldest reason for this dignity is that the person is made in the image of God (Gn 1:26-27). As such, he has intelligence and free will. Paul amplifies this freedom by seeing it as conscience which moves man to act according to a law laid down by the creator (Rm 2:15). Furthermore, for the Christian every person has a special relationship to God that is grounded in the mystery of the Son of God becoming man. All have been redeemed by His death and resurrection.

There are certain characteristics of rights in the Catholic tradition. First, there is the corresponding duty to use one's rights properly and also the duty to recognize the rights of others. Secondly, there is a hierarchy of rights. One person's right to food is a higher right than another's right to a luxury item. The more a right is necessary to ensure human dignity, the higher or more important is that right. Thirdly, there is a relation between love and justice in resolving conflicts of rights. The demands of love always fulfill the rightful claims of another, but love enables justice to see rightly. Love tempers the rigid demands of justice for the good of our neighbor. It allows one in imitation of Christ to go beyond justice in meeting the needs of others.

Even with a thorough understanding of the theory of justice and rights, it is often difficult to determine what is just in a concrete situation. To what extent does a country club have the right to determine its own membership rules? Should medical schools give preference to minority applicants in order to make up for past discrimination? Should oil companies be taxed for enormous profits? Is it objectively wrong for the United States, five percent of the world's population, to consume forty percent of its resources? People will answer these questions differently. One reason for disagreement is that we feel differently about a situation if we see ourselves as a victim rather than a beneficiary of the situation. Hourly workers in a factory tend to see a new contract in a different light than management.

This problem is being just and fair is further complicated by how we view the problem in terms of merit, equality, and fairness. For example, most people would say that it is only fair and just that the president of a company make more money than one of its secretaries, that blind people be given special help by society, that rich and poor alike are entitled to equal protection under the law. Yet, in each case we are using different perspectives for determining what is just and fair. In the first case, we are using a concept of merit—the president of a company has more responsibility than a secretary; in the second case, we are using a welfare or catch-up concept that enables blind people to catch up to the norm in some degree; in the third case we are using an equalitarian concept. In other words, it doesn't seem just to fit everything into one mold by having secretaries make as much as presidents or having blind people fend for themselves. Other examples that are more controversial include windfall profits tax, school busing, affirmative action for medical schools, the equal rights amendment, and the government allocation of scarce resources.

While many issues of justice will remain contested by people of good will, there has been an ever growing awareness of what is fair and just. In the United States of America, for example, there has been progress in civil rights. The next section will present the ever-growing development of rights and justice as seen from recent Church social teaching.

The Historical Development of Church Social Teaching

From the earliest times the Church has spoken out on issues of justice. The writings of Augustine, Thomas Aquinas, de Vitoria, and Suarez on these issues are rich. However, in modern times we can see a systematic treatment of rights and justice beginning with *Rerum Novarum* by Leo XIII in 1891 and continuing through John Paul's *Redemptor Hominis* in 1979. To understand various themes in these writings we need to sketch the historical development.

When *Rerum Novarum* was written in 1891, the industrial revolution was well underway. The worker was little more than a mere commodity in the productive process. Stressing the dignity of the worker as a human being, Leo XIII deduced basic rights which flow from that dignity: the right to a just wage, the right to organize, the right to state protection from exploitation, and the right to decent working conditions. Rejecting the extremes of socialism and laissez-faire capitalism, Leo made the dignity of the person the basis for future social teaching. Forty years later Pius XI continued the teaching of Leo in *Quadragesimo Anno*, emphasizing the dignity of the worker, the common good of society, and the responsibility of the state to promote the temporal well-being of every member of society. The principle for governing state interventions is called the principle of subsidiarity. This principle means that the state, or even lesser, intermediate powers, should never intervene to do for a lower group (family or individual) what the lower order can do for itself.

With Pope John XXIII's *Mater et Magistra* in 1961 there was a shift in focus in Church social teaching. The emphasis was placed on the global aspect of justice, the rights of all to share in the fruits of society, and the need to correct imbalances, especially, in the agricultural sector. In some ways it could be said that the oppressed working classes in the United States and Europe, championed by Leo XIII and Pius XI, are now the privileged few in comparison with the rest of the world. That is to say, the recent encyclicals are calling the workers of the industrialized world to new responsibilities. Two years later Pope John continued this stress on the world community in *Pacem in Terris*. Because of advances in science and technology, ''social progress, order, security, and peace of any one country are necessarily connected with the social progress, order, security, and peace of all other countries.''[2] Claiming that the well-ordering of society is based on the rights and duties that flow from the dignity of the person, *Pacem in Terris* gives the first systematic listing of these rights and duties in Church teaching.

With Vatican II's Pastoral Constitution on the Church in the Modern World (*Gaudium et Spes*) in 1965, there was a shift away from a social teaching rooted on a natural law of doctrine of rights. The real question facing the fathers of the council was not to promulgate a social doctrine, but to delineate the root principles and the basic laws governing the existence of the Church in the world and in history. The approach used by *Gaudium et Spes* and subsequent Church Social teaching is more inductive, scrutinizing the signs of the times with other men and women of good will. This approach, marked by humility, uses a phenomenological rather than a philosophical analysis. To be sure, *Gaudium et Spes* presents the tradition of the Church on the dignity of the person and the Church's unique contribution to mankind; but at the same time it recognizes that the betterment of mankind comes also from sources outside the Church.[3]

In *Populorum Progressio* in 1967, Pope Paul VI treated the social problems from the aspect of the rising expectations of man seeking to do more, know more, and have more in order to be more.[4] Decrying the ever-widening gap between rich and poor, Pope Paul called for advanced nations to assist developing nations not only with aid, but by establishing a more just economic order. The responsibility rests squarely with the economically developed nations. Four years later in the letter *Octogesima Adveniens*, Pope Paul extended the range of the Christian response from the economic to the political level.[5] Moreoever, he taught the need of local groups to decide effective action without waiting for direction from ecclesiastical leaders.[6] The future orientation begun in *Gaudium et Spes* is evident in the new range of problems which admit a plurality of options among people of good will. These new problems include urbanization, youth, the role of women, victims of change, discrimination, environment, and the creation of employment.

In the same year, the Synod of Bishops in their document *Justice in the World* gave an even more profound meaning to justice. "Action on behalf of justice and participation in the transformation of the world fully appear to us as a constitutive dimension of the preaching of the Gospel, or, in other words, of Church's mission for the redemption of the human race and its liberation from every oppressive structure."[7] When we realize that constitutive means essential, this indeed is a strong statement about justice. After elaborating on the unjust structures in the world today, the bishops then called for the right to development which "must be seen as a dynamic interpenetration of all those fundamental human rights upon which the aspiration of individuals and nations are based."[8]

In 1979 Pope John Paul II issued *Redemptor Hominis* which is basically a strong Christological statement governing the Church's involvement in the world. Everything must be seen from the viewpoint and within the perspective of Jesus Christ. "Given Christ and His mystery which is her very life, the Church cannot be indifferent to all that leads to the true good of human beings, nor neglectful of anything that is detrimental to that good."[9] The Holy Father then mentions many of the areas covered by recent Church social teaching. His purpose is not to delineate specific problems, but rather to explain the social implications of the mystery of the incarnation and redemption.

Urgency of Social Justice

The vast amount of Church social teaching since *Mater et Magistra* touches almost every aspect of social life. Any summary necessarily omits valuable insights. In fact, to appreciate the richness and the nuances of Church social teaching, one must read the commentaries on them. However, three themes are presented here to acquaint one with the dynamism of the Church's concern for social justice. These themes are the urgency of social justice, responsible stewardship, and the need for development.

It took mankind until about 1840 to reach one billion people. In 1975, the world population passed four billion. Conservative estimates place it at six billion people by the year 2000. At the same time, technological advances have enabled some segments of the world to take gigantic economic strides which in turn enables them through economic and political power to control the market place and to consume ever more of the available resources. Meanwhile, the majority of mankind "is deprived of nearly all possibility of personal initiative and of responsibility, and oftentimes even its living and working conditions are unworthy of the human person."[10] This would include "those people who are striving to escape from hunger, misery, endemic diseases and ignorance; of those who are looking for a wider share in the benefits of civilization and a more active improvement of their human qualities."[11]

This need for social justice is urgent too, not only because the majority of mankind is suffering, but because of the danger of even more suffering through war, whose horror and perversity have been greatly magnified by technology.[12] The main cause of war is people fighting against the injustices they experience.[13] Peace cannot, then, be a mere absence of war or a precarious balance of power between enemies. Peace must be the enterprise of justice,[14] built up day after day in the pursuit of the order intended by God which implies a more perfect form of justice among men.[15] "We have desired to remind all men how crucial is the present moment, how urgent the work to be done. The hour for action has now sounded. At stake are the survival of so many innocent children and, for so many families overcome by misery, the access to conditions fit for human beings; at stake are the peace of the world and the future of civilization. It is time for all men and all peoples to face up to their responsibilities."[16]

Responsible Stewardship

Church teaching on the responsible use of earthly goods is founded on the fundamental equality of all peoples.[17] Accordingly, no one is justified in keeping for his exclusive use what he does not need, when others lack necessities.[18] This basic teaching which is rooted in the Scriptures and Fathers of the Church has many ramifications in the world today. These ramifications include the increasing interdependence among peoples, the ever-widening imbalance of goods, the use of money, property, and power, the international component to business ethics, and the social consequences of sin.

Vatican II spoke of the ever-increasing interdependence among all peoples which involves new rights and duties to ensure the common good.[19] In the United States we have painfully experienced this interdependence while waiting in line to pay much more for a gallon of gasoline—all because someone in some part of the world raised the price of oil. Our immediate concern may be a change of lifestyle and the need to drive fewer miles in a smaller car; but, as the council fathers noted, the problems of interdependence are very complex.[20] In the case of oil, we Americans are burning up a large percentage of the world's oil even though we are a small fraction of the world's population. With some hardship we can afford it; but that is not the point. Our consumption raises the price of this limited commodity and prices it off the market for poorer countries who lack hard currencies to buy it. These poor countries in turn are then greatly crippled in operating machines necessary for farming, irrigation equipment, and transport of necessary goods. Nor can they afford modern, petro-chemical fertilizers so necessary for large harvests. Our driving habits literally affect the lives of people all over the world.

The hunger issue is an even more serious problem with one-third of mankind malnourished and almost one-half billion people seriously undernourished. Moreoever, so little food is stored that any large drought would cause the starvation of millions. Here there is an obvious linkage with the industrialized world. While overfed ourselves, we lack the will, but not the technology to alleviate much of the hunger. The complexities of this problem are too extensive for ever a cursory treatment here. An excellent analysis can be found in Lester R. Brown's *By Bread Alone* (New York 1974, Praeger Publishers).

Bishops from economically poor countries, who see so much suffering among their people, are very concerned about this linked and limited world. They are worried about the rise in the great numbers of "marginal" peoples, ill-fed, inhumanely housed, illiterate, and deprived of dignity.[21] They are also worried about the permanent damage to air and water if the high level of consumption by rich nations continues.[22] But their primary concern is the affront to their peoples' dignity that comes from being powerless in the face of the overpowering economic and political strength of the industrial nations.[23] This condition of imbalance with all its ramifications is the result of free human decisions, and it is called the social consequence of sin or simply social sin.[24]

It is not the function of the Church to give specific solutions to concrete problems.[25] However, the Church has urged her followers to participate more actively in politics as a means to redress injustices.[26] And the Church, without specifying them in detail, has called for changes in trade relations[27] and taxation practices,[28] and aid to underdeveloped countries,[29] including a "precise percentage of the annual income of the richer countries to the developing countries and fairer prices for raw materials.[30] Private property, not surprisingly, has been rethought in view of the rapid economic, political, and social changes today. *Mater et Magistra* stated the traditional teaching about the natural right to private property.[31] This was never understood to mean an absolute right because, as Pius XII taught, the state can regulate the use of private property for the common good and can even appropriate property with fitting indemnity being made.[32]

Gaudium et Spes avoids any reference to natural right and puts stress on man's responsibility in solidarity based on the absolute principle that the goods of the earth are meant for all. "A man should regard his lawful possessions not merely as his own, but also as common property in the sense that they should accrue to the benefit not only of himself, but of others."[33] Moreoever, *Gaudium et Spes* taught that the need for property as security has been reduced "in the face of public funds, rights and services provided by society."[34]

Octogesima Adveniens does not treat private property directly, but it does give guidelines for determining the use of property based on the principle of solidarity. The more fortunate should renounce some of their rights so as to place their goods more generously at the service of others. While upholding the right to private property in principle, the Church has clearly stressed the social nature of property which must be considered to set limits to private property.

Business ethics can no longer be concerned solely with the demands of commutative justice and following the laws of the state. Business activity must be concerned with reducing the glaring inequalities between rich and poor.[35] It must endeavor to establish a new structure based on justice which allows all peoples to free themselves from need and dependence.[36] Care must be taken that multinational corporations, which by and large are not subject to any government or to the common good, do not create a "new and abusive form of economic domination on the social, cultural, and even political level."[37] Business activity must be concerned with protecting the environment.[38] And above all, business activity must see that human labor is superior to all other elements of economic life. "Indeed we hold that by offering his labor to God a man becomes associated with the redemptive work itself of Jesus Christ, who conferred an eminent dignity on labor when at Nazareth He worked with His own hands."[39]

Development

Perhaps the most dominant theme in recent Church social teaching has been the need for development. The Second Vatican Council saw it as a continually growing concept which cannot be limited by a strict definition because the basic principles of justice "under the driving force of the Gospel must be applied ever anew to the changing situations of the world."[40] Pope Paul VI spoke of development as the human, civil, and temporal advancement of people who are setting out on the road to higher levels of culture and prosperity.[41] On one level, development is liberation from disease, exploitation, social inequalities, ignorance, oppressive social structures, and lack of culture.[42] On a higher level, it is a search for a new humanism that will embrace the higher values of love and friendship, prayer and contemplation, which will "permit the fullness of authentic development . . . a transformation from less human conditions to those which are more human."[43] To go from the less human to the more human must meet the "rising expectations" of mankind.[44] This task is so important that Pope Paul simply equates development with peace.[45]

Development implies that people have a right to take an active part in the shaping of their lives, to be artisans of their destiny.[46] This right of development "must be seen as a dynamic interpenetration of all those fundamental human rights upon which the aspirations of individuals and nations are based."[47] The citizens of the industrialized world have to recognize the fundamental right of people to develop. This entails a cessation of various kinds of exploitation: colonialism, neo-colonialism with its economic and political domination,[48] racial and ideological discrimination,[49] and unregulated competition in which the poor cannot compete.[50] The most important duty in the realm of justice is to allow each country to promote its own development free from political and economic domination.[51] Specifically, this means that wealthy nations must have a systematic plan for development, including the establishment of a world fund and a world authority.[52]

The Church has been a strong advocate of economic development.[53] There must be freedom from hunger, misery, disease, insecurity, and situations that do violence to human dignity.[54] However, in many places of the world and especially in South America, development has become an unacceptable term because it is equated simply with a rising gross national product. It does not tell how wealth is distributed. In other words, the unequal distribution of wealth makes the life of the majority of people more miserable in that they suffer increased violence, oppression, and domination living in a system designed to protect the rich.[55]

To correct this one-sided view of development the word, liberation, is used. Liberation is a richer term that extends beyond mere material needs. "Today men yearn to free themselves from need and dependence. But this liberation starts with the interior freedom that men must find again with regard to their goods and their powers; they will never reach it except through a transcendent love for man, and, in consequence, through a genuine readiness to serve."[56] Hence, it is a term that puts more responsibility on the rich than on the poor. "The struggle against destitution, though it is necessary, is not enough. It is a question, rather, of building a world where every man, no matter what his race, religion, or nationality, can live a fully human life, freed from servitude imposed on him by other men or by natural forces over which he has not sufficient control; a world where freedom is not an empty word and where the poor man Lazarus can sit down at the same table with the rich man. . . . Is he (the rich man) prepared to support out of his own pocket works and undertakings organized in favor of the most destitute?"[57] Pope Paul makes clear that all people should be liberated from all that makes them inferior. And the first to bear responsibility are those most able to do so, those who have the means. Through love for others they must free themselves to serve.[58]

Liberation theology is a related concept that is popular today. It is a slippery word that is used differently by various people. Basically, it implies an inductive method of reasoning that takes as its starting point the suffering of the people. It brings to this the light of the Gospel in order to bring about effective action. Because it is concerned with the causes of oppression and not just with the symptons, it tends toward involvement. It raises again the ancient question of the role of the Church in the world, that is, to what extent and in what manner should the Church be involved in the affairs of men. This is a pressing concern when a local Church sees a systematic oppression of certain people by a government or a business allied to a government. The complexity and delicacy of the Church's involvement in the world was highlighted by Pope John Paul II's visits to Mexico and Poland.

Finally, a word should be said about socialism, since more than half the world lives under some form of socialist government. The concept, rejected already by Leo XIII, was more strongly condemned by Pius XI even in its more moderate forms. "Socialism, entirely ignorant of and unconcerned about the sublime end of both individuals and of society, affirms that human society was instituted merely for the sake of material well-being."[59] Furthermore, the dignity of the worker would be sacrificed for an abundance of material goods socially produced.[60] So strong was the condemnation that "no one can be at the same time a good Catholic and a true socialist."[61] Interestingly enough, Cardinal Bourne, Archbishop of Westminster, England, quickly pointed out that Pius XI's condemnation did not apply to the socialism of the British Labor Party.

Pope John XXIII in *Pacem in Terris* distinguished the ideology of socialism from the works of socialism. Pope Paul VI, following this distinction, allows with reserve and due guarantees the possibility of a Christian who is also a socialist. He does explicitly condemn four principles of Marxist ideology which a Christian cannot hold: atheistic materialism, the dialectic of violence, the absorption of the individual in the collectivity, and the denial of all transcendence to man.[62] But having made the distinction between ideology and concrete activity, Pope Paul called Christians not to form a new ideology, but to go beyond every system and ideology to cooperate with all men to search for ways to build a more just society.[63]

Abbreviations

GS	Vatican II, *Gaudium et Spes*, 1965.
JW	Synod of Bishops, *Justice in the World*, 1971.
MM	John XXIII, *Mater et Magistra*, 1961.
OA	Paul VI, *Octogesima Adveniens*, 1971.
PP	Paul VI, *Populorum Progressio*, 1967.
PT	John XXIII, *Pacem in Terris*, 1963.
QA	Pius XI, *Quadragesimo Anno*, 1931.
RH	John Paul II, *Redemptor Hominis*, 1979.
RN	Leo XIII, *Rerum Novarum*, 1891.

Footnotes

1. *ST* 2a2ae.58.5.
2. *PT* 130.
3. *GS* 144.
4. *PP* 6.
5. *OA* 46.
6. *Ibid.* 4.
7. *JW* 6.
8. *Ibid.* 15.
9. *RH* 13.
10. *GS* 63.
11. *PP* 1.
12. *GS* 80.
13. *GS* 83; *PP* 11.
14. *GS* 78.
15. *PT* 167; *GS* 78; *PP* 76.
16. *PP 80.*
17. *GS* 29.
18. *PP* 23.
19. *GS* 23-26.
20. *GS* 26.
21. *JW* 10.
22. *Ibid.* 11.
23. *Ibid.* 12.
24. *GS* 25, 37-38; *JW* 5, 29, 51.
25. *GS* 76; PP 13; *OA* 4; *JW* 37.

26. *GS* 73-76; *PP* 81; *OA* 47-49.
27. *PP* 56-65; *GS* 85; *JW* 66-67.
28. *MM* 133; *JW* 66.
29. *MM* 150 ff.; *GS* 70, 86; *PP* 45-55.
30. *JW* 66.
31. *MM* 109.
32. *AAS* 36 (1944) 254.
33. *GS* 69.
34. *Ibid.* 71.
35. *Ibid.* 66.
36. *OA* 45.
37. *Ibid.* 44.
38. *JW* 8, 11-12, 70; *OA* 21.
39. *GS* 67.
40. *OA* 42.
41. Message for Mission Sunday, June 5, 1970.
42. *PP* 21.
43. *Ibid.* 20.
44. *GS* 64.
45. *PP* 87.
46. *Ibid.* 65.
47. *JW* 15.
48. *PP* 7
49. *PP* 63; *OA* 16.
50. *PP* 58; *OA* 44.
51. *OA* 23.
52. *PP* 50-52.
53. *MM* 163; *GS* 63; *PP* 6.
54. *PP* 1, 6.
55. *PP* 30; *OA* 15; *JW* 3, 5.
56. *OA* 45.
57. *PP* 47.
58. *OA* 45.
59. *QA* 118.
60. *Ibid.* 119.
61. *Ibid.* 120.
62. *OA* 26.
63. *OA* 38, 42.

Chapter 22

RESPONSIBILITY FOR HUMAN LIFE

Bibliography: Pope Paul VI, "Address to the General Assembly of the United Nations," *The Pope Speaks* 11 (1966) 47-47; Paul VI, "If You Want Peace, Defend Life," *The Pope Speaks* 22 (1977) 38-45; Paul VI, "Yes to Peace, No to Violence," *The Pope Speaks* 33 (1978) 35-41; Pope John Paul II, *Redemptor Hominis*, Washington, 1979, U S.C.C.; "Human Life in Our Day," Collective Letter of the American Hierarchy, Washington, 1968, U.S.C.C.; Pontifical Commission for Justice and Peace, "The Church and the Death Penalty," *Origins* 6, 389-392; B. Ashley, O.P., and K. O'Rourke, O.P., *Health Care Ethics*, St. Louis, 1978, Catholic Health Association; R. Drinan, S.J., *Vietnam and Armageddon: Peace, War, and the Christian Conscience*, New York, 1970, Sheed and Ward; J. Gremillion (ed.), *Gospel of Peace and Justice, Catholic Social Teaching since Pope John*, Maryknoll, 1976, Orbis Books; J. Sellin (Ed.,) *Capital Punishment*, New York, 1969, Harper and Row.

Introduction: The Sanctity of Human Life

Throughout recorded history human beings have valued their lives and sought to preserve and strengthen life through persistent and inventive efforts. A contemporary sociologist speaks of the deep primordial experience of being alive, the fear and awe of extinction.[1] This establishes a spontaneous sense of outrage when human life is destroyed or manipulated, rooted in a protoreligious natural metaphysic. In this sense the value of human life is experienced in an immanent way by human beings independently or religious doctrines which emphasize the sacredness of human life as reflecting the image of God.

Non-religious language speaks more comfortably of the dignity than of the sanctity of human life. The preamble of the United Nations Universal Declaration of Human Rights uses forceful terms like "inherent" and "inalienable" when it says, "Whereas recognition of the inherent dignity and of equal and inalienable rights of all members of the human family is the foundation of freedom, justice, and peace in the world. . . ." Historically, however, such convictions about human dignity have almost always been supported by the religious teachings of the world's great religions.

In the Judaeo-Christian tradition human life follows the path of God's own life in a way that radically transcends the divine reflection in the rest of visible creation. In the first chapter of Genesis God is portrayed as creating man as the crown and glory of all that He made: "Then God said: Let us make man in our image, after our likeness. Let them have dominion over the fish of the sea, the birds of the air, and the cattle and over all the wild animals and all the creatures that crawl on the ground" (1:26). In this Genesis passage, man is the image of God in the sense that he receives from God a delegation of power to rule over the world and to occupy a privileged place in the universe.

Human beings are corporeal and made of the same elements of which the earth is shaped, but also endowed with the human spirit. "The Lord God formed man out of the clay of the ground and blew into his nostrils the breath of life" (Gn 2:7). Human persons are uniquely God's image in their specifically human qualities, and it is the spiritual life principle, or soul, that makes them open to understanding and love of the infinite Love whom they reflect. Thus in the book of Wisdom, man is the image of God by his soul, spiritual and immortal: "For God formed man to be imperishable; the image of his own nature he made him" (2:23).

The Psalmist proclaimed the dignity and sacredness of human life in the lyrical words, "What is man that you should be mindful of him, or the son of man that you should care for him? You have made him little less than the angels and crowned him with glory and honor. You have given him rule over the works of your hands, putting all things under his feet" (8:5-7).

The Bible teaches that God gives each human person the wonder and the power of human life: "Truly, you have formed my inmost being; you knit me in my mother's womb. I give you thanks for that I am fearfully, wonderfully made; wonderful are your works. My soul also you knew full well; nor was my frame unknown to you when I was made in secret, when I was fashioned out of the depths of the earth'' (Ps 139:13-15). The last phrase, "depths of the earth," is considered by exegetes as figurative language for "the womb," stressing the mysterious nature of the operations which occur there.[2] Isaiah (49:1), Jeremiah (1:5), and Paul (Gal 1:15) all testify that God knew them already in their mothers' wombs, a personal relationship which all human persons have with God their creator.

The heroic mother of the seven sons in 2 M expressed the biblical doctrine about God's individual creative relationship to each human person when she said, "I do not know how you came into existence in my womb; it was not I who gave you the breath of life, nor was it I who set in order the elements of which you are composed. Therefore, since it is the creator of the universe who shapes each man's beginning, as he brings about the origin of everything, he, in his mercy, will give you back both breath and life'' (2 M 7:22-23).

Jesus attests to God's individual concern for human persons with the sparrow comparison: "Are not two sparrows sold for next to nothing? Yet not a single sparrow falls to the ground without your Father's consent. As for you, every hair of your head has been counted'' (Mt 10:29-30). Centuries later in *Humani Generis* Pope Pius XII expressed this biblical belief when he wrote "that souls are immediately created by God is a view which the Catholic faith imposes on us.''[3]

The New Testament also makes clear that all human persons have been redeemed by Christ and called to union with him. Paul states this categorically: "In Christ Jesus the Gentiles are now co-heirs with the Jews, members of the same body and sharers of the promise through the preaching of the gospel'' (Ep 3:6).

Hence, biblical revelation teaches that all human persons are enabled to overcome the wounds of original sin and enjoy the privileged role of adopted sons of God the Father. Paul Ramsey, who writes from a Christian, but not a Catholic, perspective, comments upon the sanctity of human life as follows: "Every human being is a unique, unrepeatable opportunity to praise God. His life is entirely an ordination, a loan, and a stewardship. His essence is his existence before God and to God, as it is from Him. His dignity is 'an alien dignity,' an evaluation that is not of him, but placed on him by the divine decree.''[4]

Thus, the sanctity or dignity of each human life can be seen from the ontological perspective which is emphasized in the natural law tradition or from the perspective of divine love and God's redemptive initiative which is the biblical perspective, just described in Paul Ramsey's words. In both senses, human life is a gift placed under the stewardship of human persons by God, as Thomas Aquinas remarked in rejecting suicide.[5]

Catholic theology and the continuous teaching of the Church have provided clarifications about human nature and dignity over the centuries. Augustine responded to the Manichaean errors about human nature by insisting that by being like angels we are near to God, but by being like matter we are near to nothing.[6] The Fourth Lateran Council (1215) stated that God "from the beginning of time created in the same way both orders of creation, spiritual and corporeal, that is, the angelic order and the earthly, and then the order of humanity, as it were common to both, being composed of spirit and body.''[7]

Medieval theologians rejected the Averroist theories about one intellect for the entire human race, and the Fifth Lateran Council (1513) taught authoritatively that "it (the soul) is not only truly and of itself and essentially the form of the human body . . . but is also immortal and can be multiplied in accordance with the multitude of bodies into which it is infused, has been and will be so multiplied.''[8]

In her practical teaching also, the Church has sought to uphold throughout the centuries the priceless worth of each human person, since the gift of human life transcends any comparative ranking of persons. The biblical principle of Jesus that "as often as you did it for one of my least brothers, you did it for me" (Mt 25:40) has inspired centuries of concern for the poor, the diseased, and the outcasts of society. Yet, the favored position of the noble and the wealthy class has always and still does compromise that gospel ideal.

Vatican II spoke to the modern world society with its strange mix of capitalist and Marxist political structures in terms of this inherent and immeasurable value of each human person. The fathers of the council wrote optimistically that "there is a growing awareness of the sublime dignity of the human person, who stands above all things and whose rights and duties are universal and inviolable.''[9] The council saw human persons as gifted with freedom and creativity, striving to lead lives of human dignity: ''Man as an individual and as a member of society craves a life that is full, autonomous, and worthy of his nature as a human being.''[10]

The single and most significant conclusion from this discussion of the sanctity of human life is the recognition that the existential value of human persons precedes and overshadows the varieties of human worth, productiveness, and social value that individuals achieve. As Paul Ramsey states in summary, ''A life's sanctity consists not in its worth *to* anybody. What life is in and of itself is most clearly seen in situations of naked equality of one life with another, and in the situation of human helplessness which is the human condition in the first of life.''[11]

Hence, living human persons are gifted in their very being, prior what they succeed in doing or producing. ''Too often we attribute value to human life only in terms of what one makes, does, accomplishes, or possesses; but in the Christian perspecitve the dignity of human life does not rest primarily on one's works or accomplishments.''[12]

Underpinning this existential valuing of the human person lies the understanding of the unified interrelationship of the human body and spirit. The human body and its visible activities do not stand apart from the human spirit as though different individuals could be treated differently according to the bodily and visible qualities they manifest. Rather the different bodily and visible qualities manifest the same incomparable mystery of human personhood in a variety of corporeal forms. Hence, human dignity cannot be ranked by what different individuals accomplish in the way of functional perfection; it derives from a prior source principle. Human persons possess an equal and inherent value not from what they do, but from who they are: children of God, made to His image and likeness.

However, human persons do not enjoy the gift of human dignity and destiny in a perfect and ideal world, but in a sinful and broken world marked by greed and pride, disease and despair. Hence arise the variety of situations in which human persons destroy their own lives and those of others. The remainder of this chapter will discuss the moral implications of taking human life in warfare and capital punishment—actions which may be seen as protective of peace and justice. The next chapter will discuss the morality of abortion, euthanasia, and suicide.

Killing in Warfare

In stark contrast to the secular and Christian doctrine of the dignity and sanctity of human life the wholesale killing of human beings in warfare has continually manifested the wide chasm in human history between the ideal and real. Moreover, the contemporary technological mastery of nearly incalculable nuclear energy coupled with the bacteriological and chemical discoveries of modern science has opened up the possibility of total destruction of all human life, or at least destruction measurable in the hundreds of millions of human lives. Can killing in warfare be justified today in the light of Christian revelation and Catholic teaching?

Despite the New Testament ideals on non-resistance and non-violence (cf. Mt 5:38-39), the Bible does not condemn all war as immoral. One biblical scholar has written that he finds in the New Testament "no evidence of conscious bias against the military as such."[13] The early Church Fathers seemed to take the fact of war for granted and asked only whether soldiers converted to Christianity should remain in military service.

The famous doctrine of a "just war" evolved in Christian theology with special impetus from Augustine. He envisioned war much as modern terminology describes a "police action." In his reply to Faustus the Manichaean, Augustine wrote, "A great deal depends upon the causes for which men undertake wars, and on the authority they have for doing so; for the natural order, which seeks the peace of mankind, ordains that a monarch should have the power of undertaking war if he thinks it advisable, and that soldiers should perform their military duties in behalf of the peace and safety of the community."[14]

Aquinas discussed a just war in terms of three preconditions: 1) the decision to make war by legitimate public authority, 2) the presence of a just cause, and 3) the right intention of those making war, to accomplish good or avoid evil.[15] Unfortunately, the factual verifying of these conditions, especially, the second, leaves wide scope for controversy and disagreement. In the 16th and 17th centuries, Francis de Vitoria (c. 1483-1546) and Francis Suarez (1548-1617) added the qualifications that the war must be a last resort and fought in the proper manner—without destruction of the innocent.

The Church's own association with warfare throughout history springs from her incarnational existence. Once Constantine became a Christian, the Church was inescapably linked to the political process and the rationalizing of just reasons for warfare. Various practical attempts were made by the Church to limit warfare, as, for example, the Peace of God of the Council of Chanoux in 988 which declared churches, clerics, and the common people immune from attack. Attempts were made even to outlaw new weapons, for example, the prohibition of the use of the crossbow and the longbow by the Lateran Council of 1139.

On the other hand, the approval of the Crusades by Church leaders as but one example of the justification of warfare kept alive the concept of just war. The centuries prior to, and including, the Protestant Reformation saw the emergence of mercenary armies often linked to religious fervor and intolerance. In protest against the barbaric practices of the wars of religion and the Thirty Years War, Hugo Grotius wrote his *De Jure Belli ac Pacis* in 1625. Grotius' proposals for a law of nations led to a steady development of international law.

But the industrial revolution and the great inventions growing out of it made possible the rapid deployment of huge armies over great areas. The American Civil War (1861-65) saw the entire Southern Confederacy mobilized in defense of its way of life. The Union generals in response directed crushing blows against the traditionally noncombatant and immune persons thus involved.

At the turn of the century the Hague Conferences of 1899 and 1907 established international norms to define the limited nature of war, the principle of noncombatant immunity, the rights of prisoners of war and the sick and wounded, the general inviolability of private property, and the rights of neutrals. But World Wars I and II saw most of these principles violated by both sides. The historic nuclear bombing of Hiroshima and Nagasaki culminated the expanding practice of obliteration bombing of cities so widely practiced toward the end of World War II.

The United Nations organization which followed world War II has a charter prohibiting unilateral recourse to armed force or the threat thereof. Actually the great power unity presumed in the UN collective security system has failed to materialize. The transnational ideological movements that have arisen since 1945 have freely employed psychological and economic warfare as well as subversion and guerilla activity. The Korean and Vietnamese conflicts were two major disturbances of world peace which threatened to unleash World War II and nuclear destruction despite the UN. The continuing tension in the Middle East and in Africa, the proliferation of nations stockpiling nuclear weapons, the emergence of military dictatorships in South America and elsewhere, and the maneuvers of China, Russia, and Cuba in the worldwide expansion of Communist influence all suggest that warfare is not about to disappear from the face of the earth.

One Christian response to war proclaimed by the historic peace Churches like the Quakers, Mennonites, Seventh Day Adventists, and, more recently, Jehovah's Witnesses, is total pacificism and repudiation of all use of force. Neither the major Protestant denominations nor the Catholic understanding of Christianity find this to be a Gospel imperative. This approach absolutizes peace at the expense of justice and forces a withdrawal of Christians from the realm of government and political involvement.

However, the Catholic understanding of the Gospel clearly does demand a twofold major effort: 1) a continual and unrelenting effort to "make peace," minimizing the temptation to war, and 2) a mighty effort to clarify the moral limits of just war, emphasizing especially the limiting principles of proportionality (benefit in proportion to harm done) and discrimination (immunity of noncombatants).

With regard to the first effort at "making peace" Augustine said in his day that "no man seeks war by making peace."[16] Warfare throughout the centuries is a consequence of original sin. Christians are called to overcome that sin and its grisly effect, the killing in warfare, by "waging peace." Despite the lack of biblical bias against the military, the whole thrust of the Sermon on the Mount is for peace and in that sense all Christians are called to be relative pacifists, just war notwithstanding. In this vein Pope Paul VI appealed before the UN General Assembly on Oct. 4, 1965, "No more war! War never again! Peace, it is peace that must guide the destinies of peoples and all mankind."

Realistically, the campaign to wage peace involves mighty efforts to establish international justice and a respect for the rights of nations in the economic as well as political arena. The Fathers of Vatican II described peace as "the fruit of that right ordering of things with which the divine founder has invested human society and which must be actualized by man thirsting after an ever more perfect reign of justice."[17] Hence, in the post-Vatican II era commissions have been organized in the U.S. and elsewhere for the accomplishment of "peace and justice."

The second effort mentioned above, clarifying the moral limits of just war, has preoccupied recent Popes and Vatican II as well as moral theologians. While the classical just war theory offered the possibility of just wars which were "offensive" or "aggressive" in correcting injurious actions (actions generally involving an infringement of a right), this category of just wars is now widely rejected. Thus, Pope Pius XII in his 1944 Christmas address said flatly, "The immorality of the war of aggression has been made even more evident."[18] Pope John XXIII wrote in a similar vein in *Pacem in Terris*, "It is contrary to reason to hold that war is now a suitable way to restore rights which have been violated."[19]

However, the outright rejection of "offensive" wars does not necessarily apply to "defensive" wars or wars of self-defense. Pope Pius XII admitted that such wars may still be morally justified. "There may come into existence in a nation a situation in which all hope of averting war becomes vain. In this situation a war of efficacious self-defense against unjust attacks, which is undertaken with hope of success, cannot be considered illicit."[20] Pope Pius XII was even willing to discuss using ABC (atomic, bacteriological, and chemical) warfare in such a defensive posture where a nation would be defending itself against an obvious, extremely serious, and otherwise unavoidable injustice.[21]

Ten years later Vatican II reaffirmed the legitimacy of wars of self-defense: "As long as the danger of war persists and there is no international authority with the necessary competence and power, governments cannot be denied the right of lawful self-defense, once all peace efforts have failed."[22]

Nonetheless, the council did not approve in such warfare the tactic of total warfare. Endorsing various statements of the past three Popes, it made a solemn declaration: "Every act of war directed to the indiscriminate destruction of whole cities or vast areas with their inhabitants is a crime against God and man, which merits firm and unequivocal condemnation."[23]

In this nuclear age, for example, high megaton bombs used on densely populated areas seem to violate both the principle of proportionality and of discrimination described above. In such circumstances this form of "defense" must be abandoned according to the principle expressed by Pius XII, "When the damages caused by war are not comparable to those of 'tolerated injustice,' one may have the duty to 'suffer the injustice' "[24]

Yet, this outright rejection of indiscriminate and total warfare on civilian populations does not of itself rule out all use of nuclear weapons. But the very consideration of a more limited use of such weapons does raise the specter of a world holocaust because of the proliferation of such weapons in the worldwide armament race.

Vatican II firmly condemned this arms race and said sadly, "There is every reason to fear that if it continues it will bring forth those lethal disasters which are in preparation."[25] Furthermore, the council viewed the arms race as actually breeding conditions of injustice which precipitate wars: "As long as extravagant sums of money are poured into the development of new weapons, it is impossible to devote adequate aid in tackling the misery which prevails at the present day in the world."[26] The council did not go to the point of advocating unilateral abandoning of arms development, but it did clearly insist on the obligation to exhaust every effort at accomplishing bilateral disarmament, the goal, for example, of the SALT talks.

The rejection of total war by Vatican II by no means implies that everything else is permitted if a way is justified by self-defense. Such warfare must still offer a proportionate benefit linked with the destruction it entails, must still be fought as a last resort with a hope of success and with every effort to preserve noncombatant immunity. All of these conditions were debated, for instance, in the Vietnamese War which so divided American public opinion.

The moral justification of war derives from the values which are essential to human society and to public order and harmony. The theory of the just war still stands as a Christian doctrine inspired by love. It arises from the ethics of Christian love of neighbor which permits proportionate force to protect human persons from injustice. The same imperative of Christian love, of course, sets the limits discussed above to the justification of war.

Logically, the theoretical principles which admit of just war to ward off injustice can also be extended to justify revolution and guerilla warfare. However, in addition to the difficulty of applying all the conditions discussed above to such forms of violence, another problem arises. The groups waging such "warfare" have no recognized political authority in the nations in which they act. Often it is only possible to discover in retrospect if, indeed, such groups have acted justifiably in behalf of the common good with sufficient moral justification. However, even the awesome difficulty of establishing the political legitimacy of such groups and their activities cannot rule out in principle the possibility of justifiable revolution.

Current forms of revolutionary activity and guerilla warfare frequently violate the principle of discrimination by attacking the lives and property of noncombatants, that is, of innocent civilians not involved in the alleged oppression being resisted. Unfortunately, those who turn to revolutionary violence tend to justify any violence which will undermine the established order. Such an unrestrained use of violence not only undermines justice, but also weakens the political fabric of a nation from which a new order of political authority is expected to arise after the revolution.

This analysis of killing in warfare has uncovered the complexity of moral judgments about just war. It has clearly indicated that one may not simply presume that every war is a just war. Individual citizens called to military service may find objections in conscience to their participation in a given war or even to warfare as such. This section will conclude with further reflections on conscientious objection.

Despite the theoretical justification of some killing in warfare by the just war theory, Christians have consistently taken positions of conscientious objection throughout history. A sample of this attitude can be found in the regulation, later deleted, that Francis of Assisi wrote in his original rule for his Third Order: "They are not to take up lethal weapons or bear them against anybody."

The Fathers of the Second Vatican Council spoke in general terms when they said, "We cannot but express our admiration for all who forego the use of violence to vindicate their rights and resort to other means of defense which are available to weaker parties."[27] They added, "It seems that just laws should make humane provisions for the case of conscientious objectors who refuse to carry arms provided they accept some other form of community service."[28]

Conscientious objection need not imply total pacifism, it may refer only to participation in a specific war. The U.S. bishops addressed specifically this more complex question of selective conscientious objection during the Vietnam War in 1968 and 1971.[29] They recommended a modification of the U.S. Selective Service Act making it "possible, although not easy" for selective conscientious objectors to refuse to serve in wars they consider unjust. Some other form of service to the human community would be required of those exempted. The bishops argue explicitly in their 1971 statement that not only members of the pacifist Churches like the Quakers, but Catholics also could be legitimate conscientious objectors because of "religious training and belief." Since this basis could be applied to objection to all wars as well as selective wars, it covers the possibility that there may no longer be conditions which could justify *any* wars.

This discussion of military service versus conscientious objection involves profound ethical issues. The reason for military conscription flows from the preservation of political society itself. The reasons supporting conscientious objection flow from the ethical objections to killing in warfare. Both kinds of reasons involve strong moral arguments and obligations; hence, this issue will continue to pose agonizing questions to whole nations and to individuals.

Capital Punishment

Capital punishment may be defined as the execution of a criminal under a death sentence imposed by competent public authority. The right of public authority to impose the death penalty has been widely accepted throughout history, although the frequency of its use and the crimes for which it is used have also varied widely. The twentieth century has witnessed a definite trend toward the abolition of capital punishment.

The Old Testament clearly authorized capital punishment, not only for murder, but for such crimes as blasphemy, false worship, kidnapping, striking or cursing parents, adultery, incest, homosexual actions, and bestiality (Ex 21:12-29; 22:19; Lv 20:10). In the New Testament, Paul approves the fact that the ruler carries the sword without explicit reference to the death penalty (Rm 13:4).

While the Church has never directly addressed the question of the state's right to exercise the death penalty, Pope Innocent III in 1210 stated in a profession of faith for the Waldensians that "concerning secular power we declare that without mortal sin it' is possible to exercise a judgment of blood as long as one proceeds to bring punishment not in hatred, but in judgment, not incautiously, but advisedly."[30]

Aquinas defended the established institution of capital punishment in the *Summa Theologica* arguing that if a man's sin or crime is dangerous and infectious to the community, it is praiseworthy and advantageous that he be killed to safeguard the common good.[31] Hence, Aquinas taught that by serious crime a person would forfeit his or her right to life. He viewed citizens as parts of a whole in their civic life with such basic obligations to the common good that they could be expelled from the society of the living if sufficiently dangerous.

However, vastly different judgments on "sufficient danger" to society led to vastly different applications of capital punishment. English law from the 16th to 18th centuries, for example, piled up more than 200 capital crimes, ranging from high treason to the theft of property worth a few shillings.

The most influential 18th century opponent of capital punishment was the Italian author Caesar Beccaria, whose essay *Dei Delitti e delle Pene* in 1764 rejected both the state's right to take a citizen's life and the practice of capital punishment as cruel, unreasonable, and ineffective. Within twenty years after Beccaria's essay capital punishment was abolished in Tuscany and Austria. Subsequently throughout the 19th and into the 20th century abolition spread to Portugal, Italy, the Netherlands, Belgium, Sweden, Denmark, and Latin American countries like Brazil, Argentina, Venezuela, Costa Rica, and Equador. Since World War II and its massive crimes against human life an added impetus has developed for the abolition of capital punishment. The Bonn constitution for postwar Germany eliminated it; and Great Britain, after a five year moratorium, finally abolished it in 1969. In the U.S. by 1965 twelve states had individually abolished capital punishment.

In 1972 the U.S. Supreme Court moved against capital punishment, but the burden of its decision rested on the capricious and arbitrary way it judged this penalty had been applied in various states. Hence, individual states must expect Supreme Court review of any statutes which impose capital punishment.

Pope Pius XII addressed the question of capital punishment in an allocution entitled "The Intangibility of the Human Person" on Sept. 13, 1952: "Even when it is a question of the execution of a man condemned to death, the State does not dispose of the individual's right to live. It is then reserved to the public power to deprive the condemned of the benefit of life, in expiation of his fault, when already, by his crime, he has dispossessed himself of the right to life."[32] Pope Paul VI spoke with special emphasis on the medicinal and rehabilitative role of punishment (hardly applicative to capital punishment) in an address to the Tenth International Congress of Penal Law on Oct. 4, 1969: "Moreover, the judgment and penalty ought also to tend toward the reeducation and reintegration of the guilty person in society with his entire human dignity. We congratulate you for moving always more toward this very important, human objective which is indeed worthy of retaining your full attention."[33] Significantly, Pope Paul VI that same year, 1969, abolished capital punishment in Vatican City where it had stood unused on the law books. However, the Church as a whole has moved slowly and cautiously on the issue of abolition.

The U.S. bishops in Nov. 1974 approved by a vote of 108 to 63 a simple one-sentence declaration of their opposition to capital punishment. In May 1976, the administrative board of the Canadian Catholic Conference also declared itself in favor of the abolition of capital punishment, noting that "the case for the retention of the death penalty has not been proven."[34]

The primary debate on capital punishment concerns its effectiveness in deterring major crimes. Although the statistics are often difficult to interpret, there is no convincing evidence that it is an effective deterrent.[35] It will not deter, for example, murders committed as crimes of passion nor murders which are performed by individuals who are convinced that they will escape detection or conviction.

Those who insist on the deterrent effect of capital punishment must also face the statistics which show how inequitably it is usually imposed on the poor and on minority groups. If the method of administering capital punishment is fundamentally unjust, it becomes a dubious means of safeguarding the common good and public justice. If only an unfortunate few individuals are actually put to death out of a larger class of guilty persons, they become scapegoats and are used as a means to an end.

Catholic theology has difficulty justifying capital punishment as primarily a retributive or vindictive penalty in the tradition of the *lex talionis*. The notion that a civil state must exact the punishment of a life for a life involves a kind of political expiation which may well go beyond the appropriate role of civil authority. Aquinas, for example, sounded the caution that "in this life penalties should rather be remedial than retributive."[36]

The whole weight of Christian theology leans toward the medicinal and rehabilitative role of punishment because "biblical tradition is also replete with reminders that vengeance belongs to the Lord and that He enjoins the qualities of compassion and forgiveness on those believers in the biblical revelation of God."[37]

Some contemporary Catholic theologians are even questioning the theoretical justification of capital punishment. They suggest that this institution involves the direct intention to kill a human being whereas in cases of immediate and individual self-defense one's intention may focus only on repelling an attacker. Germain Grisez, for example, finds Aquinas' justification of capital punishment very weak and argues that the juridical guilt of a criminal does not justify the killing of that person.[38]

A position paper prepared by the Pontifical Commission for Justice and Peace linked the Church's traditional opposition to abortion and euthanasia with the issue of capital punishment. It suggested that "the bishops seek first to advance respect for life that must be promoted in every situation, a position that is consistent with their positions against abortion and euthanasia. The inner coherence of this respect for life and the gospel message of healing leads them to defend life in this matter as well."[39]

Footnotes

1. E. Shils, "The Sanctity of Life," in *Life or Death, Ethics and Options*, Seattle, 1968, Univ. of Washington Press, 2-38. Ed. by Labby, *et. al.*
2. *See* footnote in *NAB*, 675.
3. *TCC* no. 205a.
4. P. Ramsey, "The Morality of Abortion," in Labby, *op. cit.*, 73-74.

5. *ST* 2a2ae.64.5.
6. *Confessions* 12, 7.
7. *TCC* no. 171.
8. *TCC* no. 205.
9. *Gaudium et Spes* no. 26.
10. *Ibid.*, no. 9.
11. Ramsey, *op. cit.*, 72.
12. G. Dyer (ed.) *An American Catholic Catechism*, New York, 1975, The Seabury Press, 223.
13. J. O'Rourke, "The Military in the New Testament," in the *CBQ* 32 (1970) 236.
14. Book 22, no. 75.
15. *ST* 2a2ae.40.1
16. *City of God* 19, 12.
17. *Gaudium et Spes* no. 78.
18. V. Yzermans (ed.), *The Major Addresses of Pope Pius XII*, St. Paul, 1961, North Central Publ. Co., 2, 86.
19. *Pacem in Terris* no. 127.
20. *AAS* 49 (1957) 19.
21. Pius XII, "Medical Ethics," Address Sept. 30, 1954, in *Catholic Mind* no. 53, 243-244.
22. *Gaudium et Spes* no. 79.
23. *Ibid.*, no. 80.
24. Pius XII, "Medical Ethics and the Law," Address Oct. 19, 1953, in *Catholic Mind* no. 52, 49.
25. *Gaudium et Spes* no. 81.
26. *Ibid.*
27. *Ibid.*, no. 78.
28. *Ibid.*, no. 79.
29. "Human Life in Our Day," Washington, 1968, USCC; statement in *Origins*, Nov. 4, 1971, vol. 1, 333.
30. *DB* 425.
31. *ST* 2a2ae.64.2
32. In *The Human Body*, Boston, 1969, Daughters of St. Paul, 205-6.
33. *AAS* 61 (1969) 711-12.
34. *Origins*, March 25, 1976, 5, 632.
35. *Origins*, Dec. 23, 1976, 6, 391.
36. *ST* 2a2ae.66.6 ad.2.
37. "Death Penalty's Future—Rhode Island Religious Leaders," *Origins*, March 25, 1976, 5, 631. Among the biblical references cited are Dt 32:3; Rm 12:19; and Ps 103:10-18.
38. *See* G. Grisez, *Abortion, the Myths, the Realities, and the Arguments*, New York, 1970, Corpus Books, 323-325.
39. *Origins*, Dec. 9, 1976, 6, 392.

Chapter 23

MORAL RESPONSIBILITY FOR
ABORTION, EUTHANASIA, AND SUICIDE

Bibliography: Sacred Congregation for the Doctrine of the Faith, "Declaration on Abortion," Washington, 1975, U.S.C.C.; T. Hilgers and D. Horan (eds.), *Abortion and Social Justice*, New York, 1972, Sheed and Ward; J. Connery, S.J., *Abortion: The Development of the Roman Catholic Perspective*, Chicago, 1977, Loyola Univ. Press; D. Horan and D. Mall (eds.), *Death, Dying and Euthanasia*, Washington, 1977, University Publications of America; D. McCarthy and A. Moraczewski, O.P. (eds.), *An Ethical Evaluation of Fetal Experimentation: An Interdisciplinary Study*, St. Louis, 1976, Pope John XXIII Medical-Moral Research and Education Center; G. Grisez, *Abortion, the Myths, the Realities, and the Arguments*, New York, 1970, Corpus Books; G. Grisez and J. Boyle, *Life and Death with Liberty and Justice*, Notre Dame, 1979, Univ. of Notre Dame Press; D. McCarthy, "Care for Suffering and Dying Persons," Washington, 1978, Bishops' Committee for Pro-Life Activities; J. Noonan (ed.), *The Morality of Abortion, Legal and Historical Perspectives*, Cambridge, 1970, Harvard Univ. Press; *Prolongation of Life*, Papers by the Linacre Center, 60 Grove End Rd., London NW 8 9NH, 1978; P. Ramsey, *Ethics at the Edges of Life*, New Haven, 1978, Yale University Press; D. McCarthy (ed.), *Responsible Stewardship of Human Life*, St. Louis, 1976, Catholic Hospital Association.

Abortion

Induced abortion may be described in general terms as the deliberate destruction of a fetus before viability. In contrast to capital punishment the victim of abortion has not reached the use of reason or violated any laws whatsoever. Christian tradition has often compared abortion and infanticide.

The Greek and Roman civilization did tolerate abortion and infanticide until the beginning of the Christian era. The worldwide movement to tolerate abortion once again which began in earnest after World War II as a partial response to population problems has so obscured the moral significance of the direct killing of the unborn that the current rate of abortions in many modern nations exceeds the rate in Rome and the ancient world.

The Old Testament does not explicitly treat induced abortion. One passage (Ex 21:22) does mention only a monetary fine rather than the penalty of "a life for a life" for accidentally causing a miscarriage. Rabbinical casuistry took advantage of this in permitting abortion in some difficult situations. But the biblical reverence for life, for children, and for God's mysterious role in procreation could never tolerate abortion in any permissive way. Germain Grisez concludes that "the silence of the Old Testament about induced abortion rather indicates that legislation against abortion was unnecessary than that abortion was tacitly approved."[1]

Neither does the New Testament explicitly forbid abortion although Paul's condemnation of sorcery or the magical practice of medicine (*pharmakeia*) in Gal 5:20 seems to have included abortifacient drugs.[2] The same practitioners of *pharmakeia* are condemned in Rv 9:21; 21:8; and 22:15. The New Testament command of love for little children and for the least of the brothers and sisters of Jesus would hardly seem permissive of either infanticide or abortion. Furthermore, the New Testament doctrine of the incarnation presented Jesus as truly human from the moment of His conception: Elizabeth proclaims the presence of the Lord in Mary's womb. The Scriptures teach that "God's role in the creation and redemption of each unique human being begins before birth, indeed from the very moment that such an individual begins to be."[3]

The most important ancient condemnation of abortion found in the *Didache* or the *Teaching of the Twelve Apostles*, composed no later than 100, links abortion and *pharmakeia*: "You shall not practice medicine (*pharmakeia*). You shall not slay the child by abortions. You shall not kill what is generated."[4] The subsequent explicit condemnation of abortion by successive Church Fathers and Church councils has been carefully documented and conveys what Noonan calls "an almost absolute value in history."[5] The Second Vatican Council declared concisely and firmly: "Life must be protected with the utmost care from the moment of conception: abortion and infanticide are abominable crimes."[6]

The protection of life mentioned by the council teaches an essential and incontrovertible duty upon the man and woman who procreate a new human being, whether they are married or unmarried, to nourish and cherish that offspring. It suggests a responsibility of their community to assist them in meeting this obligation. Assisting pregnant women with financial and medical support constitutes protection of life, whereas providing cheap or free abortions with public monies destroys life. Undoubtedly, unmarried pregnant women face immense difficulty in continuing their pregnancy and in delivering and providing for their children. But Catholic teaching has always stood for the protection of life with the possible adoption by other parents of children born outside wedlock. Catholic theology translates the misleading popular slogan of "a woman's right to choose abortion" into "a woman's right to loving compassion and practical help in her difficulty."

Murder is abhorrent to religious and non-religious persons because of the unjust attack upon innocent victims. Abortion falls under the category of murder for both religious and non-religious persons unless they have somehow reduced the human dignity and rights of that class of unborn human beings who are sheltered within maternal wombs.

Religious belief supports the full human dignity and rights of the unborn when it considers this dignity a gift of God bestowed equally and freely upon all human beings, young or old, sick or healthy, defective or normal, whether inside the womb or outside the womb. Non-religious belief supports the full human dignity and rights of the unborn when it recognizes human dignity as truly inherent to each individual, conferring equal and inalienable rights on all.

Those who reduce the human value of the unborn are faced with the necessity of postulating a value or dignity threshold which must be crossed by each human being before or after birth. Logically, this means that value and dignity are measured in terms of development or function, and this leads to an eventual elitism because some individuals develop further and function better than others. Such a perspective means that the equal dignity and rights of human persons so widely acclaimed today become merely matters of social convention adopted for practical and political reasons, not the enduring truth upon which society is grounded.

The Vatican *Declaration on Abortion* of Nov. 18, 1974, addressed the question of discrimination and a merely social or human attribution of the right to life: "It does not belong to society, nor does it belong to public authority in any form to recognize this right (to life) for some and not for others: all discrimination is evil, whether it be founded on race, sex, color or religion. It is not recognition by another that constitutes this right. This right is antecedent to its recognition; it demands recognition, and it is strictly unjust to refuse it."[7]

Because abortion touches this vital issue of the origin and meaning of human dignity and equality, it can never be an exclusively religious or Catholic issue. In a broadly humanistic perspective every act of abortion diminishes reverence for all helpless or handicapped human beings and undermines the most basic principle of social justice, the right to life itself.

Those in ancient Greece and Rome who practiced abortion could take comfort in primitive theories of human development which suggested that at first the developing being has only vegetative and then animal dignity. Aristotle developed a theory of delayed animation according to which human males receive human souls forty days after fertilization and females eighty or ninety days afterward. Christian scholars like Augustine and Thomas Aquinas accepted this philosophical theory, but still stoutly resisted approving abortions because the not-yet-ensouled beings are already actively developing and have human value rooted in their own unfolding potentiality.

The Vatican *Declaration on Abortion* in 1974 discussed these historical theories about delayed infusion of the human soul: "In the course of history . . . the various opinions on the infusion of the spiritual soul did not introduce any doubt about the illicitness of abortion. It is true that in the Middle Ages, when the opinion was generally held that the spiritual soul was not present until after the first few weeks, a distinction was made in the evaluation of the sin and the gravity of penal sanctions. Excellent authors allowed for this first period more lenient case solutions which they rejected for following periods. But it was never denied at that time that procured abortion, even during the first days, was objectively a grave fault. This condemnation was in fact unanimous."[8]

Beginning with the scientific work of the physicians Thomas Fienus of Louvain in 1620 and Paolo Zacchia of Rome in 1621, the hypothesis of successive souls in early human development was undermined by science rather than philosophy. Science today teaches that a totally new living being begins with the egg's fertilization by the sperm. Egg and sperm are haploid (have only half the requisite pairs of chromosomes and genes) so that the new being enjoys a new and unique genetic wholeness and identity from that moment onwards. This original unicellular zygote directs its own development from within like any living being using coded information from its own genetic composition which would fill a thousand volumes of an encyclopedia if written out.

Yet doubts about the immediate infusion of the human soul at fertilization still exist and three chief reasons can be noted:

1) Research has shown that twinning occurs during a period of two to three weeks after fertilization. While this may seem to undermine the definitive individuation of the zygote during this earliest phase of development, it does not undermine the fact of an internally-directed process taking place and an unfolding of a highly complex differentiation process. Therefore, twinning does not *prove* that previously no human being existed, only that this existing human being gives rise at a given point to a clone asexually or has ceased to exist and given rise to twins by asexual fission.[9]

2) Estimates of the number of all human zygotes which are spontaneously aborted at an early stage of development vary from fifteen percent to fifty percent. However, through most of human history at least fifty percent of all infants perished in infancy, so that mortality rates are hardly indicators of humanhood. Furthermore, there is evidence that some of the spontaneous losses occur because the complex process of fertilization was not itself successfully completed, meaning that no human soul would ever be expected in such cases.

3) Aristotelian philosophy taught that until an organism had developed to a point of having a central organ with the minimal structure required for psychological function it should be considered a vegetative, rather than an animal, being. But we know now, as Aristotle and Aquinas did not, that prior to the brain's development there is a sequence of primordial centers of development in the embryo going back continu-

ously to the nucleus of the zygote. The argument that Aristotelian-Thomistic concepts still support delayed infusion of the human soul on grounds of the structural insufficiency of the zygote at fertilization has been vigorously challenged by a contemporary expert on philosophy and science.[10]

The above considerations are so briefly summarized that they conceal profound and highly theoretical questions of philosophical significance regarding the role of the human soul, the relationship of soul and body, and the notions of individual subsistence. However, in this author's judgment, a compelling case cannot be made for the delayed ensoulment of the human zygote. The marvelous continuity of the life process manifests no point of radical change, whether around the time of implantation, or subsequently when brain and heart functions begin to appear, or when the somewhat arbitrary points of quickening and viability are passed.

The significant footnote no. 19 of the 1974 Vatican *Declaration on Abortion* gives two reasons *not* to rest moral judgments on the theory of delayed ensoulment just discussed: 1) Supposing a belated animation, there is still nothing less than a *human* life, preparing for and calling for a soul in which the nature received from parents is completed. 2) On the other hand it suffices that this presence of the soul would be probable (and one can prove the contrary) in order that the taking of life involve accepting the risk of killing a man, not only waiting for, but already in possession of his soul.[11]

Despite this grave caution several Catholic theologians are speculating that because of the theory of delayed ensoulment the human zygote can be considered only doubtfully human for at least the first 14-21 days so that its doubtful right to life can give way to reasons for an abortion such as rape or grave socio-economic hardship.[12]

It should be noted that a theological opinion advanced by John of Naples and Antoninus of Florence in the 14th and 15th centuries had admitted abortion of an unanimated fetus to save the life of the pregnant mother. Fr. John Connery points out that this opinion had a respectable following until, with general acceptance of immediate animation in the 19th century, it lost all practical meaning.[13]

Theologians Ashley and O'Rourke have discussed the use of the delayed ensoulment hypothesis in contemporary moral theology. They point out that the tradition of Catholic moral theology insists on following the moral probable course when serious rights such as the right to life are in question.[14] It seems that current speculation on delayed ensoulment has not shown that the human zygote is *more* probably not human during the first 14-21 days. If delayed animation should again become the accepted opinion within the Church (despite the reasoning already presented) it would seem that this older opinion of abortion to save the life of the mother, although occurring only rarely in the first 14-21 days, could be applied. That does *not* mean that the other reasons mentioned above, such as rape or grave socio-economic hardship, would also apply.

Catholic theological speculation has dealt with abortion by distinguishing direct and indirect abortion. It has permitted indirect abortion in cases where a medical procedure is directed to a pathological condition which threatens the life of a mother such as a cancerous uterus or a fallopian tube about to rupture. Pope Pius XII expressed this tradition very clearly in 1951: "If, for instance, the safety of the life of the mother-to-be, independently of her pregnant condition, should urgently require a surgical operation or other therapeutic treatment, which would have as a side effect, in no way willed or intended yet inevitable, the death of the fetus, then such an act could no longer be called a direct attack on innocent life. With these conditions, the operation, like other similar medical interventions, can be allowable, always assuming that a good of great worth, such as life, is at stake, and that it is not possible to delay until after the baby is born or to make use of some other effective remedy."[15]

This tradition applies the principle of double effect and allows the indirect causing of fetal death, but Catholic teaching has not permitted the direct destruction of the fetus by craniotomy or embryotomy.[16] The Vatican *Declaration on Abortion* reiterated that even the life of the mother cannot "ever objectively confer the right to dispose of another's life even when that life is only beginning."[17]

Fortunately, modern medical skill in performing Caesarean sections has practically eliminated the medical necessity of direct abortion to save mothers' lives.[18] Many Catholic moral theologians are sympathetic with the moral justification of abortion in the rare cases when both fetus and mother would perish without an abortion. Fr. Bernard Häring, for instance, would not consider an act to be abortion *in the moral sense* when the fetus is not truly deprived of its right to live because it could not possibly survive in the event of the doctor's failure to save the life of the mother.[19] Germain Grisez has argued that the traditional principle of the double effect can justify abortion in those cases where the single indivisible act both destroys the fetus and saves the life of the mother.[20] While such opinions go beyond the explicit teaching of the magisterium, they still restrict abortion to acts which are authentically life-saving.

Some authors are arguing that abortion can also be justified when it preserves other values which they consider equivalent to life, for example, when it averts very grave psychological or physical harm to the mother.[21] While the Catholic tradition has admitted the importance of such values in justifying resistance to unjust aggression, it has never explicitly considered these other values equivalent to life itself. In practical medicine situations are extremely rare where an abortion could be definitely known to avert grave psychological or physical harm to the mother.

In fact, the entire discussion of situations where abortion might possibly be justifiable within Catholic theological tradition remains largely academic because the overwhelming majority of abortions today do not involve such situations. The Church's Code of Canon Law applies an automatic excommunication to those who procure an abortion or who freely and willingly cooperate in performing it.[22] The purpose of such a severe penalty is to reinforce the Church's teaching of respect for the lives of tiny and helpless human beings.

While the moral wrong of abortion appears most clearly in the light of Judaeo-Christian revelation and explicit Catholic teaching, many persons of other religious persuasions and without religious affiliation also consider it gravely wrong. Hence, the effort to control abortion by law cannot be opposed as the imposition of Catholic teaching on the general public. As in the comparable issue of slavery, persons who oppose abortion cannot accept the naive solution that says abortion is a matter of private morality and should not be controlled by law. The protection of the life and rights of human beings is a matter of public morality and public concern. On the other hand, laws forbidding abortion are extremely difficult to enforce, even more so when public opinion tends to approve the practice.

Hence, it would seem that the pro-life movement cannot really succeed in controlling abortion without two significant efforts: 1) public education toward recognition of the rights and dignity of the unborn as symptomatic of a just society, and 2) public education toward recognition of the obligation of society to assist pregnant women, especially, unmarried women, in meeting their medical and economic needs during and after pregnancy.

Euthanasia

The word "euthanasia" is defined in Webster's *New Collegiate Dictionary* (8th ed.) as "the act or practice of killing individuals that are hopelessly sick or injured for reasons of mercy." The word in its ancient usage did not always connote active killing, but this has been its modern use. One of its leading defenders, Joseph Fletcher, has written: "The *direct* ending of a life, with or without the patient's consent, is euthanasia in its simple, unsophisticated, and ethically candid form."[23] Hence, this discussion begins with the moral issue of direct and active killing for reasons of mercy, but it will then discuss the related issue of allowing to die by omission of life-prolonging efforts.

While the social acceptance and legalization of abortion does not necessarily entail the acceptance and legalization of euthanasia, the two practices have one essential similarity. In both practices a human life is deliberately ended because a process of qualitative valuing has allowed suspending the principle of the inviolability of innocent human life. Abortion becomes accepted because of the theory that an unwanted child's life is not worth living. Euthanasia becomes accepted because of the theory that a life burdened with suffering or helplessness is not worth living.

Christianity has insisted that every life is worth living, that every human being is worthy of being loved just because he is human (no matter how otherwise lacking in dignity he may seem to be), because he is made to the image and likeness of God, redeemed by the blood of Christ, and destined to be with God in heaven for eternity.[24] Hence, it has condemned suicide, voluntary euthanasia in which a suffering person permits or even demands termination of his life, and involuntary euthanasia in which others decide to end the life of the suffering or helpless person.

People in primitive cultures are known to have practiced a quasi-euthanasia by abandoning aged and useless members of the community, especially in conditions of shifting residence, as among hunters and herders.[25] Among the Greeks and Romans, voluntary euthanasia of the aged was known and accepted. Seneca wrote persuasively, "Just as I shall select my ship when I am about to go on a voyage, or my house when I propose to take a residence, so I shall choose my death when I am about to depart from life."[26]

However, we have no indication that Judaeo-Christian teaching ever accepted voluntary or involuntary euthanasia. The New Testament mandate to love one's neighbor and treat the least of one's brothers and sisters as Jesus (Mt 25:40) clearly teaches unselfish care for suffering and helpless persons. In fact, the over-riding principle of inviolability of the innocent found already in Ex 23:7 ("The innocent and the just you shall not put to death") seems to have eliminated serious discussion of euthanasia among Catholic theologians until modern times.

The inauguration of involuntary euthanasia by the government of Nazi Germany destroyed the lives of thousands of mentally disturbed and handicapped adults and children.[27] In 1940, in Rome, the Holy Office was asked whether public authority may kill those who are unable to be useful to the nation because of psychic or physical defects. It replied with a categorical "No."[28] Pope Pius XII three years later in his encyclical on the Mysical Body (*Mystici Corporis*) noted that euthanasia was hailed by some as a discovery of human progress and justified by the common good. "Yet what sane man does not recognize," he wrote, "that this not only violates the natural and divine law written in the heart of every man, but flies in the face of every sensibility of civilized humanity."[29]

Recently the Second Vatican Council reaffirmed the Church's opposition to euthanasia when it listed a variety of violations of the dignity of the human person including also murder, genocide, abortion, and willful suicide. The council Fathers said, "All these and the like are criminal: they poison civilization, and they debase the perpetrators more than the victims and militate against the honor of the Creator."[30]

Eleven years later, in their 1976 pastoral on moral life, "To Live in Christ Jesus," the U.S. bishops said: "Euthanasia or mercy killing is much discussed and increasingly advocated today, though the discussion is often confused by ambiguous use of the slogan 'death with dignity.' Whatever the word or term, it is a grave moral evil deliberately to kill persons who are terminally ill or deeply impaired. Such killing is incompatible with respect for human dignity and reverence for the sacredness of life."[31]

The bishops referred to the ambiguous slogan, "death with dignity," because of widespread confusion about the moral issues surrounding suffering and death. Some proponents of euthanasia extend the term to include even foregoing extraordinary measures to prolong life and administering medications for pain relief which may shorten life. Neither of these practices is necessarily equivalent to mercy killing or euthanasia in its primary meaning.

Some contemporary discussion uses the ambiguous slogan of "respecting a patient's right to die." Catholic belief recognizes a right to life endowed upon all human persons by the Creator. This includes a right and duty to care for life with reasonable effort and a right to refuse the unreasonable prolongation of one's life. It does not include a right to reject life by suicide or voluntary euthanasia. If a state or national government were to recognize a "right" to commit suicide or to demand euthanasia, Catholic theology would consider this a false "right" comparable to the "right" to have an abortion sometimes claimed for pregnant women.

Much discussion of death centers on pain and pain relief. Proponents of mercy killing often argue that only death can relieve the suffering of many dying persons. However, contemporary medicine, especially as practiced in the hospice programs which specialize in care for the dying, can relieve severe suffering for almost all patients.[32] Proper pain medication and proper attention to the psychological components of terminal illness can relieve suffering without shortening life.

Furthermore, Pope Pius XII taught that pain medication which is judged necessary may be used even though it deprive the patient of the use of reason or shorten his life since these would not be the primary effects or intent of the medication.[33] *The Ethical and Religious Directives for Catholic Health Facilities* of the U.S. bishops apply this teaching as follows: "It is not euthanasia to give dying persons sedatives and analgesics for the alleviation of pain, when such a measure is judged necessary, even though they may deprive the patient of the use of reason, or shorten his life."[34] The principle of double effect applies here in acting for the good effect of pain relief and permitting, but not intending, the possible evil effects.

Supporters of mercy killing often suggest that dying persons or severely handicapped persons have such a diminished quality of life that a quick and easy death should be administered. Aside from the fact that death can hardly improve one's "quality of life," it should also be noted that killing the suffering and dying is the standard practice of veterinary medicine. Just as human life is totally different from animal life, so is human suffering and dying.

The historic Christian belief that every human life has inherent and essential value is opposed to the view of those who hold that a diminishing quality of life diminishes the value of life. Yet, this latter view seems to be the ethical model of those who argue that once dying has begun, acts of commission may be performed which hasten the dying process.[35] This position has been criticized as resting upon a consequentialism which redescribes evil acts in terms of desirable consequences and which permits the exalting of personal integrity and dignity as a greater good than life itself.[36] Some theologians who are sympathetic with the model of ethical analysis which might permit direct killing of the dying for proportionate reasons hesitate to recommend such a policy because it would "set human beings on a road whose direction is dangerous and end obscure."[37]

In fact, mercy killing is punishable as homicide in the U.S. and most other nations. While courts have often not applied the full penalty of first degree murder in such cases, the law itself does not recognize the motive of mercy as diminishing the gravity of homicide. Efforts to legalize active euthanasia have been made in the U.S., Great Britain, and elsewhere, but have not succeeded. Grave abuses can be foreseen in authorizing voluntary euthanasia either because of direct pressure placed on suffering persons by relatives or heirs to ask for euthanasia, or because of the indirect pressure on persons to ask for euthanasia rather than continue to burden relatives or those caring for them.

Furthermore, many of the proponents of voluntary euthanasia are equally committed to legalizing involuntary euthanasia for the insane and for severely handicapped or retarded children and adults.[38] This would effectively reduce the right to life of innocent citizens to extend only to those persons judged desirable by a majority or a review committee.

Side by side with its deep-seated opposition to mercy killing,

Catholic theology has always taught the acceptance of death when further measures to prolong life would be unreasonable. Respect for life has never meant an obligation to subject suffering persons to every conceivable form of medical manipulation which might prolong life. This constitutes medical scrupulosity.

Since the 17th century at least, Catholic moral theologians have used a distinction between ordinary and extraordinary means of prolonging human life, based on common sense and the biblical notion of responsible stewardship of human life. They have insisted on the affirmative obligation to employ ordinary means of caring for life, that is, whatever medicines, treatments, and operations offer reasonable hope of benefit for the patient and can be obtained without excessive pain, expense or other hardship.[39] Pope Pius XII employed this distinction in a discourse which outlined Catholic teaching clearly.[40]

These "ordinary" means of prolonging life are "ordinary" in an ethical and technical sense of that word used as a term of classification. Other procedures, called "extraordinary" in this classification, are considered not morally obligatory but optional, unless special circumstances mandate their use. Procedures that for a given patient in given circumstances do not offer a reasonable hope of benefit or involve excessive pain, expense, or other hardship fall into the classification of ethically "extraordinary" procedures in that situation but not necessarily in others.

Hence, standard hospital equipment which might be considered a routine or ordinary aspect of everyday hosptial operation is not automatically "ordinary" in terms of ethical obligation to prolong human life. A respirator, for example, would be an ethically ordinary means of prolonging life after lung surgery, but might well be judged an ethically extraordinary means of prolonging the life of a patient dying of an inoperable lung cancer or in an irreversible coma.

Making this distinction and foregoing some possible life-prolonging procedures may cause uneasiness for some patients and those caring for them. To avoid such uneasiness some would prefer to use all possible procedures at all times. But there is no moral obligation for this, and it could so burden physicians and patients as to create a reaction in favor of mercy killing. As medical progress continues to develop more procedures which may function in an ethically extraordinary way, the use of this distinction will become more frequent and more necessary. It will always be true that in matters of genuine doubt one should consider a procedure ordinary and obligatory, rather than the contrary.

Unfortunately, many patients for whom certain possible life-prolonging measures have become ethically extraordinary are either comatose or at lease unable to think clearly and deliberate calmly. Because the right of foregoing any life-prolonging measures belongs to the patient, the family members and attending physician must interpret the patinet's own disposition in such circumstances.

Since 1971 a document called the Living Will has been circulated for persons to record in advance their disposition toward such measures. Several states have passed legislation making such documents legally binding. Since 1974, the Catholic Hospital Association has circulated a document called "A Christian Affirmation of Life" which is not intended for legal enforcement, but is merely a religious and personal statement of one's disposition to forego extraordinary means of prolonging life.[41] This author believes that such documents may be helpful and comforting to families and physicians when forced to make decisions in behalf of patients. But he has argued that "legislation to legalize these documents . . . is unnecessary, counterproductive, harmful to the integrity of patient-physician relationships, and, worst of all, a step toward establishing a spurious right to control death or legalize mercy killing."[42]

In conclusion of this discussion of life-prolonging measures a final word must be added about terminology. The term "passive euthanasia" has begun to appear in recent years as a description for allowing a patient to die instead of actively killing that patient. If allowing death is understood as *only* omitting *extraordinary* means of prolonging life—without attempting to "induce death"—then "passive authanasia" of this kind is acceptable from the point of view of Catholic tradition. Unfortunately, the term "passive euthanasia" is often used without reference to the necessary distinction outlined above between ordinary (obligatory) and extraordinary (optional) means of prolonging life. Furthermore, some people working to popularize the term passive euthanasia have no real moral objection to active euthanasia either and do not concede any significant ethical difference between the two.

It even seems likely that some are using the term passive euthanasia today as a deliberate tactic to win acceptance for the concept of euthanasia itself, so that eventually both the omission of ordinary means of prolonging life and benevolent instances of active mercy killing would be "decriminalized" in American law. While the omission of ordinary means of prolonging life is an act of omission and not of commission and might be semantically classified as merely "passive" euthanasia, it is morally equivalent to active euthanasia and to active mercy killing within the Catholic tradition.

For this reason the term "passive euthanasia" is confusing and ambivalent. The present author feels that an acceptable term for cases of foregoing extraordinary means of prolonging life might be the description, "justifiable use of conservative therapy only," which can be abbreviated JUCTO.[43]

Suicide

In the discussion above about voluntary euthanasia it was clear that in this practice a physician or other person terminates the life of a suffering person in response to the death wish of that person. The assumption is often made that the dying person would commit suicide if he or she could do so, but someone else is needed to terminate life. The Catholic tradition has not permitted physicians or others to become agents of death even for reasons of mercy. Nor does it recognize as morally acceptable anyone's decision to commit suicide.

Suicide may be defined as an act by which one brings about one's own death and which one chooses as a means to an end which one expects will be served by one's dying or by one's own being dead.[44] Such a careful distinction excludes from the notion of suicide such acts as the profession of faith which leads to martyrdom and the foregoing of ethically extraordinary means of prolonging life discussed above.

In the Greco-Roman world of the time of Christ, suicide was both approved by groups like the Epicureans and Stoics and opposed by many like Plato and Aristotle.[45] While the Old Testament recounts six cases of suicide, it does not explicitly approve or condemn the action. The only suicide in the New Testament is Judas who is seen as the prototype of despair. Although one author rather fancifully suggests that the suicide of Judas "seems a measure of repentance,"[46] it is difficult to avoid the implicitly sinful context of Judas' self-killing. The same biblical reverence for life which grounds Christian opposition to abortion and euthanasia supports opposition to suicide also.

Formulations of Christian theology opposing suicide began to appear in the writings of the Church Fathers, especially Augustine.[47] Church councils likewise opposed suicide with the Council of Toledo in 693 punishing with excommunication those who attempted suicide.[48] Aquinas opposed suicide on three grounds: it opposes the instinct of self-preservation and the virtue of love of self, the person who harms himself does harm to the community, and suicide offends God who is the Lord and giver of life.[49]

The traditional Catholic judgment of the immorality of all acts of suicide is echoed in the Second Vatican Council's inclusion of "willful suicide" in the crimes which are offenses against life itself.[50] Theologians have traditionally excluded from such condemnation acts which are not directly opposed to life, but from which death may or will follow. In this use of the principle of double effect one may for proportionate reasons risk one's life without committing suicide and without moral fault. If one risks one's life without proportionate reason, the act may well be morally wrong, but it would not be suicide unless death were actually intended.

Fr. Bernard Häring has suggested that even acts directly opposed to life need not be considered suicide in the moral sense when some great good is accomplished by these acts, as when a spy protects the national secrets he possesses by taking a death pill.[51] Fr. Charles Curran supports this position and argues that a person may directly take his life for proportionate reasons which must be commensurate with the value of human life.[52] Daniel Maguire, in a similar vein, argues that suicide may at times be moral as, for example, "where all of the disvalues of suicide can be outweighed by ineffable pain and loneliness."[53]

Theologians who would permit direct acts of self-destruction argue from a theory of proportionalism in which the intending and doing of a physical evil like killing is justified by the proportionate values achieved. Once this theory is accepted, the discussion shifts to weighing the proportionate values. Some who accept the theory would not admit in practice that acts of self-destruction are justified because no proportionate good could come from allowing exceptions.[54]

An outstanding defense of the tradition which rejects direct suicide regardless of justifying reasons is found in the work of Germain Grisez.[55]

Grisez argues that the approach taken by proportionalism involves consequentialism and this theory implicitly measures the immeasurable and denies human freedom. He insists that a Chrstian must never do evil that good may come of it (Rm 3:8) and particularly must never do the direct evil of attacking directly a basic human good such as life itself, for any motive whatever.

Church teaching has never admitted of exceptions which might justify some acts of self-destruction. But in pastoral practice it is recognized that the majority of persons who commit suicide are so emotionally disturbed that they act compulsively or at least their perception of objective reality is so distorted by their anguish and depression that their freedom of choice is greatly restricted. Hence, although canon 2350 of the *Code of Canon Law* decrees a privation of church burial services for those who commit suicide, canon 1240 restricts the crime to those who kill themselves of deliberate purpose. Today ecclesiastical burial would rarely be denied if there is any indication that the person committed suicide in a moment of depression or impulse.

All the above questions of life and death decisions have explored the ethical and theological implications of responsibility for human life. Questions about human health and the practice of medicine also have theological implications which will be explored in the next chapter.

Footnotes

1. G. Grisez, *op. cit.*, 127.
2. J. Noonan, "An Almost Absolute Value in History," *op. cit.* 8-9.
3. D. McCarthy and A. Moraczewski, *op. cit.* 49.
4. *See* J. Noonan, *op. cit.*, 9.
5. *Ibid.*, *see* also J. Connery, *op. cit.*
6. *Gaudium et Spes* no. 51.
7. Sacred Cong. for the Doc. of the Faith, *Declaration on Abortion, op. cit.*, no. 11.
8. *Ibid.*, no. 7.
9. B. Ashley and K. O'Rourke, *op. cit.*, 227-228.
10. B. Ashley, "Critique of the Theory of Delayed Hominization," appendix to McCarthy and Moraczewski, *op. cit.*, 113-133.
11. *Declaration on Abortion*, note 19.

12. J. Dedek, *Human Life: Some Moral Issues*, New York, 1972, Sheed and Ward, 86-90; C. Curran, *Ongoing Revision*, Notre Dame, 1975, Fides Publishers, 156; *Idem, New Perspectives in Moral Theology*, Notre Dame, 1974, Fides, 186-193.
13. J. Connery, *op. cit.*, 213-214.
14. B. Ashley and K. O'Rourke, *op. cit.*, 237.
15. *See* G. Grisez, *op. cit.*, 182-183.
16. *See* J. Connery, *op. cit.*
17. *Declaration on Abortion* no. 14.
18. T. O'Donnell, S.J., *Medicine and Christian Morality*, New York, 1976, Alba House, 152-212.
19. B. Häring, *Medical Ethics*, Notre Dame, 1973, Fides Publishers, 108-109. Ed. by Garbrielle Jean.
20. G. Grisez, *op. cit.*, 332-346.
21. C. Curran, *New Perspectives*, 191.
22. *CIC* c. 2350.
23. J. Fletcher, "The Patient's Right to Die," in *Euthanasia and the Right to Death*, London, 1969, Peter Owen, 68. Ed. by A. Downing.
24. *See* J. Hardon, *The Catholic Catechism*, Garden City, 1975, Doubleday, 331.
25. J. Sullivan, *Catholic Teaching on the Morality of Euthanasia*, Washington, 1949, Cath. Univ. of America Press, 4-12.
26. *Epistulae Morales*, 70, 11.
27. *See* F. Wertham, M.D., *A Sign for Cain*, New York, 1966, Macmillan, 150-186.
28. *AAS* 32 (1940) 553-554.
29. *Mystici Corporis* no. 104.
30. *Gaudium et Spes* no. 27.
31. NCCB, *To Live in Christ Jesus*, Washington, 1976, U.S.C.C., 20.
32. Cf. R. Lamerton, *Care of the Dying*, Westport, 1976, Technomic Publ. Co.
33. Pius XII, "Anesthesia, Three Moral Questions," in *The Pope Speaks* 2 (1957) 4, 33-49.
34. NCCB, *Ethical and Religious Directives for Catholic Health Facilities*, Washington, 1977, U.S.C.C., no. 29.
35. Cf. C. Curran, *Ongoing Revision, op. cit.*, 160; D. Maguire, *Death by Choice*, Garden City, 1974, Doubleday, 126-129.
36. Cf. W. May, *Human Existence, Medicine and Ethics*, Chicago, 1977, Franciscan Herald Press, 140-142.
37. J. Dedek, *op. cit.*, 141.
38. Cf. St. John Stevas, *Right to Life*, London, 1963, Hodder and Stoughton, 45-51; Y. Kamisar, "Euthanasia Legislation: Some Non-Religious Objections," in Downing, *op. cit.*, 106-114; J. Gould and L. Craigmyle, *Your Death Warrant?*, New Rochelle, 1971, Arlington House, 130-135.
39. C. McFadden, *Medical Ethics*, Philadelphia, 1967 (6th ed.), F. A. Davis, 241.
40. Pius XII, "Prolongation of Life," in *The Pope Speaks*, no. 4, 393-398.
41. *See Hospital Progress*, no. 55, 65-67.
42. D. McCarthy, "Care for Suffering and Dying Persons," Washington, 1978, Committee for Pro-Life Activities, 5.
43. *See* D. McCarthy, "Use and Abuse of Cardiopulmonary Resuscitation," *Hospital Progress* no. 56.
44. Cf. G. Grisez, "Suicide and Euthanasia," in *Death, Dying and Euthanasia*, Washington, 1977, Univ. Publications of America, 745. Ed. by D. Horan and D. Mall.

45. Cf. St. John-Stevas, *op. cit.* 56-57; B. Ashley and K. O'Rourke, *op. cit.*, 380.
46. A. Alvarez, *The Savage God*, New York, 1972, Random House, 51.
47. Cf. St. John-Stevas, *op. cit.*, 59-60.
48. A. Alvarez, *op. cit.*, 71.
49. *ST* 2a2ae.64.5.
50. *Gaudium et Spes*, no. 27.
51. B. Häring, *Morality Is for Persons*, New York, 1971, Farrar, Straus and Giroux, 130-131.
52. C. Curran, *Ongoing Revision*, 150-151.
53. D. Maguire, *op. cit.*, 221.
54. Cf. B. Ashley and K. O'Rourke, *op. cit.*, 382.
55. G. Grisez, "Suicide," 742-811.
56. Cf. also *The Teaching of Christ*, Huntington, 1976, Our Sunday Visitor, 317. Ed. by R. Lawler, D. Wuerl, and T. Lawler.

Chapter 24

RESPONSIBILITY FOR HUMAN HEALTH

Bibliography: *The Human Body*, Papal Teaching Series, Boston, 1960, Daughters of St. Paul; W. Reich (ed.), *Encyclopedia of Bioethics*, New York, 1978, Free Press Division of Macmillan; C. McFadden, O.S.A., *Challenges to Morality*, Huntington, 1978, Our Sunday Visitor Press; *Idem, Dignity of Life*, Huntington, 1976, Our Sunday Visitor Press; W. May, *Human Existence, Medicine and Ethics*, Chicago, 1977, Franciscan Herald Press; T. O'Donnell, S.J., *Medicine and Christian Morality*, New York, 1976, Alba House; P. Ramsey, *Patient as Person*, New Haven, 1970, Yale University Press; B. Ashley, O.P., and K. O'Rourke, O.P., *Health Care Ethics*, St. Louis, 1978, Catholic Health Association.

One who receives the gift of life should care for that gift with respect and concern commensurate with the priceless value of life. Hence, Catholic theology teaches that human persons have a moral responsibility to take reasonable care of their health.

Health, however, cannot easily be defined. No specific pulse rate or blood pressure reading indicates perfect health. Physiological health signifies a generally normal or average condition of certain measurable indicators, but Christian anthropology conceives health as a desirable condition of the whole person, not merely the organic systems. Hence, Fr. Häring describes health in terms of "the greatest possible harmony of all of man's forces and energies, the greatest possible spiritualization of man's bodily aspect and the finest embodiment of the spiritual."[1]

Human health may be seen dynamically as a process of self-actualization. Not every obstacle to that process can be categorized as disease or sickness. Yet without optimal functioning, the failure to function soon leads to dysfunction. Fathers Ashley and O'Rourke point out that "A man can be healthy in this narrow (physiological) sense and yet be lazy, half-alive through lack of full use of his capacity for living, but he will not stay healthy even in this minimal way for long because his faculties will atrophy."[2]

This broader notion of health leads to a definition of health as "the optimal functioning of the human organism to meet biological, psychological, ethical, and spiritual needs."[3] The ministry of healing thus should include moral and spiritual care as well as physical and psychological care, in an integrated way. Catholic health care facilities attempt this integration as a response to the teaching of Jesus.

Illness undermines the human well-being which is health, and leads to death. "The Christian faith teaches that bodily death," said the Second Vatican Council, "from which man would have been immune had he not sinned, will be overcome when that wholeness which he lost through his own fault will be given him once again by the almighty and merciful Savior."[4] Hence, suffering and disease come from original sin whether or not any personal sin has also been involved. The struggle to maintain health thus becomes a struggle with the effects of sin. Healing becomes a redemptive mission.

Yet, every Christian knows that all suffering cannot be overcome and death cannot be indefinitely postponed. Hence, a redemptive meaning must also be found in the experience of suffering and death. Whereas suffering and death originated from human disobedience and rejection of divine love, for Christ these realities became signs of love and submission to His Father. Christians who suffer and die with Christ do so in the solidarity of His body. Paul taught this doctrine in simple words: "In my own flesh I fill up what is lacking in the suffering of Christ for the sake of his body, the Church" (Col 1:24).

This Christian doctrine of suffering with Christ does not include a masochistic pursuit or cult of, suffering. Rather, it must be balanced with the reasonable pursuit of health and healing through personal efforts and professional help. This includes personal responsibility to seek a balanced and nutritious diet, to take adequate exercise, to achieve a proper blend of work and play, and to overcome anxieties and tensions which undermine health. It also includes the seeking of competent medical, psychological, moral, and spiritual help to maintain health. It involves a personal responsibility to use reliable medications and medical procedures which were discussed above as "the ordinary means of prolonging life."[5]

Three special questions that arise in responsible care of human health will be discussed briefly: surgery, organ transplants, and the determination of death; psychological therapy and health; and human experimentation.

Surgery, Organ Transplants, and Determination of Death

With the modern development of safe surgical procedures, various forms of surgery have become routine procedures for the preservation of human health. The removal of diseased organs and malignant tumors raises no major ethical problems because the principle of totality permits the sacrifice of one part of the body for the good of the whole. Pope Pius XII stated this principle simply: "Each of these organs and members (of the body) can be sacrificed if it puts the whole organism in danger, a danger which cannot in any other way be averted."[6] He interpreted this to include even the removal of healthy organs which cause harm to an unhealthy organ with dangerous repercussions on the organism as a whole.[7]

Respect for bodily integrity forbids destruction of its functional integrity. However, organs like the appendix or tonsils may be removed according to medical judgment because of their minimal functional role.[8]

Improving bodily health by incorporating transplanted organs or tissue can be justified when medically feasible. The transplants may even come from animals (heterografts) although Pius XII cautioned that "the transplantation of the sexual glands of an animal to man is to be rejected as immoral."[9] He did explicitly approve the giving of one's body and its organs after death for transplant use.[10]

Living human donors may give one of their organs which are paired, like the kidneys, or non-functional tissue, like the cornea of a blind eye, for the benefit of another person. This cannot be approved on the strict principle of totality since the two persons do not constitute one organic whole, but simply on the principle of charity. In such cases the free and informed consent of the living donor must be safeguarded and careful calculation made of the risk to the donor.

The Ethical and Religious Directives for Catholic Health Facilities offer a norm for such situations: "30. The transplantation of organs from living donors is morally permissible when the anticipated benefit to the recipient is proportionate to the harm done to the donor, provided that the loss of such organ(s) does not deprive the donor of life itself nor of the functional integrity of his body."[11]

In the transplants of kidneys and hearts from human cadavers, physicians need these organs as "fresh" as possible and prefer to maintain their function artificially even after death is pronounced. In fact, their concerns have led the medical profession to explore appropriate criteria for determination of human death even when signs of life are maintained by artificial support systems. If the signs of life like breathing and blood circulation are being maintained without the unifying internal function of the patient's central nervous system, they are not true signs of human life and the patient is really dead. In these cases turning off the support systems is not euthanasia in any form nor even the terminating of "extraordinary means" of prolonging life. It is merely releasing a cadaver from medical manipulation.

On the other hand, if the life support system is truly supporting the internal life process and the central nervous system continues to function, the patient should not be declared dead. Recent efforts to determine death even in the presence of life-support systems, such as the Harvard criteria,[12] seek to base the determination as to whether the central nervous system is actually functioning on reflexes, responsivity, and the effort to breathe. It has been generally recognized that an electroencephalograph reading of itself does not adequately register this information. Hence, the Harvard criteria use this reading only in a confirmatory way.

Pius XII said in a discourse on Nov. 24, 1957, that the verification of death does not fall within the competence of the Church. He left this to the medical profession: "It remains for the doctor, and especially the anesthesiologist, to give a clear and precise definition of 'death' and the 'moment of death' of a patient who passes away in a state of unconsciousness."[13] Any efforts of the medical profession to designate as humanly dead those persons who are irreversibly comatose with irreversible cessation of higher brain function would be highly questionable and ethically dangerous.[14]

Psychological Therapy and Health

Since mental illness must be recognized as an obstacle to health comparable to physical illness, human persons must also cultivate mental health. Admittedly the methods of psychiatry and psychological therapy are much more complex and less empirically observable than the practice of physical medicine with results comparably less predictable. The theological anthropology of the Judaeo-Christian tradition clearly recognizes the role of human freedom and the involvement of moral weakness in mental illness.

Pius XII warned about treatments which destroy human freedom in an address on Sept. 13, 1952: "Man cannot perform upon himself or allow medical operations, either physical or somatic, which beyond doubt do remove serious defects of physical or psychic weaknesses, but which entail at the same time permanent destruction of, or a considerable and lasting lessening of freedom."[15] The Pope was not ruling out such surgical procedures as lobotomy or leukotomy entirely, but pointing out that psychosurgery can only be justified within the context of the total good and the preservation of the freedom of the patient.

Today surgical intervention to cure mental illness is not unknown, but chemical and behavioral treatments have become much more common. Standard ethical principles apply to the use of such therapies, specifically the requirement of free and informed consent and of benefit proportionate to the risk entailed. One official statement of the latter principle is directive no. 26 of the *Directives* for Catholic health facilities: "Therapeutic procedures which are likely to be dangerous are morally justifiable for proportionate reasons."[16]

The greatest single form of psychological illness affecting people today is addiction to tobacco and drugs, especially alcohol. Addiction may be classifed as physiological or psychological. Physiological addiction usually requires increasing doses of the addicting substance to obtain the same psychological effect; it involves severe withdrawal symptoms, and includes psychological dependence upon the addicting substance as well.

Regarding the culpability of those suffering addictions, Fathers Ashley and O'Rourke have commented: "Addictive behavior is voluntary in the sense that it proceeds from an inner compulsion, but it always involves a restriction of freedom, since the victim becomes less and less able to perceive alternatives of action or to choose among them.''[17]

Actual use of addictive substances by addicts will often not involve grave moral fault, but the real moral responsibility of the addict lies in the obligation to ask and receive help from others. While therapy for addiction can be highly successful, it will require intensive follow-up. In cases of physiological addiction (alcohol and some drugs) no cure can be complete, but control is assured through abstinence.

Christian theology teaches a realistic effort to overcome pain, frustration, and sorrow. It does not support the influential cultural acceptance of addictive substances which would simply overcome human problems by pills, potions, or injections. Hence, a preventive approach to addiction accords most fully with Christian responsibility for health.

Human Experimentation

Medicine cannot progress without a certain degree of experimentation, even though the use of animals for preliminary efforts can often considerably reduce the risk. Human experimentation is the recourse to treatments, drugs or surgery whose likely effects are not sufficiently established.

The Catholic hospital *Directives* offer a general principle about experimentation: "27. Experimentation on patients without due consent is morally objectionable, and even the moral right of the patient to consent is limited by his duties of stewardship."[18] The consent of the patient involves more than the mere signing of a form. To be truly human it must be reasonably free and given after adequate information has been shared.[19] Pius XII explained the reason for obtaining consent, saying, "The doctor has only that power over the patient which the latter gives him, be it explicitly, or implicitly and tacitly."[20] Fr. Charles Curran prefers to speak of the patient's participation in the experimental procedure rather than his merely giving consent for it.[21]

The moral limits to experimentation are described in directive no. 27 above as flowing from the duties of stewardship. Pius XII said, "He (the patient) is not absolute master of himself, of his body, or of his soul. He cannot, therefore, freely dispose of himself as he pleases."[22] The duties of stewardship are different in the case of therapeutic and non-therapeutic experimentation.

Therapeutic experimentation is carried on in order to improve the health of the patient by various possible means. Here the risk a patient may reasonably and responsibly undertake is in proportion to the seriousness of the disease and the relation of benefit and risk in the procedure. A person dying of cancer might well consent to high-risk experimentation without violating stewardship. Non-therapeutic experimentation, however, does not improve the health condition of the research subject, but seeks to gain knowledge or develop new techniques beneficial to others. Here the research subject performs an unselfish act of risk without personal benefit. To what degree of risk could a person expose himself or herself in this manner?

Pius XII referred to moral limits in this regard by saying that a person "has no right to permit scientific or practical experiments which entail *serious injury* or which threaten to *impair his health*."[23] In the same context he ruled out experiments which could conceivably result in mutilation or suicide.

Can proxy consent be given to expose children or the unborn or comatose persons to non-therapeutic experimentation? Christian ethicists have discussed this issue and some would rule out all such experimentation, where others would permit it provided there was only "minimal risk."[24] Those who argue in favor of such consent hypothesize that such incompetent persons can be expected to make a minimal contribution to the common good, since they are in fact members of the human community. Those who oppose such consent argue that to use such subjects is to treat them as objects or experimental animals. Fathers Ashley and O'Rourke adopt the latter position both because guardians who give proxy consent function only for the individual benefit of their wards and because the elasticity of "minimal risk" is open to an expanding interpretation.[25]

These brief reflections about human health serve merely to outline vast areas of ethical concern in the practice of medicine today. But the principles and values discussed here have comparable applications in other wider areas.

Footnotes

1. B. Häring, C.SS.R., *Medical Ethics*, Notre Dame, 1973, Fides Publishers, 154. Ed. by Gabrielle Jean.
2. *Ibid.*, 33.
3. B. Ashley, O.P., and K. O'Rourke, O.P., *Health Care Ethics: A Theological Analysis*, St. Louis, 1977, Cath. Hosp. Assoc., 33.
4. *Gaudium et Spes* no. 18.
5. Cf. D. McCarthy, "Care for Suffering and Dying Persons," Washington, 1978, NCCB Committee for Pro-Life Activities, 8-10.
6. Pius XII, "Allocution to the Italian Medical-biological Union of St. Luke," Nov. 12, 1944, in *The Human Body, op. cit.*, 55, no. 52.
7. Pius XII, "Allocution to Delegates at the 26th Congress of Urology," Oct. 8, 1953, in *The Human Body, op. cit.*, 278, no. 498.
8. C. McFadden, O.S.A., *op. cit.*, 183-199.
9. Pius XII, "Allocution to a Group of Eye Specialists," May 14, 1956, in *The Human Body, op. cit.*, 374, no. 638.
10. *Ibid.*, 381, no. 646.
11. NCCB, *Ethical and Religious Directives for Catholic Health Facilities*, Washington, 1977, USCC.
12. Cf. *Journal of the American Medical Association* 205, Aug. 5, 1968, 337-340.
13. Pius XII, "Prolongation of Life," in *The Pope Speaks*, no. 4, 396.
14. B. Ashley, O.P., and K. O'Rourke, O.P., *op. cit.*, 369-373.
15. Cf. D. McCarthy, *op. cit.*, 28.
16. Pius XII, "Allocution to the First International Congress of Histopathology," Sept. 13, 1952, in *The Human Body, op. cit.*, 199, no. 361.
17. B. Ashley and K. O'Rourke, *op. cit.*, 359.
18. NCCB, *op. cit.*, no. 27.
19. B. Ashley, O.P., and K. O'Rourke, O.P., *op. cit.*, 252-253; W. May, *op. cit.*, 17-34.
20. Pius XII, "Allocution . . ." Sept. 13, 1952, in *The Human Body, op. cit.*, 198, no. 358.
21. C. Curran, *Issues in Sexual and Medical Ethics*, Notre Dame, 1978, Univ. of Notre Dame Press, 86-87.
22. Pius XII, "Allocution . . ." Sept. 13, 1952, in *The Human Body, op. cit.*, 198-199, no. 359.
23. Pius XII, "Allocution to the Eighth Congress of the World Medical Association," Sept. 30, 1954, in *The Human Body, op. cit.*, 315, no. 545. Italics added.
24. For a summary of this discussion *see* Ashley and O'Rourke, *op. cit.*, 254.
25. *Ibid.*, 254-255.

Chapter 25

RESPONSIBILITY FOR SEXUAL ACTIVITY

Bibliography: O. Liebard (ed.), *Official Catholic Teachings on Love and Sexuality*, Wilmington, 1978, McGrath, a Consortium Book; National Conference of Catholic Bishops, "To Live in Christ Jesus," Washington, 1976, U.S.C.C.; Sacred Congregation for the Doctrine of the Faith, "Declaration on Certain Questions concerning Sexual Ethics" and "Commentaries," Washington, 1977, U.S.C.C.; *Idem*, "Observations on *Human Sexuality*," reprinted in *Origins*, 9, 167-169; W. May, *Nature and Meaning of Chastity*, Chicago, 1976, Franciscan Herald Press; P. Bertocci, *Sex, Love and the Person*, New York, 1967, Sheed and Ward; E. Schillebeeckx, O.P., Marriage: *Secular Reality and Saving Mystery*, London, 1965, Sheed and Ward, 2 vols. Transl. by N. Smith; D. Von Hildebrand, *Celibacy and the Crisis of Faith*, Chicago, 1971, Franciscan Herald Press. Transl. by J. Crosby; *Idem, In Defense of Purity*, New York, 1935, Sheed and Ward.

Introduction—Sex in Society

Responsibility for human health amounts to a form of cherishing and valuing the gift of human life itself. Responsibility for sexual activity, understood in terms of heterosexual genital intercourse, amounts to a form of cherishing and valuing the lifesharing power. This power can only be realized in the union of a male and female person, and ethical norms are needed to establish norms for the relationship of those two persons.

All known human societies have imposed limitations on sexual relations and attempted to direct them according to established patterns.

There is no evidence that a completely promiscuous human society has ever existed.[1] Marriage is a universal social institution that defines a mating relationship for the founding of a family and binds it for the protection and rearing of progeny.

This theological discussion of human sexual activity will include three sections: biblical teaching, Church teaching, and chastity and sexual morality. The next chapter will discuss specific questions about sexual activity for the unamarried and the married.

Biblical Teaching

Biblical teaching on marriage begins with the creation stories in Genesis. The Jahwist source, dated around 950 B.C., shows God remedying the loneliness of the man He had formed by creating a woman: "That is why a man leaves his father and mother and clings to his wife, and the two of them become one body" (2:24). The Priestly source, dated around 525 B.C., pictures the creation of male and female in the divine image and God blessing them, saying, "Be fertile and multiply, fill the earth and subdue it" (1:28). The two prominent meanings of sexual intercourse, unitive and procreative, are thus each presented in the beginning of divine revelation.

The descendants of Abraham treasured the procreative meaning of human sexual activity, since fertility was regarded as the greatest blessing God could bestow on marriage. To have no children meant that one's own name was "blotted out of Israel" (Dt 25:6; cf. 1 S 1:5-22).

Yet, this does not mean that married love was of purely secondary importance in the Old Testament.[2] Thus, Elkanah, the father of Samuel, protests to his wife Hannah, who has been complaining because she has no children from him: "Am I not more to you than ten sons?" (1 S 1:5-8). Jacob served his father-in-law Laban for seven years instead of paying a dowry, yet "they seemed to him but a few days because of his love for her" (Gn 29:20). Even Israel's law protected the demands of early married love, for a newly married husband was exempt from military service and any public duty for one year, "to bring joy to the wife he has married" (Dt 25:5). Although the Bible is generally silent about the intimate and private side of marriage, it was marriage lived as a faithful covenant of love which became in Israel one of the means of revealing the covenant of grace between God and His people.

Polygamy did exist among some of the leaders of the chosen people, and some theologians have speculated that God actually allowed the practice; but the Scriptures simply record the fact that it happened. Furthermore, the conception of marriage which emerges from the creation narrative is monogamous; the Mosaic Law is monogamous in spirit; and, after the exile, polygamy practically disappeared and divorce was frowned on.[3] In the wisdom literature, the praises of the good wife are best understood in the context of monogamous marriage (Pr 5:15-19; 31:10-31; Ec 9:9; Si 26:1-4).

The older historical books of the Old Testament show that the harlot was a familiar figure.[4] Custom scorned the woman who distributed her favors thus. However, extra-marital intercourse does not seem to have been forbidden the man so long as he did not take the wife of a fellow-countryman. Exodus commanded that if a man seduced a virgin who was not betrothed, he should pay her marriage price and marry her (22:15). The influence of the nature religion of Canaan with its religious reasons for unrestricted sex did influence the sexual attitudes of Israel, and on the high places secular and sacred prostitution went hand in hand.

Yet, on the basis of their understanding of God and man, the prophets like Amos and Jeremiah opposed both kinds of prostitution (Am 2:7; Jr 5:7). Hauck and Schulz in their biblical study believe that "from that time onwards any religious justification of extra-marital intercourse became impossible" and "passages which originally prohibited cultic prostitution through the sacred law of God became in the later traditions general prohibitions of fornication in Israel."[5]

In the New Testament human sexuality is treated frankly and reverently. Jesus comments on the pains of a woman's labor and the joy of her delivery of a child (Jn 16:21). Elizabeth speaks of Jesus as the fruit of Mary's womb (Lk 1:42) and a woman cries out blessing the womb that bore Jesus and the breasts that nursed Him (Lk 11:27). Paul speaks of his labor pains in bringing to birth the Galatian Christians (Gal 4:19).

The Old Testament conception of purity as an external, cultic, and ritual property is clearly transformed by the New Testament's interiorizing of the moral law. "Nothing that enters a man from outside can make him impure," said Jesus; "wicked designs come from the deep recesses of the heart, acts of fornication, theft, murder, adulterous conduct, greed, maliciousness, deceit, sensuality, envy, blasphemy, arrogance, and ob-

tuse spirit. All these evils come from within and render a man impure"
(Mk 7:20-23). Thus, Jesus says firmly in the Sermon on the Mount,
"Anyone who looks lustfully at a woman has already committed adultery
with her in his thoughts" (Mt 5:28). Yet, Jesus readily accepted conversion of the heart as when He told the penitent woman who anointed His
feet, "Your faith has been your salvation" (Lk 7:50).

Jesus rejected the practice of divorce by affirming God's plan of
indissoluble marriage. In quoting the Jahwist source in Genesis, He
appeals to the unity of two in one flesh. In the linguistic usage of the
Bible, "flesh" signifies not only the body in distinction from the soul;
but it also means the whole person as in the Genesis text or in Lk 3:6, "All
flesh shall see the salvation of God." Hence, Jesus taught that marriage
creates a unity of two in one person and not merely a union of two bodies.
This has great significance as an ideal of conjugal love.

Jesus modified the Jewish attitude which discouraged remaining
unmarried. In His response to the Sadducees He pointed out that there is a
new world in the offing in which there will no longer be any marrying
(Mk 12:18-27). He approved of celibacy "for the sake of the kingdom of
heaven" (Mk 19:10-12). Christ presented Himself as the beginning of
God's dominion or kingdom and thus that phrase meant, "for the sake of
Christ." Those who direct their whole energy and life to advancing the
kingdom of God and its presence in Christ have given up family or
property for Christ and "will receive many times as much and inherit
everlasting life" (Mt 19:29).

Paul repeated the opposition of Jesus to divorce (1 Cor 7:10-11) and
also approved of celibacy as an alternative to marriage, since "each one
has his own gift from God, one this and another that" (1 Cor 7:7).
Celibacy was not to be based on the false asceticism of the day which
taught marriage to be evil. Paul made clear to Timothy that marriage is
good (1 Tm 4:1-5); and a firm reminder in Heb (13:4) says, "Let
marriage be honored in every way and the marriage bed be kept
undefiled."

Paul clearly rejected the Old Testament double standard in sexual
morality when he told husbands that "a husband does not belong to
himself but to his wife" (1 Cor 7:4). He counseled marriage to avoid
immorality in a sober recognition of strong sexual instincts (1 Cor 7:2).
But he also saw married love as imitating Christ's love for the Church (Ep

5:22-23). In that passage to the Ephesians in which he described the bodily love of husband and wife, Paul relied on earlier passages which initiated the theme of the "body" by speaking four different times of the Church as the "body of the Lord." Paul's counsel to husbands of "Love your wives" adds an entirely new and Christian statement to the tables of neighborly and domestic duties borrowed from profane ethics.[6] He speaks not of *eros*, the love which lives by need and longing, but of *agape*, the love which bestows itself on another out of its own wealth.

Paul presents a healthy and reverent view of sexuality in using it to speak of Christ's love for His Church. He would not use that analogy if it were degrading. The two becoming one of sexual union can frankly be compared to the relationship of love betwen Christ and His Church. This reflects an optimistic view of human sexuality despite the degraded practices among people like the Corinthians.[7] With only two exceptions the Greek term for marriage, *gamos*, is used in the New Testament to describe the eternal wedding feast with God, the eschatological wedding of Christ and His redeemed.

Biblical reverence for human sexuality can be found also in the repeated condemnations of unchastity by Paul, listing it as a vice at least ten different times (Rm 1:24-27; 13:13; 1 Cor 5:10 ff; 6:9; 2 Cor 12:21; Gal 5:19; Ep 5:3 ff; Col 3:5; 1 Tm 1:10; 2 Tm 3:4). The reason that misuse of one's body and sexual powers offends God is presented eloquently by Paul in 1 Cor 6:12-20: "Shun lewd conduct. Every other sin a man commits is outside his body, but the fornicator sins against his own body. You must know that your body is a temple of the Holy Spirit who is within."

These biblical references to unchastity do not provide the kind of systematic and normative treatise on sexual morality which developed from patristic times onward and which will be reviewed in the section below on "Chastity and Sexual Morality." In fact, Bruce Malina published an influential article in 1972 making a scholarly examination of the uses of the Greek word *porneia* often translated as "fornication." He concludes that aside from a passage by Rabbi Eliezer around 90 A.D. there is no evidence of usage of the word to mean pre-betrothal, premarital intercourse which was non-cultic and non-commercial.[8] He is challenging the opinion of Hauck and Schulz, mentioned above, who see the latter development in the Old Testament as strengthening premarital chastity and who speak of the New Testament as "characterized by an unconditional repudiation of all extra-marital and unnatural intercourse."[9]

John J. O'Rourke replied to Malina with the argument that at least in 1 Cor 7:1-2 Paul includes non-cultic and non-commercial fornication in the meaning of *porneia*.[10] Although the New Testament more clearly condemns cultic and commercial fornication, there is no evidence that it tolerates non-cultic and non-commercial fornication. Malina himself notes in a footnote that the cultural setting of the first century may not have offered much opportunity or encouragement to such fornication. Surely the cultural custom of "steady dating" before marriage as practiced in the 20th century United States was not a first century phenomenon.

Scholars like Malina who question whether *porneia* included all forms of pre-marital intercourse tend to relate its usage to the Old Law and its norms of unlawful conduct. Yet, in giving the New Law, Jesus certainly transformed and interiorized the Old Testament understanding of marriage and sexual morality, a fact which must be included in the interpretations of the New Testament usage of *porneia*. Church teaching from the patristic period onwards uniformly opposes pre-marital sexual intercourse and gives witness to the Church's inclusive interpretation of *porneia*.

Church Teaching

The New Testament emphasis on reverence for one's bodily sexual powers and for the holiness of the marriage bed has permeated Church teaching. Pre-marital intercourse has been considered grave sin, as, for example, the teaching of the 13th ecumenical council at Lyons in 1245: "But concerning fornication, which an unmarried person commits with another unmarried person, there is no doubt that it is a mortal sin, since the Apostle asserts that fornicators as well as adulterers are excluded from the kingdom of God" (cf. 1 Cor 6:9).[11] Pius XI repeated this teaching in the 20th century in his encyclical *Casti Connubii* on Christian marriage in 1930: "Every use of the faculty given by God for the procreation of new life is the right and privilege of the married state alone, by the law of God and of nature, and must be confined absolutely within the sacred limits of that state."[12]

The question of the purposes of marriage has played a critical role in Church teaching on human sexuality. Up until the present century the theological reflection accompanying Church teaching relied heavily on the procreation and education of children as the primary purpose of marriage and the primary norm of marital morality. Augustine considered the concupiscence of the flesh so strong in matters of sexual activity that only the performing of the marriage act for the purpose of procreating children could free it from sin.

In the Middle Ages, Thomas Aquinas tempered this pessimism of Augustine by admitting a second possible legitimate reason for performing the marriage act: to render the marriage debt (*reddere debitum*).[13] One scholar of the medieval period has argued strongly that Thomas included here the notion of conjugal love, since the debt is a rendering of due love and not merely a transaction of justice in psychological terms.[14]

When Thomas discussed the three goods of marriage as presented by Augustine (offspring, fidelity, and sacramental bond), he related them to human persons as animal, human, and Christian, in that order.[15] Hence, marital fidelity depends on the unique freedom of human persons which is expressed in both the virtues of justice (rendering a marriage debt) and conjugal love (rendering due love). Thomas described marriage in personalistic terms as ''a certain indivisible union of souls through which each of the spouses is held to keep faith indivisibly with the other.''[16]

The twentieth century has seen an increasing theological concern for the role of conjugal love in marriage. Given the greater impersonality of relationships in modern society, the need for personal relationships is accentuated and marriage becomes the one relationship most capable of fulfilling this need. Conjugal love gives depth to sexual experience. Dietrich Von Hildebrand has written, ''Sex possesses a tender, mysterious, and ineffably uniting quality only when it becomes the expression of something more ultimate, namely, wedded love.''[17]

Hence, several modern theologians like Hubert Doms and Bernardin Krempel proposed restating the traditional ends of marriage as found in the 1918 *Code of Canon Law* which says: ''The primary end of marriage is the procreation and education of children, its secondary end is the mutual help and the allaying of concupiscence.''[18] Thus, Doms proposed that the first purpose of marriage is the personal and mutual fulfillment of the spouses which finds its highest expression in the way husbands and wives entrust themselves to one another physically, while the second purpose, the specific end of marriage, is the child.[19]

The Holy Office in 1944 spoke to this issue by insisting that the secondary ends of marriage are essentially subordinate to the primary end, not equally principal with it or independent of it. Pius XII in his address to the Italian midwives in 1951 stressed that the personal values of marriage, though not primary, are nevertheless part of nature's plan and of great importance in marriage.[20] By this time, the older language about the secondary purpose of marriage as offering mutual help and allaying of concluiscence was replaced by the description of the unitive purpose of marriage: fostering mutual conjugal love.

The Second Vatican Council avoided the language of primary and secondary ends of marriage. It stressed the traditional procreative goal simply and directly: "Marriage and married love are by nature ordered to the procreation and education of children."[21] It concluded that discussion of procreation by saying: "But marriage is not merely for the procreation of children: its nature as an indissoluble compact between two people and the good of the children demand that the mutual love of the partners be properly shown, that it should grow and mature."[22]

The significance of Vatican II's emphasis on conjugal love along with the procreative purpose of marriage can be exemplified in two post-conciliar developments. The first is a passage in the encyclical *Humanae Vitae (Of Human Life)* of Paul VI. First, he summarized the council's doctrine on conjugal love in paragraphs 8 and 9. Then, in the same paragraph (no. 13) in which he opposed actions which destroy the procreative potential of conjugal intercourse, he also taught that a marital act cannot be morally good unless it is a "true act of love:" "It is in fact justly observed that a conjugal act imposed upon one's partner without regard for his or her condition and lawful desires is not a true act of love, and therefore denies an exigency of right moral order in the relationships between husband and wife."[23]

Secondly, canonical practice of the Church's marriage tribunals has been influenced by Vatican II's description of marriage as a "partnership of life and love" (*consortium vitae*). A well-known decision of the Roman Rota *Coram Anné* of Feb. 25, 1969, asserted that the formal object of marriage "embraces also the right to a life partnership, that is, living together which is properly called matrimonial. Hence, because a spouse must have the mental, emotional, and psychological capacity to assume this relationship, "psychological impotence" has come to be regarded as an invalidating impediment to marriage, along with physiological impotence."[24]

This maturing appreciation of conjugal love is continuing to influence Church teaching about marriage and human sexuality. Some theologians find that the Vatican Council approach to the goals of marriage is reason to call for sweeping changes in Church teaching on sexuality. For example, the authors of the 1977 book, *Human Sexuality*, felt that "the (Vatican) Council's deliberate rejection of the centuries-long tradition that regarded the procreative end as supreme necessitates a thorough rewriting of the theology of marital sexuality found in the moral manuals."[25]

However, the U.S. bishops in their pastoral reflection on the moral life entitled "To Live in Christ Jesus" of Nov. 11, 1976, presented a post-Vatican II summary of Church teaching on marriage and sexuality without radically changing it.[26] For instance, they rejected the view that a marital union might die and be dissolved because conjugal love had disappeared. They taught that the love-giving (unitive) and life-giving (procreative) meanings of marital intercourse are joined in a relationship which exists not only on the biological level, but on all levels of personality.

The bishops succinctly stated Church teaching on sexual morality in four sentences: "Our Christian tradition holds the sexual union between husband and wife in high honor, regarding it as a special expression of their covenanted love which mirrors God's love for His people and Christ's love for the Church. But like many things human, sex is ambivalent. It can be either creative or destructive. Sexual intercourse is a moral and human good only within marriage; outside marriage it is wrong."[27]

The bishops explained the Church's opposition to pre-marital and extra-marital relations by pointing out that "such relations are not worthy of beings created in God's image and made God's adopted children nor are they according to God's will."[28] They cited three practical reasons to oppose such relations: 1) the unconditional love of Christian marriage is absent; 2) despite tenderness and concern that may be present, such relations tend toward exploitation and self-deception; and 3) such relations trivialize human sexuality and can erode the possibility of making deep, lifelong commitments.

Church teaching on sexual morality can only be assimilated and lived in the conscious and concentrated effort to practice the virtue of chastity. Contemporary theology emphasizes chastity as a virtue to be practiced by all human persons, married and unmarried, guiding all expressions of human love in proper proportion to the relationships of persons.[29] Sexual morality can thus be studied as the practice of Christian chastity.

Chastity and Sexual Morality

The U.S. bishops spoke of chastity in their 1968 pastoral letter, "Human Life in Our Day:" "The Christian ascetic of chastity, within and outside marriage, honors the sanctity of life and protects the dignity of human sexuality. Were there no revelation nor religion, civilization itself would require rational discipline of the sexual instinct. Revelation, however, inspires chastity with more sublime purposes and creative power. In chaste love, the Christian, whether his vocation be to marriage or to celibacy, expresses love for God Himself."[30]

The Scriptural basis for chastity has already been reviewed—it is a God-given adornment of human persons, a fruit of the action and presence of the Spirit (Gal 5:24; 1 Th 4:3-8). Patristic teaching regards chastity as the sanctification of sexuality. The eastern Fathers emphasize its mystical and transcendent character, while the western Fathers present its practical aspects.[31] Thomas Aquinas considers chastity a subjective part of the cardinal virtue of temperance, regulating by reason and will the genital powers and desires of human persons.

Contemporary theological reflection widens the notion of chastity to include sexual affections and emotions even in a non-genital context.[32] William May offers a description of this wider virtue as integrating sexual and affective loves in personal life and providing a loving and intelligent ordering of sexual desires and longings, of the need to touch and be touched.[33]

This wider understanding of sexuality reflects twentieth century personalism which has profited by the insights of psychology and phenomenology into the mysterious depths of human personhood. Donald Goergen speaks of sexuality as encompassing two dimensions, the affective and the genital. Sexuality in this wider understanding is based on the sexual identity of every person and affects their sexual attractions to others and the human relationships which develop.[34]

The older, narrower, view of chastity by which it simply regulated genital powers and desires led to the terminology of "perfect chastity" for those who have forsaken all genital experience, and "imperfect chastity" for married persons who make legitimate use of their genital powers. Contemporary trends emphasize that the same virtue of chastity should direct the conduct and relationships of the married and the unmarried and that marital chastity need not be considered an inferior form of chastity.[35] For the unmarried, chastity presumes conscious and free decisions to restrain genital impulses, lest an unhealthy repression should develop.[36]

The challenge which faces all persons in practicing chastity stems from original sin and the weakness of concupiscence which Thomas located in the concupiscible appetite.[37] But just as Church teaching presents the Christian vision of an integrated love as the norm of sexual morality, it offers the grace of Christ to fulfill that vision. The *Declaration on Sexual Ethics* of the Sacred Congregation for the Doctrine of the Faith of Dec. 29, 1975, quoted Paul saying, "The law of the spirit, the spirit of life in Christ Jesus, has freed you from the law of sin and death" (Rm 8:2). It went on to list the traditional means for living a chaste life: discipline of the senses and the mind, watchfulness and prudence in avoiding the occasions of sin, the observance of modesty, moderation in recreation, wholesome recreation, and frequent reception of the sacraments of penance and the Eucharist.[38]

The initial challenge to chastity comes from the vivid and stimulating powers of the imagination which can present sexual fantasies to both the married and unmarried persons in great intensity. Yet, one's chastity cannot be violated by the indeliberate movements of the imagination. Theologians have always considered crucial the role of consent or free response to the spontaneous function of the imagination. This was implied by Jesus when He spoke of the person who had looked *lustfully* on a woman and already committed adultery with her in his thoughts (Mt 5:28).

When chastity is considered in its narrower role as the virtue regulating genital powers and desires, it has traditionally been taught by Catholic moral theology that it is not a trivial matter to violate chastity. In other words, every direct violation of the virtue is seen as objectively capable of constituting mortal sin when undertaken with sufficient reflection and full consent of the will. This teaching applies both to the complete act of sexual intercourse outside the covenant of marriage as well as to incomplete acts which include what Fr. Bernard Häring called in the *Law of Christ* "sexual gratification."[39]

Although this teaching has more recently been criticized by Fr. Häring himself as an extreme rigorism based on the medieval concept of the sanctity of human life, it can still be appreciated in the context of contemporary personalism.[40] The contemporary emphasis on conjugal love in marriage emphasizes the unique significance of genital activity. The Second Vatican Council taught that "married love is uniquely expressed and perfected by the exercise of the acts proper to marriage." It added that "the truly human performance of these acts fosters the self-giving they signify and enriches the spouses in joy and gratitude."[41] Hence, the more sacred and sacramental these acts are proclaimed to be by the teaching Church as signs of the covenant, the more objectionable they become outside that covenant of "total fidelity" and "unbreakable unity."[42]

This doctrine that genital activity has objectively grave moral significance has been based on the principle that a natural design links even the initial forms of genital stimulation to the complete act of sexual intercourse with which it climaxes. Fr. Häring described this in 1963: "For the lesser degrees of selfish sexual pleasure, sought and enjoyed directly and with full deliberation, constitute in their intrinsic dynamism—if not necessarily in their immediate subjective intent—the way to complete sexual satisfaction."[43]

Because of this dynamism theologians have recognized the moral danger that, if incomplete genital acts were not accorded grave significance, human persons would be caught up in the onrush of sexual escalation to complete genital acts outside marriage. Dom Odon Lottin, the historian of Thomistic moral theology, explained that if complete acts were only forbidden under pain of venial sin they would be too easily committed.[44]

It must be emphasized that this estimation of the gravity of incomplete genital activity is the way the Church has taught the grave importance of genital sexuality. It by no means teaches that all such acts are, in fact, mortal sins. The 1975 *Declaration on Sexual Ethics*, mentioned above, pointed out that in sins of the sexual order it more easily happens that full consent is not fully given and added, "In this matter it is particularly opportune to recall the following words of Scripture: 'Man looks at appearances, but God looks at the heart'." (1 S 16:7).[45]

Furthermore, this doctrine about grave matter must be applied cautiously to the complex reality of human sexual behavior. While it clearly attaches grave moral significance to genital intercourse and the intimate acts which immediately precede and accompany this union, the wider questions of kissing, embracing, and touching remain problematic. Such actions need not always involve the sexual dynamism leading to genital intercourse which theologians have discussed. These actions may be expressions of affection appropriate to a relationship of persons other than the total and unbreakable unity of marriage.

One way theologians have tried to analyze actions like kissing, embracing, and touching is to consider what type of pleasure they produce. If these actions merely produce the warmth and satisfaction that relates to male-female companionship and the affective enjoyment from expressing affection, they should be moderated by chastity in the wider sense mentioned above, but do not constitute grave matter in the theological sense.

On the other hand, these actions may be prolonged to the point of genital pleasure. Genital pleasure, also called venereal pleasure in textbook terminology, arises through the bodily stimulation of the genital organs and the psychic tension which spontaneously seeks release in sexual climax. Sexual climax occurs in the female through orgasm and in the male through ejaculation of sperm.

Hence, the doctrine of grave matter can be stated in this kind of descriptive statement: for unmarried persons to seek actively or consent to venereal pleasure is grave matter. Unintended venereal pleasure can arise, especially in the problematic actions of kissing, embracing, and touching, which leads to a second descriptive statement: venereal pleasure which is neither sought nor consented to may arise without moral fault by the unmarried from actions performed for morally acceptable reasons. A proviso should be added to this second statement: the more strongly sexual desires are aroused by these actions, the more dangerous they become because of the danger of consent, and the greater the prudential reason necessary to perform them.

The above resume has outlined the basic Catholic teaching about the grave moral significance of genital activity and genital pleasure outside marriage. Theological speculation in recent years has been questioning this teaching. This comes partly from the increasing emphasis on the relational meaning of human sexual activity and a de-emphasis of the intrinsic dynamism which leads to genital climax. But it also comes from the renewed appreciation of mortal sin as a turning away from God in one's fundamental option.

According to the notion of fundamental option only those matters should be taught to involve grave moral significance which *usually* call for an involvement of a person's core freedom and basic moral orientation. Hence, those questioning the teaching on genital activity and pleasure as grave matter fear that this theological categorization establishes an unwarranted presumption of full personal engagement.[46] Fr. Charles Curran points out that this doctrine has been questioned by some theologians since the time of Sanchez even though officially upheld by the magisterial teaching.[47]

Fr. Bernard Häring, for example, in his 1978 volume of fundamental moral theology, suggests that it may be wise to accept the concept of relatively small matter in matters of the sixth commandment as in others, such as fraternal love, justice, and peace. He comments that relatively small matter may be in relation to the psychology and spiritual development of persons and "what at one time might be experienced as relatively small matter will be taken much more seriously after further conversion and growth."[48]

Perhaps because of these trends the 1975 *Declaration on Sexual Ethics* of the Sacred Congregation for the Doctrine of the Faith discussed the theology of fundamental option. It insisted, first of all, that this option can be changed by particular acts, especially when, as often happens, they have been prepared for by previous more superficial acts. It went on to insist that grave matter involves whatever is seriously disordered, for choosing such an act includes contempt for the divine commandment of charity. It restated the tradition that "the moral order of sexuality involves such high values of human life that every direct violation of this order is objectively serious."[49]

In surveying theological reaction to this document, Fr. Richard McCormick outlines his own approach. He proposes that the Vatican document can be seen as presenting the level of general rectitude, which emanates from individual intentions, dispositions, qualities, and meanings. He asserts that the individual level of rectitude in human actions fills out the meaning of these actions by including these individual and personal dimensions. He cites Fr. Curran's description of masturbatory acts that may be symptomatic of loneliness, sexual tension, prolonged absence of one's spouse, frustrated relationships, etc., as revealing their *meaning*. Then he suggests that while such acts are always a withdrawal from the full meaning (potential) of sexual behavior (and therefore are ''intrinsic disorders'') he doubts that in many of their individual meanings they constitute ''serious matter.''[50] This methodology of distinguishing moral rectitude into a general level and an individual level has been presented for situations of conflict of values in the little book *Ambiguity of Moral Choice* by Fr. McCormick.[51] It cannot be adequately discussed here. However, a similar approach has been used in two widely circulated books on human sexuality in the Catholic tradition which recently appeared.[52]

In his book, *Sexual Morality*, Fr. Philip Keane uses the term ''ontic evil'' for the elements of non-good attached to human acts, as the intrinsic disorder contained in the act of masturbation. He then proposes that in the total concrete reality of an action, including the circumstances and the end, the act need not be considered a moral evil if other factors make the level of ontic evil reasonably acceptable.[53] The individual circumstances are allowed to relativize the concept of grave matter. Thus, although actions like masturbation, petting to orgasm by unmarried couples, or homosexual actions, involve ontic evil within a Catholic theology of sexuality, there may be circumstances where they are performed with sufficient reflection and full consent of the will without being morally evil.

This methodology seems to have increasing support among some Catholic moral theologians. It involves a weighing of values to determine when circumstances can outweigh the ontic evil of certain human actions. Fr. McCormick insists on communal discernment to avoid self-justification and extreme situationism in this weighing of values.[54] The two books on human sexuality which recently appeared offer their versions of such discernment. They tend to support in general the tradition of Catholic sexual morality, but offer possibilities of exceptions to justify contraception, masturbation, pre-marital intercourse, and homosexual activity.

This author finds serious difficulty in the application of this methodology to sexual activity. The ontic evil it recognizes is usually found in the misuse of the physical and corporeal expressions of human sexuality. The justifying circumstances and ends are usually found in the desire and conscious satisfaction achieved in the process of the ontic evil. Yet, the Catholic understanding of human sexuality, built on the unique interpretation of body and soul in the integrity of the human person, offers psychosomatic integrity as a normative principle in sexual morality.

In this tradition of moral goodness the norm for sexual behavior has both psychic and somatic components. Good sex is not merely physically good or merely psychically good; it is both. The theory of ontic evil proposes that sexual activity which is physically bad (intrinsic disorder, misuse of sexual powers) is not ultimately bad because of compensating values of the psychic order.

A more satisfactory methodology in the Catholic tradition of human goodness would seem to derive from the classic principle *bonum ex integra cause, malum ex quocumque defectu* (Good when whole, evil whenever defective). This would mean that sexual activity is only good when both physically and psychically good, otherwise it remains evil. This does not mean that evil behavior is necessarily sinful because there may not be sufficient evaluative knowledge and full consent. Nor does this mean that sexual activity is primarily a physical, corporeal activity, or that the physical, corporeal activity is more important than the psychic components. It simply resists the methodology which suggests a calculus of proportionate values which may cancel out the physical or ontic evil of disordered sexual activity.

Obviously this issue of moral methodology in evaluating sexual activity is important and has profound pastoral implications. Those who propose it have confidence that communal discernment can be developed to see that it is used properly. Those who question it do so both on the theoretical grounds outlined above and on the practical grounds of the impracticality of ever developing a communal discernment of such highly personal and subjective values as the psychic dimension of sexual activity.

By way of summary of this lengthy discussion of the objective gravity of genital pleasure and activity five summary statements can be offered:

1) Official magisterial teaching continues to assert the objective gravity of actions which directly violate chastity, such as premarital intercourse, masturbation, and homosexual actions.

2) This teaching supports the historic teaching that directly intended genital or venereal pleasure outside the embrace of conjugal love should be considered an objectively grave matter.

3) In practice, Christian persons may not be guilty of mortal sin in all such instances because of traditional reasons which contemporary psychology shows to be often verified: lack of sufficient evaluative knowledge and lack of full consent of the will. In other words, grave matter will not always engage the fundamental option of core freedom, particularly in sexual matters because of concupiscence.

4) Some contemporary theologians question the inherent dynamism that links all directly intended venereal pleasure with genital climax and grave matter. Fr. Häring proposes the category of relatively small matter.

5) A contemporary moral methodology has been discussed which modifies the concept of grave matter with considerations of individual rectitude so that ontic evil or intrinsic disorder may not be considered moral evil even though freely and deliberately intended. This approach raises the difficulty of undermining the psychosomatic integrity of human sexuality.

The next chapter will examine specific questions about sexual activity by the married and unmarried in the light of the above consideration of chastity. This chapter will conclude with a brief review of celibate and virginal chastity.

Contemporary personalism and the increasing appreciation of the role of conjugal love and marital chastity do not alter the essential religious significance of celibacy and virginity. They do highlight the fact that celibacy involves the sacrifice of much more than genital pleasure. Dietrich Von Hildebrand, for example, wrote that "celibacy involves then the renunciation of a great good, the unique communion of love in marriage, the deepest source of natural happiness on earth."[55]

On the other hand, celibacy and virginity must themselves be seen in terms of their religious significance. Fr. Goergen describes celibacy as "a positive choice of the single life for the sake of Christ in response to the call of God."[56] He describes a virgin as "a person who has never had genital intercourse and chooses to abstain genitally as a form of dedication to God."[57] Pope Pius XII published a thorough study on virginity, the encyclical *Sacra Virginitas*, on March 25, 1954; and Pope Paul VI wrote a parallel encyclical on priestly celibacy, *Sacerdotalis Coelibatus*, on June 24, 1967. Both made clear that celibacy and virginity are spiritual gifts, that they do not indicate any denigration of the holiness of Christian marriage or conjugal love, and that they play a fruitful role in the life of the Church.

In Vatican II's *Constitution on the Church* the theology of celibacy and virginity is stated in one sentence: "This perfect continence for love of the kingdom of heaven has always been held in high esteem by the Church as a sign and stimulus of love, and as a singular source of spiritual fertility in the world."[58] The document referred to celibates and virgins "devoting themselves to God alone more easily with an undivided heart" (1 Cor 7:32-34).[59] This devotion to God at the cost of conjugal intimacy was described by Pius XII as "such proof of love for our divine Redeemer that there is little wonder if it bears abundant fruits of sanctity."[60]

The encyclicals on celibacy and virginity rejected the claim of some that conjugal sexual love is necessary and indispensable for human wholeness. Both emphasized the eschatological witness offered by celibacy and virginity. Fr. Goergen in his study offers the significant comment that "the New Testament presents celibacy in the context of eschatology and not as an ascetical practice."[61] Pope John Paul II in a Holy Thursday letter to priests on April 9, 1979, notes that "celibacy 'for the sake of the kingdom' is not only an eschatological sign, it also has a great social meaning, in the present life, for the service of the people of God. Through his celibacy, the priest becomes the 'man for others' in a different way from the man who, by binding himself in conjugal union with a woman, also becomes, as husband and father, a 'man for others.' "[62]

The gifts of celibacy and virginity demand at least as much maturity and personal sexual integration as the practice of conjugal love in marriage.[63] In both cases persevering fidelity is demanded, either to Christ as spouse of the Church or to a human spouse. In both cases a harmonious organizing of feelings, emotions, and passions to express properly the human power of love is necessary. It can be said that no one should attempt a lifelong commitment of celibacy and virginity who would not be strong enough in psychic development for the commitment of indissoluble marriage.

Hence, this discussion of chastity and conjugal morality concludes with the Gospel call to love God and neighbor. The virtue of Christian chastity directs the affective and genital expressions of human love in accord with every person's state in life and their personal relationships.

Footnotes

1. *NCE*, "Marriage," 9, 258-265.
2. Cf. E. Schillebeeckx, O.P., *Marriage, Secular Reality and Saving Mystery*, London, 1965, Sheed and Ward Stagbooks, 2 vols., 1, 132 ff.
3. *NCE*, "Matrimony," 9, 468.
4. *TDNT* 6, 585.
5. *TDNT* 6, 585-586.
6. K. Schelkle, *Theology of the New Testament*, Collegeville, 1973, Liturgical Press, 3 (Morality), 260.
7. Cf. D. Goergen, *The Sexual Celibate*, New York, 1974, Seabury, 28.
8. "Does *Porneia* Mean Fornication?" *Nov. Test.*, no. 14, 10-17.
9. *TDNT* 6, 590.
10. *TS* 37, (1976) 478-479.
11. DS 835.
12. Pius XI, *Casti Connubii* in J. Husslein, S.J., *Social Wellsprings* Milwaukee, 1942, Bruce Publ. Co., 2, 131.
13. *ST Suppl*. 41.4.
14. F. Parmisano, "Love and Marriage in the Middle Ages, Part 2," *New Blackfriars* 50, 649-669.
15. *ST Suppl*. 49.3.
16. *ST* 3a.29.2.
17. *NCE* "Sex," 13, 148.
18. *CIC* c. 1013.1.
19. Cf. *NCE*, "Marriage," 9, 268.
20. Pius XII, "Allocution to Midwives," Oct. 29, 1951, nos. 308-310.
21. *Gaudium et Spes* no. 50.
22. *Ibid*.
23. Paul VI, *Humanae Vitae*, July 29, 1968, in *Of Human Life*, Huntington, n.d., Our Sunday Visitor Inc., no. 13.
24. Cf. *NCE*, "Marriage," 16, 278-283.
25. A. Kosnik *et.al.*, *Human Sexuality*, New York, 1977, Paulist Press, 106-107.
26. Nat. Council of Cath. Bishops, *To Live in Christ Jesus*, Washington, 1976, USCC, 13-19; Sacred Congregation for the Doctrine of the Faith, *Observations . . . on the book Human Sexuality*, Aug. 6, 1979.
27. NCCB, *op. cit.*, 18-19.
28. *Ibid.*, 19.
29. Goergen, *op. cit.*, 51-58.

30. NCCB, *Human Life in Our Day*, Nov. 15, 1968, Washington, 1968, USCC, 9.
31. *NCE*, "Chastity," 3, 516.
32. *Ibid*.
33. *Nature and Meaning of Chastity*, Chicago, 1976, Franciscan Herald Press, 36.
34. Goergen, *op. cit.* 51-58.
35. *Ibid*., 95-103; W. Reich, "A Theology of Chastity," in *Working Papers on the Theology of Marriage*, Washington, 1967, Family Life Bureau of USCC, 37-48. Ed. by J. McHugh.
36. P. Bertocci, *Sex, Love, and the Person*, New York, 1967, Sheed and Ward Search Book, 147-148..
37. *ST* 1a2ae.85.3.
38. Sacred Congregation for the Doctrine of he Faith, *Declaration on Sexual Ethics*, Dec. 29, 1975, Washington, 1976, USCC, no. 12.
39. B. Häring, C.SS.R., *The Law of Christ*, Westminster, 1966, The Newman Press, 3, 289-312. Transl. by E. Kaiser, C.PP.S.
40. B. Häring, *Free and Faithful in Christ*, New York, 1978, Seabury Press, 1, 407.
41. *Gaudium et Spes* no. 49.
42. *Ibid*. no. 48.
43. *Law of Christ* 3, 293.
44. O. Lottin, *Morale Fondamentale*, Tournai, 1954, 490.
45. Sacred Congregation, *op.cit.* no. 10.
46. R. McCormick, S.J., *National Cath. Reporter*, Jan. 30, 1976.
47. C. Curran, *A New Look at Christian Morality*, Notre Dame, 1968, Fides Publishers, 208-209; *Idem, Contemporary Problems in Moral Theology*, Notre Dame, 1970, Fides Publishers, 164-170.
48. *Free and Faithful in Christ* 409.
49. *Sacred Congregation, op. cit.*, no. 10.
50. R. McCormick, S.J., "Notes on Moral Theology," in *TS* 38 (1977) no. 1.
51. *See* also R. McCormick, S.J., *Doing Evil to Achieve Good,* Chicago, 1978, Loyola Univ. Press.
52. Kosnik *et.al., op.cit.*; P. Keane, S.S., *Sexual Morality*, New York, 1977, Paulist Press; cf. also D. McCarthy, "Human Sexuality and Cathoilic Teaching," *Priest*, Jan. 1978, and Sacred Congregation, "Observations," April, 1979.
53. Keane, *op. cit.* 46-51.
54. R. McCormick, S.J., *Ambiguity in Moral Choice*, Pere Marquette LEcture, 1973, 96.
55. D. Von Hildebrand, *Celibacy and Crisis of Faith*, 33.
56. Goergen, *op.cit.*, 108.
57. *Ibid*., 96.
58. *Lumen Gentium* no. 42.
59. *Ibid*.
60. Pius XII, Oct. 29, 1951, no. 398.
61. Goergen, *op. cit.*, 109.
62. John Paul II, Letter, April 9, 1979, in *Origins* April 19, 1979, 8, 701.
63. *NCE*, "Marriage," 9, 266.

Chapter 26

PROBLEMS OF SEXUAL RESPONSIBILITY

Bibliography: Pope Pius XII, *Sacra Viginitas*: Encyclical Letter on Holy Virginity, Mar. 25, 1954, in *Official Catholic Teachings: Love and Sexuality*, Wilmington, 1978, McGrath Publ., 134-159. Edit. by O. Liebard; Paul VI, *Humanae Vitae*: Encyclical Letter on the Regulation of Birth, July 25, 1968, *ibid.*, 331-347; Paul VI, Address to the Teams of Our Lady, May 4, 1970, *ibid.*, 378-388; NCCB, *Principles to Guide Confessors in Questions of Homosexuality*, Washington, 1973, NCCB; Irish Bishops' Pastoral, *Human Life is Sacred*, Dublin, 1975, Veritas Publ.; Canadian Bishops, *Statement on the Formation of Conscience*, Boston, 1974, Daughters of St. Paul; C. Baars, M.D., *The Homosexual's Search for Happiness*, Chicago, 1976, Franciscan Herald Press; J. Cavanaugh, M.D., *Counseling the Homosexual*, ch. 16 "Contemporary Theological Views" by J. Harvey, O.S.F.S., Huntington, 1977, Our Sunday Visitor, Inc., 222-238; W. May, *Sex, Love and Procreation*, Chicago, 1976, Franciscan Heral Press; G. Atkinson and A. Moraczewski, O.P., *A Moral Evaluation of Contraception and Sterilization*, St. Louis, 1979, Pope John Center; J. Kippley, *Birth Control and the Marriage Covenant*, Collegeville, 1976, Liturgical Press.

The Vatican Declaration on Sexual Ethics commented that "the human person is so profoundly affected by sexuality that it must be considered as one of the factors which give to each individual's life the principal traits that distinguish it."[1] The reason is that people are designed by God to grow and develop in relationships with other persons, and, to some degree, all human relationships are sexual because all persons are sexual persons.

God is love and He created human persons in His image. Hence, human love occupies the core of human existence, and human sexuality can express human love in a unique way. No wonder sexuality has occupied considerable attention in the moral evaluation of human behavior.

The radical brokenness which entered the world through original sin can nowhere be found more obviously present than in the fragility of human love relationships, so readily soured by selfishness, exploitation, and lust. Human sexuality reflects this radical brokenness through what theologians have called concupiscence of the flesh. In the process of self-discovery and self-mastery from birth to adulthood sexual instincts must be trained, guided, and integrated under the direction of responsible freedom. Sex education presents a challenge to Christians in a fallen world. Not even adults are immune from sexual problems, since the power of sexual passion can never in this life be definitively and irrevocably channeled to the exclusive service of authentic and unselfish love.

In all four sections of this chapter problems of human sexuality are discussed in which Catholic teaching questions prevailing cultural mores. Undoubtedly, it seems unrealistic and undesirable to many. Yet, it flows from the profound respect for human sexual activity discussed in the previous chapter and from the conviction that the redeeming grace of Jesus Christ makes that respect possible, for "in Him who is the source of my strength, I have strength for everything" (Ph 4:13).[1]

The four problems below are: premarital sexual relationships; homosexual activity and masturbation; birth control; and artificial techniques of procreation. They cannot be disccused comprehensively but will be reviewed in the light of the moral teaching in the previous chapter on responsible sexual activity.

Premarital Sexual Relationships

The Second Vatican Council described marriage as "an intimate partnership of life and the love which constitutes the married state."[2] It referred to marital intercourse when it said, "Married love is uniquely expressed and perfected by the exercise of the acts proper to marriage."[3]

As discussed above, premarital sexual intercourse violates this teaching of the Church. Yet, every couple who seriously contemplates marriage must establish before marriage a profound love relationship which will be solemnized and sacramentalized in marriage and then joyfully celebrated in conjugal intercourse.

Hence, the problem to be discussed here is this: how can a couple who are attached to one another grow and develop in their human and sexual relationship without engaging in genital sexual activity? Two approaches will be taken: first, a review of the prevailing cultural attitudes and then, secondly, a review of the contrasting attitudes flowing from Christian chastity.

Cultural attitudes, found in the communication media and the advice of many counselors, represent a distorted view of human genital activity. Romantic and passionate scenes in movies and television represent it as primarily a technique to be mastered and a powerful tool to be manipulated by men and women in their encounters. It is portrayed as almost magically effective in removing barriers of misunderstanding, overcoming timidity or even antipathy, and producing the wondrous disposition of love.

Cultural attitudes tend to promise these benefits to persons at all levels of male-female relationships, from boys and girls at junior high dances to married persons. The prevailing social acceptance of couples "going steady" long before an engagement for marriage is realistic, combined with this distorted cultural picture of genital activity, leads many teenagers into premarital genital activity today.

On the other hand, the attitudes to premarital genital activity flowing from Christian chastity as described above feature a far more reverential and relational view of the significance of this activity. While all male-female relationships are frankly recognized as sexual in a broad sense, genital activity has a completely special meaning. It should not be described primarily as a technique or a tool to be used in building relationships, but as an expression and a celebration of a unique kind of relationship.

Christian chastity recognizes vast differences in the relationship of couples at junior high dances and couples soon to be engaged or already engaged to marry. In the first case, boys and girls may naturally and spontaneously manifest affection and instinctively thrill at the company of a person of the opposite sex. But their relationship in no way approximates marriage.

The couple soon to be engaged or already engaged, on the other hand, are developing a relationship which is legitimately exclusive, beginning to be possessive, and looking seriously toward permanence and indissolubility. Since this relationship is not yet totally exclusive, permanent and possessive, genital activity itself remains inappropriate. Yet such couples do have a far more serious relationship than that of the boys and girls at the junior high dance.

It is still true, in terms of the earlier discussion of kissing, touching, and embracing, that even engaged couples should not actively seek or consent to venereal pleasure. But they are in a position which one author describes as "gradual unlearning of defenses and inhibitions built up over several years in the area of sexual attitudes and behavior."[4] They have good reason for deeply affectionate kisses, touches, and embraces. They must learn two important lessons: 1) the beauty and value of expressing their love in a physical way, and 2) the mighty power of sexual activity to carry them to genital activity and climax despite their intentions to forego this. Only persons with a reasonable degree of maturity can learn and live by *both* these lessons. But, according to the ideals of Christian chastity, only such persons should permit themselves to advance to the serious relationship discussed here.

Hence, Christian chastity interprets all levels of sexual activity from simple kisses to genital intercourse as primarily the freely and responsibly chosen expressions of relationships. Cultural attitudes tend to see sexual activity primarily as building relationships. Recognizing the deep human hunger for love and companionship, cultural attitudes tend to approve indiscriminately all building of relationships, regardless of the prospects of a lasting marriage. Hence, a cultural bias encourages going steady in the teen years and the deliberate cultivation of sexual attraction and impulses between divorced or separated persons or persons of radically incompatible religious or social values.

The Christian theology of marriage sets apart the marital relationship and counsels serious and prayerful preparation for it, marked by growing intimacy and continuing control of sexual impulses. This is particularly important in the light of the sacramental and indissoluble character of marriage and the total commitment of conjugal love which is necessary. The cultural milieu, in contrast, blurs the distinction between marital and non-marital relationships. Instead of counseling discipline and restraint in preparation for the marital commitment it tends to encourage whatever sexual expressions may seem to be tools of building a relationship.

The response to the problem raised here might best be considered one of sex education and value formation. Christians will be best prepared for a healthy and wholesome development in their premarital relationships by seeing them in relation to the total giving relationship of marriage. This is the practical theology of premarital chastity.

Homosexual Activity and Masturbation

The cultural bias which credits genital activity primarily with building relationships and which implicitly teaches the indispensability of genital activity for human fulfillment can find reasons to approve homosexual activity. This question has surfaced much more openly in the United States in recent years. How should Catholic moral theology respond to this question?

First of all, moral theology should cooperate in the effort to correct the distorted image of homosexual persons as usually agents of sexual seduction and to overcome the often vicious prejudice against homosexual persons among so many heterosexual persons. Contemporary scientific studies indicate that homosexuality is a condition, a disposition, which may not at all result from the performance of homosexual acts. Persons having this disposition may or may not engage in homosexual activity; some of them live in heterosexual marriages and have produced children.

This homosexual disposition can be found in males and females and exists in varying degrees of intensity, sometimes even combined with heterosexual inclinations. A working definition of the homosexual condition useful here describes it: "A persistent, postadolescent state in which the sexual object is a person of the same sex and in which there is a concomitant aversion or abhorrence, in varying degrees, to sexual relations with members of the other sex."[5]

The origins of this condition in the life of each person are shrouded in mystery. It seems clear that the basic cause is psychological and that the condition arises early in life, and that genetic theories about its origin rest more on faith than proof.[6] The opinion of Dr. Cavanagh that homosexuality is the result of a personality or character problem in which the sexual orientation of an individual becomes fixated at an early age reflects much contemporary thinking.[7]

382   PRINCIPLES OF CATHOLIC THEOLOGY

In itself, then, the homosexual orientation of someone's personality need have no moral significance, simply reflecting what happened in the formation of that person's sexual inclinations. The pastoral letter of the U.S. bishops of Nov. 11, 1976, on moral values called for the acceptance of homosexual persons in the Christian community: "Some persons find themselves through no fault of their own to have a homosexual orientation. Homosexuals, like everyone else, should not suffer from prejudice against their basic human rights. They have a right to respect, friendship, and justice. They should have an active role in the Christian community."[8]

However, the U.S. bishops reflected the constant tradition of Catholic moral theology by teaching in the same statement that homosexual *activity* is morally wrong: "Homosexual activity, as distinguished from homosexual orientation, is morally wrong. Like heterosexual persons, homosexuals are called to give witness to chastity, avoiding, with God's grace, behavior which is wrong for them, just as nonmarital sexual relations are wrong for heterosexuals."[9]

This clear teaching reflects the constant tradition of the Church which links genital sexual activity with monogamous marriage. It holds that the act of genital intercourse expresses a total self-giving of a man and a woman and is capable of procreating a new human person as an expression of that covenant love. The same reasoning which forbids this sexual union between heterosexual persons also forbids homosexual persons to undertake genital activity. The theology of monogamous marriage makes no provision for the marriage of persons of the same sex since they have no capacity for life-sharing love. It also seriously questions the capacity for two persons of the same sex to enjoy the full unitive dimension of conjugal love. Despite the deep attraction which sometimes draws homosexual persons into relationships which seem to parallel heterosexual marriage, they still are *both* male or *both* female. The Genesis pattern of monogamous marriage calls for the complementarity of male *and* female in the unitive love of marriage.

A vigorous challenge to this moral teaching of the Church appeared in 1976 in the book, *The Church and the Homosexual*, by John McNeill, S.J.[10] He proposes that the homosexual condition is "according to the will of God," a somewhat ambiguous characterization, but, furthermore, that there is a possibility not only of morally good homosexual relationships, but of morally good homosexual activity.

Fr. McNeill's argumentation is rejected by Fr. John Harvey, O.S.F.S., a well-known moral theologian who has written extensively on the pastoral care of homosexual persons according to traditional Church teaching.[11] He points out that Fr. McNeill has bypassed the Scriptural opposition to homosexual activity by the questionable maneuver of interpreting it as opposition only to homosexual activity engaged in by heterosexual persons, perhaps in forms of sacred prostitution. This has not been the Church's own interpretation of these critical passages in divine revelation.

Fr. Harvey sums up conclusions that can certainly be drawn from Scripture: "Nowhere in Holy Scripture is the homosexual person condemned, but always the action is condemned. Nowhere is there any approval of homosexual unions, but the heterosexual union of man and wife is confirmed from Genesis to Ephesians as a perennial principle. While Holy Scripture does not say the last word about homosexuality, it gives no support to such actions."[12]

The theology of marriage and human sexuality which the Church has drawn from Scripture has insisted on the principle cited in the previous chapter, "Good when whole, evil whenever defective." Homosexual activity lacks the "wholeness" or integrity of genital activity in the divinely-designed complementarity of male and female. The position of Fr. McNeill would substitute the psychic dispositions of love as the primary determinant of moral goodness, rather than the traditional "wholeness" which includes both the physical completeness of genital activity and the spiritual dispositions of committed love between the heterosexual married couple.

Fr. Harvey has pointed out the physical/spiritual dualism and devaluation of the corioreal dimension of the human person which results from the moral legitimation of homosexual activity by Fr. McNeill: "Thus, the physical action has no meaning in itself, but derives its entire meaning from the psychic disposition and intention of the agent. Instead of confronting the meaning of the physical act, McNeill superimposes meaning. For example, he says that love makes the physical act good."[13]

Underlying the position of Fr. McNeill one finds a version of personalism in which human persons choose their own sexual identity and this choice may include a morally acceptable pattern of homosexual activity. This personalism so emphasizes human subjectivity that it may transcend the givenness of maleness and femaleness. Fr. McNeill states that "theologians who absolutize the man-woman revelation as the 'divine image' in man are guilty of raising a human creation to the level of an idol."[14] Yet, Catholic teaching has consistently held for the divine creation of marriage and firmly resists the notion that such an extreme personalism can authenticate homosexual unions as a substitute for marriage.

But the personal dilemma of homosexuals who do not have the necessary personality orientation for heterosexual marriage cannot be ignored. Fr. Charles Curran attempted to resolve it by his "theology of compromise." According to this theory, "the particular action in one sense is not objectively wrong because in the presence of sin it remains the only viable alternative for the individual. However, in another sense the action is wrong and manifests the power of sin."[15]

Here Fr. Curran would admit the evil of homosexual acts, in contrast to Fr. McNeill. But he proposes that they may sometimes be freely performed since one finds no alternative. Fr. Harvey notes the problem here: one *must* freely sin, a contradiction in terms.[16] Either one *must* act, in the sense of compulsion, and there is no freedom and no sin; or one is not forced to act and then one freely chooses evil. This has always been considered sinful and repugnant to one's loving relationship with God. Or can one freely choose evil?

Fr. Philip Keane, S.S., whose work on human sexuality was mentioned in the previous chapter, uses the methodological category of ontic evil to suggest that in some circumstances homosexual acts may be only ontic, but not morally evil.[17] In this description the homosexual person may freely choose the ontic evil of homosexual activity, but this free choice of evil need not constitute moral evil because of the circumstances.

The practical problem of discerning when the circumstances are such that homosexual activity is morally acceptable is the most obvious difficulty with this ontic evil approach. Implicitly homosexual persons are told that some of them, at some periods of their lives at least, have such a need for genital sexual activity that it becomes morally acceptable then and there. The staggering question is, Which persons at which times of their lives?

What is presented by authors like Fr. Curran and Fr. Keane as a compassionate solution to profound difficulties launches a precarious self-examination into the deepest and least accessible realms of freedom of choice so that homosexual persons may evaluate their sexual activity and choose their lifestyle. In this approach some homosexual persons will judge themselves incapable of sufficient sexual restraint to forego homosexual activity and will go in search of happiness in a rewarding homosexual union somewhat like marriage. Catholic teaching has always admitted the possibility of homosexual actions which are not fully free and responsible, but it has never created such a category of homosexual persons.

Those who place themselves in this category of needing homosexual activity by this methodology should not expect complete peace of mind. They will always wonder if they could have, in the past, or if they could, at any given moment in the present, find the moral strength to resist homosexual activity.

The theological objection to this methodology of ontic but not moral evil has already been indicated. Catholic theology has rejected the view, as undermining the unique and divinely-designed meaning of Christian marriage, that for some persons at some times genital activity outside the covenant of marriage becomes morally acceptable. It cannot accept the view which frankly admits to choosing ontic evil and hence to a deliberate misuse of the gift of human genital sexuality. Catholic theology rejects the view that "bad sex is better than no sex" which seems operative in this view.

Implicit in the rationale of this methodology is the assumption so strongly insisted upon in the cultural bias mentioned above: the indispensability of genital activity for human fulfillment. This implies that not only homosexual persons who have no hope of heterosexual marriage, but also heterosexual persons who have no realistic hope of marriage might sometimes "need" genital activity so urgently that it becomes morally acceptable for them outside marriage. Thus, widows, divorced persons, persons not psychologically suited for the common life of marriage like the severely retarded or the mentally disturbed, or persons who simply have little opportunity to find a marriage partner, might legitimately follow the rationale and choose the ontic evil of non-marital genital intercourse.

It seems clear that this hypothetical "need" for genital intimacy must not be considered morally insuperable in the context of redemption and grace. Those theologians who speculate that this need is only overcome by the grace of religious vows or priestly celibacy unnecessarily restrict the gifts of the Spirit in healing human weakness. Lay persons have a title to this healing power in their sexual difficulties because redemption is not restricted to priests and religious. Chastity is a gift from God which He does not deny to those who ask it properly. Paul taught that "He (God) will not let you be tested beyond your strength. Along with the test he will show you a way so that you may be able to endure it" (1 Cor 10:13).

Christian anthropology recognizes the need for some forms of psychological intimacy as far more essential to human growth and perfection than genital activity. On this basis the pastoral advice in the NCCB's 1973 publication, "Principles to Guide Confessors in Questions of Homosexuality" suggest that homosexual persons break out of homosexual environments and reintegrate themselves into the heterosexual culture, "but seek to form stable friendships among both homosexuals and heterosexuals."[18]

Just as unmarried persons, with the help of God's grace, can forego genital activity as their relationship progresses, so homosexual persons can form deep and strong friendships without genital activity. Fr. Harvey summarizes this goal of Christian chastity: "Nothing is more important than to lead the homosexual person into an examination of the different forms of positive real relationships which he can form to develop himself as both a lovable and loving person, indeed as a sexual person, but without the need of genital intercourse."[19]

The Vatican Declaration on Sexual Ethics included in its closing paragraphs a helpful review of Catholic teaching about the virtue of chastity as liberation from sin to serve Christ in the newness of life. Such pastoral guidance is indispensable in assisting homosexual persons. The declaration in its brief discussion of homosexuality had distinguished homosexuals who may be transitory or at least curable from those who may be incurable. Its comments about care for the latter group of homosexuals summarize Church teaching in this critical area: "In the pastoral field, these homosexuals must certainly be treated with understanding and sustained in the hope of overcoming their personal difficulties and their inability to fit into society. Their culpability will be judged with prudence. But no pastoral method can be employed which would give moral justification to these acts on the grounds that they would be consonant with the condition of such people.''[20]

This discussion of homosexual activity has not focused on the physical form such activity may take. The genital activity of persons of the same sex cannot include genital intercourse in which the male is physically united to the female through the insertion of the penis into the vagina. Instead it includes a whole range of activities which produce male sexual climax or female orgasm. One generic description of this homosexual activity, whether it involves male or female persons of the same sex, would be mutual masturbation.

This section will close with a discussion of solitary masturbation or self-stimulation to sexual climax. The previous reflection on efforts to justify homosexual activity in some circumstances relied on the possibility that the love-expressive aspects of this activity might render it morally acceptable. Such considerations have no role in the discussion of masturbation.

Rather, the most prominent concern about the act of masturbation in contemporary moral theology questions the gravity of this act. Traditional Catholic teaching includes it under the heading of objectively grave matter, even in individual instances. This traditional teaching has always admitted that impulse, habit, and circumstance could prevent the act from becoming a subjectively grave sin.

However, older theologians who defended this position with reference to male masturbation often relied on a biology which considered the male sperm almost as precious as a human embryo. Contemporary biology asserts that the average male ejaculation contains 150-160 million sperm. Modern medical studies have not documented the significant ill effects formerly thought to be caused by masturbation. Psychological studies have linked masturbation among adolescents with the process of sexual-discovery and have noted that it may be a symptom of various personality problems.

Hence, Fr. Charles Curran argued in a 1968 book, *A New Look at Christian Morality*, that masturbation should not be considered gravely wrong in itself because it does not represent a substantial inversion of a very important order of nature.[21] The Church's traditional teaching on grave matter in matters of human sexuality was reviewed in the previous chapter. There it was noted that the teaching of the grave importance of genital activity is the way the Church has taught the grave importance of human sexuality itself. Hence, the Church's teaching has the effect of inculcating respect for genital activity, whereas the person uninformed by this teaching might well trivialize such activity.

The Vatican Declaration on Sexual Ethics reviewed this issue and reasserted the traditional teaching "that masturbation is an intrinsically and seriously disordered act."[22] The document reviewed psychological opinions which suggest reasons why the deliberate character of the act may be reduced so that serious sin may not actually occur. But it added cautiously that "the absence of serious responsibility must not be presumed; this would be to misunderstand people's moral capacity."

Fr. Keane's book on human sexuality appeared after the Vatican declaration and used the "ontic but not necessarily moral evil" approach to masturbation. He admits frankly that this is not in accord with present magisterial teaching but would like to support his position as "in accord with the deepest instincts and traditions of the teaching Church on masturbation."[23]

However, the same objections to Fr. Keane's approach here as in reference to homosexuality above must be noted. In brief, what criteria does a person use to judge that in a given case or series of cases masturbation is only ontic evil and need not be resisted? Does this not corrupt the Christian doctrine of chastity into a case of "bad sex is better than no sex?" In short, does this not subjectivize the moral evaluation of human sexual and genital activity? Guilt is necessarily measured subjectively, but is the moral norm or ideal also to be measured subjectively?

This is not to say that present Church teaching insists that all individual acts of masturbation are grave sins—the Vatican declaration makes clear that this is not the case. But Church teaching makes clear that despite the frequency of masturbation problems among adolescents, the act is still contrary to a person's sexual good, something like falling down in contrary to a person's ambulatory good, although most children fall down when learning to walk.

Birth Control

The problem of birth control in marriage did not originate in the 20th century, any more than did contraception or the use of abortion as a form of birth control. However, the population explosion, the development of modern contraceptives, and the shift from an agrarian economy where large families may be an economic asset to an industrial economy have all magnified the birth control problem.

Catholic teaching has consistently opposed sterilization and contraception since the days of the Fathers as acts destructive of the procreative potential of conjugal intercourse.[24] When the procreation and education of children was identified as *the* primary purpose of marriage, as it was up until Vatican II, the teaching seemed clearer than it has to some theologians. Contemporary Catholic theology includes a maturing appreciation of conjugal love as essential to the well-being of marriage. Furthermore, the approbation of methods of natural family planning admits that couples may deliberately intend to avoid procreation even while exercising the conjugal act.

Hence, the focal issue of the birth control problem today could be formulated in this question: If a married couple have sufficient reasons to regulate the birth of more children, does it make any significant moral difference whether they do so by avoiding the fertile times in their lovemaking cycle or if they use a contraceptive or sterilizing procedure to eliminate their fertility?

Pope Paul VI in his highly criticized encyclical, *Humanae Vitae*, in 1968 reaffirmed the Church's teaching with a firm, "Yes, it does make a difference." Pope Paul relied on the creative intention of God, expressed in the very nature of marriage and its acts and manifested by the constant teaching of the Church, in answering that vital question. The Pope taught as a norm of natural law that each and every marriage act must remain open to the transmission of life. Natural family planning does not interfere with the marriage acts themselves, whereas contraception and sterilization do: they deliberately and directly eliminate the life potential of these acts.

Although this specific moral doctrine cannot be found explicitly taught in the Scriptures, it can easily be linked to the biblical reverence for the marriage covenant (a sign of Christ's love for His Church) and for human life, parenthood, and the life power. The early Church condemned potions (*pharmakeia*) which probably included both contraceptive and abortifacient agents.[25] Lawrence Cardinal Shehan, former Archbishop of Baltimore, speculated in a thoughtful article on what would have happened if the contraception controversy had erupted after Cardinal Newman wrote his famous study on the development of doctrine in 1845.[26] Cardinal Newman may well have described the Church's development of its moral doctrine on abortion and contraception from the biblical revelation as an example of the authentic development of doctrine.

In recent years countless articles and books have challenged the Church's historic position on the objective moral evil of contraception. One significant aspect of this conviction which the Church has held firmly as a kind of instinctive intuition will be discussed in introductory comments.

To legitimize the removal of procreative potential from conjugal intercourse opens up in principle the possible legitimacy of conjugal intercourse outside the marital covenant. John Finnis argued in an important article in the British *Heythrop Journal* that the contracepted act need no longer signify a total and indissoluble commitment.[27] It becomes an act expressing great psychological and physical intimacy, a passionate embrace, but not necessarily a marital act.

While it is true that the natural act is naturally procreative and symbolic of a total commitment, the weighing of proportionate values which permits the act in marriage to be contracepted cannot, in principle, be excluded from a comparable application by unmarried couples.

For example, if John and Mary are married and cannot afford more children, they may choose contraception or sterilization by calculating that the values offered by their no-longer-procreative embrace outweigh the disvalues (ontic evil) of their contraception or sterilization. But such a calculus of values could, in principle, justify the no-longer-procreative embrace of Paul and Elizabeth who are deeply in love but unmarried. Why cannot the harmless benefits of the no-longer-procreative embrace be extended beyond marriage, at least when the values are sufficiently, even if rarely, high enough? The moral compromise of justifiable contraception in marriage introduces, at least in principle, the compromise of non-marital sexual intercourse. Some theologians could undoubtedly admit of this, but it raises one more objection from the theology of marriage to justifying contraception.[28]

Having introduced these preliminary comments, it must now be noted that Church teaching forbidding contraception is not presented in terms of values and disvalues as commensurate and discrete elements factored into the moral judgment. The Church's teaching is presented as a normative principle flowing from the divine plan in creating man, woman, and marriage. It is, of course, possible that with divine omniscience one could establish accurately the preponderance of disvalue over value in the justification of contraception. That divine omniscience may represent the collective impact on the whole human community of the individual instances of justifying contraception.

For the Catholic tradition in morality does maintain that evil acts have evil consequences and are not evil simply because of a divine *fiat*. The problem mentioned here is the comparative calculation that some attempt in justifying contraception. Paul VI himself appealed to the evil consequences of contraception in his famous encyclical (no. 17) without basing his teaching specifically on them. Interestingly, also, the most persuasive reason many women today avoid contraceptive medications is the harmful outcome on their physical health.

The strong sympathy for justifying contraception often grows from the conviction that notable good consequences can occur. Some married couples have testified that contraception has made possible a more loving relationship because it eliminated anxieties caused by fear of an unwanted pregnancy and permitted more spontaneous and frequent acts of conjugal intercourse.

The danger in weighing such desirable good consequences lies in the fact that they are subjectively conditioned and impossible to measure objectively. A more convincing indication of good consequences of marital contraception would arise if it could be shown to lead to more stable marriages in which couples more fully and evidently manifested the virtue of Christian charity in all their relationships. Yet, although it seems that many Catholic couples are using contraception today, there is little evidence of increasing stability in marriage, the contrary is the case. One preliminary analysis has even named the contraceptive pill and the intrauterine device as major factors in increased divorce rates.[29]

Despite the mixed outcome of values and disvalues from marital contraception alluded to here, some Catholic moral theologians are proposing the model of ''ontic but not necessarily moral evil'' here as in other matters of sexual morality. In fact, this methodology began to be popular in the 1960's when the great contraceptive debate was at center stage.[30]

The description of Fr. Keane is to the point: "It does not seem arguable that the ontic evil of artificial birth control becomes a moral evil in all sets of circumstances. If a couple face serious medical, psychological, or economic problems, their need for the human values involved in sexual communion would seem to give moral justification to their use of birth control devices."[31]

Note in this statement the phrase, "their need for the human values involved in sexual communion." This "need" was discussed above as more directly a need for psychological intimacy, affection, and love than a genuine need for genital activity. Yet, the high degree of emotional and volitional strength and maturity necessary for a married couple to cultivate love and intimacy without genital activity cannot be overlooked. Yet, the basic question for speculative moral theology raised here is this: should a difficult and idealistic moral teaching beget a theological analysis in which acts contrary to that teaching are no longer evil in their objective moral reality?

The encyclical *Humanae Vitae* was a restatement of a difficult and idealistic teaching of the Church. And it was not simply a statement of marital ideals, but a statement that contraceptive acts of themselves are morally evil acts.[32] It is true that today many people have what theologians call a "perplexed" conscience or even a conscience formed in good faith which permits these acts. This simply means that they are not fully culpable of the moral evil of their acts.

Theologians and others who dissent from this Church teaching often point out that they do not countenance the so-called "contraceptive mentality." This is the mentality which selfishly excludes parenthood from marriage or considers it a purely optional accessory for those inclined that way. However, William May, a husband and father and lay Catholic theologian, argues that contraceptive acts necessarily beget this "contraceptive mentality."[33] He writes that "there is a definite relationship (between individual acts and a person's moral identity) inasmuch as we shape or 'create' our moral identity by our willingness to choose to act in certain ways."

The U.S. bishops in their 1976 pastoral letter, "To Live in Christ Jesus," taught that "though there is a difference (between individual acts and the contraceptive mentality) even . . . an act of contraceptive intercourse is wrong because it severs the link between the meanings of marital intercourse and rejects one of them.''[34]

What about natural family planning? Echoing the statement just cited from the U.S. bishops: it does not sever the link between the meanings of marital intercourse and reject one of them. Pope Paul VI explained the difference between contraception and natural family planning because contraception impedes the development of natural processes whereas the natural method makes ''legitimate use of a natural disposition.''[35]

This means that contraception destroys the life potential from conjugal intercourse (as abortion destroys life itself) whereas natural family planning respects the life potential, foregoing the pleasurable experience of conjugal intercourse rather than violates it. The principle of the inviolability of innocent human life is hence reflected here in the key principle of the ''inviolability of the human life process.''

Could the determined practice of natural family planning generate its own version of the ''contraceptive mentality?'' It could. Hence, the practice must only be undertaken for sufficiently serious motives. However, the likelihood that couples who unselfishly observe periods of abstinence from their marital privileges will fall victim to the selfish contraceptive mentality is rather minimal.

The far greater difficulty with natural family planning has been the notoriously low confidence couples have placed in its reliability and their generally suspicious attitude that it is impractical, impossible, or destructive of married love. Fortunately these difficulties have been reduced considerably in the past decade.

Natural methods of family planning only became systematically effective with the work of the Japanese doctor Kyusaku Ogino and the Austrian doctor Hermann Knaus working independently in the 1920's. The earliest system of natural family planning was called the ''rhythm method'' based on the calendar cycles of women's menstrual periods. This method was ineffective for a significant number of couples, but the prominent forms of contraception like the condom that were used at that time were not nearly 100 percent effective either.

As subsequent well-publicized research developed chemical contraceptives with much higher effectiveness, it was not well publicized that natural family planning was becoming much more effective with the use of the basal body temperature to discover the time of ovulation. This was no longer the old and scorned "rhythm method."

In 1968, as Pope Pius XII had before him in 1951, Paul VI called upon medical science to provide a sufficiently secure basis for a regulation of birth founded on the natural rhythms of the body.[36] Much more progress has been accomplished since then, notably through scientific study of the mucuous discharge which accompanies fertility and which can be used with other indications in what is called the symtothermal method of natural family planning. When it is used alone, this is called the ovulation or Billings method after Drs. John and Lyn Billings.

In the U.S. the Couple to Couple League, founded in 1971, now has 250 professionally trained and certified married couples who teach the symtothermal method of natural family planning in over forty states.[37] They are convinced that this method can be reliable for every couple willing to learn the signs of fertility, even those with very irregular fertility. The periods of abstinence from intercourse range from 8-14 days each month, roughly similar to the abstinence for ritual impurity by the Jews of the Old Testament.

These teaching couples not only demonstrate in their lives and teaching that natural family planning is neither impossible nor impractical. They also witness to the paradoxical outcome that this method, instead of destroying marriages, can even enrich and strengthen them. This author attended the first National Convention of the Couple to Couple League near Cincinnati in July, 1978, and would not expect to find anywhere a group of 100 couples so happily and deeply in love. A sociological study at Catholic University has also recently documented that three quarters of the couples practicing natural family planning have found positive benefit in it and only two percent would not recommend it to others.[38]

This discussion of the problem of birth control has only offered an overview of the most serious moral problem facing married Catholics today. But it has indicated that the moral analysis of conjugal intercourse which justifies contraception in marriage is part of a larger framework which has been caricatured above with the slogan, "Bad sex is better than no sex." Hence, the firm teaching of Paul VI may eventually be seen as a prophetic proclamation of "good sex" and authentic conjugal love.

The doctrine Pope Paul reaffirmed was not proclaimed in the format of an infallible proclamation. It may very well be still infallible because of the universal ordinary magisterial teaching in a serious matter of morals.[39] But if it is a true doctrine as Pope Paul proclaimed it to be, the source of that truth is the Paraclete, of whom Jesus said, "When he comes, however, being the Spirit of truth, he will guide you to all truth" (Jn 16:13).

Artificial Techniques of Procreation

Much of the controversy over birth control has debated the propriety of interventions in human activity which are described as "merely" biological interventions. For instance, the assumption of those in the previous discussion who would justify contraception in marriage is that the physiological manipulation which impedes procreation can be overlooked because of higher, more personal and spiritual values. This raises the problem of dualism mentioned above in the discussion of homosexuality and of playing the corporeal and spiritual elements of the human person against each other.

Since genital sexual activity seems to be primarily physical and biological, is not the Catholic tradition of respect for this activity a kind of biological tyranny? Cannot the person as subjective agent give primary meaning and moral significance to physical and biological activity? Should not human persons be delivered from the restrictions of medieval and static natural moral law in the name of a new and liberating personalism?

Catholic theology and magisterial teaching actually do teach a form of Christian personalism in the context of incarnational theology. By the interpenetration of the soul and body Catholic theology teaches that there are *no* merely biological functions of human persons. The human person cannot in this life achieve an angelic withdrawal from corporeal experience nor can corporeal activity ever be reduced to a subpersonal realm and manipulated as such.

In this anthropology the Church teaching on the moral inseparability of the procreative and unitive elements of conjugal intercourse stands as an eminently "personalist" teaching. Pope Paul VI spoke as a personalist in *Humanae Vitae* when he said, "Human intellect discovers in the power of giving life biological laws which are part of the human *person*" (emphasis added).[40] For human persons life is both corporeal and spiritual. The procreative process is an interpersonal experience which shares this psychosomatic characteristic. In this sense contraception is both anti-life and anti-personal.

This final discussion will raise the issue that artificial techniques of procreation are not anti-life in an immediate sense, but they are anti-personal. There is good reason for saying that these techniques should be opposed on essentially the same ground as contraception—sundering the inseparable link between the two meanings of conjugal intercourse and eliminating one of them. This time it is the unitive meaning which is eliminated.

The Second Vatican Council clearly presented marriage in the context of Christian personalism. It is a mutual giving of two *persons* demanding total fidelity and an unbreakable unity between them.[41] This personal unity is psychosomatic, neither corporeal nor spiritual alone. Thus, the council taught that the acts of married persons must be "truly human" to foster the self-giving they signify.[42] It implicitly taught this corporeal-spiritual interpenetration within genital activity of human persons when it said, "Man's sexuality and the faculty of reproduction wondrously surpass the endowments of lower forms of life; therefore, the acts proper to married life are to be ordered according to authentic human dignity and must be honored with the greatest reverence."[43]

Animal breeders have long known how to manipulate animal reproductive functions. Among humans the process of artificial insemination means any act of fertilization which takes place not as a result of sexual intercourse, but as the result of sperm being introduced into the vagina by means of an artificial process.[44] This practice can be readily distinguished from "assisted insemination" both practically and in moral significance as Pope Pius XII did when he described the latter as "the use of certain artificial means destined simply either to facilitate the natural act, or to enable the natural act, normally carried out, to attain its proper end."[45]

In 1949 Pope Pius XII spoke out firmly against artificial insemination.[46] He first condemned it outside matrimony and in matrimony but using sperm obtained from a donor (A.I.D.). Then he approached the use of artificial insemination within marriage from the husband very carefully (A.I.H.). First he pointed out that the legitimate desire of infertile parents to have a child does not of itself morally justify the mean used. He indicated that acts against nature (masturbation) could not be used in procuring the male sperm. Then he concluded that these were not only reasons for caution, but that the technique of artificial insemination must be excluded altogether.

Two years later in his address to midwives he returned to this theme and situated the sanction against it in explicit terms of the Christian personalist approach to marriage and sexuality: "The marital act, in its natural setting, is a personal action. It is the simultaneous and direct cooperation of husband and wife which, by the very nature of the agents and the propriety of the act, is the expression of the mutual giving which, in the words of Scripture, results in the union 'in one flesh.' There is much more than the union of two life-germs, which can be brought about even artificially, that is, without the cooperation of the husband and wife. The marital act, in the order of, and by nature's design, consists of a personal cooperation which the husband and wife exchange as a right when they marry."[47]

Hence, it seems clear that the primary objection to A.I.H. is its violation of the integrity of the act of conjugal love and not the problem of acts against nature (masturbation) which may be used in obtaining the male sperm.[48] William May has reviewed the issue of the moral significance of masturbation when not undertaken for selfish pleasure but for the unselfish purpose of procreation. He argues strongly that even here the "apologia for well-intentioned masturbation" implies a dualistic understanding of the human person and fails to consider the psychosexual dynamics of masturbation.[49]

Those theologians who adopt the "ontic but not necessarily evil" approach discussed here are inclined to admit the possible legitimacy of both masturbation for A.I.H. and the process of A.I.H. itself. Their reasoning parallels their case for justifying contraception in marriage: in special conditions of desire for a child without other possible means of pregnancy the principle of proportionality implies that the ontic evil is not a moral evil.[50]

Furthermore, this approach cannot rule out universally even artificial insemination from a donor other than the husband (A.I.D.).[51] Moral theologians are, of course, aware of added objections here: the privation the donor experiences in being "used" only as a biological and not a human father, the rejection of the husband who does not provide the sperm, the wife's ambivalence toward her husband, and the child's possible stigma as representing division rather than unity in marriage.

In summary, the version of Christian personalism in Church teaching which forbids these practices is opposed by the moral methodology which accepts the personalism in principle but makes exceptions to its applications in practice. The birth of Louise Brown in England on July 25, 1978, signaled an extension of this difference of moral evaluation into a new realm: *in vitro* fertilization, the process by which a new human being begins to exist in a laboratory process of fertilization, followed by implantation in the uterus of a mother.

In May, 1956, when Pope Pius XII was repeating for a third time the Church's opposition to artificial insemination he included a one-sentence sanction against *in vitro* fertilization: "On the subject of the experiments in artificial human fecundation *in vitro*, let it suffice for us to observe that they must be rejected as immoral and absolutely illicit."[52]

As in the case of contraception, this teaching stands as a universal prohibition, not directly based on the observable preponderance of evil consequences over good consequences in this procedure. The teaching rests on the same intuitive certitude about the wholeness of human genital sexuality rooted in the biblical revelation discussed at the beginning of the previous section on birth control.

It is, of course, possible that the practice of *in vitro* fertilization will soon begin to manifest a preponderance of negative consequences as the use of thalidomide did, or as the use of the contraceptive pill now seems to be suggesting with increasing urgency. The great unknown in *in vitro* fertilization is the full effect of this procedure upon the human being who begins life in a laboratory. Little significant parallel research from the animal kingdom existed when Louise Brown was successfully brought to birth. She is literally the subject of radical human experimentation. Considering this and the 100 tiny embryos who were sacrificed in the process of producing Louise Brown, one sees massive ethical objections to what was done, even from the perspective of consequentialist analyses.

But now that the experiment seems to be working and the risks may be minimized, it is safe to predict that consequentialist analysis will become more and more favorable. The genuine benefit of the procedure—that childless couples will have their own children—will be emphasized. The "ontic but not necessarily moral evil" approach will become, perhaps more and more permissive of the procedure when performed for couples with marriages that are stable and promise a loving home for the wanted child.

Some ethicisits will even speak of the parents' right to bear their own children as helping justify the procedure. Pope Pius XII anticipated that rationale over twenty years ago. In his address which condemned the procedure he said, "The matrimonial contract does not give this right (to a child), because it has for its object not the 'child' but the 'natural acts' which are capable of engendering a new life and destined to this end."[53] A child is a human person and no human person has a right to another.

The philosophical and theological objection to *in vitro* fertilization will not go away. They are not based on an obscurantist view that technology is evil. They are based on the conviction that technology serves human persons legitimately when it plays a therapeutic role— overcoming diseases and defects of nature. Artificial methods of human reproduction do not correct a defect of nature—they replace nature with technology. The mother of Louise Brown was not a patient who was cured. Hence, the procedure can be described as an *abuse* rather than an acceptable use of technology.

Both this discussion of artificial techniques of procreation and the previous considerations of premarital sexual relationships, homosexual activity and masturbation, and birth control have questioned prevailing and culturally accepted practices from the perspective of Church teaching and Christian personalism. These questions have been raised, not for the sake of impeding genuine human progress or authentic moral development, but in pursuit of wisdom and Christ's own vision of marriage and responsible sexual activity.

The questions have been raised because, as Pope John Paul II wrote in his first encyclical letter, *Redemptor Hominis*: "We must ask ourselves, with absolute honesty, objectivity and a sense of moral responsibility, the essential questions concerning man's situation today and in the future. Do all the conquests attained until now and those projected for the future for technology accord with man's moral and spiritual progress? In this context is man, as man, developing and progressing or is he regressing and being degraded in his humanity?"[54]

LAUS DEO SEMPER

Footnotes

1. Sacred Congregation for the Doctrine of the Faith, *Declaration on Certain Questions concerning Sexual Ethics*, Dec. 29, 1975, Washington, 1976, USCC, no. 1.
2. *Gaudium et Spes* no. 48.
3. *Ibid.* no. 49.
4. R. O'Neil and M. Donovan, *Sexuality and Moral Responsibility*, Washington, 1968, Corpus Books, 141.
5. J. Cavanagh, M.D., *Counseling the Homosexual*, Huntington, 1977, Our Sunday Visitor Press, 38.
6. Cf. Cavanagh, *op.cit.*, ch. 6, 59-75.
7. *Ibid.*, 58.
8. NCCB, *To Live in Christ Jesus*, Nov. 11, 1976, Washington, 1976, USCC, 19.
9. *Ibid.*
10. Kansas City, Sheed, Andrews and McMeel, Inc.
11. Cf. Cavanagh, *op.cit.* ch. 16, 222-238; cf. also J. Harvey, O.S.F.S., "Homosexuality as a Pastoral Problem," in *TS* 16 (1955) 86-108, and "The Controversy concerning the Psychology and Morality of Homosexuality," in *AER* Nov. 1973, 624.
12. Cavanagh, *op.cit.*, 227.
13. *Ibid.*, 223.
14. McNeill, *op.cit.*, 105.
15. C. Curran, *Catholic Moral Theology in Dialogue*, Notre Dame, 1972, Fides, 216-217.
16. Cavanagh, *op.cit.*, 236.
17. P. Keane, S.S., *Sexual Morality, A Catholic Perspective*, New York, 1977, Paulist Press, 87.
18. NCCB, *Principles to Guide Confessors in Questions of Homosexuality*, Washington, 1973, NCCB, 11.
19. Cavanagh, *op.cit.*, 238.
20. *Op.cit.*, no. 8.
21. C. Curran, *A New Look at Christian Morality*, Notre Dame, 1968, Fides, 201-221.
22. *Op.cit.*, no. 9.
23. *Op.cit.*, 70.
24. J. Noonan, *Contraception*, Cambridge, 1965, Harvard; New York, 1968, Mentor-Omega.
25. *Ibid.*, passim.
26. L. Card. Shehan, "Humanae Vitae: 1968-1973" in the *Homiletic & Pastoral Review*, Nov. 1973.
27. J. Finnis, "Natural Law and Unnatural Acts," *Heythrop Journal* 11 (1970) 365-381.
28. For a fuller explanation of this "slippery slope" consideration, *see* G. Atkinson and A. Moraczewski, O.P., *A Moral Evaluation of Contraception and Sterilization*, St. Louis, 1979, Pope John Center.
29. R. Michael, *Two Papers on the Recent Rise in U.S. Divorce Rates*, Stanford, 1977, National Bureau of Economic Research.
30. A key article in the 1960's was P. Knauer, "The Hermeneutic Function of the Principle of Double Effect," in the *Natural Law Forum* 12 (1967) 132-161. More recent and influential articles include: J. Fuchs, S.J., "The Absoluteness of Moral Terms," *Gregorianum* 52 (1971) 415-457; L. Janssens, "Ontic and Moral Evil," *Louvain Studies* 4 (1972) 115-156; Richard A. McCormick, S.J., *Ambiguity in Moral Choice*, Milwaukee, 1973, Marquette Univ. Dept. of Theol.

31. Keane, *op.cit.*, 125.
32. R. McCormick, who dissented from the teaching of *Humanae Vitae*, points out that this is the teaching in "Notes on Moral Theology," *TS* 40 (1979) 83-84.
33. W. May, *Human Existence, Medicine, and Ethics*, Chicago, 1977, Franciscan Herald Press, 79-80.
34. *Op.cit.*, 18.
35. Paul VI, *Humanae Vitae*, July 29, 1968, *Of Human Life*, Huntington, Ind., Our Sunday Visitor Press, no. 16.
36. *Ibid.*, no. 24.
37. A thorough and competent discussion of natural family planning including a coherent explanation of the reasons for choosing it (pp. 1-75) can be found in J.& S. Kippley, *Art of Natural Family Planning*, 2nd ed., Cincinnati, 1979, Couple to Couple League, Intl.
38. Sr. M. Peter McCusker, S.M., *Couples' Perceptions of the Influence of the Use of Fertility Awareness Methods of Family Planning on Their Marital Relationship*, Washington, 1976, Cath. Univ. of America.
39. J. Ford and G. Grisez, "Contraception and the Infallibility of the Ordinary Magisterium," *TS* 39 (1978) 258-312.
40. *Op.cit.* no. 9.
41. *Gaudium et Spes* no. 48.
42. *Ibid.*, no. 49.
43. *Ibid.*, no. 51.
44. B. Ashley, O.P., and K. O'Rourke, O.P., *Health Care Ethics: A Theological Analysis*, St. Louis, 1978, Catholic Hospital Assoc., 228.
45. Pius XII, Address to Delegates at Fourth Intl. Congress of Catholic Doctors, Sept. 29, 1949, in *Love and Sexuality: Official Catholic Teachings*, Wilmington, 1978, McGrath Publ., 100.
46. *Ibid.*
47. Pius XII, Address to Midwives, Oct. 29, 1951, in *Love and Sexuality, op.cit.*, 118.
48. Ashley and O'Rourke, *op.cit.* 292.
49. May, *op.cit.*, 50.
50. Keane, *op.cit.*, 140.
51. *Ibid.*, note no. 95, 217.
52. Pius XII, Address to the Second World Congress on Fertility and Sterility, May 19, 1956, in *Love and Sexuality, op.cit.*, 177.
53. *Ibid.*, 178.
54. John Paul II, *Redemptor Hominis*, March 4, 1979, Washington, 1979, USCC, 48.

INDEX OF PERSONS

INDEX OF SUBJECTS